*Selected Essays 1963–1975*

TURTLE ISLAND FOUNDATION
BERKELEY : CALIFORNIA
1 9 8 1

*Selected Essays 1963–1975*
*Carl O. Sauer*

© 1981 by the Netzahaulcoyotl Historical Society

ISBN 0-913666-46-7 (paper)
ISBN 0-913666-45-9 (cloth)
LCCN 81-52865

Some of these essays first appeared in the following periodicals and anthologies: *Annals, Association of American Geographers; American Anthropologist; Climate and Man: Yearbook of Agriculture, 1941; Festschrift für Ad. E. Jensen; Geoscience and Man; Heidelberger Geographische Arbeiten; Historical Geography Newsletter; Ibero-Americana; Landscape; Land Use Policy in the United States; Man's Role in Changing the Face of the Earth; Man and His Habitat; Mitteilungen der Osterreichischen Geographischen Gesellschaft; New World Journal; Population and Economics; Social Life of Early Man.* Grateful acknowledgement is made to the editors of all of these publications.

A special thanks to James J. Parsons and Lewis Mumford for consultation on this text, and to Ellen Brent for her tireless attention to the detail of its preparation.

*Selected Essays: 1963–1975* is published by Turtle Island Foundation for the Netzahaulcoyotl Historical Society, a non-profit educational corporation engaged in the multi-cultural study of New World literature and cultural history. For more information, address: Turtle Island Foundation, 2845 Buena Vista Way, Berkeley, California 94708.

# Contents

# Introduction

In editing together the essays in this text, I had initially most wanted to bring to the reader some of the more important writings Carl Sauer composed after the publication of *Land and Life* in 1963 right up until the author's death in 1975. Indeed, on the very day of his death Carl Sauer was preparing something of a bicentennial overview of our native landscape, and the notes for that essay were found on the table next to the author's favorite reading chair. Carl Sauer, it seems, only came to stop writing these essays on the day that he died. The more deeply I became involved with this project, however, the more I came into contact with certain essays and monographs published before *Land and Life,* essays every bit as rich and provoking as anything contained in that still-seminal collection. The scope of this current project thus changed until finally I realized a new collection of just this magnitude and size was very much in order.

Whatever the breadth and richness of this new *Selected Essays,* I did quickly note that there was no good way to improve on the overall categorical or section layout of Sauer's work provided by his good friend John Leighly, editor of *Land and Life.* My own chosen categories for this text are thus mere faint echos of those first suggested by Dr. Leighly; and what this all goes to prove, I suspect, is whatever the apparent diversity of the author's concern, Carl Sauer was really writing about the very same subject all of his working life. *Man's Role in Changing the Face of the Earth* was in fact the name of the revolutionary symposium Dr. Sauer co-chaired with Lewis Mumford and Marston Bates back at Princeton in 1952; man's roles in changing the face of North America was in truth the underlying subject Carl Sauer wrote about, in one form or another, throughout his professional career.

These new *Selected Essays* begin therefore with a section entitled "Agriculture, and the American Colonial Frontier," a section which includes, right at the first, three interlocked essays focusing on the impact upon the Eastern Seaboard of the arrival of certain European agricultural systems and practices, and the consequent spread of these practices to the Middle Border states. In fact one of these essays, "The Settlement of the Humid East," had become more or less lost inside a massive tome, *Climate and Man, Yearbook of Agriculture, 1941;* whereas the other two essays, altogether representing Carl Sauer's main concern at the time (a concern which would bring him in touch coincidentally with the historical botanist, Edgar Anderson), had up until Sauer's death never been published in any form. The European absorption of old Indian fields, and the quiet continuity of habit and practices which seemed to have prevailed, is of course an extraordinarily critical turning point in our own immediate economic history. It is therefore all but shocking how little literature other than these Sauer pieces exists on this subject; and it would be even more shocking, I believe, were these Sauer observations to be lost to obscurity forever.

The section concludes with both "Homestead and Community on the Middle Border," at first appearance perhaps a most controversial choice, and Sauer's final writings on this subject, "Status and Change in the Rural Midwest—A Retrospect." Indeed an earlier version of the "Homestead" essay does appear in *Land and Life,* a version which inadvertently omitted Dr. Sauer's tough words on the limitless frontier school of American historical thinking. It was Carl Sauer's one request that if ever I did get around to editing a new collection of his essays, this one essay be reprinted intact. I remain, of course, only most honored to finally reprint it as such in the pages of this new collection.

"Culture Origins" finds Carl Sauer in his world-thinking mode, a cap he tended to don often enough in his retirement years. It only *seems* to be true, I guess, that the older Dr. Sauer became, the further back in time he began to look for the actual beginnings of his story. The breadth of insight and range of these three essays will be clear enough to even the most casual reader. In reviewing them I can't help but think of the title Sauer's friend, the late poet Charles Olson, would eventually choose for his own collected poems, *Archaeologist of Morning*. Carl Sauer is very much the Archaeologist of Morning in these three pieces. I think Dr. Sauer was additionally pleased that one of these essays, "Sedentary and Mobile Bents in Early Societies," had become over the years such an important essay for feminist scholars and Women's Studies programs all over the world.

"The Road Back to Mexico" has been for me the most difficult section of this book, and I can only hope I have done justice to Sauer's firm command of this line of pursuit in the pages I have selected for inclusion in this text. The first piece is a mere abridgement of Dr. Sauer's comments on a Paul Kirschoff Southwest piece printed in the *American Anthropologist,* and yet it is, I believe, quite representative of the kind of synoptic overview for which ultimately Carl Sauer would become famous throughout the whole of his career. The other two pieces, "Aboriginal Populations of Northwestern Mexico" and "Colima of New Spain in the Sixteenth Century," represent large, and perhaps entirely too generous, selections from the original *Ibero-Americana* monographs which bear the same names. It was Jim Parsons, former Chairman of the Geography Department at the University of California, Berkeley, and Sauer's own successor in that position, who reminded me of the author's importance in terms of the whole "Berkeley School of Population Demographics," strategies which Dr. Sauer first worked out in this very paper; and, as for "Colima"—well "Colima" is a favoured paper for so many Sauer enthusiasts, I knew only to reprint as much of that paper as I could in this volume.

On the surface "The American Historical Geographer" might appear to be the most academic section of this volume, and the section least likely to be of interest to the general reader. On examination, however, I doubt if such an assumption would actually hold true. In this section Sauer presents nothing less than a history of American geographers and American geographical thinking; a treasured view of one of his beloved German geographical predecessors, Ratzel; and a particularly articulate call to his fellow geographers never to abandon "the fourth dimension of geography," the dimension of history, or time. In the end what had originally appeared to me to be almost a dry area of inquiry becomes one of the most fascinating sections in the entire book.

And finally we come to "The Agency of Man on Earth," the star-spangled feature film section of the text which, presumably, most of Sauer's readers have been waiting for all along. "Plants, Animals and Man" was in fact the first paper Dr. Sauer ever presented to this editor, and the first time really I ever became aware of just how much information the good Doctor was able to pack into a simple English paragraph. Each of the three essays in this final section represents nothing less than a somewhat self-contained, entire environmental history book concerning the impact of man, and his various migrations, upon the natural landscapes of this planet. That we would have any impact at all, of course, is still something just vaguely realized by most politicians; even as, in our own time, many more people are becoming aware that as the oil and natural resources flow, so flows the support and foreign policy of most leading modern and competitive nations. At the end Carl Sauer could only muster a bittersweet smile at such a new and wide-scale recognition; after all it was the subject he had been teaching the entirety of his professional life.

The book concludes then with "The Agency of Man on the Earth." If any paper could be considered summary of the whole of the man's thinking, then this would, I suppose, be the paper. And yet we have the whole of the rest of this volume, and many others, to prove there is precious little truth to that. "I just start with simple themes," Carl Sauer once told Charles Olson, "and then take them as far as I can take them. No more than that. Let the great historians worry about the grand encyclopedia. Everything I have ever said is limited, both as for theme, time and area of concern." This is of course the very same man who, when once dismissing the work of an overly-ambitious colleague, remarked: "Poor Doctor X. He never did learn to master the art of understatement."

Carl Ortwin Sauer was born in Warrentown, Missouri, on Christmas Eve, 1889; and pardon me if I don't again recall that in certain semi-rural German-American communities around the turn of the century this was also considered the night when certain barnyard animals began to talk. Man and animal—what meaning this actually has is of course beyond me, yet I am strangely haunted by this fact, and I would again make note of it here. Carl Sauer was born that Christmas Eve in 1889, and eighty-five years later he died on a typically chilly Bay Area summer day in his "garden" house on Arch and Rose in Berkeley, California, July 18, 1975. Those of us who knew the man, and prized his conversation and intellect almost above all else, thus lost a friend and a teacher of the first magnitude. At his death the American people as a whole lost one of the most articulate scholars this century has yet to produce. And indeed, the very Earth—my God, the American Earth—lost a man who had become the very voice and conscience of benign and intelligent American land-management thinking. Like so many of the leaders of the various Native American cultures he had come over the years to so very much admire and respect, Carl Sauer, it now seems, may even have been born to teach us all how to walk softly, and ever so much more knowingly, in balance with the lasting treasures and resources of our continent.

*Bob Callahan*
*Berkeley*
*May 1981*

*Selected Essays*

# I. Agriculture and
## the American
### Colonial Frontier

# 1. The Settlement
## of the
### Humid East

Whereas ocean air flows freely during all seasons over the European shores of the Atlantic, the Atlantic seaboard of the United States is only occasionally and in part influenced by its position on the ocean. Since the weather usually moves from west to east, the usual storm tracks pass from western Canada or the Rockies eastward by way of the Great Lakes and New England. Much of the air that gets to our Atlantic coast has passed over a wide stretch of land beforehand. Such continental air may have been greatly chilled in winter or similarly heated in summer before it reaches the seaboard. Thus our eastern seaboard areas are largely subject to extremes of heating and chilling like those in the interior of the continent, although they have intervening periods of weather that is tempered by air from the ocean. Our Atlantic states have hotter summers and colder winters than the countries of western Europe. Other continental qualities of the climate are a rather abrupt change from winter to summer and the fairly marked development of summer thunderstorms, with rains more intense but of shorter duration than in coastal Europe.

---

"The Settlement of the Humid East" first appeared in *Climate and Man, Yearbook of Agriculture, 1941* (U.S. Dept. of Agriculture: Washington, DC, 1941) and was reprinted in *New World Journal* (Turtle Island: Berkeley, 1977) pp. 17–30.

The European colonists became well aware of these differences while recognizing the generally familiar nature of the weather. One of the earliest observations was by Capt. John Smith, who likened the summers of Virginia to those of Spain but its winters to those of England, and who said also, "The like thunder and lightening to purefie the air, have seldome either seene or heard in Europe."

Peter Kalm, visiting this country from Sweden, wrote under date of September 23, 1748:

> It is true that in Pennsylvania, and even more so in the lands farther to the north, the winters are often as severe as in Sweden, and therefore much colder than in England and the southern countries of Europe. I found, for instance, that in Pennsylvania, which lies by 26 degrees farther south than some provences of my fatherland, the thermometer of Celsius fell 24 degrees below freezing. And yet I was assured that the winters which I spent there were not of the coldest, but quite ordinary. It is also true, however, that if the winters are at times hard, they do not last usually a great while. One can say properly that in Pennsylvania ordinarily they do not endure more than 2 months, and sometimes not that long. It is unusual if winter holds for as much as 3 months. Further, the summer heat is very strong and constant. In Pennsylvania, most of April, all of May, and the following months until October are as warm as June and July in Sweden. Cherries are often ripe in Philadelphia on the 25th of May; and, not infrequently, wheat is harvested in Pennsylvania by the middle of June. All of September and half, if not all of October, constitute the pleasantest season in Pennsylvania.

EUROPEAN AND AMERICAN VEGETATION

In most cases, the colonists were at no loss to identify the native plants and animals which they found on the western side of the Atlantic. It would be impossible, indeed, to cross an ocean anywhere else and find as little that is unfamiliar in nature on the opposite side. In all the lands of earliest colonization, from Massachusetts Bay south to Virginia, flora and fauna were closely related to those in the European homeland and indicated to the settlers that they were still under familiar skies and seasons.

Except for some stretches of sand, the east coast was a land abounding in hardwoods. Above all, there were oaks of divers kinds. Ash, elm, beech, birch, maple, poplar, willow, linden, and holly were other familiar trees, even though the American species differed somewhat from those of Europe.

Hardwoods conspicuously different from those of north Europe were the chestnut and walnut; the English had enough experience of the Mediterranean to guess right as to names of both of these, but they also found hickories and pecans, for which Indian names were adopted, and the noble tulip tree, which they misnamed "yellow poplar." In the north, the colonists found white and red pine mingled with the hardwoods; on the sandy coast, pitch pine; southward from Virginia, forests of yellow pine. Such stands were a new experience to the immigrants, for pines are few in western Europe. Still more novel were the coniferous trees met with in the swamps from Chesapeake Bay south. For want of a better name, the colonists called these trees cypresses, though they are not closely akin to the Old World cypresses. The eastern juniper was similarly mislabeled "red cedar." It was obvious that America possessed a wealth of fine trees far beyond that of the European homelands.

The wild berries were remarkably similar on both sides of the Atlantic and served as an important food supply to the more northerly English colonists. The wild grapes of the New World attracted much attention from the settlers, for in most of northwestern Europe, grapes, either wild or cultivated, did not grow. English, Swedish, and German settlers commented upon the abundance and merits of the American grapes.

This was indeed a lustier land to which the settlers had come, a land of hotter summers and colder winters, of brighter and hotter sun and more tempestuous rain, a land suited to and provided with a greater variety of vegetation than the homelands of Europe. In one important respect only was it strikingly inferior to northwest Europe—the quality of the grasses. There was grass aplenty, both in wet, low meadows and parklike openings or glades in the upland woods, but mostly it furnished rather poor feed. Some, like the broomsedge or broomstraw (eastern *Andropogons*), became coarse and harsh as it grew. Almost none of the native grasses withstood trampling and grazing. The annual grasses died off if heavily pastured, because they did not get a chance to seed; the perennials had delicate crowns that ill stood the abuse of heavy grazing. In clovers and other herbaceous legumes, a similar inferiority may be noted for the eastern American flora as compared with the European.

## INDIAN ECONOMY OF THE EASTERN WOODLANDS

All the native tribes encountered by the early colonists had basically similar ways of making a living. They are usually all classed by anthropologists as Eastern Woodland Indians. Their houses were made of logs or poles set upright; or in some cases strips of heavy bark, as of the chestnut, were tied to a framework of poles. They made dugout canoes by hollowing the trunk of a tulip tree or some other light, strong wood, or used bark canoes, as in the north. The household vessels were largely of wood and bark. The hard maples were carefully tapped for the spring sap, which was boiled down to sugar. From woods borders, berries and edible roots were gathered in quantity. Walnuts, hickory nuts, chestnuts, and the sweeter acorns provided winter foods of importance. Woodland browse and glade and marsh grasses supported game in an amount and variety that greatly impressed the newly come Europeans, who rarely had been given the chance to hunt at home. Many of the Indian uses of forest resources were copied or adapted by the settlers. The products of the woodlands were important to them for many years, as these products had been to the Indians.

From the woodland Indians, the colonists learned ways of farming that greatly helped, if indeed they did not make possible, the successful establishment of settlements in the new country. First of all the whites learned a valuable short cut to land clearing, the deadening of trees by girdling. In Europe, where they were accustomed to open fields and plow land, when additional land was cleared the trees were carefully cut down and the stumps dug out for firewood. In the New World, the clear field, the plow, and the seeds of Old World agriculture all gave way largely to the Indian methods of forest girdling and planting in hills and the use of Indian crops.

The basic Old World crops were field crops, such as small grains, planted in plowed ground, either broadcast or seeded in rows. The Indians used digging stick and hoe for farming, had no regular, rectangular fields, such as plowing requires, and disregarded stumps and dead trees. The planting was usually done in "hills," often by setting several kinds of seed, such as corn, beans, and squash, in each heaped-up mound of earth. By such procedure, the cultivator secured a much greater food supply than would have been possible under European modes of farming, without the labor of getting the soil ready for the plow and without requiring draft animals or equipment other than hoe or mattock.

Not only in the early colonial days of the Atlantic seaboard but for two and a half centuries thereafter the pioneer settler used Indian tillage and Indian crops. He continued to do so until he had advanced westward to the far interior margin of the lands of humid climate. The best known solution of how to farm in a hardwood country, with a minimum of tools and without the necessity of costly clearing, had been worked out by the aboriginal agriculturists of the New World.

The barking or girdling of trees let the full sunlight onto the forest floor in a few months' time and thus made it ready for planting. The ground commonly was burned over before being planted, to free it of dead branches, dry leaves, and the light herbaceous vegetation that was present. The forest topsoil was dark with leafmold, rich in potash, and congenial to the heavily feeding Indian corn. In a few years wind and weather completed the task of bringing down the dead timber. The deadened hardwood trunks and roots decayed rapidly in the moist, warm summers.

With one or two exceptions the plants cultivated by the Indians had originated far to the south of the United States under tropical or subtropical conditions. The list of native crops includes several kinds of corn, such as dent, flint, and sweet corn, various kidney or navy beans, squashes or pumpkins, the common sunflower, and the Jerusalem artichoke. Somewhat doubtfully the last two are credited to the eastern United States as the original place of domestication. Excepting the Jerusalem artichoke, these are all annual plants which, in contrast to most of the crops of northern Europe, require warm weather for starting. A large part of our humid East is as warm in summer as a tropical region. Summer in the middle Mississippi Valley is as warm by day or night as summer in the tropics, perhaps warmer. Hence, carrying the warmth-loving domesticated American annuals northward from Mexico and Central America to the eastern woodland areas involved no very serious problems for the aboriginal cultivators. It may be assumed, however, that it took many generations for agriculture to spread from Mexico to Chesapeake Bay. As it spread, a gradual selection of plants that would mature in a shorter and shorter growing season took place. These in turn became the parents of our modern commercial corn, beans, and pumpkins.

## COLONIAL BEGINNINGS NOT AGRICULTURAL

When the English first began their activities in the New World, they had little concern about places suitable for agricultural settlement. Farming was forced upon the colonists; it was not the object of their coming. The early Englishmen who came to America came to seek a northern way to the Orient, to bar the way of Spanish or French expansion, to seek wealth in furs and in codfish, herring, and mackerel, to find precious metals like those of Mexico and Peru, or at least to secure profitable cargoes of medicines, spices, dyewoods, or naval stores. Stockholders in trading ventures put up the funds on which attempt after attempt at settlement was made and failed—in Newfoundland, in Maine, in North Carolina, and in the tropics—largely because settlements were started for all reasons but the suitability of climate and soil for farming. The fact that any group of overseas colonists needed above all else to sustain themselves by the products of their agriculture was understood very slowly.

## PLANTATION CROPS FROM TROPICAL LANDS

Even the colony of Virginia, first overseas English settlement that endured, was extremely reluctant to engage in agriculture. In its floundering beginnings, it depended on imported supplies and food traded or taken from the Indians. Four miserable years after the founding of Virginia, the new government of Sir Thomas Dale applied a rigorous regime of enforced agricultural labor, which pulled the colony through. The Englishmen gave some attention to the growing of Indian crops, and European livestock was turned out to range through the woods. Swine in particular did well on the mast of the hardwoods and increased rapidly. Smith reported as late as 1618 that only 30 or 40 acres of European grain had been sown—in soil prepared with a single plow.

Meanwhile, apparently in 1612, the cultivation of tobacco was begun. This was not the harsh native tobacco *(Nicotiana rustica)* used by the Indians of the eastern woodlands, but the cultivated tobacco *(N. tabacum)* of the American tropics. During the sixteenth century Spaniards and Portuguese had introduced this Indian ceremonial plant to European trade and its seeds to European gardens. The use of tobacco spread rapidly into France and England. In both countries it was planted to some extent before the founding of Virginia. It is not definitely known how this tropical tobacco came to Virginia. The first plantings probably were of seed that had been brought from England. Fortunately for the success of the Virginia colony, the experimental introduction of tobacco was made just at the time when the English were acquiring the tobacco habit, before any English colony had been established in the tropics, and under an economic policy that emphasized production of goods by Englishmen.

It cannot be claimed that Virginia had any peculiar climatic advantage in the growing of tobacco. But Virginia had an advantage in being the only English colony at the time and in the indifferent quality of the leaf tobacco produced in England; and the long and equable summers of Virginia, amply supplied with moisture, free of hot dry winds and sudden sharp drops in temperature, proved sufficiently congenial to the growth of this delicate plant of tropical origin. This was the climatic discovery the Virginians made for New World agriculture.

In later years, the major expansion of tobacco was westward in the same latitude as Virginia, continuing to the western edge of the woodland country. A secondary spread took place southwestward, through the Piedmont. After Virginia and the lands north of the

Ohio were involved in tobacco planting, and by the middle of the nineteenth century, St. Louis was the greatest tobacco market, with tobacco fields stretching west across Missouri to the Plains.

The next introduction of tropical crops came primarily by way of Charleston, S.C. Shortly after Virginia became a tobacco-planting colony, English settlements were established in the smaller West Indian islands, most significantly in Barbados. The rapid growth of settlement and plantations soon crowded this and other islands, and an overflow of population was directed to South Carolina after 1670. Sugar cane, indigo, Barbados, or sea-island, cotton *(Gossypium barbadense)*, and rice were introduced as plantation crops in the lowlands around Charleston. Similar introductions took place around New Orleans in the eighteenth century by the French, largely influenced from Haiti. Florida entered only slightly into this plantation development, not because of unsuitable climate but because of lack of rich lowlands with deep soil. From the sea-island coast of South Carolina to the delta of the Mississippi, tropical climatic conditions prevail during most of the year. The principal difference in practice here as compared with that in the West Indies was that whereas such tropical crops as sugar cane and sea-island cotton were treated as perennials in the islands, winter frosts required annual planting in South Carolina and Louisiana.

Last and greatest of the plant introductions in the southern plantations was that of upland cotton, *(Gossypium hirsutum)*. The manner of its appearance in the South is obscure. A domesticated plant of Mexico, it was, like many New World plants, taken to the Mediterranean by Spaniards in the sixteenth century, and soon it was cultivated to some extent along the entire length of the Mediterranean shores. Its introduction to the English colonies was perhaps by way of southern Europe. In the eighteenth century upland cotton was rather commonly planted on a small scale in the southern colonies, chiefly for domestic use. Commercial planting was made possible by the invention of the cotton gin, and the first area of upland, or short-staple, cotton plantations was in South Carolina and Georgia, inland from the old sea-island cotton section.

The climatic background of upland cotton is quite different from that of the sea-island species. The latter needs a large and frequent supply of moisture and a very long, warm growing season, reflecting its fully tropical origin. The upland, or Mexican, cotton was bred in a land with much less moisture and a shorter growing season. The spread of upland cotton was principally westward from South Carolina. Historically, tobacco dominated the upper South and cotton the deep South. This segregation of the cotton belt from a tobacco and general-farming belt to the north was not wholly a matter of length of growing season. Two quite different farming systems were in process of spreading westward. Cotton planting pioneered the westward movement through the warmer section of the humid eastern hardwood country. The black prairies of Alabama and Mississippi proved the suitability of the crop to prairie-land cultivation. When settlement reached them, the rich prairies of central Texas were rapidly and most successfully added to the cotton belt.

It is somewhat doubtful whether the history of our cotton culture proves the superior climatic adaptability of our South, in particular of the Southeast, for cotton. Perhaps it records only the establishment of a crop in an area with a reasonably suitable climate, the long dominance of the South in world markets resting largely upon its prior development of cotton growing and marketing.

## AGRICULTURE IN THE NORTHERN COLONIES

New England was not settled because of agricultural attractions, nor did agriculture become the chief interest of the colonists. Fish and furs, oaken ship timbers, spars and masts of white pine, and iron made from ore raked from the floors of coal bogs were early products, characteristic of the natural resources of New England. Farming was in many cases a part-time occupation. It appears that New England has scarcely grown enough food for its needs at any time. Lack of sufficient areas of good soil and a climate marked by a brief growing season and little summer heat placed it at a disadvantage compared to the colonies farther south.

In the planted fields local kinds of short-season Indian maize, beans, and pumpkins were grown side by side with small grains from England, and it appears that the Indian crops gave the more satisfactory returns.

In the second half of the seventeenth century, English grasses began to make a noticeable improvement in pastures and meadows. The manner of their spread is obscure, but it appears that, sown here and there, they naturalized themselves rapidly and soon displaced the poor native grasses. The cool New England climate was fully congenial to the introduced European grasses and to white clover, in contrast to that in the southern colonies. In the eighteenth century, one of these European grasses, long established in New England, became perhaps the first important sown hay crop of America, first under the name of "herd's grass" and then as "timothy grass." With the improvement of hay and pasture, more attention was given to livestock, especially for meat production. Rhode Island and the Connecticut Valley were especially known in later colonial times for their beef, mutton, and draft horses. These are the chief earlier expressions of the climatic suitability of New England for grass rather than grain and other tilled crops.[1]

## DOMINANT QUALITIES OF AMERICAN FARMING DERIVED FROM THE MIDDLE COLONIES

The basic pattern of the American farm is derived chiefly from the middle colonies, and thus from a continental European as well as from an English background. It was to the middle colonies that the greatest number of people came who were by birth and training tillers of the soil. Their coming was delayed sufficiently so that they

---

1. From Jared Eliot's "First Essay on Field Husbandry in New England" (1747): "English Grass will not subsist without a Winter. In the Southern Colonies the less Winter the less Grass. In Virginia, North and South Carolina, they have no English Grass at all. Where there is no English Grass, it is difficult to make Cattle truly fat; so that Winter brings its good as well as its evil Things." In his Second Essay (1748) he added: "Red Clover is of a quick Growth and will supply our Wants for the present; a few Months brings it forward to an high Head: There are few People yet know the Value of this beneficial Grass." (In *Essays Upon Field Husbandry in New England and Other Papers, 1748–1762,* Columbia Univ. Studies, 1934.)

brought with them some of the new agriculture that changed western Europe so greatly in the eighteenth century.

Unlike New England, the middle colonies were not generally settled as closely knit township communities but as single farmsteads. Unlike the owners of plantations on the southern seaboard, the land operators to the north were themselves the tillers of the soil, occupants of single-family farms.

The contributions of Europeans to the colonies from the Hudson to the upper Chesapeake were varied. The Swedes and Finns are credited in particular with the introduction of the log cabin, which became the standard house of the frontier until the sod house of the western prairies took its place. The Dutch contributed better breeds of livestock and interest in dairying, and played a role in the introduction of European grasses and clovers. The Scotch-Irish, under which the terms *Irish* and *Scots* are also included, provided a large proportion of the intrepid backwoodsmen who first ventured into the wilderness. It is also probable that they established the culture of the potato.[2]

The German settlers as a group were most preoccupied with becoming permanently established as farmers wherever they settled. They were less mobile than the Scotch-Irish and so are often considered as forming a second wave of settlement behind the latter, who constituted an advance guard in the movement inland. The Germans were general farmers, accustomed to animal husbandry. They practiced manuring and, largely, crop rotation. Notable improvements in grain growing and stock breeding are credited to them. Architecturally they were the creators of the basic American barn, combining barn, stable, granary, and wagon shed under one commodious roof in the so-called Swiss, Mennonite, or bank barn. In contrast to the English colonists, they stabled animals in bad weather and were accustomed to stall feeding. Other items of importance to American farm settlement credited to the colonists from the Rhine are the

---

2. Earlier introductions of potatoes occurred, but their cultivation did not become common until the eighteenth century. Then they appear in localities with colonists from Ireland, such as New York, and in the back country of New England where Scotch-Irish settlements were made.

introduction of the rifle, the Conestoga wagon, and the stove to replace the English fireplace.

From all northwestern Europe, farmers poured into the colonies during the eighteenth century, settling from the Mohawk Valley to Pennsylvania and in the back country of Maryland. Here lay the largest bodies of rich land, with a familiar climate, convenient to the seaboard. All the accustomed crops and livestock of Europe thrived here. The Old World pattern of general farming, with emphasis on the feeding of livestock, was transferred here to the New World with one major modification—Indian corn was quickly fitted into the agricultural economy and greatly increased the livestock capacity of the farms. Maize was found to be a stock feed superior to anything known then or now in northern Europe. Corn, oats, wheat, rye, clover, and European grains formed a crop combination that provided the means of keeping more livestock and of obtaining sustained high yields. In late colonial and post-colonial times, these general-crop and stock farmers spread this basic American way of farming westward and southwestward. Indeed, when these farmers, reinforced by New Englanders and new arrivals from the north of Europe in the second quarter of the nineteenth century, encountered the prairies in the Old Northwest Territory between the Ohio River and the Great Lakes, they quickly found the technical means of occupying them. The prairies are still a part of the humid East, scarcely differentiated climatically from the woodlands by which they are surrounded on the north, east, and south. The same crops succeed in both areas. The summers of Iowa are as hot as those of Pennsylvania and as much characterized by rains from thunderstorms, and so Indian corn found admirably suited conditions across the whole breadth of the prairie country. Fall, winter, and spring weather in the prairie states are equally congenial to the small grains, grasses, and clovers from northern Europe. Hence the middle-colony pattern of farming easily became the famous corn-clover-oats rotation of the prairie states, with hogs as the primary market product.

In the development of the forested Great Lakes states, corn was largely eliminated by reason of the reduced summer warmth. Here the pattern of agriculture became almost identical with that of the climatically very similar Baltic countries. Dairy products, potatoes and other root crops, and some small grains constitute an agricultural complex suited to short, cool summers. New Englanders and Scandinavians were dominant groups that found a continuation of accustomed climatic conditions in the new country.

# 2. European Backgrounds
## of American
### Agricultural Settlement

## Origins of Our Pioneer Settlers

### THE SIGNIFICANCE OF THE MIDDLE BORDER

In the shaping of our rural life, first importance attached to those groups that undertook and carried out the task of converting the new land into settled farms. In most cases these were not the first pioneers, but a second group of comers who have been called, aptly, the "men of the Middle Border." The advance scouts of European civilization in the New World were the reckless, feckless backwoodsmen who fought the Indians and tarried briefly in one spot, soon to drift forward again into the wilderness as the true settlers caught up with them. The footloose breed of the First Border were in good part running away from the prospect that most appalled them, the steady toil of the settled communities behind. Much has been written and romanticized about the first thin wave of frontiersmen. We are not concerned with these passing prospectors of the new lands, but with the people who followed them, the men of the Middle Border, who

"European Backgrounds of American Agricultural Settlement" first appeared in *Historical Geography*, Volume 6, Number 1 (California State University, Northridge: Northridge, California, 1976), pp. 35–57.

put down roots and, working together, made the farming settlements.

The early settlers brought with them not only their families and chattels, but skills and attitudes from the old homes which they had left. They brought habits of tilling the soil and of handling livestock, familiarity with certain crops, preferences as to homes and furnishings; in short, accustomed ways of rural life. Some of these habits were dropped under the changed circumstances of their new homes, but much experience that they brought along continued in the pattern of living. Behind the homes, crops, and animals of the present-day farms of the United States is a varied background of age-old learning. Our present agriculture takes us back not only to the men who cleared the American land and broke the sod, but to more distant forebears who developed many of the basic forms of our farming in European countries. In this country we have been at farming for two or three or at most eight or ten generations, but behind these are long accumulations of experience in the Old World, developed in climates and soils similar to much of our own land.

## SOURCES AND PERIODS OF RURAL IMMIGRATION

Overseas migration started from a small and contiguous strip of territory on the North Sea. As time went on, emigration spread to more and more adjacent lands, but at all times a rather small part of Europe furnished most of the stock of rural settlers. It should be remembered that by "settler" we mean the people of the Middle Border. It is true that ultimately all of Europe contributed heavily to American immigration; this is not true for land settlement. Many European stocks came too late. These latecomers entered American life, mostly through jobs in town. When they did get out onto the land, it was not onto new land, but onto going farms, and then these people had to fit themselves into an established rural situation. It was only those who came early enough to be properly called settlers who had an important hand in creating the basic forms of American agriculture.

The people who cleared the new lands, planted them, and set the forms of American agriculture were mostly near neighbors in the

Old World, where they practiced a similar husbandry, tilled soils that were of related origin, and were nurtured in common under moist skies of high latitudes, close to the sea. Our agriculture, in brief, is derived from farming ways and skills, learning, and preferences that were developed in the moist, cool lands of northwestern Europe. We may begin therefore with considering whence, in what order, and with what equipment of knowledge the farmers of Europe came to our country. The three and a half centuries of our history may be divided into four periods of rural immigration: (1) from 1607 to the end of the seventeenth century; (2) the eighteenth and first half of the nineteenth century; (3) from about 1850 to about 1890; and (4) from 1890 to the present.

## THE OLD COLONISTS

During the old colonial period (seventeenth century), the settlers overwhelmingly were from the south of England. Next in importance were those from the mouths of the Rhine, largely Dutch. Finally there were a few hundred Swedes and Finns from the Baltic. The English settlers in general came from a strip of land a hundred and fifty miles long, and little more than half as wide, stretching from the Bristol Channel to the mouth of the Thames. A short extension of this strip from the mouth of the Rhine to the German border adds the homeland of the Dutch colonists. It should be noted that a large part both of the Dutch and, to a somewhat lesser degree, of the English colonists of this first period, were townsmen rather than farmers.

## THE MIDDLE PERIOD

The next period (about 1700 to 1850) starts with the founding of Pennsylvania. Penn, his associates, and his successors became colonizers on a great scale. They invited the oppressed and underprivileged and engaged most actively in the rental and sale of land to common settlers and to other landed proprietors from New York to the Carolinas at the same time.

During the eighteenth century almost the whole of the British Isles, in particular the western and northern parts, became involved in a great overseas migration. Thus, the more or less Celtic peoples of the favored back country, Scotch-Irish, Irish, Scots, and Welsh, came as wave on wave of settlers to the whole length of the Atlantic seaboard. These non-English islanders furnished probably the largest contingent of the eighteenth century, the major body of settlers who moved into the Appalachian country and across into the drainage of the Ohio.

The last great expression of this British Isles migration was the mass movement from Ireland in the second quarter of the nineteenth century. Though many of these later Irish immigrants remained in the cities, many others took part in the rural settlement of the states of the Great Lakes and of the upper Mississippi.

On the continent, Penn's agents found kindred religious groups along the Rhine, such as the Mennonites, eager for new homes and guarantees of religious freedom. The founding of Germantown in 1683 was soon followed by a flood of German home-seekers, mostly small farmers. It continued without interruption through the eighteenth century. These German farmer immigrants entered at first through Philadelphia and in smaller measure through New York. Soon, however, Baltimore and southern ports as far as Savannah were discharging boatloads of immigrants originating from the Rhine lands. Every part of the Rhine Valley contributed, most of all the middle portion, in particular the Palatinate and the little principalities nearby. A second center of major importance was the upper Rhine country, including Switzerland. Groups of especial significance in American agricultural development were colonists, largely Mennonites, from the canton of Bern, at the northern foot of the Alps.

The early years of our republic brought a lull in the German immigration. When it resumed in force in the second quarter of the nineteenth century, the same lands that had given rise in colonial times to the so-called Pennsylvania Dutch settlements again contributed heavily. Also a belt of country immediately to the east, from Westphalia to Württemberg, was drawn into the stream of migration. These later colonists entered chiefly through New York and Gulf ports and found their way to the Middle Border from Ohio and

Wisconsin through Missouri to Texas.

To the middle of the nineteenth century, the British Islands and the Rhine Valley supplied nearly the whole of our farming stock. Some modification of this statement needs to be made for the French settlements of the Mississippi Valley. In the upper Louisiana settlements about St. Louis, the stock was predominantly from the north of France, as were the numerous Acadians found throughout the territory. Normandy and Brittany appear to have been especially represented. In lower Louisiana, numerous pioneer farmers were brought to the lower Mississippi by John Law's great land promotion, which we remember as the Mississippi Bubble. These were predominantly German-speaking farmers from the middle and upper Rhine, the same stock that came at the same time to Pennsylvania. Finally there were the French Creoles, properly speaking, centered about New Orleans, and derived from various parts of France. Agriculturally, the latter were significant chiefly as sugar, rice, and indigo planters.

### THE LATER NINETEENTH CENTURY IMMIGRATION

From 1850 on, the districts situated to the east and southeast of the North Sea contributed heavily. Steamship lines by that time had been established across the Atlantic and the ports ef Bremen, Hamburg, and Gothenburg became points of embarcation for the New World. The plains of northern Germany contributed Low German farmers who arrived in time to take a large part in the settling of the prairie states (1850–1870). At the same time Czechs from Bohemia came into the prairies of the north and of Texas, and a great Scandinavian migration set in after the Civil War, too late to get much of a slice of the corn belt. It found its place in the forest lands of the upper Mississippi and in the grasslands west and north of the corn belt.

During this period there was also a rather important movement of farmers from the Mediterranean to California. These included both Italian Swiss and north Italians from the southern slopes of the Alps and the Po Valley, and also south Slavs from Istria, Dalmatia, and Croatia. The head of the Adriatic Sea, therefore, formed a new center of emigration to the most distant part of the United States.

Both groups have been especially important in the development of wine, fruit, and truck growing in California.

A distant source of colonists at this time was located in southern Russia. The so-called Russian Mennonites were a part of the same Rhenish non-conformist farming stock that contributed to early Pennsylvania. At the same time that many of them moved across the Atlantic, another body began moving eastward, attracted by the guarantee of freedom of conscience. They settled finally in the Black Earth country of the Ukraine and also on the lower Volga, hard against the borders of the dry steppe and the hordes of Asiatic nomads. Whole colonies of them came to the United States in the 1870s when the Russian government revoked the guarantees against military and other public services. Four generations of living on the dry borders of southern Russia had markedly altered their farming practices. They were almost the last group of agricultural immigrants to have a notable effect on American farming.

## THE LATECOMERS

The immigrants of the past half century have been absorbed mainly into industry and commerce. They came for the most part too late to find new land. Finnish peasants, starting as woodsmen or miners in the upper Great Lakes, became in good measure the pioneers in the adjacent cut-over lands of upper Michigan, Minnesota, and Wisconsin. Slowly and stubbornly they opened agricultural settlements in the woods about Lake Superior. Near great industrial centers in the East, secondary agricultural settlements by Slavs and Mediterranean people have in part replaced the older stock and modified to some extent farming practices.

## *Climates and Vegetation in the Countries of Europe*

### MILD WINTERS OF THE NORTHWEST

From the North Atlantic Ocean air flows in over adjacent Europe almost continuously. This air is laden with moisture and so it is neither readily nor rapidly heated in summer nor greatly chilled in winter. Northwest Europe has a markedly oceanic climate.

The sea influences are most striking in winter, when moist air penetrates deeply with every storm that moves in from sea to continent. In spite of high latitude, the land of northwestern Europe is kept supplied throughout the winter with relatively warm air from the ocean. This moist air blankets the earth against great loss of heat radiated into the atmosphere. Winter skies are likely to be gray, but winter temperatures remain extraordinarily high considering the latitude. The entire Atlantic coast of Europe has a January mean above freezing. All but a few mountain spots in the British Isles have mean temperatures above freezing in mid-winter, as does the Rhine Valley as far south as northern Switzerland. From Basel to Belfast, from Bergen to Brest, winter weather brings night frosts, but only a few days that do not warm up well above freezing.

How well this influx of sea air moderates average winter temperatures is shown by the 30° F. line for January. It reaches inland nearly to the borders of Bohemia and extends well up into southern Sweden. The winter averages of Stockholm are about those of New York, but Stockholm does not know the blizzards that may block the streets of New York. To find such winter cold, one must go farther east in Europe, to southern Finland or to the east side of the Baltic where continental winter air brings sub-zero minima.

The contrast between the full oceanic climate of England and the partially continental climate of Sweden is recorded by Peter Kalm, an eighteenth century Swedish naturalist. On his way to the New World, he had his first view of an English winter. Under the date March 7, 1848, he wrote:

> The air in England is much softer than in Sweden. Its inhabitants in part have to thank their more southerly position for this; in part they owe it to the sea that is all about them. The land here already is quite green. Here and there a hedge still holds a little patch of snow, since there was, only fourteen days ago, an extraordinary snowfall. Cattle are already grazing in the fields, so that the farmers are not under necessity of providing for them. There are entire winters when they are not driven in at all but seek their feed throughout the year in pasture and field. For the cows, there is commonly provided a shed into which they are

driven at night, at times of bad weather, for which occasions a supply of hay is stored. Sheep, however, are never brought under roof, but must stay out at all seasons, by night and day. Only for very delicate lambs is occasional provision of shelter made. Thus during the heavy recent snow, all that was done was to drive the flock to a haystack to feed there while the ground was buried by snow. It is therefore not difficult to keep a lot of live stock in these parts. These farmers know little of the burden of providing feed in winter, such as we experience.

In the houses, fire is kept going all day long. When, therefore, it becomes quite cold, every one moves up to the chimney. Here one sits, warmed through on one side and freezing on the other. The ground, however, is so little affected by frost that they plow all winter long. There is scarcely a month in the year in which something is not being planted. At this time, a considerable part of the summer rye, of the barley, and of the legumes were already sown. Beans and peas mostly had been planted by the end of February; some of them had been broadcast at the middle of that month, and part at its beginning, and so it is with other similar plants. The lakes, rivers, and brooks were ice-free, and though an occasional fish-pond was covered with ice at the end of February because of the unusual cold weather, at this time all were free of ice. It is something extraordinary when the Thames freezes over at London. Most of the inhabitants of the city see such an event only once or twice in a life-time. Although snow falls occasionally in winter, it usually remains no longer than three days.

## THE MOISTNESS OF THE NORTHWEST

The other most distinctive quality of northwestern Europe's climate is the abundance of moisture at all seasons. There is no dry season; there are no long dry spells. Even the parts more remote from the ocean hardly ever experience a drought. Precipitation is not heavy as to total, nor intense in an individual rain. The rainier portions, close to the sea, have around forty inches annually; the drier, more inland localities, thirty or somewhat less. Rainfall is well distributed through the seasons. The season of maximum rainfall shifts from winter to summer in going from the northwest to the southeast. There is a winter maximum in Ireland, in fall over England and the coastal continental regions, but the upper Rhine has a summer maximum.

Humidity of the air is high and evaporation correspondingly low. Saturation of air and also of soil is highest in those parts most freely exposed to sea air, namely, western Ireland, northwestern Scotland and western Norway, as well as Brittany. Here rain, mist, and fog are the rule rather than the exception; bright days come infrequently, and the ground underfoot is rarely dry. Normally the west of England, the Low Countries, and Normandy are also pretty wet, being only a little less exposed to the sea than the areas previously mentioned. On the other hand, eastern England, in particular East Anglia, and the German part of the Rhine Valley, enjoy a situation of less moisture; they have enough to insure favorable plant growth, but they also have more clear weather and better drained and aired soils. In these last two areas, rainfall averages less than thirty inches, and the amount of sunshine is highest for all northwest Europe.

## NATURAL VEGETATION IN THE NORTHWEST

The climate is extraordinarily favorable to vegetative growth. The westernmost parts, like Ireland, are green the year around. Some winter pasturage is available in all parts of the northwest. Meadows and pastures remain green throughout the summer. Because of the mild winter, cold frost does not penetrate deeply. Thus a few sunny winter days are sufficient to start growth of some plants and to bring out flowers in sheltered spots.

Our literary expressions of the seasons derive from this part of the world. Here, March is a spring month and spring lingers about as long as summer or winter. By the end of April, drifts of apple and pear blossoms dot the countryside, and in July the gold of the grain fields sets off the green of meadows and woods. Autumn lacks the high color of our eastern woodlands and its Indian summer quality. In northwest Europe, autumn changes gradually with increasing wetness to the wintry alternation of rain, snow, and passably fair weather. The trees and bushes lose their leaves slowly and undramatically in fall, beeches and oaks continuing in foliage through a good part of the winter.

From northwest to southeast, moisture conditions differ sufficiently to give rise to important contrasts in the native vegetation. Coniferous forests generally are wanting in all this part of Europe. For natural stands of pines, spruce, and firs, one must go into eastern Germany, upper Scandinavia, or to the mountains, for these trees are expressions of more continental climates.

In the coolest and moistest parts of the farthest northwest, there is little tree growth. Here moors and bogs prevail, with grass and some trees on the better drained slopes and steppe soils. Much of Ireland, Scotland, and the Low Countries was apparently never really forested, but was a land of woods and meadows interspersed with larger stretches of lowland bogs and upland moors. The occurrence of peat bogs is an indication of a climatic margin on which tree and grass become restricted to the most favorable soils and slopes. On many uplands in Scotland and Ireland, heather, bracken, and mosses form an aggressive company of plants that crowd out the more exacting grasses and trees.

The greater part of northwest Europe had a natural covering of deciduous woodlands on the uplands and of meadows on the lowlands. Such was the character of most of England, of southeastern Scotland, and of all but the extreme lower part of the Rhine Valley. One should not think of dense, dark forests, but of more or less open woods, with grasses and herbaceous plants growing under the trees and in natural openings. Valley floors, including that of the Rhine, appear to have been ordinarily too wet for woodland growth. They constituted the major natural meadows, apart from the coastal marshes. In them, however, certain water-tolerant trees, such as willows and alders and, in part, elms occurred.

The upland woods have minor evergreen elements in holly, ivy, and yew, but mostly they are composed of oak or beech. Oak and beech often grow in separate stands, and the beech in particular not infrequently forms nearly pure stands. The variety of trees in these woodlands is not great as compared to most of our hardwood forests.

Linden, ash, elm are less common forest trees of northernmost Europe.

The woods' margins and openings are especially favorable to a number of small trees and shrubs. Here are to be counted the wild apples, pears, plums, cherries, sloe, and hawthorn. Here also belong the hazelnut, the blackberries, raspberries, gooseberries, blueberries and currants. The climate is excellent for berries. To this day the picking of wild berries is an important item in the income of many peasant communities. In addition, sunny slopes of the hill country along the upper Rhine had a wild grape that is one of the parents of the vineyard grapes of that section.

The native meadow flora is very rich in terms of useful members, the richest by far in the world. Native to it are most of the important perennial hay and pasture plants of our own present-day agriculture. The superior blue, rye or ray, bent, orchard, and meadow fescue grasses are natives of the meadows of northwest Europe. Among the wild clovers of this section are the wild red clover *(Trifolium pratense)*, white clover *(Trifolium repens)*, and lesser forms of *Trifolium* and *Medic* or *Medicago*. Important characteristics of the grasses of this section are that they are highly nutritious, that dominantly they are vigorous perennials, that they form a compact turf or greensward, and that they thrive under repeated mowing or grazing. These qualities are not similarly combined by any other grass vegetation elsewhere and therefore the native meadow and pasture plants of northwest Europe have proved of the greatest importance in the modern animal husbandry of distant parts of the world as well as in their home lands.

We may rank the meadow and pasture grasses as the most important plant contribution of this region to the outside world. Perhaps next would come the apples, pears, cherries, and berries, as partial parents of our familiar domesticated forms. Next should be mentioned the native wild members of the mustard family *(Brassica)*, originally plants of the woodland openings and meadows which are ancestors to our garden cabbages and turnips.

All of the plants that have been taken into cultivation from this part of the world still preserve a marked preference for the moist and cool climatic conditions of their ancient home. Well-flavored apples, plump, firm heads of cabbage, and sweet turnips still grow best where the summers are cool and where there is no lack of moisture.

## SOIL AND CLIMATE IN NORTHWESTERN EUROPE

Soil qualities reflect closely the climatic conditions, for soils are in part the result of the weathering of rock material and in part are formed by the incorporation of organic matter. Hence, it is inevitable that an important soil change should take place in the direction of climatic change, from northwest to southeast. In general, there is an increase in desirability of soils southeastward. At the northwest, the soils are generally extreme podsols; that is, their upper parts consist of heavy accumulations of raw organic matter. Beneath, they are largely leached of their mineral plant food and characteristically have a tight subsoil. Such soils are very acid, low in fertility, and poor in natural drainage. They tend therefore to accentuate the climatic tendency toward saturation of the ground. To the southeast, under lessened atmospheric humidity and higher evaporation, much more desirable forest soils have formed. Thus, in the climatically most favored part of the British Isles, in mid-Germany, and in Switzerland, chocolate brown upland soils have formed, rich in broken-down humus, not excessively leached, and of a structure and texture that provide for good drainage and root penetration. The more desirable climatic conditions are therefore reproduced by a more desirable group of soils. These in turn support the more varied and useful natural vegetation, and they are the lands best suited to cropping.

## CLIMATIC AREAS AND MIGRATION: NORTHWESTERN EUROPE

If we now return to the historical sequence of overseas migration, some interesting associations can be traced between climatic conditions and migrant groups. In the first period of American colonization, it should be noted that the English settlers came from the physically most advantageous part of the kingdom. Their land was one of mixed hardwoods and meadows, of deep, rich soils, of beneficently reduced humidity, and of very mild winters. The Dutch homeland had more heavy marsh soils—excellent, however, for grass growth when drainage was improved. It too enjoyed a long growing season; for native grasses, a nearly continuous growing season. The general agricultural attractiveness of the Dutch country was somewhat less than of eastern England, because of poorer climatic conditions for the ripening of grains and of fruits.

In the second period, the added areas of emigration show a reversal of advantage as between the British Isles and the continental areas. The newly contributing parts of the continent are much more favored as to climate than the new areas of emigration from the British Isles. The Scotch-Irish, Irish, Scots, and Welsh came from one of the least favored parts of northwest Europe as to climate, soils and natural vegetation. Theirs was a background of dripping skies and soggy soils, of bog and heath, of bracken and moss invading meadows and pastures, of crops that failed to ripen, of mildew, mold, must, and rust. By comparison, the Germans of the Rhine lands had adequate sunshine, reasonably bright fall seasons, better drainage, mellower soils, a country that was good not only for meadow and pasture, but for grain fields, orchards, and even vineyards.

## CLIMATIC BACKGROUND OF THE LATER
## NINETEENTH CENTURY SETTLERS FROM NORTHERN EUROPE

The rural migrants from northern Europe of the second half of the nineteenth century may be segregated into a northern and southern group, the Scandinavians and Low Germans forming the northern lot; the South Germans and Bohemians, the southern group. Both groups were accustomed to more continental winters than were the earlier comers, and to greater need of winter feed for stock.

The northerners had experienced rather short crop seasons, cool, moist summers that presented difficulties for the ripening of grain and the curing of hay, and soils that were of the podsol type, though less extreme than those of western Ireland. In so far as they moved into our north-central states, they exchanged their climatic habitat for one of longer and more severe winters, and of brighter and somewhat warmer summers. But the general contrasts between their old homes on the Baltic and their new homes in such a state as Wisconsin are not very great.

The more southerly group, South Germans and Bohemians, knew fairly long and warm summers, which were occasionally touched by droughts. They had a markedly better climate for grains and fruit trees than the north, and one in which the valley lowlands still were generally satisfactory for meadows. That neither group lived in a land radically dissimilar from that of the Rhine and of England is shown by the fact that beech and oak were also the forest trees of these more easterly lands.

## CLIMATIC BACKGROUND OF THE
## COLONISTS FROM THE MEDITERRANEAN

Neither was the home country of the Italian and south Slav colonists as different as their location on the Mediterranean might suggest. They came from the least Mediterranean part, climatically speaking, of the Mediterranean shores. The area at the head of the Adriatic Sea has winter temperatures much like those of southwestern Germany, the principal difference being that there are more days of bright sunshine in winter. The summers are, however, markedly warmer. Rainfall is considerably heavier, though there is also more clear weather. Rain is abundant at all seasons of the year. The sheltered southern exposure of the foothills of the Alps provides favorable conditions for fruit and wine. The lack of summer drought tends to keep meadows and pastures continuously green, in contrast to the summer brownness of really Mediterranean lands.

## THE CLIMATIC BACKGROUND OF THE
## RUSSIAN MENNONITES

The Mennonites and associated immigrants from south Russia are the only numerous American settlers who were acquainted in their old homes with severe and frequent droughts, with great summer heat, with dry, cold winters, with blizzards and high winds. They knew the continental extremes of interior Russia, which they were to find again as they settled in our western plains. On their native steppe border, they experienced frequently long, hot summers that grew drier as the season wore into fall; as well as brief, uncertain rains, and dry winds that sucked the moisture from the soil.

## CLIMATIC BACKGROUND OF THE FINNS

The last group to be considered, the Finns, came from the opposite climatic margin of eastern Europe. To a far greater degree than the Swedes and Norwegians, they knew sub-arctic cold. A narrow southern fringe of their country along the Gulf of Finland has summer warmth enough for deciduous hardwoods and protection from unseasonable frost. Northward lie coniferous forests, cold bogs, and swamps. More than any group of American settlers, these hardy northerners had pioneered against the cold limits of agriculture. In their own home, they had been engaged for generations in slowly and stubbornly driving northward the limits of agricultural settlement.

## SUMMARY

We may summarize the ancestral climates of our farm settlers by saying that until the last quarter of the past century, they came from temperate climates, knowing winters scarcely more severe than those of the Carolinas, and summers no hotter than those of New England. The growth period was relatively long and for grasses, in part, almost continuous. Excess moisture was a far greater problem than drought. They were indeed differentiated as to climatic background, principally coming from excessively wet or from favorably humid lands. Hardwoods and lush grass dominated the native vegetation. Only the two latest groups brought with them experience of widely divergent climates: the Finns coming out of the northeastern lands where agriculture meets limiting cold and the Mennonites out of the southeast of the continent from the dry margin of the interior steppes.

## Basic Crops Before the Eighteenth Century

### FARMING BROUGHT TO EUROPE FROM ASIA

European agriculture did not originate in Europe. The knowledge of tilling the soil and the fundamental crops were both introduced thousands of years ago from southwestern Asia. The plants that were cultivated in Europe were mostly strangers, therefore, to its climates and soils. We may think of them as coming first into southeastern Europe, where climate and soil conditions were still rather similar to those of their Asiatic homelands. The farther they spread north-westward, the more did the physical environment change. Ancient farmers overcame this change partly by gradually breeding new strains or races of their crop plants. But we shall see that agriculture was forced to take on new forms and to drop certain crops as it took hold in lands of greater moisture, less sunshine, and less warmth.

It is important to remember that from the distant beginnings of agriculture to about the eighteenth century, farmers had little more to work with than the crops and animals that were raised far back in the Bronze Age. During all this time, fields were plowed and planted principally in order to raise grain, which supplied the starch and a good deal of the protein in the diet of the people. To a far greater extent than is true today, the farmers of northwest Europe made their living by the growing of small grains.

### BARLEY

Supposedly the oldest grain cultivated in Europe is barley. It appears to have been brought from southwest Asia up the Danube by the earliest cultivators of the soil as their basic crop, and to have been the means by which agriculture was spread to the far ends of the European continent. Barley is the most northerly grain grown in Europe today, and it also spreads southward toward the desert of North Africa farther than any other grain.

The quality of this plant that made it so very useful in the spread of agriculture is its ability to thrive under a greater variety of climatic conditions than almost any other crop. It matures faster than any of the common grains and hence can be grown farther poleward than others. It is remarkably tolerant not only of cool weather, but also of hot, dry conditions. It grows in most soils of moist as well as of dry climates. To these advantages must be added the fact that it usually outyields the other small grains. Its principal disadvantage is in its use in the kitchen. It does not make "risen" bread and its taste is somewhat harsh as compared with other grains. As meal it may be baked into thin, hard cakes, or it may be boiled as gruel or soup. An improvement in its palatability was discovered very long ago by malting it and therewith using it for brewing beer. Especially in northwestern Europe, which was poorly supplied with vegetables, fruits, and sources of sugar, beer through the ages has played a very important role in the food of the people. As they came to have more desirable grains for direct use in the kitchen, barley growing continued to remain important for malt and beer.

### WHEAT

Wheat is almost as old in agriculture as is barley, and it may have come into European farming at the same time. Wheat, however, has been unable to spread as far as barley because it is a more exacting crop. As it was taken northward by the spread of agriculture, wheat encountered uncongenial, sour podsol soils, as well as weather too cool and growing periods too brief to suit it. As it was taken westward it met with summers that were too rainy and cool, and soils that were too soggy. Wheat needs a longer growing season and more sunny weather in the latter part of its growth period than do the other non-tropical small grains. It needs a soil of good substance, not too acid, not too high in organic matter, not too sandy. Much of the country of northwest Europe has one or more qualities that are unsuited to wheat. In consequence, wheat did not establish itself continuously across northwestern Europe as a field crop as did barley. It took hold only in what we should call the better regions, the areas of diminished humidity and of brown loam soils. Wheat became the staple grain of southeastern England and of the better lands of southwestern Germany. Beyond those areas, both toward the Atlantic and toward the northern continent, it gives way to oats or rye.

## OATS AND RYE

It has been suggested that oats and rye originally were weed plants, or at least inferior grains that were mixed accidentally with wheat seed. Grain as broadcast in primitive farming was an uncleaned mixture. Under this view, in the good wheat lands, oats and rye remained subordinate plants in the grain fields. However, as grain came to be sown in the more northerly lands and on the poorer soils, wheat failed to mature or yielded poorly, whereas the oats and rye made a stronger growth and ripened their seed. Thus, it is thought, that in the primitive grain fields of the north, oats or rye gradually replaced wheat.

The conditions under which rye and oats are most vigorous are somewhat different. Both do much better in cool summers than does wheat; both mature in somewhat less time. Oats, however, are much more tolerant of wet weather than is rye, whereas rye does better than other grains on thin, sandy soils. Therefore, oats had an increasing advantage as agriculture occupied the windward marine coasts of northwestern Europe, whereas rye became the most successful grain as farming spread eastward to the lands about the Baltic. Here the ice sheets of the glacial period had spread large surfaces of sandy and gravelly soils, on which no grain except rye does at all well.

At the dawn of history we find these regional qualities of the small grains already well established: barley, the most generally distributed grain, but of limited direct use as a bread-stuff; wheat, dominating the deep, mellow soils of the sunnier and drier parts; oats, the grain of the wet western parts of the British Isles and Norway; and rye, constituting the bread grain of nearly the whole of the northern part of the continent. Wheat is the staple grain or "corn" of England, France, and parts of southwestern Germany; rye of the Baltic countries; oats of Scotland and Ireland. These conditions go back beyond the memory of man and have become fixed in various food habits.

## LEGUMES

With regard to plant proteins, northern Europe was in a decidedly poor situation. The two most valuable legumes available were the

common or garden pea *(Pisum sativum)* and the horse or broad bean
*(Vicia faba),* called sow bean by the Germans. The garden pea is a
cool-climate plant, but as its name indicates, it requires a superior
soil and careful attention. It has never been much grown as a field
crop. The horse bean is also somewhat exacting as to soil, requiring a
fertile soil that is at the same time well drained; it flourishes under
cool and rather moist summer weather. Except in England, it did
not become an important food. None of the other plants that we call
beans and peas were known to north European agriculture until
recently.

## OIL AND FIBER PLANTS

Vegetable oils were also few and decidedly inferior or costly to get.
Although beechnuts and poppy seeds were pressed for oil, the chief
sources were flax and rape seed. Both flax and rape grow well in
northwest Europe, though they incline to produce stalk and leaves
rather than seeds. The harvest of their seed is somewhat tedious and
costly and great skill and care is needed in pressing the oil so as to get
a product free of unpleasant taste. It is significant that both plants
seem to have been grown more and more for leaf or fiber and less and
less for oil. Flax indeed was the most valuable tilled crop after the
grains, providing a fiber second in importance only to wool. Flax for
fiber thrived best on rich, heavy lands, with high atmospheric moisture. In such parts of the Low Countries, it became the dominant
staple of agriculture. It was also important on the fatter soils of
Ireland and along the Baltic.

## THE BRASSICAS

Rape was a most important ancient forage crop in the northwest, one
of the very few plants at hand that could be grown for the feeding of
livestock. Rape belongs to the genus *Brassica* of the mustard family.
This genus was and still is of the greatest importance in northwest
European farming, and in part the forms that have been made into
domestic plants originate in this part of the world. For untold generations, the people of northern Europe got from one mustard-like
plant or another their principal vegetables and part of their stock

feed. Some brassicas were developed for size and tenderness of leaves into the plants we call cabbages and kales. Others were selected for their roots until they became the turnip and rutabaga. Not the least of their value lay in the possibility of keeping them in storage during the winter months. In our garden cultivation this whole group of plants still shows marked preference for the cool, moist growing weather of the lands from which they came.

FRUIT

The supply of fruit was in considerable part from wild berries. Since northwest Europe has an excellent berry climate, there was no great incentive to domesticate berries, for berry bushes flourished wild on woods borders and the edges of the fields. Berrying is to this day an important source of income for the poor country people all over northwestern Europe. Our garden berries largely have been developed in the last few centuries, many of them since the time of the colonization of our Atlantic coast.

Apples, pears, and cherries were improved from wild ancestors to a considerable range of domestic forms. Beer was the drink of the open, low country, but cider, made from apples or pears, was the common drink in the rolling hill countries such as the Kentish hills south of London, in Normandy and Brittany, and in various hill regions along the Rhine. A well-drained, sun-facing slope marked the chosen spot for orchards. Only on certain hills of the Rhine Valley was there warmth and sunshine enough to grow grapes for wine. The wine grape and tree fruits, including sweet cherries and some plums, were in cultivation before the time of the Romans in much the same localities where horticulture is still important. The prune possibly was added during Roman occupation, but became selected into forms suited to more northern climes.

THE CROP COMPLEX

Such was the assemblage of crops available to those colonists who came to America before the eighteenth century. All of these plants had been selected for their capacity to withstand, in greater or lesser degree, the cool and moist weather that characterizes the northwestern lands of Europe: barley, oats, and rye overshadowing wheat as grain; garden pea, horse bean, flax, and rape providing, rather inadequately, proteins and fats; vegetables, chiefly cabbage, turnips, and kale, but also beets, carrots, parsnips, onions, and leeks; orchard fruit in apples and pears, with sweet cherries and plums in selected sites, and wine grapes restricted to the one area of greatest sunshine.

## The Older North European Animal Husbandry

### PRIMITIVE STOCK KEEPING

The farmers of northern Europe, as far back as we know anything about them, have been accustomed to handling animals at the plow, to milking, and to the arts of animal husbandry in general. The woodlands, being deciduous and open, furnished grass and browse through the year for cattle, sheep, and horses, and mast of oak, beech, and roots for swine. The natural meadows provided a crop of summer hay and pasturage at other seasons. Thus, long ago, before many fields had been cleared or drained for the plow, there was large provision by nature of animal feed.

### RANGE AND UTILITY OF STOCK

Cattle were the chief animals kept, and marked the wealth of the farmer. Oxen were the draft animals of north Europe. Cows were kept so as to have a continuous supply of milk. The least common and most costly animal was the horse. It was not ordinarily employed for plowing in the old days; rather, it was used as a pack and riding animal and, in part, for the hauling of wagons where these were used. Many farms had no horses at all. The importance of sheep-raising was greatest in the chalky, sandy, and stony uplands of thin and harsh pasturage. Sheep were as valuable for meat and tallow as for their wool, the principal source of clothing.

Dairying is the foundation of north European husbandry, not only of cattle, but largely as well of sheep and goats. Fresh and sour milk, curds, butter, and cheese provided, together with grain, a cheap and sufficiently balanced basic diet.

Meat was not daily food except for the rich. In most production, swine held first place and rounded out the economy; they foraged in the woods and used the waste of the kitchen and the surplus or spoiled milk. Somewhat similar was the status of geese, rarely absent from a farm; they were foragers in meadow and marsh, and scavengers about the village. Roast goose, goose grease, feather pillows and comforters, and quill pens were familiar items in the life of all northern Europe.

## ANIMAL PRODUCTS MORE IMPORTANT THAN GRAIN

Nowhere else in the world was agriculture as much dominated by the many uses made of the domesticated animals. Nowhere else was as much of the time of the farmer and the farmer's wife devoted to the care of the livestock and the preparation of livestock products. Not crops, but animal products were the first objective of farming. Not the plowed fields, but the meadows and grazing lands made up the larger and more important part of the rural land. Each rural community was surrounded by garden, field, meadow, pasture, and woodland that together formed an economic areal unit, which fed, and largely clothed and furnished itself, and which disposed to nearby towns of its surplus, animal products being usually the chief of these surpluses. The products of the land were utilized primarily for feed and forage, and only secondarily for seeds and fruits for human consumption.

## CHARACTERISTIC LAND UTILIZATION

Usually one of the largest fractions of a community's land was in woodland, not dense forest. This supplied pasture, browse, fuel, and building material. In times of shortage, twigs and even bark were collected for the feeding of stock. The open pasture lands, usually dry uplands, were in large measure commons on which all the farm animals, from horses to geese, were driven to graze.

Especially important in determining the wealth of a community was the extent and quality of its meadow land. There a form of husbandry developed that is almost peculiar to northern Europe—the cutting and curing of crops of hay. The name meadow signifies the place that is mowed. In this oceanic climate, as we have seen, the lowlands were likely to be permanently wet. The low, flat lands, such as the valley floors, were therefore not commonly available for plowing. They needed deeper and closer ditching than was generally possible in the days when the only ditching tool was a spade. The oldest meadows were ordinarily the least wet parts of the lowlands. As more land was needed, ditches were dug through lower lowlands, sufficient to make them suited for grass, but hardly enough to permit plowing. The meadow was a fully permanent form of land use, and received a good deal of care, for the meadows determined how much milk could be produced in winter. With continued mowing from generation to generation, a selection of meadow plants took place. The ones that did not thrive under repeated cutting were eliminated; the more vigorous perennials remained. A similar selection occurred through pasturing; plants that could not stand repeated grazing and trampling disappeared, and the ones that did made up the pasture. Thus, meadows and pasture, by no other process than mowing and grazing, unless it be ditching, came to be composed of vigorous, perennial grasses and clovers, plants which have furnished us with our most widely valued hay and pasture plants.

The fields also were invaluable for grazing. We have seen that fields were planted mostly to some small grain. Fall-sown grains were regularly used for winter pasture. In this climate, volunteer, palatable weeds and grass came freely into the stubble, so that pasturing of the stubble was also common. Straw was mixed with hay as feed. A little grain was fed and a bit of forage, perhaps rape, often was planted.

Of greatest importance, however, was the practice of fallowing. During the period of which we speak, crop rotation was not yet practiced. A field was planted to grain for two or more years and then allowed to lie fallow for a year or longer. This not only rested the land, but it gave additional pasture surface, and the animal droppings helped fertilize the land against its return to tillage. Under the local climatic conditions and vegetation, fallow lands provided reasonably good grazing almost at once. The fallow ground also acquired animal manure, some fixation of nitrogen from volunteer legumes, and an increment of green manure when it was plowed for reseeding to grain. This handling of fallow land at least made for a balanced, if not an intensive, agriculture. By means of it, the organic content of the soil was maintained, soil deterioration was effectively prevented, and the value of animal manure recognized.

The total picture of the older land use is in brief one of a fairly good balance of man, livestock, and vegetation. It was built on a climate that was more favorable to the growth of leaf and stalk than for the ripening of seed. Basically, what was sold from the land was animal surplus rather than crop.

## Comparison of Farming in England and the Continent Before the 18th Century

The areas of most advanced agriculture in northern Europe were along the Rhine. Along the middle Rhine, fruit orchards and vineyards bordered grain fields and pastures. The lower Rhine specialized in the raising of flax and meadow culture, while on the Swiss borders dairying was well balanced with grain cultivation. Reasonably improved breeds of dairy cattle were raised both on the upper and lower Rhine, and specialized cheese-making skills were well established. In all of the Rhine lands, stall feeding was widely practiced; this allowed the most economical use of hay and fodder and also permitted the full amount of animal manure to be saved. The barn and stable were important, and sometimes the most imposing structures on a farm.

In southern England, on the other hand, there was greater emphasis on pasturage and less on feeding of livestock than on the continent. England was then still a country whose first export was wool, itself an indication of less intensive use of land than along the Rhine. Very open winters and a relative abundance of land favored a less laborious and less productive livestock husbandry. Stall feeding was little practiced. Stock fended for itself, supplemented by occasional hay placed in ricks. Hay and grain were sometimes stored under roof, but were often stacked out of doors, a practice that seems to have been little known on the continent.

A conspicuous difference in the rural landscape of England and the continent was provided by the common use of hedges in England and their absence on the continent. The hedge wasted land, but it also provided firewood. As to the heating of houses, the English situation was curiously more primitive than on the continent. In the British Isles, a simple fireplace was used for cooking and heating, wasteful and inefficient as compared to the heating stoves, of brick, tile, or cast iron, generally used on the continent. Coal was available to some of the English towns, but the country people were obliged to bring together with difficulty fuel enough for the insatiable fireplaces. Firewood was provided, in no small measure, by the hedges, and by the practice of cutting back the young shoots of heavily trimmed trees (coppicing).

## The Agricultural Revolution, Principally of the Eighteenth Century

Agricultural production was kept at a fairly uniform and rather low level by the two limiting conditions, namely, the necessity of fallowing the fields and the dependence for animal feed on hay and pasture. Red and white clover were present as part of the native growths in the grasslands, but they were not seeded in the older days.

### CLOVER AS A SOWN CROP

In the latter part of the sixteenth century, the revolution of agriculture by clover set in, though for a time very slowly. At this time, the Low Countries were in close commercial contact with Spain. From some northern part of Spain, which has an oceanic climate similar to that of the Low Countries, a superior form of red clover was brought to the lower Rhine and became known as Brabant clover. Little by little it spread along the Rhine as seeded meadow and, after a while, as a field crop. The spread, however, was very slow, and it was not until well into the eighteenth century that farmers became widely aware that red clover could take the place of the fallow. When they did so, they of course made the change from fallowing to crop rotation. One of the most important agricultural innovations of the eighteenth century was the realization that clover was valuable as a field crop and as a soil builder.

Thus began an experimentation with other clovers. Alfalfa was introduced successfully in the sunny lands of southern Germany. Crimson clover came at the beginning of the nineteenth century from Spain into the Low Countries. Alsike, best suited to wet soils, was not cultivated until well into the nineteenth century, and then through the segregation of seed in the meadows of Sweden, where it grew wild.

The more intensive agriculture spread outward from the Low Countries. Their commercial connections provided unusually favorable opportunities for bringing in new seeds and even stock from other lands. Dutch and Flemish development of clover culture was accompanied by improvement of drainage and by the development of better breeds of cattle, horses, and swine. Thus was pioneered the shift to an intensive livestock husbandry that secured increasingly higher yields from tilled land, which became capable of continuous cultivation.

DEVELOPMENT OF THE STOCK BEET

At the same time that red clover was coming into use as a sown crop, ancient garden beets were being developed into the stock beet. Beets—white, yellow, and red—had long been grown in gardens for their juicy roots, and other forms had been specialized as greens (mangold). Out of several of these, the stock beet took form during the eighteenth century, apparently in Germany and Switzerland. The result was a plant which grew both a large amount of tops and large beets, fairly high in sugar content. From these stock beets, the sugar beet was later formed by selective breeding, principally during the Napoleonic period. The stock beet was added to the field crops, first in Germany and adjacent countries, then in Scandinavia, especially in Sweden, and thereupon in England. Its cultivation substantially increased the amount of stock feed available, made possible the keeping of more livestock, added to the farm manure supply, improved the tilth of the soil, and ultimately led to sugar production in lands outside the tropics. The beet is most at home in the cool summer lands of northern and central Europe, and has a good deal of tolerance for moist air and somewhat acid soils.

## INTRODUCTION OF THE POTATO

The third great crop in the agricultural revolution of northern Europe was the potato, the history of which is still poorly known. Some of the confusion about its past rests in its name, which is properly only the name of the sweet potato *(batata)*, a plant unrelated to the common, or Irish, potato. In numerous old accounts, it is impossible to say whether the sweet or the Irish potato is described.

The common potato was the basic starch food of the Indians of the cool regions of the South American Andes, and of the natives of much of the cool coast country of Chile. Together with many other products of the New World, the Spaniards introduced it into Europe, perhaps between 1560 and 1570. It was soon planted as a vegetable in gardens in Spain and Italy, but attracted little attention. In part, the reason may be that in the Mediterranean climates, the potato hardly finds suitable conditions as a field crop, but is grown as an early vegetable, maturing before the heat of summer. By the end of the century, it was also known in gardens of Germany and the Low Countries. More significantly, it had also been introduced into the British Isles.

Until about the middle of the seventeenth century, it seems to have been little more than a rather widely distributed garden curiosity in Europe. Then it became important as food for the common man in Ireland. Its name of Irish potato is not unwarranted, for it was in Ireland that the potato became, for white people, a major food rather than a subordinate vegetable. Its spread thereafter through Europe was closely associated with hunger: failures of grain crops, devastation by war, and exploitation of peasant by landlord all helped the dissemination of the potato. Where people had enough good bread-grains, they had no interest in the potato; but when people did not have enough to eat, they learned to know its great merits. From Ireland, potato cultivation spread to western England, where it was of some importance by 1700. In the second half of the eighteenth century, it became a staple on the continent, especially all through northern Germany. In the first half of the nineteenth century, it completed its penetration of Scandinavia and the Russian lands.

The migration of the potato is a most interesting and significant illustration of a crop in search of a congenial home. In the New World it had not spread north of the Andes prior to the coming of the Spaniards; tropical heat barred its expansion northward. In the Mediterranean lands, it was grown generally as a short season crop, between winter and summer. Gradually (we do not know just when) it was introduced to the coolness and moisture of Galicia and northern Italy.

When the potato invaded the oats belt of farthest northwestern Europe, however, it found conditions greatly to its liking. Here it encountered a land of cool summers, rainier than its Andean home country, yet having the important qualities of similar temperatures during the growing season. Here it took hold not as a commercial crop but as a subsistence crop of the small farmer, planted and tended by spade, hoe, and mattock. It grew well in the good, loose soils, but it also produced reasonably well in sand and in peaty soils where grains failed. Also, it yielded four to ten times as much food as did an acre of grain. An acre of potatoes might feed a family and leave some surplus for a sow and a cow. Thus, the food situation of the Celts of the farther British Isles improved and, with lessened hunger, the population increased.

Similar events took place on the continent, where the potato invaded the rye belt about the Baltic in the latter eighteenth century. Soon it was a more important human food and a greater foodstuff than rye. It enabled people to make a better living from a smaller tilled area. It permitted the tillage of poorer soils and improved the tilth of the fields. It provided additional feed for all livestock and hence increased the supply of manure. A large increase in population took place and much new land was cleared and drained for agriculture. Especially between 1750 and 1850, north Europe, from Ireland east across Russia, came to depend on the potato as the first item of plant diet.

## NEW WORLD LEGUMES

A second New World crop, the bean, was spread rapidly over northern Europe. All the common beans we know, excepting the soybean, originated in American Indian agriculture, whether we call them string, pole, or snap beans, navy, kidney, or lima beans. The merits of boiled and baked beans were quickly recognized by the Spaniards and Portuguese of the New World, and the crop was soon planted widely in the Mediterranean. Numerous domesticated forms, like the frijol of central Mexico, came from cool uplands of the New World and were easily acclimated to northern Europe. The double utility of the plants, as a green vegetable and for the dried beans, made them welcomed in north European gardens. They spread far more rapidly than the potato, so rapidly in fact that their New World origin was forgotten until the latter part of the nineteenth century.

## SUMMARY

Four crops combined to revolutionize north European farming, mostly between 1700 and the early nineteenth century. Red clover, stock beet, and potato together made possible an enormous increase in the capacity of the land to feed livestock. Animal and green manure and bacterial nitrates were more easily acquired, and the tilth of the soil was greatly improved. As a result, agriculture became intensive, where before it had been extensive. The potato and beans contributed directly to the human food supply, and, indirectly, all of them to the dairy and meat supply available for the local population. Our first American colonists came too early to have been touched greatly by the European agricultural revolution. The eighteenth century immigrants brought with them parts of the newer husbandry. Those who came in the nineteenth century knew the full effects of the revolution in crop rotation and animal husbandry.

# 3. The March
## of Agriculture
### Across the Western World

If history often suffers by being restricted within the frame of national boundaries, the history of human learning is even more ill-
suited to being confined by political limits. Especially is this true of
the history of agriculture, which at most times is determined only
subordinately by politics or national culture. Yet of the spread of
agricultural skills, the most important culture traits possessed by
man, we have slight comparative knowledge. We speak of agriculture in the United States as though it were a conceptual unit, which
it is only in somewhat greater degree than would be a study of agriculture in Missouri. In either case, the political framework is significant only insofar as government has directed the course of agricultural development. By way of contrast, we may regard agriculture as
the employment of crops and animals for the most economical satisfaction of the most important material wants of man. The invention
and spread of agricultural traits, the development of agricultural
complexes or systems, and the solutions of environmental problems
attained thereby then become the objectives of inquiry. In these
terms, we may attempt a necessarily inadequate outline of the

The abstract for "The March of Agriculture Across the Western World" first
appeared in *Proc. Eighth American Sci. Congress* held in Washington, May 10–18,
1940, 5:63–65, 1942. The paper itself, however, is printed here for the first time.

growth of agriculture in the New World. The sequence of time may perhaps be generalized into five periods, each of which has added its increment of agricultural learning to the agricultural institutions as they now exist.

## THE ABORIGINAL STAGE

Indian agriculture in most parts of the New World is not an antiquarian matter. The aboriginal cultivators found and bred a series of crops for almost every climate in which agriculture is now practiced in this hemisphere. For the most part, the geographic limits of agriculture have not been greatly advanced by the coming of the white man. In many places we have not passed the limits of Indian farming at all. The most important exceptions are the far west of the United States, the Pampas of the Argentine, and the far north of the northern continent. The question of the lack of agriculture in the Pampas is most interesting, and the reasons therefore are still unsolved, but these reasons are certainly not climatic.

Since primitive agriculture was dependent solely on the labor of men and women working with planting stick, foot plow, or hoe, the most serious barriers to primitive cultivation were found in heavy soils and a cover of sod. In the utilization of broken terrain and forest land, on the other hand, the aboriginal systems were highly effective.

In general, it may be said that the plant domesticates of the New World far exceeded in range and efficiency the crops that were available to Europeans at the time of the discovery of the New World. In grains Europe had nothing to match Indian maize as to productivity, food value, utility for hill lands, and varietal adaptations to many climates. Starchy root crops were almost wanting in Europe, whereas America, south of the United States, had one or more excellent ones for every climate, among them some, such as manioc and potato, that are unequalled in the world in food produced per unit of tillage. In plant proteins and fats, Europe again was poor and the New World richly supplied by cultivated plants. Especially in the subtropical lands, that is, the edge of the *tierra templada* against the *tierra caliente,* there was characteristically an embarrassment of agricultural riches: different kinds of corn, flour, and dent, but perhaps also flint, pop, and sugar; beans, including a large color and dietary range of the kidney beans, both as dry beans and for green vegetables; sweet potato, manioc, and other tubers; tomatoes and chiles; avocado, cacao, papaya, pineapple, and other fruits in number; Barbadoes cotton for the tropical lowlands and, in more temperate lands, the upland cotton that is ancestral to virtually all commercial cotton of today.

The ancient Indian plant breeders had done their work well. In the genial climates, there was an excellent, high yielding plant for every need of food, drink, seasoning, or fiber. On the climatic extremes of cold and drought, there still were a remarkable number of plant inventions that stretched the limits of agriculture about as far as plant growth permitted. One needs only to dip into the accounts of the early explorers and colonists, especially Spanish, to know the amazement with which the Europeans learned the quality and variety of crop plants of Indian husbandry.

Native methods of tillage were remarkably benign in their effects on the soil. Planting and cultivation did not give rise to furrows or even commonly to lineal rows. The "hilling" of the plants tended to break the surface into a maximum number of small elevations and depressions that were favorable to arresting the movement of water down slopes. Hill cultivation (temporalis) was in effect a long term rotation of wild woody growth and of crop plants. It is, nevertheless, apparent that in the long run soil has been stripped in considerable amounts from hillsides. It is probable that when we know much more about the geography of American archeology, we shall have a variety of evidence as to the deterioration of crop lands through ancient agriculture, and that less appeal will be made to climatic change in accounting for the failure of such settlements.

THE BLENDING OF OLD WORLD
AND NEW WORLD AGRICULTURE

The New World was not explored nor first appropriated by Europeans for the sake of farming. This is true of every nationality that established colonies across the Atlantic. All of them knew or soon learned, however, that they had to feed themselves by products raised locally. In considerable measure the Spanish colonists were able to use the Indian populations as purveyors of food; in other cases, at least part of the energy of the colonists was directed to the production of food.

The period from 1492 to about 1620 is of a special interest since it laid the basis for the world-wide agricultural revolution, which is usually not recognized until much later. This is indeed the time of the greatest exchange of breeding stock of plants and animals between the Old World and the New.

All the European colonial groups recognized very soon the quality, range, and productivity of the Indian crop lands. During the sixteenth century, the Spanish and Portuguese settlers and sailors fed themselves largely on maize, manioc, potatoes, and beans, with resulting important changes in culinary habits. At the same time, a large scale introduction of New World plants took place into the Mediterranean countries of Europe. Well before the end of the sixteenth century, the cultivation of cotton, tobacco, maize, beans, and capsicum or chile had spread from end to end through the Mediterranean lands. The sweet potato had been widely introduced and the true potato partially. From this base a gradual dissemination took place northward, with the increasing elimination of the climatically less plastic varieties. France, the Low Countries, and the British Isles in particular served as experimental grounds in the selection of American crop plants.

The Old World, in its turn, provided both subsistence and commercial crops to the Spanish and Portuguese colonies. For the most part, these crops were grown chiefly about the larger centers of white population for the supply of the more prosperous classes. Wheat, for instance, remained in most sections a luxury commodity, the principal exception thereto being provided by Chile, where it soon became the staple, in a land climatically more congenial to wheat than to maize. Most numerous was the introduction of fruits and the garden vegetables of the Old World. About these transfers of Old World plants to this side of the Atlantic, we are even less informed than concerning the dispersal from the New World into the Old.

Of greatest significance was the bringing of all kinds of livestock and poultry from the Old World and thereby the gradual establishment of elements of animal husbandry in the agricultural practices of the native cultivators. Thus an elaborate blending of the domesticated plant and animal resources of both hemispheres provided on both sides of the ocean a large enrichment of agriculture. Specifically, this was a time of trial of environmental adaptations and economic utility of newly available plant and animal resources, and resulted in the formation of a large number of new agriculture complexes or economies.

During this century, for various reasons, terrific reductions took place in many areas of the Indian populations. Initial abundance of labor gave way to chronic labor shortage. It is possible that the latter part of the sixteenth century saw the areas of formerly most advanced native civilization and most dense populations at their lowest level. This shortage of available labor was made good only partially by the introduction of Negro slaves. Numerous areas became so reduced in population that fields and villages became abandoned in large measure. This vacated, open land was then utilized for the establishment of stock ranches. Repeatedly it can be shown that rise of livestock and decline of agricultural settlements go hand in hand. By the end of the sixteenth century, the stock ranches had also moved out into broad areas of grassy or brushy steppe and savannah which had been of minor utility to Indian agriculture. Northern Mexico and northwest Argentina are illustrations of this process. The majority of the mining districts of Latin America had been opened during the century. The great and continuous demands of the mines for work stock, leather and rawhide, tallow and meat, made stock-raising commonly the most profitable use of land for long distances around the mining districts. The mines, indeed, in general provided the markets of greatest purchasing power, and, hence, dominated the development of agricultural economy.

Here and there, in especially advantageous climatic situations, the first foundations of the plantation system were laid. The discovery that sugar cane could be grown well in the New World without irrigation made American cane plantations the prototype of virtually the whole development of the subsequent growth of plantations of the world. Of New World crops, cacao, cotton, and tobacco in particular are introduced into plantation economy.

Old World methods of land use applied to New World conditions set up new forms of attrition of the surface, in particular in mining areas which became in some measure centers of soil erosion. Often they were completely denuded of their trees, in some cases even of their brush and coarse grass, to supply the mining centers with fuel. In many cases, the old mining camps to this day are characterized by almost complete lack of woody growth. In addition, the necessity of pasturing a large amount of work stock around the mines resulted in a serious over-grazing and baring of the surface. It should be remembered that the mines required not only a large number of pack and draft animals but that animals were the principal source of motive power for operating mine hoists, grinding the ore, and performing the process of amalgamation in the patios of the mines.

## RISE OF PLANTATIONS IN THE
## SEVENTEENTH AND EIGHTEENTH CENTURIES

While the Spanish were elaborating a mining economy that provided for commercial stock and crop raising, the Portuguese pioneered plantation agriculture. Almost simultaneously, they introduced the Old World sugar cane to the tropical coast of Brazil, and began the planting of tobacco and cotton. Production of these crops as monoculture by forced labor on large land holdings was joined with partial processing and direct merchandising to European markets. Thus the plantation system was born in the tropics of the New World. Sugar and alcohol in particular became major commodities of world commerce.

The Portuguese success in Brazil was followed in the seventeenth century by the intrusion of Dutch, English, and French plantation colonies into the New World. The profits of the trade in sugar and alcohol were the mainspring of colonial activity (other than Spanish) throughout the seventeenth and eighteenth centuries. The West Indian sugar islands were far and away the most important American possessions of England. In colonial Virginia, an originally tropical American product, tobacco, introduced probably by way of Europe, formed a lone extension of plantation agriculture into extratropical lands. French colonists of the West Indies in the eighteenth century introduced in coffee a second major plantation crop from the Old World.

Characteristically, the plantation specialized in one commercial crop, though many things may have been grown for the needs of the plantation laborers. Climatic advantage, suitability of soils, and shipping advantage resulted in marked localization of the plantation districts, usually sharply segregated as to commodity. Functionally the Portuguese, English, and French plantations on the one hand, and the extratropical settlements of each nation on the other, were in a position similar to that of the Spanish mining districts and their supply areas of stock ranches and farms. Extratropical southern Brazil complemented the sugar country of the Beijamar by animal, grain, and lumber products, as the continental English colonies supplied the British West Indies. New England, chiefly, was made possible by Barbados, Jamaica, the Leeward Islands, and the plantations of Virginia.

Of soil exhaustion and soil erosion in the tobacco fields of Virginia we are informed. We know less of the effects of sugar planting. It appears that the decline of Barbados, in early years the richest English colony, was partially caused by diminished productivity of the land. Many of the cane plantations of the West Indies were laid out on low slopes. Irrigation was often added to such plantations, especially on drier parts of the islands. In the course of time, it seems that the continued application of water and clean cultivation caused permanent and perhaps widespread damage. The subject, however, has been scarcely investigated.

## FARMING SETTLEMENTS INITIATED
## IN THE EIGHTEENTH CENTURY

Farming is a rather late and localized development in the New World. Basically, in its genesis, it is associated with the English colonies of the mainland of North America and is derivative from the agricultural communities of northwestern Europe. There is perhaps a tendency in American historical studies to overemphasize the role of New England and the southern colonies in this respect. Early New England was concerned with agricultural production as a matter of necessity rather than with farming as a chosen way of life. The economy of early New England was a town economy in which commerce and manufacturing, rather than tilling of the soil, played leading roles. Virginia and Carolina were plantation foundings, it is true, with a backwoods fringe. These early backwoods settlements, however, contained little that was germinal for the development of the farm. If we consider the farm to be a family institution, concerned in its earlier period primarily with supplying the family with most of its necessities of life and uniting crop and animal husbandry, this development took place on an important scale only at the beginning of the eighteenth century.

The basic form is developed mostly in the middle colonies of English America. It is a phenomenon of woodland settlement of a variety of origins. The log house is an important element, for it enabled the pioneer to erect adequate buildings without recourse to saw mills and carpenters. The log house is made by one tool, the axe. It is now agreed that this structure was introduced on the Delaware by the Swedish and Finnish settlers. The taking over of a superior maize from the Indians by the European settlers is another step of importance. It appears that in Pennsylvania and Maryland the settlers acquired valuable forms of high yielding, dent corn from the Indians, supplying not only the basic food for the family but a foodstuff for livestock. In this area we have a very early industry of fattening hogs and of feeding work stock with corn. From sources as yet not sufficiently known, improved livestock, horses, cattle, and swine become established between the Hudson and the Potomac. The American barn and farm wagon are developed in the same area. The single farmstead reflects the self-contained family unit and becomes the dominant mode of rural living, having beginnings in the middle colonies. These developments were made possible by a large emigration at the beginning of the eighteenth century of rural folk from northwestern Europe. This is the great inflow of Germans from the Rhine, including German-speaking Swiss, principally Mennonites from the canton of Bern, which was a group of particular importance in transferring important agricultural traits. It also involved great numbers of Scotch-Irish, Irish, and Scots who established themselves in particular on the outer fringes of settlement. The introduction at this time, and largely by these groups, of grass and clover culture and of the Irish potato added greatly to the productive equipment of the farmer. Increasingly mingled as to human stock and blended as to farming practices, the eighteenth century rural immigrants spread southwestward through the Piedmont and mountain valleys behind the plantation colonies of the south, and westward across the mountains into the fringes of the interior prairies. The inclusive period of the development of the American farm may be set between the dates of 1700 and 1825.

Partial parallels can be noted in Spanish and Portuguese territory, again principally in extratropical woodlands. From Spain a type of small husbandmen came in numbers, in particular out of Galicia and Asturias and the Basque provinces. These people were accustomed to animal husbandry related to that of northwest Europe. They raised feed for swine and milk cattle. They were subsistence farmers in their own lands. A similar situation was true of the north Portuguese. Chile, Venezuela, the south of Brazil, and perhaps Colombia provide illustrations of colonization reminiscent of the American pioneer farm. During the nineteenth century, in particular, south Chile and southern Brazil show important developments of farm settlements. An adequate distinction has not yet been made between the aristocratic *latifundia,* usually derivative from the background of the *encomiendas,* and employing native labor, on the one hand, and the small peasant or yeoman colonization, basically democratic, on the other hand.

THE EXPORT AGRICULTURE OF HUMID GRASSLANDS

The last great expansion of agriculture may be designated as the hundred years from 1820 to 1920—from the beginning of steam transport to the end of the World War. Previously, agriculture had been carried on for home consumption or for short distance trade, but only in the case of valuable specialty products—such as sugar, coffee, and indigo—for the supplying of distant markets. With steamboats on rivers, lakes, and sea, and soon steam trains on land, long hauls of bulky, low-priced and somewhat perishable farm products, mainly foodstuffs, became possible. This torrent of cheap food and foodstuffs, increasing for a century and directed primarily to western Europe and the northeastern United States, made possible the extraordinary industrialization and increase of population of those lands. The increased agricultural production was realized chiefly by the plowing up of two of the greatest extratropical grasslands of the world, centering about the prairies of the Mississippi Valley, with adjacent Canada, and the Pampas of the La Plata Basin. These grasslands were extraordinarily fertile but had been, until then, inaccessible to agriculturalists. Of heavy texture and held by a dense mat of grass roots, these soils required the steel plow and tools perfected at this time, as well as powerful draft animals.

About 1920, the centuries-long process of agricultural expansion is drastically checked; suddenly there are no more large tracts of fertile land that can be brought into production at low cost. The frontiers of settlement had moved out from the Mississippi and the La Plata in similar, headlong manner until they encountered permanent barriers of aridity in the west in both cases; in the north, they met limits of cold; in the other, the almost equally serious climatic problem contained in the region of El Gran Chaco.

We are not yet in a position to cast up the balance sheet of the century just past with its optimism of endless land resources. Such optimism as to the availability of new lands for old led to an exhaustive cropping and large scale loss of surface soil, and largely corrupted the older peasant thriftiness of seeking an equivalent return to the soil for that which had been removed therefrom. Soil depletion, soil wasting, and soil drift increasingly laid hold on lands of initially high fertility. In these youngest agricultural lands of the New World, the incidence of soil destruction is perhaps more menacing than in any of the older categories of land use.

This sketch of events, under its five headings, is a suggested program of an almost undeveloped field of comparative study. Actually, we know little of cultural origins of New World agriculture as to land tenures, crops and cropping practices, rural populations and their employment, or kinds, quantities, and values of products. As general background, three types of studies in particular are needed:

1. We need to know where and in what number people lived on the land. Population studies usually deal with the contemporary scenes, or are casual estimates of early days. Until we know what the labor reservoirs and shortages were, and what was the number of urban consumers, we are guessing in the dark about colonial, economic structures.

2. We need to know the destructive effects on soil, surface, and native vegetation in each agricultural period. If such destruction of surface took place many years ago, as through overgrazing about old mines or on colonial pulque plantations, it may be misconstrued as normal erosion. This field therefore requires studies in normal erosion forms and soil profiles under various conditions of climate and terrain in order to determine the features of induced erosion. It also requires close documentary knowledge of the locations and kinds of destructive economic processes.

3. We need exact knowledge of the domesticated plants and animals as to their spread over the New World. These living things are themselves a documentary record of the past which has been little regarded. By good fortune we have, in some cases, written records of occurrence of introduction of a crop or domestic animal. But where there was no such record, the plant or animal may still exist to give us the clue to cultural spread. Students of geography, economic history, anthropology, agronomy, animal husbandry, and genetics need to develop a working association to such ends in all the countries of the New World. Collaborators are needed in every agricultural region, in particular in those of aboriginal and colonial importance.

In terms of native plants, we know shockingly little about the kinds, occurrence, growth characteristics, and utilities of our American crop plants as compared to our knowledge of the wild New World flora. Only a few students have as yet given us glimpses of the varietal distribution and ecology of such important domesticates as maize and beans. In most literature, maize is maize, and beans are beans, and that's the end of it. Yet a careful regard of the varietal range of these two major crops will tell us more of the early movements of human culture than any means of inspection other than archeology, and it will tell us certain things that the archeologic record will never disclose. The host of minor native domesticates, some of them very ancient, is even less regarded. Nor are we much better informed about the introductions from the Old World of such things as citrus and stone fruits, small grains, and breeds of livestock. Many an archaic form of these survives in back-country localities in the New World, that can probably no longer be found in the Old. Cumulative observations along such lines might well begin with brief and rather random notes on noted presences of distinctive forms of any plant or animal domesticate. Soon the participation of geneticists will be needed to place such items as to phylogeny. Gradually, distributional synthesis can be attempted to chart the spread of these items as culture traits. This sort of inquiry has not only great possibilities for the enrichment of studies in culture history; it would have as well the most practical application of helping to save the work of past generations for future generations of plant and animal breeders. Ironically, the present spread of scientific agriculture and of breeds, strains, and varieties from United States breeding stations is rapidly extinguishing in area after area to the south of us the older, more primitive forms, with their greater range of genetic diversity , unknown as to their long-range breeding value.

These three forms of inquiry, on population change, on destructive exploitation of land, and on domesticated plants and animals, can only be developed by regional specialization. In all of the countries of the New World, we need men and women who will patiently observe and record and interpret such data, and who will then have the opportunity of comparing their findings and building them into larger generalizations. These themes, in themselves of interdisciplinary character, are eminently adapted for consideration in this and successive American scientific congresses.

# 4. Homestead and Community
## on the
## Middle Border

A public anniversary in the present American mood is likely to consider the date as a determinate point between the past and the future. The past thus is of interest chiefly because it shows what change has taken place and what its direction has been. The present is the base from which we project the future. Perhaps more than any other people, or at any other time, we are committed to living in a mundane future, confident we shall control it by anticipation, that is, by planning the march of the material progress desired.

The immediate instrument of change is provided by the spiraling advance of technics that appear to put limitless material possibilities in our hands, and it is of these that we think primarily. What we have gained, at least for the present, is the ability to produce many more goods of more kinds for more people. We not only think to hold the horn of plenty but we believe we can and should pass it on to the rest of the world. Capacity to produce and capacity to consume form a reciprocating system that we desire to expand without end.

An edited version of "Homestead and Community on the Middle Border" appeared in *Landscape,* 12(1):3–7, 1962, and it was this version which appeared in *Land and Life,* John Leighly, Ed., (University of California: Berkeley, 1963). At Dr. Sauer's specific request we reprint here the original, unedited, version, as it first appeared in *Land Use Policy in the United States,* Howard W. Ottoson, Ed., (University of Nebraska: Lincoln, Nebraska, 1963).

Growth in material wants and in the ability to satisfy them and so to stimulate new wants is what we are agreed is progress. We measure progress by such things as gross national product, income per capita, standard of living (a term we have introduced to the world; perhaps it is the most widely known of all American phrases), level of employment, new construction, and other quantitative indices of an expanding economy. The system, insofar as we have seen it work, depends on continued acceleration and perhaps on being kept jogged by the stimuli of debt and taxes as well as of consumption and obsolescence. The American image is becoming that of the compulsive spender of neo-Keynesian doctrine. Thorstein Veblen formed his thesis of conspicuous waste too soon by a generation.

Output grows with input and so on, requiring more and more engagement of expert technicians. The objective of growth necessitates making and carrying out more and more decision about public policy, which becomes an increasingly limited and coveted prerogative. For the individual and the community the choice as to how one would live becomes more restricted in the interest of the will and authority of what is proposed as the commonweal. Reducing the risks of livelihood we also diminish the diversity of purposes and ends of individual living, once richly present in rural America.

On this occasion we call to remembrance an event of a hundred years ago when American life differed greatly from the present mode, mood, and meaning. We may take a look back over a formative span of our history which lasted for several generations, a long time as our history goes. In its first part we were a rural nation, the first major shift to city living coming as the result of the Civil War and its industrial mobilization. Thereafter, population flowed more and more from country to city but the ways and values of rural living continued for two more generations to have much the accustomed meaning and content. We are here in fact taking part in an Old Settlers Reunion, as descendants of those who left their previous places and conditions of life to take part in making a new West, the Promised Land which a chosen people came to possess. In the western migration there was an Old Testament sense of fulfillment that should not be forgotten.

The Homestead National Monument, situated where wooded valley met upland prairie, is a model geographic expression of the manner in which the West was settled. This first homestead as taken under the act lies well out into the farther and later part of the Midwest. Its specific location records still the original pioneer requirement of a living site with wood and water, requisites that the building of railroads soon made unnecessary. When this tract was taken up, only three young and raw towns were in the Territory of Nebraska, all of them on the Missouri River. Through them emigrant trails led to Oregon and California, bearing westward over prairie and wooded stream, in a land still ranged over by Indian, buffalo, antelope, and deer. In very short order the wild land was brought into cultivation and fully settled. By mid-century, the westward course of homesteading had begun to cross the Missouri line at the west, to be halted later by dryness farther on. In simple outline, I should like to direct attention to the peopling of that part of the interior we know as the corn belt. The wheat belt is another, though derivative, story. What sort of rural living was established on the Middle Border; what were its attainments and satisfactions, its lacks and failures?

The date of the Homestead Act marks conveniently for our recall a moment of significance in the mainstream of American history, the great westward movement of families seeking land to cultivate and own. This movement began from states of the eastern seaboard, swelled to surges across the wide basin of the Mississippi-Missouri and ebbed away in the high plains. To the south and north there were other westward movements sufficiently different in kind and route as to be left out of present consideration. The Middle Border, as it has been named appropriately, was the wide, advancing wave of settlement that spread over the plains south of the Great Lakes and north of the Ohio River, making use of both waterways as approaches. Its advances made Cleveland, Toledo, and Chicago northern gateways. At the south it gave rise to border cities on rivers, such as Cincinnati on the Ohio, St. Louis at the crossing of the Mississippi, and Kansas City on the great bend of the Missouri. The Mississippi was crossed in force in the 1830s, the Missouri River into Kansas in the border troubles prior to the Civil War. Although it did not begin as such this became the peopling of the prairies, the founding and forming of the actual Midwest.

The Homestead Act came pretty late in the settlement of the interior. Land had been given free of cost to many. It had been sold at nominal prices and on easy terms by public land offices and by canal and railroad companies. The squatter who settled without title was generously protected by preemption rights and practices that grew stronger. Many millions of acres had been deeded as homesteads before the act and many more continued to be acquired by other means afterward. Land was long available in great abundance. The price in money of the wild land was the least cost of making it into a farm. Public land offices were set up to get land into private hands quickly, simply, and cheaply. Under the Graduation Act lands were reduced in price according to the length of time they had been on the market, the last cut being to twelve and one-half cents an acre. Canal and railroad lands were priced to sell. The railroads were well aware that revenue from farm traffic would be their largest return. The land seeker was induced to buy railroad land because he knew that he was given facility of transportation. The theme that land was a commodity for speculation is certainly true, yet it may be over-stressed and oversimplified. The settler knew that the price of the farm was mainly in the work of all the family, in making out or doing without, in minimizing wants and spending. Largely, our farms could not be reproduced from wild land at present prices, wages, and standards.

Advantage of location was of first importance in selecting the home site. The original entry of a tract was because of its immediate suitability as a homestead rather than because it would continue to be most desirable; locational advantages change, as might productive capacity. Settlers were in process of regrouping themselves in neighborhoods of their liking. The drawbacks of one place having been experienced, a better location might be sought farther on. Property passed from one hand to another at a price reflecting, perhaps, the improvements made more than rise in land value. The term "land speculation" is not fully adequate or appropriate. The relinquisher was paid for the worth he had put in, the purchaser received a partially improved farm. The early succession of owners largely was a passing from financially weaker to stronger hands. The border was pretty fluid in its first years. Those who moved on are forgotten, or appear only as names of patentees and first conveyors of title. Those who remained and took root became the Old Settlers. There were various kinds and conditions of people who moved into or across the Middle Border, the restless and the sedentary, the overflow from older settlements farther east and the immigrants from Europe for whom this was a first opportunity to live on land of their own.

The famous frontier thesis of Professor Turner was adapted from a theory of social evolution that was popular late in the nineteenth century. According to it, mankind everywhere has gone through the same series of stages of progress from simpler to more advanced skills and societies. The succession is held to be the same, the rate to differ with the environment. It was an attractive, simple theory of history, not borne out by the facts anywhere. Turner picked up the general idea and thought to reproduce the whole supposed history of human experience in the short span of the American frontier. Thus he saw our frontier as a "field for comparative study of social development," beginning with Indian and white hunter; followed by the "disintegration of savagery by the entrance of the trader, the pathfinder of civilization"; then by the pastoral stage; the raising of unrotated crops of corn and wheat in sparsely settled farming communities; intensive agriculture; and finally, the industrial society. He saw each stage present "in the march toward the West, impelled by an irresistible attraction. Each passed in successive waves across the continent." This plot of a westward-moving pageant in six scenes was good drama but was not our history.

As corollary to this theory of cultural succession he proposed one of cultural regression, namely that whoever entered a new scene or stage reverted from his former ways to accept those of the "stage" he was joining. Thus, the wilderness "takes him from the railroad car and puts him in the birch canoe and arrays him in the hunting shirt and moccasin. It puts him in the log cabin of the Cherokee and

Iroquois and runs an Indian palisade around him . . . he shouts the
war cry and takes the scalp." A half truth. Every migrant group loses
some of the elements of its previous culture in fitting itself into a new
environment, whether wilderness or city. It may also introduce some
traits of its own. The spell of a uniformly determinate course of social
evolution as cast by the anthropologist Lewis Morgan and the sociol-
ogist Herbert Spencer took hold of Turner, who passed it on to his
pupils.

The first three stages or waves of Turner did not exist in the
Middle Border. The next two were not stages but the entry of differing cultures.

From the Indian, the American settler acquired learning that
was important for his survival and well-being, mainly as to agricultural ways. The settler was still a European in culture who had the
good sense to make use of what was serviceable to him in the knowledge of the Indians of the eastern woodlands. This learning began at
Jamestown and Plymouth and was pretty well completed before the
Appalachians were crossed. It contributed Indian corn, along with
beans and squash, as the basis of frontier sustenance. The seed corn
the settler took west with him was dent corn from Indians of the
middle seaboard and flint corn from those of the northeast. Mainly
he appears to have grown yellow dent, presumably acquired from
Indians in Pennsylvania. A preferred parent in breeding our races of
hybrid corn has been the Lancaster Surecropper, an old kind from
eastern Pennsylvania. The Indian corn, beans, and squash of the East
were well suited to western climate and soils until settlement got
well beyond the Missouri River. The settler took over Indian ways of
woodland clearing and planting. He prepared corn for his staple food
in Indian ways, from succotash and hominy to corn cakes. He had
learned back east to make maple syrup and sugar after the Indian
fashion and continued thus to supply himself as far west as sugar
maples grew. He brought with him the Indian art of dressing buck-
skins and making apparel. These were new learnings. Professor
Turner possibly was right in attributing the stockade to Indian example but, if so, it too was learned from the Indians of the Atlantic
states. The Indians, of course, did not have log cabins.

Little seems to have passed from the Indians of the interior to the settlers. The Indian culture west of the Appalachians was still significantly based on cultivation, more largely so than is thought popularly to have been the case. Whether the western Indians contributed any strains of cultivated plants had little attention until we get much farther west, to the Mandans of the upper Missouri and the Pueblo tribes of the Southwest. The Pawnee were a numerous village-dwelling people living toward the western margin of the humid country. One might expect that some strains of plants they cultivated passed on to the white settlers. Did their earth lodges suggest the dugout house of the pioneer, a curious and unusual form of dwelling? The Caddoan tribes to which the Pawnee and Wichita Indians belonged were anciently established farmers as well as hunters living between the prairies and high plains (witness the Coronado expedition) and might have had something to add to the trans-Missouri frontier.

The American entry into the Mississippi Valley encountered the Indian tribes in an advanced condition of disturbance, dislodgement, and dissolution. In most of our early accounts they are described in terms of disdain, deprecation, and disgust, without awareness that what was being witnessed was the breakdown of a native society. The Delawares, Wyandots, and Shawnees had been driven far from their homes. The Spanish government in upper Louisiana invited them to a haven west of the Mississippi. Briefly they built and occupied farming villages there, but the Louisiana Purchase soon dislodged them again to drift west beyond the borders of Missouri. The Illini tribes were broken early, beginning with Iroquois raids that stemmed from French and English rivalries. American penetration about the Great Lakes pushed Pottawatomis, Kickapoos, Sacs, and Foxes to pressing upon tribes that lived beyond the Mississippi. The old resident tribes did not like the new ones, the whites liked neither. The Missourians in particular, carrying on the Indian hating of the Kentuckians and Tennesseans, would have none of them. The remnants of a score of tribes were piled west beyond the Missouri line, some from as far east as Pennsylvania and New York. In the territories that were to become Kansas and Nebraska they were given reservations between the native Osages, Kansas, and Pawnees until most of them in a last remove were taken into the Indian Territory. (The original Kansas City, Kansas, was named Wyandot and began as a village of those Indians.)

Dispossessed of title to home, deprived of their economy, and losing hope that there might be another start, many were reduced to beggary or lived as pariahs about the white settlements. Their debauch was completed by alcohol, a thing wholly foreign to their ways, which became for them a last escape. Objects of despair to each other, and of contempt and annoyance to the whites, the time was missed when the two races might have learned from each other and lived together.

The French settlements, nearly all in river villages, were the meager reality of a vast colonial design of a New France that was planned to reach from the St. Lawrence to the Gulf of Mexico. The French habitants contributed little to the ways of the Middle Border. Some of their villages remained as enclaves in the American land. They were indifferent farmers. Despite the rich alluvial lands by the side of which they lived, they were often short of food. Some were fur traders in season, ranging far up the rivers, and instructing a few Americans in the fur trade, but this had precious little to do with the settlement of the interior. Some showed Americans, such as Moses Austin, a very primitive way to mine and smelt lead. The Americans got the word "prairie" from them to replace the name "barrens," which had been given to grassy uplands in Kentucky and was still used in Missouri around the time of the Louisiana Purchase. The French were easygoing, amiable people who did a little of various things and some of these well, but they were not the pathfinders of a French, much less an American, civilization, nor did they think of themselves as such. The romantic attribution to the trader of being the pathfinder has its proper place in the western mountains and beaver streams, not in the interior prairies and woodlands.

Most of the earlier American pioneers of the Mississippi Valley came by a southerly approach. They were known as Virginians and Carolinians, later as Kentuckians and Tennesseans, and in final attenuation as Missourians. They came on foot and horseback across the Cumberlands and Alleghenies, usually to settle for a while in Kentucky or Tennessee and thence to move on by land or river and cross the Ohio and Mississippi rivers. The relocations of the Lincoln and Boone families are familiar examples. Turner's stages are not properly descriptive of the order or manner of their coming. By his scheme they would need to be distributed through his four first stages, least apparent in the second. Actually, they do not sort out as such separate waves.

The border had an element that came in for unfavorable comment in almost every early account, of persons who had taken to the backwoods because they did not fit into an ordered society, either because of their indolence, or perhaps for some misdemeanor or crime. They were the shiftless and the reckless, sometimes called drifters in the language of the West, the flotsam carried on the advancing wave of settlement, but not the first, nor a distinct wave. Violence was not marked in the history of this border except for Kansas where ruffians enjoyed a license through the approaching civil conflict. Some such "out" groups became lodged permanently in the poor corners of the Midwest. But largely they drifted on into the farther Southwest and far West. Some got stranded on the overflow lands of the Missouri and Mississippi, others in the "hollers" of the hill lands adjacent. They were early in the history of settlement and chose to live segregated from the rest, usually marrying among their own kind. Of all settlers these were the most fully self-sufficient. A patch of cleared ground was in the woman's care; a litter of hogs ranged free. The men fished and hunted and loafed and kept hound dogs. In the steamboat days money could be had by cutting and loading firewood. When the railroads came there were ties to be hacked. They would work to sell something when they wanted money; employment they avoided. They were indifferent to increasing their income or to owning property. Some were defectors from civilization; I knew two of the most famous names of Virginia among them. They were considered to be predominantly a farther fringe of the Southern poor whites, usually bearing English surnames, in part a residue from the least fit part of those shipped to the colonies. I do not think that Turner's view of cultural regression on the frontier applies; the frontier gave room for antisocial elements as well as for the builders of society.

The main contingent of pioneer settlers were a different breed. Theodore Roosevelt hailed them as Scotch-Irish, Mencken stressed their Celtic tone and temperament, Ellen Semple saw them as Anglo-Saxons of the Appalachians. Whatever their origins, and they were multiple, those were the backwoodsmen who brought and developed the American frontier way of life. They were woodland farmers, hunters, and raisers of livestock in combination, and very skilled in the use of axe and rifle. Trees were raw material for their log cabins and worm fences, and also an encumbrance of the ground, to be deadened, burned, or felled. The planting ground was enclosed by a rail fence, the livestock ranged free in wood or prairie. When the New Englander Albert Richardson reported life in eastern Kansas in the time of border troubles (*Beyond the Mississippi*) he said he could tell the home of a settler from Missouri by three things: The (log) house had the chimney built on the outside and at the end of the house; the house was located by a spring which served for keeping food in place of a cellar, and one was given buttermilk to drink. He might have added that there would be corn whiskey on hand and that if the family was really Southern the corn bread would be white.

This colonization was early and massive, beginning by 1800 and having the new West almost to itself until into the 1830s. At the time of the Louisiana Purchase American settlers already held Spanish titles to a million acres in Missouri alone, mainly along the Mississippi and lower Missouri rivers. They moved up the northern tributaries of the Ohio River as far as these were wooded; they filled the river valleys of Illinois and those of eastern Iowa and even penetrated north somewhat into Wisconsin and Minnesota. Their homes and fields were confined to wooded valleys, their stock pastured on the upland prairies. Nebraska alone of the mid-continent remained almost wholly beyond the limits of their settlement.

Viewed ecologically, their occupation of the land was pretty indifferent to permanence. Trees were gotten rid of by any means, the grasslands were overgrazed, game was hunted out. They were farmers after the Indian fashion of woods-deadening, clearing, and planting, and made little and late use of plow or wagon. The impression is that they gave more heed to animal husbandry than to the care of their fields or to the improvement of crops. Central and northwest Missouri, for example, the best flowering of this "Southern" frontier, developed the Missouri mule early in the Sante Fe trade, and later bred saddle, as well as trotting, horses, and beef cattle. I do not know that it contributed anything to crop improvement, unless it was in bluegrass pastures.

There was self-sufficiency of food to this frontier but also there was a well-marked commercial side. It had things to sell or exchange for merchandise, above all tobacco, not a little corn whiskey, hogs on the hoof, in some cases hemp or cotton—all items that could be put on boat or horseback or driven to more or less distant markets. The settlers brought with them knowledge as to how tobacco should be grown, harvested, cured, and packed for shipment.

Corn and tobacco were the two crops planted in the new clearings in the woods, and they continued to be grown on the same land so long as its fertility lasted. Several acres of tobacco gave the needed purchasing power to the small farmer. Tobacco growing also attracted slave-owning planters north across the Ohio and especially west across the Mississippi, beginning with the Spanish government that freely granted land and sanction of slavery. From the beginning, the backwoods farmer, the hunter of the long rifle, and the slave-holding planter mingled in this stream of American colonists; they might indeed be the same individuals. When the corn and tobacco fields began to fail under the clean cultivation these crops required, more virgin woodland was at hand or farther on. The effects of soil exposure to slope-wash by continued planting of corn and tobacco in early days may still be seen from the Muskingum Valley across Missouri to the Kansas border in surfaces of light color and tight texture that reveal the loss of the original topsoil.

This migration of the early nineteenth century came without benefit of constructed facilities of transportation, of public or private capital, or of most of the products of the newly begun machine age, except for the river steamboat. The people came in bands of kindred and friendship to settle in contiguity that was less than close clustering and more than wide dispersal. Their locations quite properly bore the name of a "settlement," identified perhaps by the name of the leader, or of the stream along which their homesteads were strung. Thus, the group Daniel Boone led to Missouri was known both as the Boone Settlement and as the Femme Osage Settlement, the French name of the principal creek. The colony of families the senior Bollinger led from North Carolina across the Mississippi to Missouri was known by his name and as the Whitewater Settlement. Largely such transplanted communities were of kith and kin that maintained close connections even though each household lived on its own homestead. The lonely family cabin, removed far from and isolated from its neighbors is mostly a myth, even as to Daniel Boone himself. Sociability, not aloofness, was the quality of life sought. Much of the work was done by mutual aid; leisure time was time for meeting, a word of special meaning in the vernacular of the frontier. Such were the people and the life that Mark Twain knew so well and portrayed with affection. They enjoyed discourse in all forms and on all occasions, respected those who excelled in it, and produced an able lot of politicians, lawyers, ministers of the gospel, and school-teachers.

The great northern immigration began in the 1830s and depended from the beginning on improved transportation, the Erie Canal, steamships on the Great Lakes, stout and capacious wagons. It continued to demand internal improvements (the term of the time for public aid to communication), first canals and soon railroads, rarely constructed and surfaced roads. Wagon transport, however, was important and a wagon-making industry sprang up in the hardwoods south of the Great Lakes. It may be recalled that the automobile industry later took form in the same centers and by using the same skills and organization of distribution. Canals, most significantly the Illinois and Michigan Canal completed in 1848, linked the Great Lakes to rivers of the Mississippi system for shipping farm products to the East. Railroads were first projected as feeder lines to navigable waters. The first important construction, that of the Illinois Central, was chartered in 1850 to build a railroad from Cairo, at the junction of the Ohio and Mississippi rivers, to La Salle, on the

Illinois and Michigan Canal and on the Illinois River. It was given a grant by Congress of two million acres of land. Its principal early support was by the sale of lands in tracts from forty acres up; its continued success depended on the produce of the farms and the goods needed to be shipped in. The pattern was adopted and given an East-West orientation by other rail lines that quickly spread their ribbons of steel westward, often in advance of the farm homesteads.

This last great movement of land settlement was out onto the prairies and it differed largely in manner of life and kind of people from the settlement of the woodlands. It depended on industry and capital for the provision of transportation. It was based from the start on plow farming, cast iron or steel plows to cut and turn the sod: plows that needed stout draft animals, either oxen or heavy horses. By 1850, agricultural machinery had been developed for cultivating corn and harvesting small grains and was responsible for the gradual replacement of oxen by horses as motive power.

The prairie homestead differed from that of the woodlands in the first instance by depending on plow, draft animals, and wagon. It, too, grew corn as the most important crop. In part the corn was used for work stock but largely it was converted into meat and lard by new, large breeds of swine developed in the West. Stock was penned and fed. Fences were needed, not to fence stock out of the fields but to confine it. The livestock was provided with feed and housing. The farm was subdivided into fields, alternately planted to corn, wheat, oats, clover, and grass, arranged in a rotation that grew the feed for the work animals and for the stock to be marketed. A barn was necessary for storage and stables. This mixed economy, its cash income from animals and wheat, spread the work time through the seasons, and maintained the fertility of the land. It was a self-sustaining ecologic system capable of continuing and improving indefinitely and it was established by the process of prairie settlement. There was no stage of extractive or exhaustive cultivation.

By the time of the Civil War—in a span of twenty years or so—the prairie country east of the Mississippi, the eastern half of Iowa, and north Missouri were well settled. Some counties had reached their highest population by then. My native Missouri county had twice its current population in 1860. More people were needed to improve the land and to build the houses and barns than it took to keep the farms going. Some of the surplus sought new lands farther west, much of it went into building the cities. These people who settled the prairies were farmers, born and reared, out of the Northeast or from overseas, first and in largest number Germans and thereafter Scandinavians. They knew how to plow and work the soil to keep it in good tilth, how to care for livestock, how to arrange and fill their working time. They needed money for their houses and barns, which were not of logs but were frame structures with board siding. The lumber was mainly white pine shipped in from the Great Lakes, long the main inbound freight source. These settlers needed money, as well as their own labor, to dig wells and drain fields. The price of the land again was the lesser part of the cost of acquiring a farm. The hard pull was to get enough capital to improve and equip the homestead and this was done by hard labor and iron thrift. This is a sufficient explanation of the work ethic and thrift habits of the Midwest, often stressed in disparagement of its farm life. In order to have and hold the good land it was necessary to keep to a discipline of work and to defer the satisfactions of ease and comforts. The price seemed reasonable to the first generation who had wrested a living from scant acres in New England or to those who had come from Europe where land of one's own was out of reach.

Dispersed living, the isolated family home, became most characteristic of the "Northern" folk on the frontier. In Europe, nearly everyone had lived in a village or town; in this country, the rural village disappeared or never existed. Our farmers lived in the "country" and went to "town" on business or pleasure. The word "village," like "brook," was one that poets might use; it was strange to our western language. The nature of frontier life has often been ascribed to the ways of the Scotch-Irish who have been credited with or held responsible for almost anything that took form or place there. Thus, the dispersed farmsteads have been credited to the fact that some lived on small tracts in Scotland, as so-called cotters. Over here, they were conspicuous in the forward fringe of settlement but it cannot be said that it was the Scotch-Irish who broke the conventionally ordered pattern of rural living in villages. The nucleated New England town early acquired outlying farm homes in number. The Pennsylvania German settlements early included farm as well as village habitation. Land was available to the individual over here in tracts of a size beyond any holdings he might ever have had overseas. The village pattern was usually retained only where religious bonds or social planning prescribed living in close congregation.

Normally, the land holding was the place where the family lived and this identification became recognized in the establishment of title. The act of living on the occupied land was part of the process of gaining possession. As time went on, prior occupation and improvement of a tract gave more and more weight to preemption rights; living on the land protected against eviction and gave a first right to purchase or contract for warranty of ownership. The Homestead Act was a late extension of the much earlier codes of preemption by which possession by residence on the land and improvement could be used to secure full and unrestricted title.

The General Land Survey established the rectangular pattern of land description and subdivision for the public domain. Rural land holdings took the form of a square or sums of squares, in fractions or multiples of the mile-square section of land. The quarter section gradually came into greatest favor as the desired size of a farm and became the standard unit for the family farm in the Homestead Act. Thus, four families per square mile, a score or so of persons, were thought to give a desirable density of rural population. The reservation of one school section out of the thirty-six in a township, for the support of primary public schools, provided an incentive for the only kind of public building contemplated in the disposal of public lands. Four homes to the square mile and about four schools to the six-mile-square townships gave the simple general pattern for the rural geography of the Midwest. The pattern was most faithfully put into effect on the smooth upland prairies. Here the roads followed section lines and therefore ran either north-south or east-west and the farmsteads were strung at nearly equal intervals upon one or the other strand of the grid. It is curious that this monotony was so generally accepted, even a clustering of homes at the four corners where the sections met (and giving the same density) being exceptional.

Little attention has been given to the site where the house was placed, or to the assemblage of the structures that belonged to the farm. The choice of location was greatly important, as in exposure to wind and sun, for example. We may take a largely forgotten instance, malaria. Presumably, malaria came with the French, carried up the Mississippi from the south. The French were subject to chills and fever but kept on living in the river bottoms. The Americans also suffered thus, but soon began to select their living sites accordingly. The general idea was that the sickness came from the miasmas forming from stagnant water; the answer was to build the house on a ridge where the wind would sweep the miasmatic air away. The river bottoms long had a bad reputation. The Illinois Valley was malarial through most of its length, the early settlement of Bureau at the southward bend of the upper river, for instance, having been relocated for that reason. It would be of interest to determine the distribution of malaria at various times, the flare-ups and gradual recession, and the effects on living sites.

The logistics of home location is an attractive and hardly investigated field of study, as is indeed the whole question of the rural landscape and its changes. The location of house and farm buildings involved conservation of energy in the work on the farm, cultural preferences of different colonizing groups, microclimatic adjustments, and esthetic satisfactions. The relation of water, drainage, and sanitation was unrecognized, the toll paid in typhoid and "summer complaint."

Building was starkly utilitarian and unadorned. Neither the log cabin of the woodlands, nor the box-shaped frame house of the prairies, nor yet the sod house of the Transmissouri country (made possible by the sod-cutting plow) was more than compact and economical shelter, varying but little in each form. Ready-cut houses of standard simple patterns were already offered by railroads to buyers of their land, an early form of tract housing. Quality of house and quality of land seem to be in no relation. The embellishment of the home and the planting of the yard were left mostly to the second generation, for country town as well as farm. The history of the dissemination of ornamental trees and shrubs might be revealing, perhaps to be documented through the nurseries that sprung up from Ohio to Nebraska (mainly post Civil War?).

The economy from its beginnings was based on marketing products, but it also maintained a high measure of self-sufficiency. Smokehouse, cellar, and pantry stored the food that was produced and processed on the farm. The farm acquired its own potato patch, orchard, berry and vegetable gardens, diversified as to kind from early to late maturity, for different flavors and uses, selected for qualities other than shipping or precocious bearing. The farm orchards now are largely gone and the gardens are going. Many varieties of fruits that were familiar and appreciated have been lost. A family orchard was stocked with diverse sorts of apple trees for early and midsummer applesauce, for making apple butter and cider in the fall, for laying down in cool bins in the cellar to be used, one kind after another, until the russets closed out the' season late in winter. The agricultural bulletins and yearbooks of the past century invited attention to new kinds of fruits and vegetables that might be added to the home orchard and garden, with diversification, not standardization, in view. Exhibits in the county and state fairs similarly stressed excellence in the variety of things grown, as well as giving a prize for the fattest hog and the largest pumpkin.

The Mason jar became a major facility by which fruit and vegetables were "put up" for home use in time of abundance against winter or a possible season of failure in a later year. The well-found home kept itself insured against want of food at all times by producing its own and storing a lot of it. The family, of ample size and age gradation, was able to provide most of the skills and services for self-sufficiency by maintaining diversified production and well-knit social organization. This competence and unity was maintained long after the necessity had disappeared. As time is measured in American history the life of this society, and its vitality, was extraordinary.

Looking back from the ease of present days these elder days may seem to have been a time of lonely and hard isolation. It was only toward the end of the period that the telephone and rural mail delivery were added. The prairie lacked wet-weather roads. In the hill sections, ridge roads might be passable at most times; on the plains, winter was likely to be the season of easiest travel, spring, that of immobilization by mud. The country doctor was expected to, and did, rise above any emergency of weather. Life was so arranged that one did not need to go into town at any particular time. When the weather was bad the activities of the family took place indoors or about the farmyard. In our restrospect of the family farm as it was, we may incline to overstress its isolation. The American farmstead did not have the sociality of the rural villages of Europe or of Latin America, but the entire family had duties to learn and perform and times of rest and diversion. It depended on a work morale and competence in which all participated and in which its members found satisfaction. Perhaps it suffered fewer social tensions and disruptions than any other part of our society.

Though living dispersed, the farm families were part of a larger community which might be a contiguous neighborhood or one of wider association. The community, in some cases, got started on the Boone pattern of a settlement of kith and kin. A sense of belonging together was present to begin with or it soon developed. The start may have been as a closed community; it was likely to continue in gradual admission of others by some manner of acceptance. Consanguinity, common customs, faith, or speech were such bonds that formed and maintained viable communities through good times and bad. The Mennonite colonies are outstanding examples. The absence of such qualities of cooperation is shown in the Cherokee strip, opened as a random aggregation of strangers.

The bond of common customs and language showed up strongly in the German settlements made between 1830 and the Civil War, and in the Scandinavian settlements of somewhat later origin. Both were attracted to districts where some of their people had chanced to locate and tended to increase about such nuclei. This clustering, a partial segregation, gave protection from cultural alienation and loss and afforded time to adjust and contribute to the common ways of life. Although the Germans were sharply divided as to confession, they were drawn into areas where German speech was used, however strong the difference in creed or dialect. Most of their settlement took place before 1870 and included people not only from the states that were to join the German empire, but from Switzerland, Austria, and later from Russia.

The country church played a leading part in social communication, differing again according to the particular confession. Catholic and Lutheran communicants had more of their social life determined by their church than did the others. Their priests and pastors were more likely to remain in one community and to exercise merited influence on it. Parochial schools extended the social connections. Church festivals were numerous and attractive. Sunday observance was less austere. The Methodist church, on the other hand, shifted its ministers, usually every two years. In a half century of service my grandfather was moved through a score of charges in five states. The high periods of the Methodist year were the winter revival meetings and the camp meetings in summer after the corn was laid by. For some, these were religious experiences; for others, especially for the young people, they were sociable times, particularly the camp meeting, held in an attractive, wooded campground where one lived in cabins or tents on an extended picnic. Almost everyone belonged to some church and in these churches found a wide range of social contacts and satisfaction.

The churches also pioneered higher education, founding colleges and academies across the Middle West from Ohio into Kansas before the Civil War and before the Morrill Act fathered the tax-supported colleges. These church-supported small colleges, about fifty of which still exist, first afforded education in the liberal arts to the youth of the prairie states and they did so by coeducation. Their students were drawn by their church affiliations, not only from nearby but from distant places. In these colleges, humane learning was cultivated and disseminated. Their campuses today are the Midwest's most gracious early monuments of the civilization aspired to by its pioneers.

Country and town were interdependent, of the same way of life, and mostly of the same people. By a tradition that may go back to the town markets of Europe, Saturday was the weekday for coming to town to transact business (note the pioneer implications in the term "to trade") and to visit. The town provided the services, goods, and entertainment that the farm family required. In time, it also became home for the retired farmer. Farmstead and its particular town were linked in community by factors beyond the one of economy of distance. When the railroads were building across the prairie, they laid out what seemed a most rational spacing of town sites for shipping and trading centers. Some grew, some withered away, and some never got started. Quantitative measurement of radius of trade never has been enough. The choice of direction and destination in going to town had other reasons than economy of energy expended. One liked it better in one town than in another, a matter of social values and affinities that are ponderable but not measurable.[1]

The era of the Middle Border ended with World War I. Hamlin Garland introduced the name in 1917 in his *Sons of the Middle Border,* a retrospect he made in middle age. Willa Cather, growing up on the westernmost fringe of Nebraska, drew its life in quiet appreciation in her two books written before the war. Then she saw her world swept away. Some of us have lived in its Indian summer, and almost no one was aware how soon and suddenly it was to end.[2] A quarter section was still a good size for a family farm and the farm was still engaged in provisioning itself as well as in shipping grain and livestock. It was still growing a good crop of lusty offspring. The place of the family in the community was not significantly determined by its income, nor had we heard of standard of living.

---

1. Lewis Atherton, *Mainstreet of the Middle Border* (1960), has a large documentation and itemization of life in the country towns. His composite picture is later and less attractive than are my own recollections. He stated that he was not relying on his own memories or family tradition. I, however, have done so, not knowing a nearer approach to objectivity than by putting such recall to reflective scrutiny. This is not sociologic method, but do systems of analysis bring enough understanding of what we are, or of what we were? A literary genre in disparagement of rural life and country town originated toward the end of the period with its ugly geography of Winesburg, Spoon River, Zenith, and Main Street.

2. I made field studies in northern Illinois and in Missouri from 1910 to 1914, when rural life was much more like that of Civil War time than of the present.

The outbreak of the war in 1914 brought rapidly rising demand and prices for supplies to the Allies and to American industry. Our intervention in 1917 urged the farmer to still more production: "Food will win the War"—in the war that was to end all wars. He made more money than ever before, he had less help, he was encouraged to buy more equipment and more land. The end of the war saw a strongly industrialized country that continued to draw labor from the rural sections. Improved roads, cars, tractors, and trucks made the horse unnecessary and thereby the old crop rotation broke down. Farming became less a way of life and more a highly competitive business for which the agricultural colleges trained specialists, engineers, chemists, economists, to aid fewer and fewer farmers to produce more market goods, to widen their incomes against the rising cost of labor, taxes, and capital needs. This became known as "freeing people from the land," so that now we have about a tenth of our population living on farms (among the lowest ratios in the world) and these are not reproducing themselves.

The Middle Border now belongs to a lost past, a past in which different ways and ends of life went on side by side. We have since defined the common welfare in terms of a society organized for directed material progress. For the present at least, we control the means to produce goods at will. We have not learned how to find equivalent satisfactions in jobs well done by simple means, and by the independent judgment that gave competence and dignity to rural work. The family farm prepared youth well for life—there or elsewhere. It enriched the quality of American life and it will be missed.

# 5. Status and Change
## in the Rural Midwest,
## A Retrospect

There is no substitute to my mind for knowing some part of the world well, by intimate and repeated observation. Obviously this cannot be a great part and probably it will be by comparison of rather small parts. Perhaps what I am saying is that geography is and has been regional and experiential, which is not the same as saying that regional geography is the objective of all geography. I do enjoy a good *Landeskunde* as I enjoy browsing through a well-drawn atlas to visit places I know and others that I shall never see. This is the immemorial curiosity of mankind to know something significant and interesting of places that are different from one's own place.

To unlettered folk geographic lore may be little more than the small world of their own territory. Within those limits the natives have competent identification of the differences in terrain, vegetation, productivity, habitation, amenities, hazards. They have given the names that we have adopted in large measure into our vocabulary. The descriptive names proper to all geography are in part unique and locational, place names, and in part qualitative and comparative, characterizing features as belonging to a class.

"Status and Change in the Rural Midwest—A Retrospect" first appeared in *Mitteilungen der Österreichischen Geographischen Gesellschaft*, Band 105, Heft III (Austria: 1963).

Geography is the attempt to identify and understand the differences in terrestrial space and this is as true of the university seminar as of the aborigine. Whatever the academic disciplines that use it, and they are numerous, the geographic method is understood as the inspection of the areal distribution and difference of whatever is being studied. It is to gain insight into the multiform Earth and its life that we pursue our inquiries, knowing that we who may be thus called as to profession are only a modest part of the representatives of such interest.

In the early years of academic geography in the United States I was sent (1910) to make a study of the upper Illinois Valley for the state geological survey. The purpose was to be an educational bulletin for teachers and residents of that area, to instruct rather than to discover. It was a *Landeskunde* of sorts for which I lacked model and preparation. Unschooled observation though it was, it was independent observation and I found out some things. The fertility of the upland was due to a well-marked mantle spread indifferently over different glacial materials and rock surfaces, later to be recognized as loessial, though not the kind of loess found along the Mississippi and Missouri rivers. The distribution of prairie and woodland, strongly outlined by change in relief, began a continuing interest in the origin of grasslands. There were other glimmerings: that Indian sites were governed by considerations other than those of the whites who followed them, that pioneer settlements were relocated because of malaria, that first water and then rail transport determined the changing logistics of townsites, that the farmsteads were dispersed in terms of farm size and these were changing. Elementary questions that brought some awareness that the scene then presented was the result of almost eighty years of settlement by people of certain ways, and some anticipation of further rural change. A good expression of the corn belt, prosperous and stable, which made sense as to its character.

The attitude at the time was that geographers should do regional studies, without too much concern as to how these should be done. It was not yet the time when the boundaries of regions or their hierarchies were taken seriously. In time it was thought there would be a series of regional monographs illustrating the diversity of environment and ways of life across the country. The kind of area might be a political unit or a "natural region," the larger overview would come by the increase of such studies to be based on field observation. The common background we had was a reasonable ability to identify land forms. How to deal with the presence of man on the land was undetermined beyond estimating the fit of his activities to his physical environment. This was facilitated by turning to census enumerations of population and production of goods plotted on maps, disclosing differences in activity and success by differing qualities of natural resources. Description thereby tended to become somewhat derivative from enumerations in the categories provided for by censuses.

At the time of my study of the Ozark Highland of Missouri (1913–14) the bias was to undertake study of a large area. My inclination was to the St. Francois Mountains, which were thought too small and therefore a large reconnaissance took the place of an intensive field study. The result was not entirely disadvantageous because it gave some insight into the then still marked cultural differences, a small survival of French settlements, a large German fringe at the east and north, New Englanders at the southwest, and the major interior core of hill people mainly derived two generations earlier from Tennessee and Kentucky. The inner Ozarks were a still lustily viable remnant of frontier life, self-contained, relying on rifle and axe as well as one-horse plow, clearing fields by deadening trees, fencing out stock that ranged free, still using rail fences and log houses and barns. Cultural diversity and persistence impressed themselves on the observer, become somewhat aware of the retention of group ways under mild pressures from outside. Contrasts in mode of life were still marked and these were based on cultural conservatism as well as on environmental limitations.

After World War I the University of Michigan set up a summer field camp on the Cumberland River in southern Kentucky. One of the reasons for choosing this base was that its people were of the stock of the original settlers who maintained old ways and attitudes. One of the student exercises here was to make a map of land use along with a map of physical land forms. In trying to assign the entire surface to forms of utilization it became apparent that there were tracts of declining utility, passing from one use to a lesser and different one, in some cases approaching no use. Land deterioration was expressed in soil loss by ablation and erosion of gullies. Fields that no longer served for tillage became pastures or were abandoned to weeds and brush. Plants thus became indicators of the degradation and beginning reconstitution of the land. A regional study of the Pennyroyal followed in which representative localities were studied as to the state of the land, a pioneering attempt to show man-induced soil erosion and vegetation changes.

The first objective in a regional study was to make proper identification of the things noted. The recognition of the forms of the land and its mantle presented least difficulties, for these have been most widely observed and named with reasonable validity. The terms thus available largely are genetic and were so used, intrenched meander, doline, ground moraine, flood plain, colluvium, loess, descriptively proper and intelligible in terms of their origin and development. This is said not as discounting inquiry into land forms *per se,* but as needed in this case only insofar as the terrain is described more readily. The attention to man-induced erosion attempted to show the state of surface and soil at the time of observation and thus to provide a datum for subsequent induced physical change.

The effects of human disturbance of vegetation were sketchily presented. Red cedar, sassafras, persimmon, and hawthorn were colonizing old fields. There should have been some mapping of types and stages of such invasion, which documentation would be of considerable interest at the present. The scant identification and failure to show plant distributions in tension sites was not due to ignorance of what the plants were. These aggressive weedy plants, grasses, shrubs, or trees were familiar. What I failed to see adequately was that here an ecologic process was under way that should have been documented as of that moment of time. Nor did I see at all clearly the extent to which Ozark woods were modified by burning or not burning, by open ranging of livestock, and cutting of logs. A rather common blind spot among geographers, not to see the trees for the forest.

In retrospect also I wish that I had been more attentive to cultural elements and variants rather than to aggregates and common qualities. Here I had not dispensed with the blinders to which we were accustomed from economic geography, the domination by numbers, so many of such and such aggregates of people, distinguished as to occupation. Or so much corn, so many hogs, so much pasture land, such and such means of transportation at such distance from place of production. The oversimplified categories and sums of the census takers may come between us and recognition of what is or should be apparent to our eye and mind as significant. The unquantified and unquantifiable qualities of living in a particular tract that was their own began to be of concern as based in part on traditional values. How these were expressed in household and community, their structures and functions presented an unexplored field for which the experience in inquiry was lacking that had been developed in Europe and for primitive societies. The brevity of our national history and its dominant direction had left these areas of Missouri and Kentucky as unconsidered and unimportant backwaters, almost as deviants and laggards bypassed by the great stream of national development and destiny. This was however their attraction: that they had ways of life of their own that might be understood and appreciated in their own terms rather than considered as failing to come up to a general norm and standard.

In 1923 I moved to California to other lines of interest than synoptic regional studies. Since then I have had only casual contacts with the Midwest of my earlier years, with the exception of the spring of the present year of 1963. [Ed. note: the original date of publication of this paper.] Having now had occasion to revisit scenes observed forty and fifty years ago, a comparison of then and now raises thoughts about the nature and purpose of geographic observations. These three field studies were starting jobs, first delineations of what I thought at the time were the significant expressions of certain kinds of people living in a certain kind of place or environment. Of necessity they bear the stamp of the date at which they were done.

The scenes I had tried to describe and interpret in three midwestern areas would have seemed more familiar to one who had known them at the time of the Civil War than they will be to a person who sees them today. What I had tried to do as functional geography is now a record of superseded ways of life. In a fashion I had caught a late moment of a rural life that was to fade away very soon. I had tried to be aware of changes that were under way, in some degree to place the scenes then observed between the past and an indicated future. What I did not foresee was the greatly accelerated pace and direction of change. Probably there was an emotional bias involved that had attracted me to geography, getting satisfaction out of the diversity of the Earth's surface and its inhabitants, even seeing in the course of organic evolution the suggestion of natural order as continuing accommodation of greater diversity. What I overlooked therefore was the latent power and ambition of technology and political economy to standardize, organize, and integrate life into an inclusive system in which cultures were dissolved into a total society.

The family farm was the basic unit of the rural Midwest, homesteads that were dispersed upon the land the household utilized and usually owned. The farm produced most of the food the family required and the feed for its stock. A large measure of self-sufficiency characterized farm life, from the most meager Ozark hill farms to the rich black prairies of Illinois. One grew, stored, and processed the meat, milk, eggs, vegetables and fruit needed. When the roads were impassable by mud or high water one busied oneself about house and barn. Elementary schools were spaced within walking distance and usually the children could walk to school whatever the weather. Country churches were of more uncertain attendance by reason of weather but the more devout and sociable families were inclined to get to Sunday meeting by carriage or wagon despite the weather. Poor roads were the most obvious handicap to country living but life was well adjusted to the isolation imposed and this gave substance and solidarity to family life.

Improvement of rural communication was well started a half century ago. In the more prosperous sections telephone lines had been provided. Rural Free Delivery of mail had been established, was resulting in some road improvement by grading for better drainage and occasional surfacing with gravel, and gave rise to the mail-order houses that sold almost everything by catalogue. Henry Ford had put his Model T automobile into production and thereby became the first author of the new revolution.

The First World War brought an industrial boom to northern cities and drained labor from the farms. Trucks and tractors, as well as self-powered agricultural machinery, entered rural use in the decade after the war. The horse quickly became superfluous and much land that had been planted to oats, and some hay and pasture land, became available for row crops. Hybrid maize brought larger yields and more demand on soil fertility. Soybeans became the second crop on the more fertile lands and contrary to first opinion also demanded more fertilizer. Crop rotation tended to disappear, clover and grass giving way to the more profitable seed crops. The Second War brought a new and strongly continuing wave of urban employment. Commercial fertilizer replaced organic manuring and chemical sprays reduced the necessity of cultivation. Fewer and fewer men could operate large farm units with greater and greater yields. The open market economy gave way to a politically managed economy of increasing complexity and direction, using rewards and penalties. Taxes increased steeply, in considerable part for public services, as for road construction and consolidated schools. The farm had become a mechanized enterprise, minimizing the labor employed, and requiring cost accounting. The farmer had become a specialized producer or he went to the city to work in a factory or for other urban wage.

The agricultural revolution came earliest and proceeded farthest in the more fertile and more advantageously situated districts. In the Ozarks some moved to the highways to gain employment on road maintenance, in services to tourists, in part-time factory employment. A good many farms passed into the hands of city people for retirement or weekend occupation. The properties may still be farms nominally but their possessors get little or none of their living thus. Southern Kentucky is somewhat less changed, in part because of the great increase in demand for cigarette tobacco, tobacco growing not having been mechanized. Here one still sees horses and even mules on farms. A small farm may provide a sufficient cash income for a family from a few acres of tobacco, enough to keep them on the place as owners or tenants, using a rotation with pasture, pasture sod being beneficial to the quality of tobacco leaf desired. Here also the corn fields largely have been replaced by grass on which cattle graze, and even some sheep are still seen, now absent in other parts, as are horses and mules. This is the least altered rural land of the interior to my knowledge, except for the dairy country of Wisconsin where the family farm still is viable and represents a way of life.

As to impressions of change this returning visitor received: First, the wilderness is moving back in. The forms of abandonment of land are various. At one extreme is the utter devastation left by strip-mining of coal, which chewed up areas where coal beds could be exposed by stripping off the overburden. The more agriculture has become mechanized, the more has it selected the smoothly lying lands. The hill farms are out of business even where the soil is productive, as it is in the loess-covered uplands along the southward flowing rivers. Without benefit of quantitative demonstration the farmer has experienced the cost of steepness and irregularity of slope, mainly in the utility of machinery but also in the retention of fertilizers. In some cases the hill fields have gone into pasture for beef cattle, or for dairy cattle where there is an urban market for fresh milk. To a greater extent they have been repossessed by wild growth. In early spring the tawny patches of last year's growth of broomsedge *(Andropogon)* outline more recently abandoned fields. The succession of plants that recolonize the land is varied and leads through brush (sumac and poison ivy—both *Rhus*—being conspicuous) to pioneering kinds of trees. Red cedar *(Juniperus virginiana)* flourishes especially well in old fields and pastures and may be seen occasionally in a solid stand that outlines the rectangular lines of a former field. There is a great lot more of cedar than there was when I knew that part of the country. Some parts are becoming cedar woods, which they never were in the past. Sassafras has also become more abundant; the persimmon, the third familiar member of these early tree invaders seemingly less so. Secondary woodlands have replaced a good deal of land that had been cleared with much labor two, three, or four generations ago.

The former woods are undiminished in area and increased in density. Formerly they were harvested for railroad ties, posts and poles, domestic lumber, staves, and especially for firewood. These uses have diminished or disappeared. The practice of burning the woods for additional pasture has pretty well stopped, as has the ranging of pigs and cattle. Reproduction of seedlings is high, utilization low, management rare, and stands become excessively crowded. In the Ozarks a small beginning has been made to reestablish the pines that had been nearly eliminated at the beginning of this century.

The Missouri Conservation Commission has been doing an outstanding job in managing wild life and thereby of managing wild and also agriculturally occupied land. When I tramped the Ozarks as a young man I never saw a deer or wild turkey. The former now are probably more abundant than they were when the white settlers came, also increasing remarkably in the northern, largely prairie counties of the state. Wild turkeys have been successfully reintroduced. Quail, squirrels, and rabbits are responding well to conservation management. Fishing is well maintained in streams large and small and in artificial ponds and reservoirs. The large number of sportsmen from cites and towns has become the main support game and wild land management, of wild life refuges, of state forests and parks. The Ozarks in particular have become a major recreation area, not only for sportsmen and sports, but for the enjoyment of a near approach to the wilderness that urban dwellers may desire to turn to at times. The occasional need to retreat from the city is one of the interesting and perhaps promising phenomena of our current urbanization.

As to the farm scene, these impressions of then and now present themselves. First of all is the uncertainty as one drives by as to whether the farmstead is the home of a farmer, of a part-time farmer, of a person who has retired to the country, or of someone who works somewhere else at something else. Farmhouses often were solidly and sometimes attractively built. Many are on all-weather roads of convenient access to cities. They may be bought at considerably less cost than a comparable place in town and the taxes are likely to be much lower. The consolidation of farms into larger operations, whether by purchase or rental, is leaving a surplus of houses. This, I suppose, is in part included in what is known as urban sprawl. Historically it is a farmhouse, but is it so functionally? Whether or not the census taker has rules for a proper distinction between a farm family and a non-farm rural family I do not know. If the yard is unkept and cluttered I am pretty sure that the occupants are not resident farmers, as I am if it has a tennis court or paddock. An historical identification I might make, an actual one perhaps not. Since farming is a numerically declining way of life, houses of current styles are not commonly farm-houses. My recognition may tell whether the house has the end chimneys and long verandas of southern mode or otherwise tells something of what kind of people built it and whence they came. Largely they are monuments of generations that are past, of days of lumberyards stocked with northern white pine for framing and weatherboarding, of local brickyards. Function is a matter of time, circumstance, and taste and to say a house is a house is less than identification or giving of meaning.

The barns in particular tell of the passing of the family farm. Largely, these are no longer needed. Some have been remodeled to serve other ends. Some have been torn down and others are falling down. Passing by you look at the barn to get a summary at-a-glance of the fortunes of its farm. The barn of the Midwest had different forms and sizes according to the kind of farming and farmer but it was likely to include in one structure such functions as the stable for the work stock and milch cows, above it the loft for keeping the hay, bins on the ground floor for feed oats and some of the feed corn, other bins for the seed saved for the next crop, a harness room, and space for some of the machinery, all under one roof. The work stock is gone and so are the milch cows and there is no more need for hayloft, stable, or bins. The utility of a common structure has disappeared and so have the varied activities of the barnyard about it. If beef cattle are raised these are not stabled, but are given their rations of baled hay, grain, or mixed prepared feed in the open or from feed racks. Poultry is gone from the barnyard and if pigs are kept it is likely to be by movable pens where they are fed in number for mar-keting. Milk and butter, eggs and dressed poultry, fresh meat, ham, and bacon are now bought in town by farmer and town dweller alike. Stable manure has been replaced by commercial fertilizer. The barn is obsolete because it was built for many purposes and the farm of many purposes is gone or going.

The farm orchard, once as ubiquitous as the horse, is now about as rare. The common element was the apple tree of which there were numerous kinds, early and late ripening, preferred for eating out of hand, for baking, cider, apple butter. Some were favored varieties brought from the East with the original settlers. Others were of local origin, Missouri providing several kinds that became widely grown. A well-kept orchard had a dozen kinds or more. Sour cherries, also known as pie cherries, were perhaps next in importance. Plums were likely to be natives, introduced from Indian sources, such as the Chickasaw and Wild Goose, but also the dark blue damson, its name telling of its remote home in the Levant. Peaches were grown in the always recurring hope that the year would escape a late spring frost to nip the bloom. Pear trees, it seems to my memory, grew tallest and lived even longer than the apple trees. Some men knew how to take cuttings for grafting or budding, or there were the nurseries in number and even tree salesmen who drove about with their wares and brightly colored catalogues. This spring I stopped on occasion to find an ancient apple or pear tree surviving in a flourishing stand of red cedar, or some forgotten planted plum in a thicket of briars. Once I saw hemmed in by cedars an Indian peach, a small frost-resistant form that in manner unknown was handed on from Spaniards to southern Indian and to pioneer American settlers, and which reproduced "true" from the pits.

The kitchen garden and its topography also are passing into oblivion. The potato patch of several kinds early and late, the beds of carrots, beets, turnips, cucumbers, melons, beans and peas climbing on tented poles, tomatoes, rhubarb, asparagus, cabbages, and berries. In season fresh, for the rest of the year stored, canned, or dried, these supplied cellar and pantry with the needs of the family. Along with the care of the poultry they were the care of the women of the household. One could make a fair guess of national and sectional origins by what was grown in the gardens.

The country schoolhouses have given way to consolidated schools, served by buses. The country church is holding somewhat better, in part because it may be flanked by family burial plots and sentiment may hold a balance against convenience. The statistically minded could plot the reduction in rural churches by population and the differential tenacity by church denominations.

Formerly there were general stores and blacksmith shops to be found in the open country. Now one may see an occasional service station for gasoline and soft drinks, and here and there even a "beauty parlor" of a hairdresser, or an antique shop which has collected old handcrafted furniture to sell to the passing tourist. The fortunes of the country towns are various but have not been good in most cases unless a factory moved in to provide employment. The county seats have fared best, the business of government at all levels tending to ramify more and more. The general store of family ownership and management persists but is being largely replaced by groceries and specialty stores belonging to merchandising chains. The decline of hotels is especially notable, the accommodation of visitors and passing travelers having shifted to the food and sleeping facilities purveyed by new structures (motels) built along the highways that bypass the town. The more heavily traveled highways are assuming more and more the aspect of an unending *Strassendorf* catering to the wants of private cars, trucks, and buses, replacing the older town plan related to railroad station, main street, and converging roads upon a town center.

The nature of rural commerce is greatly altered in the direction of standardization of product, mass production, and governmental credit and fixing of prices. In older days livestock, grain, wood in its marketed forms were made as cash sales to buyers of such staples. A host of lesser and occasional products were known as "produce" disposed of by "trade." The keeper of the general store was also a trader, exchanging the goods on his shelves for diverse items brought in by people from the country. Such produce he sorted and stored to be shipped mainly to "produce firms" in the cities. The farmer was of secondary importance in this exchange; he might bring his surplus of cured hams and bacon, of salt pork and lard and hides. The farm wife was the principal participant in produce trade. By custom the poultry, eggs, and butter were hers to dispose of. He might have the disposal of the fruits of the orchard, she of those of the garden. In the Mississippi Valley that I knew there were no markets such as in Europe but Saturday was a sort of market day when the country people came to town to trade produce for store goods or for money, the cash price being somewhat less than the trade value. The business extended beyond the products of husbandry, especially for the young folks and the poor hill people, who grew very little. In winter dressed game was brought, mainly rabbits, and pelts of fur-bearing animals. In autumn nuts were gathered of hickory trees, walnuts, butternuts, and pecans. In summer wild berries were picked and in early spring roots and bark were taken, to be shipped as flavoring and medicines to be processed in the cities, ginseng, sassafras, and wild cherry being among the best known.

Such were characteristics of the social geography of the early part of this century, largely lost in the changes that were soon to set in. Some of them I described at the time, many I failed to note although they were familiar to me. What I tried to record was a then-functioning way of life, its origins and relevance to the kinds of place and kinds of people. They were beginner's exercises with some awareness of the differences in the qualities of living as well as of livelihood, of becoming and being. The rising forces of change into new directions that we call progress largely escaped me. I must confess that they did not then have special appeal nor do they have such now. I could not anticipate the two world wars nor the enormous impact they would have on ways of life. Nor did I foresee that a free economy was to change into central control by a welfare-oriented state. That I was viewing the approaching end of an era was somewhat foreshadowed by the beginnings of a new mode of transportation. The American scene had experienced two such revolutions, first by steamboat and then by railroad. The third, by internal combustion engine and improved roads, began to appear in the second decade. With it came not only a new pattern in the transport of goods and persons but a new interest in the experience of motion. When the first automobiles came to my home town there existed a single stretch of eight miles of smooth road to a neighboring town. People who had cars soon formed the habit of evening drives back and forth over this stretch for the sheer exhilaration of rapid motion, not in order to get to another place. The sedentary home and community centered life began to give way to wider, more frequent, more casual, and more rapid mobility. The American has become habituated to relocating himself beyond the proper call of bettering his position, a new restless nomad. Also many find satisfaction in speed of motion rather than the enjoyment of new scenes. One of the new experiences in revisiting the Midwest was to see the many speedboats on trailers en route to the numerous lakes, mainly built by the Corps of Engineers across lesser rivers. Nominally constructed for navigation and flood control they serve primarily for recreation and especially for boats that dash back and forth for the sake of the sense of speeding they give.

The landscape of the Midwest has been greatly changed in the past fifty years. The cities have taken over the countrysides. What was functionally good then has been largely replaced by other ways of life, cast in a different economic and social pattern, to a large extent fashioned by a new political economy. The social geography of the early part of the century is now no longer functioning, the vestiges still apparent in process of attrition or absorption into another and more generalized convention of living. Social geography soon becomes historical geography, and never more rapidly so than at present. I call to mind Alexander Rüstow's pregnant phrase of the *Ortsbestimmung der Gegenwart*. It may be possible to gain insight into how people live in a place by knowing how that living was fashioned. This I take as the objective of regional description, an appreciation of the qualities that are expressed in a particular habit and habitat. Their projection into the future is another matter that involves imponderables that cannot be predicted merely from present trends.

*II. Culture*
    *Origins*

# 6. Concerning
## Primeval Habitat
## and Habit

OF HUMAN LINEAGE AND TIME

When it became apparent that the diversity of life had come about by long process of evolution, as documented through paleontology, the place of man in the phylogeny of the primates became a matter of major interest. Thus it came to be inferred that the great or higher apes who resembled him most were also his next of kin. During the latter part of the past century the search for a missing link between man and apes was followed actively. Such was the interest and the interpretation of Dubois when he found in Java in 1891 the bones to which he gave the name *Pithecanthropus erectus,* the erect ape man. South African finds early in the present century were ascribed to *Australopithecus* as southern apes and until lately remained in dispute as to whether they were apes, men, or intermediates. As late as 1933 Professor Hooton called his book on human evolution *Up from the Ape.* Interest in the behavior and learning of the great apes, in particular of the docile chimpanzees, has been somewhat ambivalent. Would they throw light on human ways because they and we were of common and near origin or did they illustrate certain traits of paral-

"Concerning Primeval Habitat and Habit" first appeared in *Festschrift fur Ad. E. Jensen,* (Klaus Renner Verlag: Munich, 1964), pp. 513–524.

lel evolution, informative without inference of phyletic derivation? It now appears assured that the hominid line has followed an evolutionary course independent of that of the higher apes and perhaps began to do so even earlier than these. The ape man is no longer being looked for but his fictional image has not wholly disappeared from thought about human traits.

The bones of early humans are still very few, perhaps too few for the numerous classifications into which they have been sorted. Also, they are missing from most of the sites at which their simple tools have been found. The rock shelters at Choukoutien behind Peking gave the first proof of both in association, leaving no doubt about remains or tools. Peking Man was shown to be a near relative of Pithecanthropus; the latter was accepted as early man of Java. On somewhat meager evidence Peking Man has been assigned to the Second Interglacial Stage, Java Man by recent potassium-argon dating is given an age of five hundred thousand years, which might be earlier than that interglacial. Heidelberg Man also has been put into the same interglacial stage but may be earlier by a good deal. The discovery at Swanscombe on the Thames is best documented as to where it belongs in the Pleistocene sequence, safely in the Second Interglacial. The remains at Steinheim are thought also to be of that stage. Of these major and other early minor finds, all made before 1959, only Swanscombe is securely placed as to Pleistocene stage and an approximate absolute age is given only for hominid presence in Java. In physical type the Swanscombe and Steinheim specimens are considered to differ least from late humans, Heidelberg to be most primitive, and those of Peking and Java are cautiously labeled by some as of archanthropic or paleanthropic grade, whatever that may mean. The phyletic classification of these early representatives is in little more satisfactory state than are the estimates of their several ages. At the moment the Second Interglacial seems rather overcrowded with a diverse lot of human kind scattered through far parts of the Old World. (A preliminary caution may be entered here against thinking that this was a generally "warm period.")

In 1959 Dr. Louis Leakey made the first discovery of a hominid to be named *Zinjanthropus*. The discovery site in Olduvai Gorge of

Tanganyika also yielded an assemblage of worked stones that were recognizable as fashioned tools and to which the name Olduwan Culture has been given. In addition there was refuse of bones of animals that had been collected and eaten and these were of Villafranchian fauna. The site, therefore, was of high antiquity unless such animals lasted there well beyond their usual time. The discovery attracted much attention and, being buried under volcanic tuff, the newly developed method of dating by potassium-argon was applied, an age of one and three-quarter million years being found. Zinjanthropus, Olduwan culture, and Villafranchian fauna were thus certified as of common age, acceptable for the animals but unimagined for man and the making of tools. The new precision method of geochemistry has opened up the reconsideration of human antiquity and in particular of the African record of man and past climates. The previously known Kafuan culture (without human remains) may be still earlier and provisionally is considered as possibly extending the presence of tool-making humans in East Africa to a span of two million years.

## OF GEOLOGIC TIME AND ITS DIVISIONS

Various approaches to the history of the Earth were being followed in the nineteenth century and were expressed in a variety of terms of geologic time, which in part are still in alternative and overlapping use. The German "Diluvium" and the English "Drift" recall the days when the mantle of clays and sands spread over the lowlands of northern Europe was attributed to the Great Flood of biblical lore. As the idea of a catastrophic deluge gave way to the mounting evidence of a long series of events, a fourth part of earth history, Quaternary time, was added to the then current threefold division of the geologic scale. The term Pleistocene was introduced independently to express the time of first appearance of a large number of living mammals or their near relatives. When Boucher de Perthes, powerfully supported by Lyell, established the presence of Paleolithic Man during the deposition of the Drift, the Age of Man was extended into such earlier time. The Drift became recognized as of glacial origin and thereby the Great Ice Age was demonstrated. All of these terms continue to be used in some uncertainty as to their synonymy but jointly they express the nature and significance of the latest geological time.

Alpine studies, especially by Penck and Brückner, proved a succession of glaciations with intervening stages of deglaciation. Penck estimated the four Alpine glacial and three interglacial stages to have occupied six hundred thousand years. A similar succession of continental ice sheets was found to have spread from the Scandinavian highland over the north European lowland. In North America five continental glaciations were identified and named Nebraskan, Kansan, Illinoian, Iowan and Wisconsin. The two earliest, Nebraskan and Kansan, reached south to and across the line of the lower Missouri River. By later revision the Iowan stage was merged into the Wisconsin and thereby agreement with the four European stages accepted.

The continental ice sheets of North America spread into lower latitudes and were far more extensive than in Europe. Except for the Nebraskan stage the surfaces formed by each have remained exposed over large areas. They differ greatly in the weathering they have undergone and in the modification of their surfaces. The later Wisconsin moraines and their outwash are nearly as they were deposited and have young soils. The older the exposed drifts the greater the loss of original surface features and the more advanced the development of their soil profiles. The most notable contrast is between the Illinoian and Kansan drifts. The Kansan, widely exposed over northern Missouri and southern Iowa, is deeply leached and converted into colloidal clays, has well-established surface drainage and many streams that have cut well into underlying bedrock. Where the Kansan is overlaid by Illinoian drift it is found to be in an advanced state of weathering, showing that it was exposed for a long time during the intervening interglacial stage (the Yarmouth). The southern margin of the Kansan drift has been obscured by deep and intricate erosion. The striking differences in appearance of age of the several North American drifts are not matched in Europe.

The early estimates of glaciologists that the successive American drifts occupied a span of a million years have continued to be acceptable. In his study of the formation and warping of the terraces of the lower Mississippi Valley Harold Fisk came to the same estimate of age. The "million years" is an informed guess in round numbers, based on field experience by various observers in different terrains, within and beyond the area covered by ice.

The coincidence of stages between New and Old World is more inferred than proven but the resemblances are rather strong and a general mechanism of circulation of air and sea is most probable. The disparity in chronology is unresolved but is unlikely to remain so since absolute measure of time is now at hand by geochemical means. The astronomical calculations of Milankovitch involve unacceptable premises and contrary facts of climate, present and past.

The limits of Quaternary/Pleistocene time have been in need of being extended at both ends. It is most likely that we are living in an interglacial phase rather than in postglacial time. To the original four stages of Alpine glaciation other earlier ones have been added. Paleontology has long known that the more important faunal innovations and displacements, both on land and sea, came well before the beginning of the conventional Ice Age and that these reflect an altered climatic regime. Thus a time of Plio-Pleistocene Transition was recognized, a terrestrial one named Villafranchian, marked by a fauna of wide extension in Africa and Europe. It has become apparent that Günz or Nebraskan glaciation did not properly begin the latest geological period. The International Geological Congress of London in 1950 resolved that Pleistocene time should include Villafranchian, thereby more or less doubling the time span of earlier use. By revised definition Villafranchian is Lower Pleistocene, the former Lower becomes Middle Pleistocene, and the Middle is merged into the Upper Pleistocene. The acceptance is well established in the earth sciences, in archeology still somewhat irregular.

An absolute measure of geologic time is now offered by potassium-argon (K/A) dating of volcanic materials, applied and refined by J. F. Evernden and G. H. Curtis of the Department of Geology in the University of California at Berkeley.[1] They were called on to date the Zinjanthropus site. The unanticipated high age they found

---

1. Method and determinations to latest date are given in their article, "The Potassium-Argon Dating of Late Cenozoic Rocks in East Africa and Italy," in press by *Quaternaria*, which I have been privileged to use.

required continued retesting and resampling of the volcanic beds of Olduvai Gorge, and a wider study of the local vulcanism, all confirming the early determination. Tests of volcanic materials taken in Italy and Java add to their early human chronology. They conclude their latest exposition thus: "Five years from now few questions about the general time-scales of Pleistocene glaciations and of human cultural evolution will remain to be answered." Zinjanthropus, Olduwan culture, and Villafranchian fauna have been placed in well-determined stratigraphic context, and the discovery site is affirmed as dating 1.75 to 1.8 million years. Olduvai Beds I (Zinjanthropus-bearing) and II previously thought to have been formed during the "Kamassian Pluvial" but were shown here to involve a span of the order of a million years and therefore too long to be the correlates of a single glacial stage, as had been held.

In the United States repeated vulcanism in the Sierra Nevada offers possibility of determining the glacial series. The Bishop tuff, overlying a till on the east side of the Sierra, has been found by Evernden and Curtis to date at 980,000 years, giving support to the views of our early glaciologists as to the length of our Ice Age. The still unknown correlation of the continental ice sheets with glacial deposits of our western mountains is made difficult by the absence of vulcanism in the eastern half of the country.[2]

PLEISTOCENE CLIMATES

The cause of the Ice Age and of its alternation of stages still is unsettled. It was a complex lot of happenings to the air that was recorded on land and sea. The record has parts that are only beginning to be read and that are inscribed in strange tongues, the latest of which is in readings of Pleistocene vulcanism. Marine terraces anywhere may record glacial and deglacial stages by rise and fall of the world ocean. Sediments on sea floors yield information as to stages of the Ice Age and their duration. At the present the most meaningful

---

2. The group at Berkeley thinks that it has now bridged the time gap that had separated K/A from radiocarbon dating. It may be therefore that the only limits to absolute dating of the past are in the availability of suitable volcanic (or organic) matter.

interpretations are coming from vulcanologists and oceanographers whose materials may be far removed from any glaciated area. Thereby a description of the entire earth during the Ice Age is becoming possible bit by bit, and thereafter perhaps a satisfactory explanation may be made of this strange episode of earth history.

A good deal has been learned lately about the last deglaciation, as a rapid recession of ice margins that was under way ten thousand years ago and gradually played out, to come approximately to a halt around four thousand years ago. This melting is thought to imply a major and brusque change in the circulation of the atmosphere to the climatic pattern now prevailing, in which there are dominantly meridional and frequent exchanges and confrontations of cold and warm air masses, the so-called cold and warm fronts. The present world climates thus are taken to be a model of interglacial conditions.

Fuller interpretation requires more knowledge of the upper air circulation. The older interest in extraterrestrial factors, such as the solar constant, is now replaced by concern with the dynamics of air and sea that will fit the historical facts of the Ice Age in its contrasted and successive stages. The facts are of several kinds and still are in need of being gathered and put into relation.

To call a glacial stage "cold" and an interglacial one "warm" conveys neither sufficient nor proper information. To accumulate snow that is changed to glacial ice, snowfall is needed in excess of melt; the greater the snow and the less the loss by melting, the greater the growth of the ice mass. The requisites are provided by air that has high absolute humidity, by temperatures ranging below and above freezing but not greatly so, and by cloudy skies. If Scandinavia were chilled in summer and warmed in winter it would be in good position to develop another ice cap by massive drift of wet sea air against high land.

Equatorward from the ice margins a wide zone of increased raininess has been inferred, a pluvial stage thereby substituted for the glacial one of higher latitude or altitude. This is an oversimplification that has been misleading. Past "pluvial" conditions have been reported from the Mediterranean south to the far extremity of Africa and have been assigned to particular glacial stages of the Alps. However, the meteorological mechanism that could effect this is unknown and probably unavailable. It is known that at such times aridity was less in extratropical latitudes, the Great Basin of the western United States being an example. In presently arid parts of the United States that extend into northern Mexico extensive lakes were formed, as in the Wisconsin stage. The land surfaces and soils about them show little evidence of former raininess. It is assured that evaporation was then very much reduced, which would have come about by greatly increased cloudiness and lessened annual range of temperatures. From such evidence it is not proper to construe a simultaneous and general increase of precipitation, humidity, or cloud cover across the low latitudes.

Interglacial conditions are represented, it is thought, by the present circulation of air and sea and the contemporary pattern of climates with their extreme differentiation as to heat and cold, wetness and dryness, seasonal change, contrast of maritime and continental air, and an equatorial zone that has remained least subject to climatic alteration.

Least is known about changes in Pleistocene climate in low latitudes. In high mountains such as the Andes the lower limit of permanent snow was well below present levels. This has been construed to show a general lowering of temperature, still held by some to have been worldwide and cause of the Ice Age. A general chilling of the atmosphere, however, would have reduced its moisture-holding capacity and operated against the forming of continental ice caps. The former glaciers in tropical high mountains may perhaps be accounted for by greater cloud cover associated with a somewhat freer and deeper flow of warm and moist air from the lowlands and the sea. On the improper premise that when ice fields were forming in high latitudes it was also raining more in low ones it has been construed that former and formerly-larger lakes in central and southern Africa (and also in the Andes) mark the "pluvial" equivalents of European glacial stages, without measure of age and without resolving the atmospheric circulation thereby implied. The question of such "pluvial" stages is considered below under the Olduwan environment. The large taxonomic diversity of xerophytic plants in much of Africa, endemic to that continent, indicates the persistence there of climates of drought. Minimal Pleistocene dislocation of climates is most assured for the lowest latitudes.

## AFRICAN HEARTH OF MANKIND

Darwin had seen in Africa the center of primate evolution and therefore the probable place where man originated. The discovery of Australopithecus again raised the interest in African origins. Other finds of interest but of uncertain age followed. Leakey in the course of hunting for fossil vertebrates made archaeologic finds in equatorial East Africa, climaxed by the Zinjanthropus discovery of 1959 in Olduvai Gorge in Tanganyika.

The soon-famous Olduvai Bed 1 contained Zinjanthropus, his tools, and the bones of Villafranchian animals he had consumed, snugly buried by tuff deposited from "nuées ardentes," a primordial Pompeii. The discovery came shortly after it had become possible to measure geologic time by geochemical alteration of certain minerals, which fortunately were present in unweathered and uncontaminated state in the Olduvai tuffs. The astonishing age of Zinjanthropus, one and three-quarter million years, has been reaffirmed. Olduwan artifacts are reported also from later horizons and as continuing for about seven hundred thousand years. Found in a different locale, the so-called Kafuan culture, based on dressed pebbles, is considered earlier than Olduwan. It has not been dated and is unacceptable to some. The tenor of the evidence adduced is that highland East Africa has been occupied by tool-making early humankind for about two million years, far back into Villafranchian time, the fauna being in agreement.

Potassium-argon tests have been made on other and later sites in East Africa, which have led Evernden and Curtis to assert "that early estimates of the ages of nearly all early African stone age cultures were in gross error, all estimates being far too young." Their inquiry is setting up a far longer chronology for Pleistocene Man in Africa than had been construed and one, as will be noted below, that breaks down the bracketing of "pluvial stages" with European glacial stages such as had come into acceptance in African archeology. The upset is great but the validity of the method and its application have not been seriously challenged.

For the very long continuance of Olduwan culture, perhaps the most disturbing of their findings, they propose that "the creatures fashioning these tools were performing to the limits of their abilities and the slow pace of evolutionary change prevented more rapid cultural development." For this duration of Olduwan culture, accompanying skeletal material is lacking. It may be suggested on the other hand that neither somatic evolution nor cultural innovation can be deduced from the persistence of a way of shaping stone. Early human learning was very slow, not merely because the human brain was less evolved but because learning builds on learning and there was as yet little to build on. The collecting life followed by such folk had little urgency to diversify and improve their stone tools. The record is silent as to what they may have been doing with perishable materials, what they thought about and communicated to one another, how and where they lived, what sort of society they made. They may have been doing nothing much different, in particular if they lived in isolation. The isolated Tasmanians of the past century were of Lower Paleolithic skill in tool making, which gives no basis for assessing their mental capacity.

What Olduvai has provided is the earliest known presence of man and his work. It supports African origin but it has not discovered such origin.

OLDUWAN ENVIRONMENT AND HABITS

The Olduvai beds have been examined in stratigraphic detail by R. L. Hay,[3] throwing important light on the environment of the time. The Zinjanthropus site was on or near the shores of a rather strongly saline lake, fed by streams descending from volcanoes to the east and south. Bed II, overlying the former conformably, also was formed at the time of a moderately to strongly saline lake, appearing to Hay to suggest a climate like the present one. At the time of Bed

---

3. *Science,* vol. 139, 1963, pp. 629–633.

III evaporation still exceeded precipitation, and in that of Bed IV there were indications of desert aridity. Olduwan culture found in Beds I and II was given a span of seven hundred thousand years by Evernden and Curtis, the two later beds perhaps adding another similar length of time.

The lakes of the present time in that region are salt. Those of the time of the Olduvai beds were such also and that time is measured as extending over two-thirds of the Pleistocene period (in the revised usage). The record is of conditions of marked excess of evaporation over precipitation, as at present, at times of somewhat greater aridity, at no time much less than now. The climate differed little from that of today. Such dominance of dry season in equatorial latitudes on the western side of the Indian Ocean is very good indication that the monsoonal regime was operating then as now, and as strongly. Before these studies were carried out by joining stratigraphy to K/A change, the lower beds at Olduvai were thought to have formed in much less time, to be of younger age, and they had been considered to mark locally the "Kamassian Pluvial Stage," not noting the evidences of their aridity. At Olduvai there is no evidence of any pluvial stage or in fact of significant climatic change from Early Pleistocene to the present. The scheme of a succession of African "pluvials" and of their coincidence with European glacial stages is unsupported at Olduvai and needs to be reexamined elsewhere.

The continued existence of a monsoon climate of dominant dry season in East Africa being acceptable and resembling present conditions, continuity of biomes is also to be accepted. Local exceptions need to be made for the building or destruction of volcanoes and for the sinking of the rift depressions, but in general the land mass stood about as now. In two million years the larger mammals experienced evolutionary changes but not radical replacements. The vegetation, it may be inferred, was a scrub savanna except on the volcanoes, and consisted of drought-tolerant shrubs and trees intermingled with grasses and herbs, both annual and perennial, with narrow gallery forests of more mesophytic character along the streams. The growing interference of man has since then replaced scrub savanna with more and more open grassland. The small terrestrial animals were locally resident, the large ones moved with the season according to the availability of feed, in the manner of the big game of the present. The ancestral fauna, it may also be inferred, was more dependent on browse and less on grass.

The environment of the interior as represented by Olduvai is ill-suited to the origins of humankind. Dry seasons greatly reduced the availability of food and water. Plant growth slowed or ceased at time of drought and game wandered farther in search of sustenance. The wearing down of human teeth indicates some dependence on hard plant food, which such a climate provides neither in variety or abundance. The time is far too early for a hunting society that could live in mobile predation of big game and there is no evidence of hunting weapons or skills. It is sometimes suggested that primitive man could run down game that was fleeter of foot and longer of wind than himself by relays of pursuers. He might do so if he planned properly but it is a poor exchange of energy for a return in food, incapable of sustaining a group. The Olduwan animal refuse is revealing. It consists of remains of small things such as lizards, snakes, and the like, curiously also of fish bones, and of infants of large animals, including giraffe, pig, and ostrich, the kinds of creatures that could be knocked over with a stick or taken by hand. Nothing suggests the skill of hunters. The example is rather that of a waterside camp about which foraging was rewarding and, it may be suggested, the foraging activities were mainly by the women.

The camp that became buried under hot ashes was of some permanence, as shown by the accumulation of tools and refuse. It was also a habitation site in the open air. The land was ranged over by feline and canine predators that took their prey both night and day. Having poor night vision, man retires at night to a common shelter against the chill and the unseen dangers of the dark. How could he protect his kind from the night-prowling predators for which he would be attractive and easy prey? That he was somehow able to do so is shown by the exposed situation of the living site. An enclosure might serve, fire would be most effective. The absence of any sign of hearth, charcoal, or burned bone has been taken to mean that he did not know the use of fire. How else might he have attained the security of his nights in the open? The site at Olduvai gives our earliest insights into human living and raises some unanswered questions.

Olduvai shows that humans had learned at a very early time how to live at favorable spots in savannas of the interior, to live there in the presence of other competitors for the same food, some of which were formidable predators, and to continue to live there despite the perils of vulcanism. It also tells of uncertain and marginal sustenance. These were not the circumstances under which mankind may be thought as having taken his origin and begun his cultural ascent. Rather they bespeak a venture into a difficult and hostile environment where he was able to maintain himself.

## AS TO PHYSIOLOGICAL BIAS

The course of human evolution, divergent from that of other primates, may be read in part in anatomical and physiological differences that point to an ecologic niche apart from the rest of his biologic kin. Alone among his order man walks upright on the soles of his feet, heel to toe, with his forelimbs shortened into arms that are freed from any service for locomotion on land. His unspecialized hands gave him unique freedom to develop manual dexterity in various directions. The human hand, foot, limbs, and erect posture were fully acquired, it appears, while his brain and skull were still in long process of evolution. Of his kindred he alone walks and runs freely, makes his home and secures his food wholly on the ground. He is most naked of the primates and most provided with active sweat glands and therefore required to drink most often; also he is especially sensitive to cold and heat. Of his kind he is most omnivorous, yet his jaws are of only moderate power and his teeth are undistinguished for ability to tear or grind and they last him poorly.

The course of human infancy and youth is slowest and longest and thereby has given a different direction to human society. The human infant remains helpless longest of all creatures. It does not cling but must be carried. It is most backward at locomotion and requires to be fed, led, and protected longest. Dependence is reduced gradually as childhood advances but is not terminated at adolescence. Man is last to be full grown, to attain full use of his physical

and mental powers. Least precocious of all creatures, his development continues longest and proceeds farthest. Thus the bonds between parent and child are not broken when there are later offspring
but are continued and diversified. So are those between siblings.
This continuity sets human society apart from all others and is in
large measure its foundation. Enduring acknowledgment of consanguinity, identification of kind of kinship, and observance of incest
taboos are peculiarly human qualities. Delay of maturity may well
have lengthened in the course of human evolution but it is built into
the particular course followed by our kind.

The primates in general lack the quality of paternal provision
and participation that is present in numerous other groups. Among
them the responsibility for feeding and looking after the young rests
upon the mother. With the human mother such care continued to be
given to all her progeny. As against a current vogue of thinking
human society as beginning as a band or horde under the control and
at the will of the strongest male, the older thesis is preferred, that, as
Lewis Morgan and Sir Henry Maine thought, it began with the
maternal family. The titillating model of promiscuous bands of
monkeys and baboons is not a proper preview of human society, nor
is it fully applicable to the higher apes. Aside from the hope that we
may have been destined to a better state than baboons, the requirement of continuing provision and supervision of offspring by maternal care meant family life, which properly has been considered as
matriarchal and matrilineal in character. The mother founded the
family and directed it, the father was brought into it. This appears
to be the simplest inference derived from the "premature birth" of
the human infant, as it has been called, and of its slow and long
growth to maturity.

The responsibilities of the mother incline her to as sedentary a
life as is possible, to require a home where she can get provisions for
her brood at short range and have a convenient and secure shelter.
The currently advanced view of primordial society as a stage of free
wandering common to early man is quite contrary to the sedentary
inclination and need of the mother, on which the survival and success of the race depended. Free wandering is not desired by any

society, not even a nomadic one. Those who have been forced into meager and adverse environments, such as Australian aborigines and other desert people, move about as little as they must, keep the same camp to which to return if they can, and leave the children and infirm at the base if possible.

## AN ECOLOGIC NICHE

Neither tropical rain forest nor savannas appear suitable as nurseries for our lineage. The first needs were for ample and proper food and water, shelter, and limited hazard. The pristine habitat should make functional sense of human anatomy, including the erect carriage of the body and proportions of the limbs. Specialization was lacking for the taking or ingestion of particular foods, flesh or plant. It is apparent that in most ecologic situations man was at a disadvantage with other primates and still other competitors for food. A superior and available niche for *Menschwerdung* was available by seashores of East Africa.

In Villafranchian times the level of the ocean stood considerably higher than at present, as marked in various parts of the world by "pre-glacial" marine terraces. To the south of Mombasa, for example, at this time the coast should have lain well inland from its present position, against the margins of the continental massif, resulting in the cutting of sea cliffs and building of intervening beaches. Such an articulated coast, located on an ocean of good tidal range such as the Indian Ocean has, is suited to primitive human occupation. It may be remarked that the great cats and most primates are not attracted to seacoasts. Here, it is suggested, was an unpreempted niche having the qualities favoring human evolution and cultural beginnings. Although to my knowledge no such sites have been found or looked for in East Africa, elsewhere, in South Africa, Morocco, Algeria, and Portugal, the inner margins of high marine terraces have revealed the earliest living sites, where beyond the tropics "pre-glacial" man was living by the side of the sea.

Professor Sir Alister Hardy has recently proposed that certain features of human anatomy may be accounted for by adaptive evolution experienced under somewhat amphibious living. While foraging along shore hominids thus became accustomed to going into the water, and learned to swim and dive in search of food. Such natant habits, if acquired early enough, could operate by selective evolution to develop the symmetry, erectness, and grace of carriage of the human body, the proportions of limbs to trunk, and of arm to leg. He also thought that such functional redesigning of primate anatomy, which does impress as an improvement in line and motion over that of the apes, might include loss of body hair, the streamlined pattern of the remaining hair tracts, and the topography of subcutaneous fat as distributed for buoyance. Hardy's genial thesis derives from large experience of adaptation of form to swimming.

Food habits and needs of man differ strongly from those of other primates and indicate origin in a different habitat. The food chain that is started with plankton offered him full nourishment from the sea. Coastal living and dependence on the sea avoids deficiencies of diet. It affords a diet high in protein and in unsaturated fats, and is provided with salt, iodine, and all minor elements. The peculiar human needs of nourishment are entirely satisfied by food from the sea. As Hardy has asked concerning human anatomy, it may be asked whether human physiology also reflects a seaside phylogeny? By way of comparison hunters on land, though well supplied with meat, are likely to have need of fat, since most game yields lean meat, as shown among our Indians of the eastern woodlands who added the fat of nuts to their diet. The extensive aboriginal trade of sea salt into the interior of tropical America made good the deficiency of salt and iodine felt by the inland peoples.

The tidal shores of the Indian Ocean provide diversity and abundance of food, daily and throughout the year. Shellfish are sessile or move in a narrow and short range. Low tides expose the sea bottom for collecting and bring more of it into diving range. High tides and storms cast things on shore. Twice a day and twice each lunar month the shore changes its offerings. The shallow seas offshore in East Africa are superior pasturage of sea turtles. Marine mammals and fish are stranded occasionally. There is edible kelp in quantity and behind the shoreline other plant and animal foods may be had, as is the case also at river mouths. Beachcombing yields materials of wood that has been seasoned in salt water, shells of useful shapes and sizes, and cobbles that have been sorted and shaped by wave. For untutored man the provision of food and prime material was vastly greater and more continuously available than he could find in the interior. These were his for the taking, uncontested by other creatures.[4]

Such shores offered the best opportunity to emergent humanity—food and water without seasonal limitation, tools prepared by nature, and life without fear. A living site could be chosen by fresh water, perhaps in the shelter of bank or cliff where they might stay and congregate and have leisure to begin social living. Permanence and increase in population expressed themselves in forming communities of kindred. The basis was established for human society.

Here also was the best prospect of origin of the bilateral family. I recur again to the Hardy thesis. In swimming and diving there is no significant advantage of sex and least of age. When European discoverers got overseas they were amazed to see the aquatic skill and enjoyment of the inhabitants of warm and temperate coasts. Whether very primitive like the Tasmanians and natives of the Gulf of California or of advanced culture like those of the South Seas and the Caribbean, both sexes were adept swimmers and divers. They swam for a purpose and for the pleasure it gave. Every one, young and old, went into the water. Such joint activity, referred back to primeval times, would provide for the participation of the males in getting food and in sharing responsibilities.

As one place became fully occupied there was another farther along the coast waiting to be colonized. The resources of the sea were everywhere familiar and usually ample. Drinking water was likely to be found at intervals along shore, even if the interior was arid. The seasons inland hardly mattered. Coastwise expansion under similar ways of living could continue all about the Indian Ocean and

---

4. I have just read the article by Gisela Petri-Odermann, "Das Meer im Leben einer Nordwest-Australischen Küstenbevölkerung," in *Paideuma*, May, 1963. An illuminating account of primitive life on the opposite shore of the Indian Ocean, relevant to the inferred primal ways of the African coast.

beyond, to the Pacific and Atlantic. Settling inland—whether in savanna, forest, or desert—required other skills and offered reduced satisfaction.

The same was true of high latitudes, which must not be thought to have lacked cold winters during interglacial times. Winter in northern China seems to have been as severe when Peking Man lived there as it is now. He made good use of fire, about which curious notions have formed. One is that he more or less dates the beginning use of fire. Another is that later and elsewhere it was not used until early Würm time. Still another holds that fire was employed to keep warm a long time before food was prepared by its aid. All such ideas rest on the lack of evidence of fire in such sites, which is no proof that it was not used.

Man's early presence in wintry lands is attested by every Early Paleolithic site in Europe beyond the shores of the Mediterranean. It will hardly do to say that he protected himself by wrapping himself in skins. To provide the family with pelts required not only the ability to take them but to dress them so that they would stay soft, and to piece them together, involving a number of skills that were not acquired easily and early. That he lived where it was cold is fair presupposition that he used fire. Its traces often are erased by accident of time and weather. Some are likely to be found; there are some now which are explained away as natural fires only because the sites are very old. Even the mile high, open air site at Olduvai raises the surmise that it makes sense as a fire-guarded encampment. Having fire, man was enabled to go forth to possess the world; without it, he was a primate narrowly limited to suitable parts of the tropics.

*Note:*

The geographical localizations of cultural beginnings were considered by me in a Wenner-Gren symposium on early human society, held at Burg Wartenstein, Austria, in 1959 and published as "Sedentary and Mobile Bents in Early Societies" in *Viking Fund Publications in Anthropology, No. 31,* pp. 256–266.

The theme was further developed in "Seashore—Primitive Home of Man?" in *Proceedings of the American Philosophical Society,* vol. 106 (1926), pp. 41–47. "Fire and Early Man," in *Paideuma,* Band VII, pp. 399–407.

# 7. Sedentary
## and Mobile Bents
## in Early Societies

GLOSSES ON THE GENERAL THEME

My original title, "Farther Roots of Agricultural Society," is here rephrased for better accord with the general theme as it was developed in the discussions. The conference put major emphasis on primate biology for reconstructing the social life of early man. Man as an animal was compared anatomically with his various kindred, in particular as to size and topography of the brain. Behavior of monkeys, baboons, and the great apes was considered at length, especially their sexual conduct. Thus there were implicit assumptions and explicit inferences that the social life of early man involved a group of behavioral patterns exhibited in simian individuals and communities. My interests as historical geographer lie far afield from such mechanistic biologic thinking and turn to questions of how man explored his habitable world, learned skills and communicated them to others of his kind, and diversified his ways of living; in short, how he became maker of culture.

A serious difficulty with the simian model is that the males are dominant (also there is an order of dominance within each group),

"Sedentary and Mobile Bents in Early Societies" first appeared in "Social Life of Early Man," Sherwood L. Washburn, Ed., *Viking Fund Publication in Anthropology, No. 31,* (Washington, DC: 1961), pp. 256–266.

that they are promiscuous, are food-snatching instead of sharing, and are indifferent to their offspring. The most that can be said for them seems to be that they will rally round for defense and attack. How then has the psychologic and cultural gap between the simian groups and the most primitive human society been bridged? The biological version of "humanization" retains the dominant male, but places him and his subordinated horde in a new environment that requires a change in food habits from "frugivorous" to "carnivorous." This may be explained by migration—leaving a forest home to occupy "open savanna" habitat—or by climatic change—desiccation shrinking the cover of vegetation. In either case the male is thought of as turning to hunting game, which he brings home to share with his womenfolk and children. The type of the alpha ape is transformed into *paterfamilias*, who recognized his dependents and accepted the responsibility of caring for them. I do not see that such a reversal in primate behavior is explained either by migration into a new environment or by climatic change. The dominant simian male I should judge to be the wrong exemplar for the forming of human society.

The lineage of man has been developing for a very long time and so has that of the apes. The length of divergent evolution limits the propriety of drawing inferences from living pongids to primordial man. On the other hand we are acquiring new knowledge of hominid evolution. Dr. Hürzeler was invited by his sponsor, our host foundation, to show the remarkably preserved *Oreopithecus* remains he has been collecting from central Italy, probably of Upper Miocene age. If these are hominid, they will mean another advance, morphologically and also geographically, toward the knowledge of human origins. We were also briefed at some length on the current status of australopithecine studies, again a subject in which the foundation has been interested. Their hominid filiation, as has been advocated previously by J. T. Robinson and Le Gros Clark, had favorable attention. The rudiments of culture found with *Australopithecus* open up new vistas of the threshold of humanity. South Africa and now also East Africa are at present the centers of greatest interest for human origins. South Africa is, however, at a farthest end of the Old World land mass. In such a cul-de-sac location archaic forms are more likely to survive or to undergo terminal variation than new and successful lines of evolution are likely to originate. This remote land's end is, rather, an area in which relict hominid groups survived beyond their time. It will be interesting to see whether their origin may be traced to lands farther north and more favorably situated for evolution and dispersal.

The larger question is, I think, of cultural origins and growth beyond the reach of biologic determinations. Phylogeny, mental capacity, ideas, and culture are not in a single series. The Lower Pleistocene has yielded primitive human remains and artifacts, both showing slow progression toward more advanced forms, the osteologic materials being the more scanty, discontinuous, and less consistent. But may we say that there ever was one Rubicon of evolution, as marked by the acquisition of brains of a certain size and conformation, at which we can aver that humanity began?

## ENVIRONMENT IN THE ICE AGE

Conventionally and conveniently the Ice Age is considered as the "Age of Man." There is sufficient evidence in both Europe and North America that the so-called First Glaciation (Güns, Nebraskan) was preceded by at least one widespread glaciation, which was followed by a deglaciation. This agrees with paleontological inclinations to place the Villefranchian (Blancan of North America?) as of Quaternary rather than Pliocene age. The Sicilian marine high terrace (of interest to early archeology) thus would record the first interglacial stage. It also seems most probable that we are still living in the Ice Age and are experiencing an earlier phase of an interglacial stage. At a rough estimate the earth has been undergoing extreme climatic changes and displacements of climatic regions for the past million years. The known history of mankind falls into a geologic time of maximal climatic instability and contrast.

Glaciers formed and continued to grow only so long as more snow fell in winter than was melted in summer. Glaciation depended on high relative humidity, extending pretty much throughout the annual cycle; in other words, on reduced winter cold and summer heat. There was less sun and more cloudiness over high and

middle latitudes and especially over continental interiors. Equatorward from the ice margins pluvial zones extended far inland. Desert
areas were at their minima. Least is known of tropical conditions
during glacial stages, though there is evidence of somewhat lowered
temperatures. Ewing and Donn lately have advanced interesting ar-
guments that the Arctic Ocean was open during glacial stages; this
would have fed more snow to the northern margins of the icecaps and
greatly tempered the winters of the far North.

Present weather may be considered characteristic of interglacial
conditions, with polar and tropical air masses strongly developed
and circulating vigorously. Areal climatic contrasts are now accentuated as to seasonal heat and cold and also as to extremes of aridity and
humidity. It should also be noted that the Arctic Ocean is wholly
frozen over in winter and helps to refrigerate the high latitudes.

It is therefore not proper to speak in too general terms of cold
glacial and warm interglacial phases. A good deal is being learned of
what happened in and at the end of the last glacial stage, provisionally summed up thus: The last interglacial stage (Riss/Würm, San-
gamon) seems to have merged slowly into the "Fourth" glacial stage
as a lengthy time of moderated weather in intermediate and higher
latitudes. The spread of the continental icecaps proceeded gradually
to a culmination, followed by recessions and gradually diminishing
readvances. Somewhat more than ten thousand years ago a sharp
swing took place into the great deglaciation that we call postglacial
time and that is construed as marking the establishment of the contemporary pattern of atmospheric circulation. Early Würm time
saw the yielding of Mousterian to Upper Paleolithic cultures in Europe and the replacement then of Neanderthal man by modern
forms. It is, however, gross oversimplification to read this change in
terms of the rigors of glacial cold.

The Pleistocene climate swings were accompanied by large alterations in flora and fauna. A good deal has been inferred, though
little is actually known, about the thermal tolerances and water re-
quirements of specific animals and plants of importance to man.
Growth and decrease of icecaps and of deserts alternately spread and
shrank available ranges. Undemanding and mobile forms had the

best of it; ecologically the times favored pioneers. Some plants increased or decreased; animals came or went, but only in some cases may the change be attributed to temperature change or to rainfall. Some plants are disseminated quickly; some germinate freely on mineral soil; some fail to reproduce under increased shade. The conditions involved in plant successions have made ecology a complex and interesting study, more and more cautious about climatic effects. The climatic explanation of grasslands has failed in case upon case, be they tropical savannas or mid-latitude prairies or steppes. The identification of Pleistocene herbivores with particular climatic conditions and vegetation is similarly dubious. Of the three living species of bison, which are interfertile and perhaps only geographic races, the European Wisent and the American woodland bison lived in woodlands and largely on browse, and only our plains buffalo was mainly grass-consuming. Few herbivores can be claimed as necessarily dependent on grass rather than browse; palatability and availability were main determinants of their feeding habits. The frequence, presence, or absence of specific plants or animals depends on so many biotic, edaphic, and climatic elements that inference of a single cause, such as climatic change, is rarely valid.

Sea levels the world over fell with each glaciation and rose during each deglaciation. These glacial eustatic changes are estimated to have had an amplitude well in excess of a hundred meters. Since the last glacial recession began, about ten thousand five hundred years ago by radiocarbon determination, sea level appears to have risen by more than thirty meters, and it is fairly certain that most of this occurred in the first half of the time elapsed. This rise is thought to be about one-third of the total since the maximum of the Fourth Glaciation. The seacoasts of the world as we know them are very young, developed within recent geologic time. Those on which Paleolithic man lived, and also much of their adjacent lowlands, lie well submerged. Only the landward remnants of the highest sea stages reached in interglacial times are exposed to our view.

The eustatic fluctuations of sea level have also had worldwide effects on lowland rivers flowing into the sea. As sea level rises, either the entering stream course is drowned or it builds its bed higher, aggrading the valley floor laterally and especially upstream.

The great lowland flood plains of today, too, have been fashioned by the last deglaciation. When sea levels were lowered, the valley floors were trenched. The glacial succession of cutting and filling was first and fully documented for the Mississippi River and tributaries from the Gulf of Mexico to above the junction of the Ohio River; how far it applies to the upper valley has not been worked out. At interglacial times the valley floors were subjected to flooding, deposition of alluvium, and the forming of swamps. In glacial stages drainage was accelerated and coast plains were eroded into ridges and valleys. The Arctic Coast plains of eastern Siberia and Alaska, both of which remained unglaciated, then were well drained, with less, or even without, tundra and permafrost. Was such the time when woodlands of aspen and birch and conifers prevailed in the Yukon and the New Siberian Islands and there were mammoths and bison? And an open Arctic Ocean moderated conditions for hyperborean living?

## BIOLOGY AND THE FAMILY

If the simian horde and its dominant male are in part irrelevant and in part incompetent to serve as models for primordial human society, we need to consider the human female as to our beginnings. She has always lived, of necessity, closer to the daily biologic realities and responsibilities than has the male. Why should she be cast in a subordinate and passive role as to our social origins?

The human infant is born prematurely as compared with the other higher mammals. It has been proposed that this prematurity was progressive in human evolution, the female pelvis not continuing to enlarge along with the increase in size of the foetus and its head. Care of the progeny least developed at birth falls upon the human mother; the time during which the infant remains wholly dependent is longest in humans and may have grown longer as evolution went on.

The period of suckling among primitive peoples is usually at least two years. It may determine the spacing of pregnancy in part; when the next child is born, the elder one, though probably weaned, still must have its food prepared and provided. The cluster of dependent children grows, and dependence is lessened only gradually as the brood increases. There is no break until after puberty is attained, and then it is only partial. The mother continues to watch over, feed, and instruct her young through childhood, the male parent in time taking on the training of the boys. However much or little he may participate, she is the center and creator of family life. Family ties are lasting; no primitives lack recognition of kinship, which may take forms much more elaborate than those in civilized societies. The enduring family is a major human innovation; it is due to the role of the mother and has a singular biologic base. It involves awareness of the past and anticipation of a future and is expressed in a sense of history.

It was the woman's daily task to forage for food for her offspring. This reduced her mobility and shortened the radius over which she could range at collecting. If she covered less ground, she learned to know its food potentials more intimately. Also she trained the young ones with her to recognize what was to be taken or avoided and how to go about collecting.

How the putative father was attached to the family circle is more uncertain. He ranged at will, probably with other male companions more often than alone, and it is not probable that he originally set out on such excursions with any idea of bringing back food to share with others. When he came back hungry, his woman may have saved something for him and gradually conveyed to him the idea that if he wished to be assured of bed and board he had better help to provide.

As the male came to accept association with a particular woman and her offspring and thus his part in parenthood, the bilateral biological family came into being. The mother always had her family in mind; the father had to be brought into it, overcoming his reluctance toward domestication. Altruism, prime requisite for social advance, begins with the mother in the care and affection for her own, extends to the kindred, and becomes interfamilial aid. The trend, encouraged by the woman, is toward monogamy. Regard for others beyond and above the call of glands is the postulate of humanity.

The figure of the hunter, male of course, has been overstressed for both primordial and primitive man. Humans were not choosy as to what they ate or how they got their food so long as it agreed with them; food specialization came with cultural specialization. Man is omnivorous, with a dietary range approached by very few creatures. This quality, original or acquired, has had much to do with his success. The bones of larger mammals found in some early archeologic sites are not enough to prove hunting economy or skills; we do not know whether part was secured by scavenging or represents disabled and infirm aged or young individuals. The club may be conceded to earliest man; the wooden spear already required considerable skill in the making and use. Modern primitive societies, although all of them have some specialized hunting skills, continue to depend primarily on collecting in many parts of the world. For the majority of tribes of upper and lower California the food procured by hunting game was minor and hardly of critical importance.

An extension of the theme that early man was a carnivore and ruthless killer is the attribution to him of cannibalism, the illustrations cited being australopithecine and Peking Man. The imputation is one of serious abnormality; beasts do not prey on their own kind. Cannibalism is not a trait of primitive peoples or of hunting tribes, nor is it a matter of food economy anywhere so far as I know. It has existed perhaps only in certain agricultural societies, where it has a sacrificial ceremonial character. The adduced evidence for early man is to be taken with reserve; there are other interpretations, such as funerary cult for Peking Man.

WOMAN AND FIRE

Although we are dealing with man of the Old and Middle Stone Age, it was less the stones he shaped than the fire he employed that provided the greater range to his artifices and stimulus to cultural diversity. With the use of fire he entered on the promethean road that has led to the technology of today. It is, however, with Vesta rather than Prometheus that I am concerned, with woman as the keeper of the fire.

The capture of fire brought with it the duty of keeping it "alive," as we still say. Ages may have elapsed before the art of making fire was discovered, and then the making of new fire was not easy. Continuous possession of fire is a theme of ancient religions as sacred or eternal fire, in the care of female attendants.

Keeping the fire is the duty and privilege of the woman. Her sessile inclinations, rooted in the care of her family, were strengthened by adding the care of the fire. Hearth and home are synonymous. The hearth fire gave security against the great predators, especially at night. It invited evening gathering for social activity and leisurely discourse. The social hours, firelit after sunset, were best suited for exercising the faculty of thought and the fashioning of speech. As woman learned to cook, new food potentials were developed. Animal foods may be eaten raw, though their taste is varied and improved by cooking, which also makes foods keep better. Man's ability to digest raw starch and the seed proteins is slow and therefore limited. Women were the original food chemists and botanists. They experimented with roots, stems, and fruits at the hearth and learned to identify in the field which ones could or could not be made palatable. Proper application of heat made available plants that were bitter and poisonous. Where heat alone did not suffice, soaking and washing in water was learned (we do not know when). Before there were carrying containers, collecting perhaps concentrated on large units, such as the digging of underground starchy stems, tubers, bulbs, and corms. However, natural containers were often available, such as carapaces, the shells of large mollusks, and the large and tough leaves of some plants. We should also consider the utility of stone tools in cutting starchy stems of aroids *(Alocasia)*, *musas (ensete)*, palms (sago), etc., all requiring preparation by cooking. We may be confident that recognition and experimentation went on and that a new success at the hearth was reported out from woman to woman and group to group; also that, the more successful the cook, the firmer her position in the society.[1]

---

1. Perhaps in time there may be enough known of early hearths to tell something of what went on, such as whether there were raised hearths or cooking pits—the latter indicative of steam-cooking.

## AGE AND ORIGIN OF FIRE-USING

Choukoutien has been called the earliest center of fire use, but how old is it? As in other early Paleolithic sites in eastern and southern Asia, there is very great uncertainty as to age. Current interpretations incline toward Middle rather than Lower Pleistocene age, not perhaps on the basis of better evidence. There is still the question of the "eoliths" (Red Crag) of the Ipswich area of East Anglia, which are acceptable geologically and satisfy some competent archeologists but not others. These are acknowledged as bearing proof of fire, though fire has hardly been considered in the controversy, since it has been assumed that natural fires could have swept the site.

The inference of natural fires should not be accepted as casually as has been done here and elsewhere in archeology. About fires from volcanic action there is of course no doubt. The easy assumption of lightning fires in sites that are under scrutiny as to human occupation is not proper. Where thunderstorms are rainstorms, and such is the case for very much of the world where early man lived, the chances of natural fire are extremely slight. (We must eliminate the conductors and dry fuels that have been provided by modern man.) Mountainous areas in arid and semiarid lands do set up dry-season turbulence with lightning discharges into inflammable plant matter. Such fires occur under conditions of low humidity and are accompanied by little or no rain. These, however, are exceptional regions, hardly involved in the early archeologic problem. It would be of importance to know whether or where charcoal is known from any of the great body of Pleistocene and Pliocene alluvial deposits beyond the time of human presence. The occurrence of charcoal, burned earth, and fire-crazed or fire-broken stone needs to be considered with care as circumstantial evidence of the presence of man.

The capture of fire by man raises psychological (it has been suggested psychiatric) questions. Dr. Galdston has called our attention to the orgasmic quality of pyromania. How did fear of fire become fascination and excitation, how did fire worship come, and how was the sacred fire linked to fire of domestic utility?

The capture of fire may well have come about as a discovery in food-collecting following after a natural fire. As the source of such a fire I should prefer vulcanism. Italy and the eastern Mediterranean, the East African Rift, and especially the Sunda volcanic arc all are in such favorable position with regard to early man. The first premise is a natural fire that swept across part of a collecting range, killing and roasting animals trapped in its path. The next is the entry of humans into the burned area, the collection of carcasses, the enjoyment of their improved taste, and the recognition that this was an easy way to get a lot of better food. The third is that someone picked up a brand and started another fire. (The original version is by Charles Lamb as *A Dissertation on Roast Pig.*) Then fire was brought to the living place and given to the care of woman. Whatever that first use of fire, if there was a decisive moment to the course of human events, this was probably it. We need to know the various myths of the getting of fire, the fire cults and divinities, and the cremation customs in order to add insight to old, very old, aspects of culture.

## DIVERSITY OF HABITAT AND HABIT

Physiology supports the guess that mankind may have originated in some temperate land, without extremes of heat and cold or of aridity and humidity. An inland origin is assumed. Those who would have primordial man leave the forest and stray out into the open savanna rely both on the hunter image and on the postulate of wide grasslands at that time.

It may be proposed that, wherever man came from, the discovery of the tidal sea was a major event. The seashores must have had the strongest attraction for primitive and artless folk. Here was abundant and diverse food, waiting to be picked up or dug twice daily, and less subject to seasonal fluctuation than were land supplies. Fish and sea mammals were stranded occasionally. In season there were the eggs and young of sea fowl to be got at rookeries. There was edible seaweed and salt for seasoning. Driftwood supplied ever-replenished fuel and good stuff for tools, being seasoned in salt water instead of decaying on land. Headlands and coves provided tough, wave-selected, and wave-shaped cobbles, better than those fashioned by stream corrosion. May not man have been helped to learn the kinds and shapes of stones most useful to his lithic industries by living along the sea?

Primitive man could hardly find a better prospect than in beach-combing, which was also conducive to social grouping and to reduced mobility. In arid lands coastal sites are more likely to provide drinkable water than are interior ones, for various reasons of physical geography. In cold lands a harvest of food may still be possible at the edge of salt water when the land is locked by frost and snow. The dispersal of settlement along arid coasts and into high latitudes was invited by moving farther along shores provided with familiar foods and materials. The wider exploration and occupation of the world must have been greatly helped by following the coastlines. In later days we find the strandloopers as backward peoples, possibly because they lacked the challenge necessary to progress. In the infancy of humanity, however, such habitat meant better opportunity for food and other raw materials and more chance for social living. It does not matter that there is slight archeologic evidence of the early habitation of coastlines; all but the higher sea margins of the interglacial levels are now submerged as are, of course, the marine lowlands of the glacial stages.

There can be hardly any doubt that man sought out the shelter of a natural roof wherever he could. Under an overhang of rock he might be out of the wet and wind, with a dry floor to sleep and sit on, and with less nightly chilling of the air than in the open. Such shelters provided the preferred, perhaps the first, home in any clime and became virtually a necessity when fire was kept. Mankind found rather than built its early homes. Suitable shelter niches are provided where differential weathering and erosion produce longish shallow recesses. Sedimentary or volcanic beds, flat-lying and differing in resistance to weathering, form such rock shelters, in particular when they are undercut by stream or wave. Where the sea meets the land, unless the latter is very low, one rarely need seek far to find such shelters, including some that have been notched by storm waves. Inland, as in uplands formed of limestone and shale or of sandstone or interbedded lava and ash, recesses are fashioned by the downcutting and lateral erosion of streams. In all cases these are ephemeral geologic features, being made, crumbling away, and being replaced. We know them mainly as used by Upper Paleolithic or later folk, but it is improper to infer, as has been done, that men turned late to inhabiting them. I refer, of course, to rock-shelter habitation, not to ceremonial use of deep and dark caves. The sequential geomorphologic processes have erased older abodes as they have ancient kitchen middens.

The primordial habitation patterns were determined by abundance, diversity, ease of securing food and water, and availability of shelter, and also, I suspect, very early by a good supply of fuel. These conditions were provided by seashores and in some valleys. If these are the right trails, they take us into areas of accentuated relief, both coastal and interior, of varied, abundant, and useful flora and fauna, either marine or terrestrial localities of superior advantage for population increase, social grouping, sedentary trends, and cultural variation.

As occupation spread into arid lands, or when aridity spread, increased mobility was exacted. Of such necessities the men became the principal providers of food, the scouts and trail-makers, and the leaders of the group on the march from camp to camp. Thus emerged protohunting groups and, one may infer, primacy of the male. The high latitudes perhaps were accessible only to hunting societies. Boreal and subboreal vegetation is rather poor in plants edible by man and also in the lower and smaller animal life that can be had by simple means of collecting. Such areas would await the development of hunting skills.

Our knowledge, our terminology, and in some measure our interpretation of Paleolithic man is still predominantly European, except for the current African discoveries. It is only from the Upper Paleolithic that hunting cultures are clearly known. The Middle Paleolithic has uncertain indications of such specialization, as in the Mousterian points. The long Lower Paleolithic has yielded only artifacts of kinds that may have served for many uses, such as the so-called scrapers, choppers, and bi-faces or "hand-axes." Hand-axes are serviceable for cutting and splitting, for taking bark and bast, and for adzing, digging, and pounding, but they are not very suitable for killing game or for combat. It has been suggested that the makers of "core" tools were woodland-dwelling collectors and that those of "flake" industries were ancestral to hunting societies and their militant offshoots. Despite evident oversimplification, there may be something to the contrast.

The ancient users of hand-axes and choppers are known especially from the great passageway of mankind that runs between the western shores of Europe through the Mediterranean and the Near East across India (Soan culture) and Burma (Anyathian) to the South China Sea. It is from somewhere in these attractive lands that the derivations of later agricultural villagers are to be sought. The Mousterian of Middle Paleolithic, borne by the Neanderthal race, mainly, it would seem, an endemic growth in the shelter of the European peninsula, will hardly serve as an antecedent. It was inundated and swept away by incursions of the great hunters of the Upper Paleolithic. The last of these, the reindeer hunters of Ahrensburg, have now been dated as contemporaries of the first town of Jericho, the earliest known agricultural date. The conventional sequence of Paleolithic, Mesolithic, and Neolithic may still fit Europe and its borders as sequences, not as developmental stages. The hunters came from elsewhere. The cultivation of plants and the keeping of domestic animals were brought to Europe from the outside, apparently also borne by new peoples. Since the arrival of the first Aurignacian elements, Europe has been invaded many times by new cultures and new peoples, perennially a colonial land, especially for the East.

The hunters radiating from inner and northern Asia brought masculine societies. The roots of agricultural living are to be sought elsewhere, as in southern Asia, by the diversification of skills proceeding from collecting, with the forming of larger and more sedentary local groups.

As it is inferred that the mother had the major role in the making of earliest human culture, so her influence continued to find in genial climes new means of expressing itself in household and vicinal skills. Culture growth takes a long time to gain momentum; the simplicity, persistence, and slow diversification of the artifacts of the greater part of Paleolithic time illustrate the slow accretion of learning.

As familiar and mistress of the hearth, woman continued to learn most about plants and their uses. The lore of curing was hers, especially as to simples. Plants that could not be made edible by cooking alone might be made so by first leaching them. Soaking and pounding opened the way to extracting and felting plant fibers and gave the start of textile skills, which have remained chiefly in woman's domain. It was discovered that certain plants macerated in water would stupefy fish, which then were easily collected and cooked without ill effects. Comparative ethnology indicated this as a primitive and perhaps earliest mode of fishing; there seems to be no sex limitation in this manner of taking fish, which otherwise is men's work. Fresh-water fish communities, as I have tried to show elsewhere,[2] gave the best conditions for beginning agricultural life.

These matters take us far beyond the half light of what we know of archeology, but their linkage is through a progressive collecting economy in which the women were free to develop their bent toward sedentary living, the arts and goods of the household, and pacific community life. The great and decisive advance by steps leading to agricultural life was made by securely sedentary communities, living with sufficient leisure in certain amply rewarding situations and enjoying the stimulation of communication between settled groups.

---

2. Carl O. Sauer, "Environment and Culture during the Last Deglaciation," in *Proc. Amer. Phil. Soc.*, 92:65–77.

# 8. Man's Dominance
# by Use
# of Fire

## HEARTHS OF EARLY ARCHEOLOGIC RECORD

The discovery of human occupation of caves or rock shelters at Choukoutien, west of Peking, gave first proof (1927–1936) of the use of fire by early man. Peking Man, as he has been named, lived here in comfort and for some time. The roof and walls of limestone gave opportunity to heat the enclosed space of his living quarters, and the floors preserved his hearths. It does not follow, as has been construed, that here man learned the use of fire to protect himself against cold.

The time of Peking Man has been estimated, insecurely, as falling within the Second Interglacial, in terms of European Pleistocene chronology following the Mindel Glacial. The presence of early man in Europe at that time has been securely established at Swanscombe in the Thames basin. In Germany remains at Steinheim and Heidelberg have been placed in that interglacial, those at the latter perhaps being earlier. All are open-air sites and lack hearths. Other European sites of similar age, one in Hungary and one in France, have been since reported as having hearths. All are in fairly high latitudes,

"Man's Dominance by Use of Fire" first appeared in *Geoscience and Man,* Volume X, April 20, 1975, pp. 1–13.

between 40° and 50°N. All are of unknown age in years, and, with the exception of Swanscombe, of uncertain position in the glacial succession of events.

The Choukoutien materials were studied exhaustively, fauna and flora (hackberry, for instance) indicating climatic conditions resembling the present. It is misleading to designate glacial stages as cold and interglacial ones as warm. Icecaps formed when snowfall was heavy and remained as ice throughout the year when winters were mild and summers cool and cloudy. Icecaps wasted when winters were cold and snowfall was light, and summers were sunny and warm. We live at a time of atmospheric circulation with maximum seasonal range of temperature, in what is in fact an interglacial climatic pattern. Early man in northern China and in northern Europe lived under climatic conditions like those of the present. He had learned to cope with winter cold and a short growing season, suggesting that he had learned to store food, as well as to heat his quarters.

The divisions of Pleistocene time are given quite different durations according to the measure used. The Second Interglacial (between Mindel and Riss) is considered as having been the longest of the deglaciations. Peking Man and Java Man, both assigned to that stage, are held to be near physical relatives. The age of Java Man has been determined by potassium-argon tests as eight hundred thirty thousand years.

Man, the naked primate, although not the "naked ape," had the use of fire when he moved into lands of winter cold. With fire he made the artificial climate of his habitations from England to northern China. His hearths are well preserved under the sheltering roof of rock at Choukoutien. They are wanting at open-air sites that have been exposed to removal by weather, rain, runoff, and wind. Possessing fire, man could enlarge his ecological range to whatever lands offered sustenance. The proposal that now and then he picked up "natural fire," presumably set by lightning, used it locally and briefly, but did not make it a way of life, negates the curiosity and learning that has marked the course of mankind. It implies repeated opportunity to find natural fire, use it, and then abandon its use. It also implies that Peking Man, significantly advanced in the shaping of artifacts, was unconcerned about seeing what he could do with fire other than to keep warm. In place of the casual use of fire, the alternate explanation is that man carried fire with him as his most prized acquisition, keeping it long before he learned to make it.

## AFRICAN ORIGIN OF MAN

Charles Darwin thought that Africa, south of the Sahara, with the greatest diversity of primates, was the place of origin of mankind. In 1924 the Taungs skull was found in Bechuanaland in South Africa, first of the lineage named *Australopithecus,* meaning southern ape. The discussion of what kind of primates these were went on for decades, the name affiliating them with apes. Later they were accepted as primitive hominids. Their age was indeterminate, other than that the limestone recesses in which they were found had long been subject to alteration and collapse. There was evidence of the use of tools; that of fire has been advanced and disputed.

In 1932 Louis Leakey began his long and patient search for vestiges of ancient man in what was then Tanganyika. Olduvai Gorge had been an important collecting area for vertebrate paleontologists. Its walls—beds of volcanic tuff, ash, and cinders—expose diverse bones of animals buried by ash falls or washed in by mud flows. Leakey occasionally found artifacts, and in 1959 Mrs. Leakey discovered the first human skull. J. F. Evernden, then of the Department of Geology of the University of California, Berkeley, took samples from the discovery site to use in the lately developed geochronology by alteration of potassium to argon. The potassium silicates of the Olduvaian volcanic beds gave the first dating. In 1961 Garness Curtis and in 1962 Richard Hay of the department at Berkeley began their field study of the Olduvai beds and thus established their chronology and the sequence of geomorphic events and determined that humans had lived there 1.75 million years ago. Later Richard Leakey found more and earlier (2.6 million years) remains at Lake Rudolf in Kenya, the age established also by potassium-argon determination.

Olduvai provided a new key to the human past, which was much older than had been thought before. Rift valleys in northeastern

Africa, their formation accompanied by vulcanism, are known to have been inhabited by mankind for millions of years, living in areas of marked and long dry season, with a vegetation and fauna adapted to alternate dry and wet periods—summer rain at the north, winter rain at the south. Richard Hay has closely studied the beds in Olduvai Gorge, finding only minor changes in salinity throughout, at times somewhat more, at others less, dry than at present, indicating persistence of a climate similar to the present.

The famous camp in Olduvai Bed I was buried by a fall of hot ash, a primordial Pompeii. It lay beside a shallow lake that provided water for man and animals, including fish and amphibians. The remains of the larger mammals are mainly of young ones, perhaps clubbed at the watering place. No hunting or fishing skill is indicated: Louis Leakey spoke of its people as scavengers. Water determined the camp's location in a land of little water. Lake Rudolf, inhabited a million years before Olduvai, was of similar environment.

For a million years, man lived in the presence of volcanic eruptions despite an occasional toll of human life. The hazards were offset by advantages, among them the rewards of collecting after volcanic heat had fired vegetation, the blaze overtaking fleeing game and suffocating small animals in their burrows and on the ground. Mud flows or ash trapped living things and shortly supported a new plant cover and animal population. The beds of Olduvai Gorge hold a stratified animal graveyard.

The habitation at the discovery camp of Olduvai was an open-air site at the margin of the Serengeti Plain, then as now browsed and grazed on by diverse game, which in turn was and is preyed upon by great cats and other carnivores. Unprotected humans were easy and attractive prey. They had neither weapons nor walls to give them safety, yet they lived here in the open. The one available safeguard was fire, a hearth that would keep predators at a distance day and night, especially at night. It may be suggested that long familiarity with volcanic fire led to taking brands with which to experiment and thus to find that fire gave man safety. Humans who dressed stone into tools for particular uses may be expected to have had the curiosity to learn what they could do with fire. Stone implements last, hearths do so only rarely.

## MAN'S ECOLOGIC NICHE

The familiar model of primordial man is one of living on savanna plains of grass and scrub, trailing herds of game as these grazed and browsed, subsisting by scavenging and picking off crippled, infirm, and young herd animals, in time learning how to hunt, following herds that moved with the alteration of wet and dry season. It is thus implied that for the major part of his existence, he was highly mobile, living in small bands, led by dominant males, the females submissive to male demands. The basis of human society is construed as organized about a male hierarchy similar to that of the herd animals they followed.

A quite different primordial habit and habitat may be inferred from human biology. Man alone has enduring family ties. The human infant is born prematurely as compared to other primates, is wholly dependent on maternal care, and remains so longest. It is slowest to become ambulant and to begin to take care of itself. Childhood lasts longest and puberty comes latest. There is no time at which maternal rejection comes and recognition of parent and offspring ends. Not the male-dominated band, but the family, cared for and trained by the female, is the basis of human society. Kinship systems are most elaborate in primitive cultures, especially by matrilineal descent. The thesis that human society is paternal is a Judeo-Christian one, made an academic doctrine in the Victorian nineteenth century.

Men might roam, but the women sought a place at which to stay, a home where the offspring could be left in safety, a place convenient to the daily provision of water and food, where supplies and possessions could be stored. The homemaker was as sessile as possible, with the least radius that would provide sustenance and the least obligation to move with seasonal scarcity. The savannas thus are an improbable choice for the origins of human society.

Man is the only biped among the primates. Apes are in part arboreal, getting about on the ground and in trees on all fours. Baboons, least arboreal, forage largely on the ground but climb into trees or cliffs to sleep. Man walks erect and flatfooted, lives and sleeps on the ground. That he is a good walker and even a comparatively good runner gave him the means to range about, but such mobility is distorted by construing the males as trailing fleet and far-moving game, their women and children following along. The image of the primordial wanderer as the founder of human culture is biologically improper and is placed in a disadvantageous environment.

A non-arboreal primate lacked advantage in a land shared with other primates. His opportunity for food and shelter was narrowed by his restriction to the ground. The greatly increased mobility postulated brought him into competition with other predators and scavengers. Instead of the savanna habitat, a niche was needed in which man had assurance of provision at all times.

Such a habitat has been proposed by Sir Alister Hardy,[1] professor of marine biology at Oxford University. The human body, as he outlined, is excellently suited to float, with legs and arms, hands and feet of superior adaptation for swimming. Swimming may be learned as early as walking, and as easily. The direction of human evolution that Hardy proposed was indicated by bodily adaptation to living on land and water. Waterside habitat, in particular at the seaside, was the available place for the evolution of a primate of distinctive anatomy and physiology, of the only primate at ease in water.

I have suggested the proper niche at hand as in the Indian Ocean coast of East Africa, an area where daily tides provide food twice a day the year round, without regard to season. Seafood provided much protein, salt, and iodine, a good human diet. Cobbles and driftwood were available for man's use, and rock shelters to live in. There was no lack of food and only small hazard. Here was freedom from want, permanence of habitation, and the stimulus of the diversity of shore and sea. Instead of the severe seasonal limitations on the

---

1. A. Hardy, "Was Man More Aquatic in the Past?", *New Scient.*, v. 7, pp. 642–645.

savannas, the seashore gave opportunity to stay put, have a home, and establish a society based on family.

## SPREAD INTO EURASIA

Recent discoveries have affirmed the African origin of mankind and have greatly extended its age. The earliest sites known are in the interior, where the environment, because of its seasonal extremes, is here considered as unsuited to human origins, Lake Rudolf being the least disadvantageous. At a distance of several hundred miles, the coast of the Indian Ocean offers an appropriate ecologic niche with daily food, seafood rich in protein and fat (in contrast to the diet of other primates), invitation to permanent habitation, and the attractions of beachcombing for shells, cobbles, and driftwood. It is suggested that this was the cradle of our lineage and that from here man began his spread both along farther seacoasts and into the interior, where his presence has become known in a stressful environment of dry season and vulcanism.

Primordial man lived in warm lands. Sensitive to cold and unprotected against it, he would have established himself in wintry lands by adaptation of habit, by learning how to keep warm. By the time of the Second Interglacial, he is known to have lived from England to northern China in the open air and under rock shelters, and in places his hearths have been found. The currently held explanation that the use of fire was casual and occasional is an argument *ex silentio,* based on the inference that where a site showed no use of fire, no fire was used. The alternative, which I think is correct, is that he took fire with him as he began his occupation of higher latitudes.

Prehistoric archeology had its beginnings and long its main interest in western Europe. In the course of time, certain stone objects were proposed as crudely shaped by man and older than the earliest Paleolithic implements. These so-called eoliths were long the subject of controversy about whether their shapes could be produced by natural processes of rock fracture, and about their age, which in general appeared to be pre-Pleistocene, therefore too great for the objects to have been artifacts. Eoliths reported from the Red Crag beds at Ipswich on the coast of East Anglia are fractured flints lying on a surface beneath the earliest English moraine. The locality was examined repeatedly by competent persons who agreed that the stones are eoliths, judging by their shapes, surfaces, and assemblage.[2] Some of the flints have crackled surfaces, admitted to be the result of heat. The earlier interpretation that they had lain in hearths has later been replaced by attribution to lightning, a conjecture without support and proposed for an unlikely coast. The late knowledge of the great age of man and his early dispersals should reopen the eolith question.

More than nine-tenths of human time, as it is now known, falls into the Paleolithic period, so named by French archeologists before its age or extension was foreseen. The record is of stone artifacts, shaped by blows to serve as tools, and of very little else. Men who selected rocks to make into serviceable tools lived for countless generations in the presence of active vulcanism. Despite occasional disaster they were attracted, as men have ever been, by the advantages of such habitat. Man chose to live where he had the benefit of volcanic fire. He appropriated it to his use, it may be submitted, and thereby made the lands of the world accessible to his habitation.

Thus man entered diverse biotic communities or ecosystems and modified them. Habitation was as permanent as possible, on the premise that the mother selected the location for water, yield of provision, and shelter. The biota of such territory was modified, at one time benefited by repeated harvest, at another, diminished thereby. The accumulation of refuse about the habitation altered the soil's pH, and thereby the occupant organisms. The longer a site was used, the more it changed. A superior living site was unlikely to be abandoned so long as it served the interests of the occupants, a sort of first principle of bionomics applied to man. At times fire escaped and spread. Man, being observant and curious, learned early that fire aided in collecting food, both plant and animal, and thus began the practice of setting fire to vegetation. Alteration of vegetation began wherever man brought fire.

---

2. W. J. Sollas, *Ancient Hunters* (London: 1924), pp. 97–105.

## NEANDERTHAL MAN AND MOUSTERIAN CULTURE

The discovery of a different kind of man, Neanderthal Man near Düsseldorf in 1856, was linked to a culture, first described at Moustier in southwestern France. At first considered of western European origin, the culture is now known to have had a vast range that extended from Morocco, through the Zagros Mountains of the Near East into Manchuria, across a great diversity of climates and biota. The Neanderthal breed and Mousterian culture existed from the Third Interglacial through a major part of the Fourth Glacial, a span of about a hundred thousand years; it was succeeded about forty thousand years ago by Cro-Magnon Man of the Aurignacian culture. The age of *Homo sapiens,* modern man, is first of record in Europe and adjacent Mediterranean lands. Neanderthal man is now recognized as an early subspecies of *Homo sapiens.*

Mousterian culture brought major innovations: stone projectile points were fashioned, attached to spears and used in hunting big game. In the ice-free plains of European and Asiatic Russia, mammoths provided a major part of the subsistence. Rock shelters served as habitations where available. Large game was butchered before it was brought in, which suggests that hides were removed and dressed. It has been claimed that this culture introduced the use of fire for cooking, indicating an inordinately delayed lack of interest in what man might do with fire. Giant game, such as woolly mammoth, was taken by organized hunting, perhaps the earliest hunting society. Mousterian sites are the earliest to give evidence of religion. The dead were given formal burial, along with their possessions and provisions, and frequently were covered with red ochre—in one case, with a blanket of flowers. Because the spirits of the departed were friendly, interment was at the living place. A remarkably similar way of life was established across the breadth of Eurasia, from Morocco to Manchuria, from warm to cold climate, from dry to humid lands. It lasted twice as long as time since.

## MAN IN THE NEW WORLD

A rigid doctrine was established, during my student years, that man immigrated to the New World after the end of the Ice Age, that he came with few and undetermined skills, and that, in the course of a few thousand years, he repeated independently the stages of cultural progress of the Old World to the high level of the native societies of Peru and Mexico. In the New World, rapid, multiple, parallel invention was the counterpart of slow diffusion of learning in the Old World. The inhabitants of America were held to be one race, American Indians (Amerinds) of Mongoloid stock. Small groups of these people were thought to have entered the continent through Bering Strait and possibly by way of the Aleutian Islands. This passage was thought to have taken place over several thousand years, at about the time of the end of the Paleolithic and the beginning of the Neolithic period in Europe, these various groups developing independent cultures. The most highly developed of these cultures, such as those of the Mayas, Incas, and Aztecs, were recognized as approximately comparable to the cultures of Egypt and Mesopotamia during the third millenium B.C.

The beginning of postglacial time was unknown until radiocarbon dating, effective since about 1950, determined that the wasting of the ice front in Wisconsin occurred some eleven thousand years ago. Archeologic sites of about that age in the western Great Plains, beginning with the discovery at Folsom, became the base of the chronology of man in the New World. The tenet of the postglacial peopling of the New World was retained and given a date of about eleven thousand years. In 1969 the Geological Survey of Canada published a map of the late extent of glaciation in Canada as a continuous ice cover from the Atlantic to the Pacific coast as late as eight thousand years ago. At that time hunters of now extinct big game were still living on the high plains of Texas and to the south, and in Puebla and Oaxaca, people were planting and tilling cultivated crops. The doctrine of the postglacial entry of man to the New World, propounded when nothing was known of time, continues to disregard the evidence.

Reports of early man in this country were ignored or rejected, including those made by highly competent geologists and paleontologists. As a result sites have been lost, others have been disregarded, and but a few continued to be studied.

The Santa Barbara Channel area, rich in resources of sea and land, held the largest and most advanced population in California at the coming of the Spanish. Also, its archeologic sites are many, diverse, and of markedly differing ages. As director of the Santa Barbara Museum of Natural History, David Banks Rogers gave close attention for many years to these sites, their sequence, and their relation to changes in the environment. His book *Prehistoric Man of the Santa Barbara Coast,* published in 1929, is an able reconstruction of human geography carried back from the time of Spanish contact to the earliest recognized presence of man. It relates sites and content of archeologic horizons to changes of land and sea and finds a succession of different cultures instead of the *in situ* evolution favored at the time. His earliest well-defined occupants, whom he called the Oak Grove People, lived only on knolls on the Santa Barbara Coast plain, from which he inferred that they lived during a notably higher stand of the sea. That this was at a remote time was further indicated by the greatly weathered condition of the milling stones always found at these sites. Grinding of seeds and acorns being held to a be a late trait, their presence has been used against the early age of the Oak Grove sites. I had the opportunity to visit a number of them in time to be impressed by Rogers' account as being based on careful observation without theoretical bias.

The Santa Barbara Museum staff was complemented by Phil C. Orr, a vertebrate paleontologist experienced in the study of Pleistocene elephants. Orr became concerned with the dwarf mammoths of the Channel Islands and their human contemporaries. Santa Rosa Island, undercut by waves and eroded by excessive grazing, has been for years the object of his attention, focused on animal and human bones and artifacts. Thus began the discovery of mammoth bones in fire-baked depressions and in proximity to stone tools. The paleontologist became archeologist and made use of radiocarbon dating, available by that time, with the precaution of having members of laboratories do their own sampling. Age beyond the prudent limit of radiocarbon determination, for instance, as in excess of thirty-seven thousand years, brought the rebuttal that the mammoths were killed in these pits by lightning. This explanation was applied to repeated events in a marine climate where any thunderstorm is front-page news! Geophysicist Rainer Berger of the University of California at Los Angeles joined Orr in rebuttal with an important study of heat effects of lightning on mineral substances.[3]

The Mojave Desert also has been of interest for archeologic sites about dry lakes and waterless stream channels, with the Yermo-Calico locality lately in the news because Louis Leakey had given his endorsement. There was a time when the desert did not exist, and the land was inhabited by makers of primitive stone implements, the question being how long ago. The association of sites and surfaces of a past geomorphology points to late Pleistocene time. A study of dry Lake Chapala in Baja California also makes a case for occupation during the Wisconsin glacial stage.[4]

In northern Texas a cluster of a dozen hearths was studied before they were submerged by construction of the Lewisville Dam. They contained the charred remains of modern and extinct mammals and hackberry seeds. The charcoal was beyond the testing limit of the laboratory at thirty-seven thousand years. Three large limestone cobbles—sculptured heads—were found at the base of gravel pits in the highest terrace of the Trinity River, which contain bones of mammoth, mastodon, horse, camel, and ground sloth. The heads are in the Texas State Museum and are illustrated in Newcomb.[5]

There are other vestiges of man in the New World during the latter part of the Ice Age. Santa Rosa Island and Lewisville record his presence as being earlier than thirty-seven thousand years, which was the limit to which charcoal could be tested for radioactivity. The chronology of the Wisconsin stage of glaciation is still in dispute. There was a partial deglaciation earlier, of uncertain extent and time, which coring of the sea floor by the Lamont-Doherty Geologi-

---

3. P. C. Orr, "The Fire Areas on Santa Rosa Island," *Natl. Acad. Sci., Proc.,* v. 56; "Geochronology of Santa Rosa Island, California," *Symp. on Biol. of Calif. Islands, Proc.,* Santa Barbara Bot. Garden, pp. 317–325.

4. B. Arnold, "Late Pleistocene and Recent Changes in Landforms, Climate and Archaeology in Central Baja California," *Univ. Calif. Publ. Geogr.,* v. 10, n. 4.

5. W. W. Newcomb, *The Indians of Texas* (Austin: 1961), pp. 9–12.

cal Laboratory places at forty to fifty thousand years ago. Northern Siberia and lowland Alaska remained unglaciated, open to hunters accustomed to extreme winter cold. The problem was how to go south from Alaska, for which the proper time, by present information, would have been forty thousand years ago or earlier. This is before Cro-Magnon Man appeared in Europe and when Mousterian culture still prevailed across northern Eurasia. At any rate, the doctrine of the postglacial entry of man to the New World is obsolete.

## HUNTERS AT THE END OF THE ICE AGE

In Europe a succession of hunting cultures appeared in the latter part of the Ice Age, consisting of mobile people who specialized in mass hunting of a particular kind of game. They used the new technique of pressure flaking, by means of which they fashioned blades and projectile points of superior effectiveness and distinctive design.

In North America hunters with remarkably similar habits and skills appeared later and for a shorter time, from about eleven to eight thousand years ago. They are named by their differing types of projectile points, from the size of which it has been inferred that they also used a new arm, the dart thrower. The earliest makers of Clovis points in the United States hunted mammoths and other big game. They were followed by the makers of Folsom points, known as hunters of giant extinct bison; and these were succeeded by the Plainview people, who also hunted the giant bison and once left the remains of a hundred victims in one heap near Plainview, Texas. Clovis, Folsom, and Plainview are place names from the western Great Plains, where these cultures were first discovered. Their range has been extended east and north of the Great Plains and far into the eastern woodlands.

Mammoths and giant bison were browsing rather than grazing animals. They and their hunters disappeared together. The end of the Ice Age was brought about by a change in the general circulation of the atmosphere that took place in a short time and brought the modern pattern of climates. Our Southwest and adjacent Mexico became arid and unsuitable for mammoths and bison. They and their hunters, however, disappeared as well from the lands to the east where there was no adversity of climate. The question is unresolved but cannot, I think, be attributed solely to climatic change.

These big game hunters had their major habitat in the central and southern Great Plains, finding there the best hunting lands for their principal game. In modern times this is grassland, known for its low-growing (short) grasses, but where tall grasses grow also. Elephants feed by browsing on shrubs and trees and the great bison was of similar habit. Except for our plains buffalo, the genus *Bison* of Europe and North America inhabits woodland, as did its extinct forms. The inference that the plains were woodland has support from buried soils, from the growth of trees and shrubs on valley sides or on "breaks" below the upland plain, and from recent woody invasion of the plains, as by shinnery oak in the Staked Plains of Texas and by sagebrush in the north, largely as the result of the exclusion of fire. The modern pattern of vegetation is set by the configuration of the plains, the smooth upland surface being grassland, the rough terrain having woody growth.

The big game hunters, from Clovis to Plainview, occupied western plains for three thousand years, during which there was time and occasion to alter the biota. The mass kill of bison by Plainview hunters was excess destruction, an overkill unlike the normal predation of hunters. The animals were stampeded over a high bank to their crippling fall, to be butchered. When the Spaniards became acquainted with the wild cattle, as they called the plains bison, they found that these herds were not alarmed by attack. Horsemen killed what they wanted by gun or lance without disturbing the herd. The one force competent to set it into panic flight was fire. At Plainview it is presumed that this was the case, that the fire was set by man so as to drive the herd to an appointed place, convenient for the kill. The Plainview hunters were among the last of the ancient hunters, living at the time of the last of the giant bison and participating in their extinction.

Recurrent fires, it is inferred, reduced the habitat of the large browsing game. Grassland replaced a mixed vegetation of trees, shrubs, and herbs. The ancient hunters of the High Plains set fires and thereby helped to eliminate the game on which they depended.

After its disappearance the plains were repopulated by a fauna that fed on grass and herbs—the plains buffalo, pronghorn antelope, plains elk, jackrabbits, and prairie fowl. Other people, of less specialized hunting skills and of more restricted area, are of obscure record for the long interval prior to the historically known tribes.

## DIFFERING VIEWS OF PREHISTORIC MANKIND

The human lineage has been traced for millions of years in East Africa, currently accepted as man's original home. The sites are in the interior of northeastern Africa, in lands of long and severe dry seasons, with shortages of food and water. A superior ecologic niche for earliest man was at hand in the shores of the Indian Ocean. It is suggested that the use of fire was learned early, perhaps by familiarity with volcanic fire. The possession of fire enabled expansion from warm parts into those of marked cold. Peking Man was the earliest assured user of fire, but not its discoverer, all human presence beyond the tropics being attributed to the possession of fire. Mousterian culture flourished from the time of the Third Interglacial, well into the Fourth Glacial and is known from Morocco to Manchuria. During that time access was open from the unglaciated plains of northeast Siberia to lowland Alaska, and man entered as hunter of big game, including mammoths. Long before the icecap in Canada receded to open a passage south, immigration had taken place into the area of the United States and farther south; the earlier interglacial conditions are as yet undetermined.

Having fire, man was able to live wherever he found subsistence, appropriating new environments to his use, becoming a member of new ecosystems, and beginning to alter them. Hearth was home, the base of family life, shelter, place of collection and preparation of supplies, its location determined by economy of provision. Human society was not founded or developed by drifting, homeless bands. The mobile hunters moving about with the game are a late, specialized way of life, related to grasslands and grasslands game.

Man, through his continuing presence, altered the vegetation by introduction and suppression, by permitting fire to escape, by using fires to aid in collecting and, in late hunting cultures, to drive game.

Recognizing that natural fires made for more productive collecting of small creatures, man later became aware that burns became stocked with plants palatable to animals and men that occupied the newly sun-exposed ground. Dominant intervention by man came when the benefit of periodic burning was known. By the time of the hunters of ten thousand years or so ago, grasslands were in the process of occupying plains in North America and perhaps elsewhere.

A different version of man's use of fire is current. A recent expression by Leopold and Ardrey[6] gives the earliest known evidence of the use of fire as three hundred to three hundred fifty thousand years ago, at Choukoutien, also near Budapest, and in the south of France, all three associated with the Mindel glaciation. (This is according to a shortened and invalid glacial calendar.) The thesis further states that the use of fire was so sporadic for hundreds of thousands of years that man was unlikely to have depended on it, in Mousterian times hearths being found at most sites but absent at others. They infer that in Africa the continued use of fire began only fifty-six thousand years ago. About forty thousand years ago, hearths appeared so decisively in Syrian caves that nearly half the artifacts have been distorted by heat. Shortly thereafter Cro-Magnon man made universal use of fire and displaced Neanderthal man: "The universal use of controlled fire made cooking possible."

GRASSLANDS AND OPEN WOODS:
EARLY HISTORICAL ACCOUNTS

In his second voyage, Columbus went inland from the north coast of Haiti to explore a large, open, and populous plain, which he called the Vega Real. The name persists in La Vega, the second largest northern town of the Dominican Republic. Soon the Spaniards adopted the island Arawak name *savanna* for open plains and *arcabuco* for thickety tracts. Peter Martyr, who collected information in Spain from those who had been overseas, wrote of savanna plains. Las Casas, early resident of Haiti and Cuba, described "the innumerable *campinas,* level and clear as they were, which they call in their lan-

---

6. A. C. Leopold and R. Ardrey, "Toxic Substances in Plants and the Food Habits of Early Man," *Science,* v. 176, pp. 512–514.

guage savannas." Oviedo wrote in his natural history of the Indies: "This name savanna is given to land without trees but of much herbage, tall and low."[7]

As they entered the mainland, the Spaniards continued to use the Arawakian name. From Darién horseback parties rode west and south along savanna trails, taking advantage of ease of travel, provisions, and Indian services. When Balboa set out from Darién in 1513 to discover the Pacific Ocean, he passed through savannas to reach the Gulf of San Miguel, where he had his first sight of the Pacific from the top of a bare hill. A river that he followed down to the gulf, now in heavily forested country, still bears the name *Rio Sabanas.* Eastern Panama, today tropical rain forest, had numerous savannas, populated by Indian settlements. An almost continuous savanna extended from the Bayano Valley, a hundred miles east of the present city of Panama, for another two hundred miles west of Panama to the Gulf of Montijo, the lowlands clear and without arabucos.[8] Under Spanish occupation the natives of the Antilles soon died out and those of the Isthmus of Panama were reduced to remnants. Within a few decades, the savannas became largely wooded, most rapidly and completely so in eastern Panama.

Savannas were grassy plains in tropical lowlands, without trees except for tall palms scattered throughout them. Other trees depend on the sensitive tissue of the sheath of cambium and thus were eliminated by repeated burning, but palms survived. Savannas were formed and maintained by burning: they reverted to forest when burning ceased.

Spaniards first applied the name "savanna" to tropical lowlands in which there was an alternation of wet and dry or partly dry seasons. The term referred mainly to grasslands about the Caribbean, on the mainland especially in northern Venezuela and Colombia, but not because there was a season of rain and one of no rain.

As they moved into the interior of New Granada (Colombia), the Spaniards found humid grasslands both in temperate and cold climates, which also were known to them as savannas. The province of

---

7. G. Friederici, *Amerikanistisches Wörterbuch* (Hamburg: 1947).
8. Carl O. Sauer, *The Early Spanish Main* (Berkeley: 1966), pp. 285–288.

Antioquia consisted of grassy benches above river canyons, and long slopes of Andean *cordilleras* in grass at intermediate and partly into high altitudes; little of it is a plain and in good part it exhibits strong relief. This exceptional hill and mountain savanna had been occupied in prehistoric time by an advanced culture competent to clear it of forest cover. The lush montane pastures attracted settlement by Spanish cattle-raising small farmers, the *Antioqueños*. Farther in the interior, the *Sabana de Bogotá* is, at an altitude of eight thousand feet, a cold and cloudy basin in *tierra fría*, differing greatly from the normal savanna.

Modern climatology has appropriated the term "savanna" to a different and restricted meaning, that of tropical climates with strong contrast of wet and dry seasons, arid for months, even for the greater part of the year. Where weather records are lacking, xerophytic vegetation has been taken as an indicator of such climate.

Farther south in the Andes, Quechua and Aymara words were incorporated into the Spanish vocabulary, *puna* (for the bleak, cold altiplano) and *pampa* for the more genial treeless plains. Spaniards coming to the grassy plains of Argentina named them pampas, as they did lesser ones in Chile. The large northern savanna, the lowland drained by the Orinoco River, was explored by men unfamiliar with that term and was known from the time of its discovery as *Llanos del Orinoco*.

### NORTH AMERICAN VEGETATION AS SEEN BY SPANIARDS IN THE SIXTEENTH CENTURY

The first Spanish account of vegetation in the United States was that by the Ayllón party in coastal South Carolina (1526), describing a land of pines and oaks, both live and deciduous, grapevines, laurels, sumac, palmettos, blackberries, and other plants native to that coastal plain. There was no mention of open country.

Cabeza de Vaca gave an account of Florida as he saw it in 1528, from Tampa to Tallahassee and St. Andrew Bay, as being in part open woods. The start was along the sandy coastal plain. Near Apalache (Tallahassee) the country changed in appearance, more fertile and well peopled. There were nut trees, laurels, liquidambar, cedars

(*Juniperus*), *sabinos* (bald cypress), live and deciduous oaks, and palmettos. There was mention of very good pasture for cattle and of open woods but none of grasslands.

Cabeza de Vaca and his companions told of their shipwreck on the Galveston Coast and the seven years in Texas, of Indians setting fire to the Texas plains to hunt *venados* (either deer or antelope), of going up river bottoms at the beginning of cold weather to gather pecans, and in summer to cactus thickets to collect prickly pears. They remembered well the food they had or lacked but did not mention seeing any buffalo.

Coronado set out in the spring of 1541 on the long ride from the pueblos of New Mexico to central Kansas. Beyond the Pecos River, his party came to the Great Plains and buffalo herds "like fish in the sea." The accounts speak of a sea of grass in which horse and rider were lost if half a league away from the party. Strips of woods marked the eastward courses of streams. At the escarpment that is the eastern edge of the High Plains, the group descended a canyon (Palo Duro at Amarillo, Texas), well wooded and inhabited, to be guided northeast across rolling prairies to central Kansas, where the Wichita nation farmed and hunted in a land of prairies and woods. This was a fertile land of ample rainfall, but the Spaniards had not come to grow crops or raise herds and turned back. Early in the next century, Governor Oñate of New Mexico led a mounted party across the high grassy plains to the Wichita villages. The buffalo plains were known to the Spaniards by that name, or simply as *llanos,* the part south of the Canadian River later as *Llano Estacado.*

De Soto arrived in Tampa Bay in 1539 with six hundred men, their mounts, and a large herd of swine, brought from Cuba to serve as provision. At his death near Natchez three years later, his estate was credited with seven hundred swine, perhaps more than at the start. Despite those animals lost by drowning in crossing rivers and by straying, those taken by Indians, and those given as presents, the herd thrived, mainly on mast. For four years the expedition ranged north and south, back and forth across ten states of the South—a host of Spaniards, their horses, hog herd, and captive Indian bearers. The records are in good detail and include descriptions of vegetation and game. There is no mention of open grasslands, but the rate at which the host freely moved implies that it was rarely impeded by dense forest and that the swine could be kept under control as they foraged.

While Coronado and De Soto were in the interior, Cabrillo was sent by ship to explore the coast of California. At a bay (now Ensenada), the men saw savannas with vegetation like that of Spain and herds of antelope grazing. Farther on they entered the " 'bay of smokes,' of plains, and groves" (area of Los Angeles), and "many smokes inland."[9] (It was October, the latter part of the dry season.) The Santa Barbara Channel area contained many Indian villages, fine plains with groves and savannas on the mainland, mountains in the distance. At that season the natives were supplementing their fishing by harvesting acorns. The reconnaissance continued north to Monterey and beyond, along a mountain coast of pine trees. At later times the mingling of grassland and oak groves on the coast of southern California was noted as being in contrast to the northern coast.[10]

## FRENCH OBSERVATIONS

France sent Verrazzano in 1524 to explore the Atlantic coast and this he did, from Cape Fear to Cape Breton. South of Hatteras were great woods, in part open and in part dense, and also beautiful champaigns. He named the country to the north Arcadia for the beauty of its trees, some of the woods being open. The ship remained in Narragansett Bay for two weeks, which gave leisure to visit the land, with "champaigns twenty-five to thirty leagues in extent, open and without any impediment of trees,"[11] the woods thereabout passable in any direction by an army. This is the earliest account, somewhat exaggerated, of the prairies and open woods of southern New England. Having passed a high land with dense forests of conifers (Maine), they sailed by a more beautiful and open land (Nova Scotia).

---

9. Carl O. Sauer, *Sixteenth Century North America,* (Berkeley: 1971), pp. 154–155.

10. Ibid., 1971.

11. Ibid., p. 57.

In 1534 Cartier made careful exploration of the Gulf of St. Lawrence, noting prairies on the Magdalen Islands and along Prince Edward Island. These may have been marshes, as in later usage on the Bay of Fundy. In the second voyage (1535), Cartier went up the St. Lawrence River as far as the island of Montreal, where there were oaks as fine as in France. The ground was covered with acorns, and there were large champaigns with cornfields, with the Indian town of Hochelaga situated in their midst. He wrote of Indian clearings around the principal town, the great valley being a deciduous woodland including yews (hemlock).

The brief French occupation of Florida (1564–1565) yielded good observations on vegetation—pines, oaks, nuts, laurels, hollies, palms, cedars, cypress, and so on—with praise of the great green valley (St. Johns River) for its beautiful prairies and herbage for pasturing livestock.

During the seventeenth century, Canada took outline in the form of St. Lawrence Valley settlements and Great Lakes fur trade and missionary posts. Mainly there was forest country—hardwoods and conifers—about the Great Lakes. To the south were open woods and beyond them, prairie plains. Southern Ontario was an open woodland with good hunting of deer and turkeys and a few buffalo. On Lake Michigan, Green Bay gave access south to prairies interspersed with oak groves (on moraines and drumlins). At the southwest edge of Lake Superior, Chequamegon Bay was the gateway to Ojibway villages on lakes in northwest Wisconsin, where wild rice gave abundant harvest. Sioux lived west of the Ojibway across Minnesota, woodland farmers at the east, buffalo hunters on the grasslands to the west. Prairies rimmed the woodlands from the Red River Valley of the north across southern Wisconsin, south of Lake Erie into the Iroquois land of northern New York. All were visited by the French and attentively described.

Beyond Canada, La Salle projected the colony of Louisiana to extend from the head of Lake Michigan to the mouth of the Mississippi River and southwest into Texas. His grant included the monopoly of the trade in buffalo hides and wool, which was expected to be a large source of revenue. The enterprise began in the upper Illinois Valley. Tribes of the friendly Illinois confederation lived and farmed in the valley and hunted on the prairie. La Salle built one fort on Starved Rock overlooking the Illinois River and the Indian village of Kaskaskia on the valley floor. (Now a state park near Ottawa, Kaskaskia shortly was moved to the mouth of the Kaskaskia River in southern Illinois.) A second fort was built downriver at Peoria, where there was a large Peoria Indian village. Frenchmen at these posts described in vivid detail the wooded valleys trenched in the upland prairie plains, the prairies extending from the valley rim to the horizon, and the buffalo trails leading to water and shade. They wrote about the people of the villages moving out into these plains to hunt, about the women preparing the meat and dressing the hides, and especially about the practice of burning the prairies in late fall to assure a good stand of grass the next spring. Occasionally Indians of prairie tribes from beyond the Mississippi River came to visit the French posts.

La Salle's last venture was on Matagorda Bay in Texas. Buffalo in fair to good numbers were found from the coast, northeast to the Caddo Indian country (northeastern Texas), and a few to the east across Arkansas to the Mississippi River. A century and a half earlier, Cabeza de Vaca and his companions knew no buffalo in the Texas coast plains. The buffalo's range had extended eastward, as in other areas, and this suggests that woody growth was being replaced by herbaceous vegetation.

## CLIMATE OF GRASSLANDS

The founders of plant ecology, in particular Frederick Clements and H. C. Cowles, construed a system of plant societies that developed through stages to a stable climax. Both men acknowledged their debt to William Morris Davis' cycles of landforms. In each case events and time were replaced by a model of succession that continued until the flora was in equilibrium, fully adapted to its environment, climate being most important. Cowles took us into the dune belt around the south end of Lake Michigan to note the change from the fresh dunes to the oldest, on which the mesophytic climax was like that of the loamy ground moraine. In the long run, climate, not soil, determined the vegetation. Extensive grasslands were regarded as climax vegetation, with a different climax for a prairie climate, a Great Plains climate, and (for the tropics) a savanna climate. In what manner herbaceous flora had an advantage that excluded woody plants was not made clear.

Grasslands are not found where there is year-round wetness or aridity, nor at climatic extremes of heat or cold. The North American arid lands dominantly exhibit woody growth as in Sonora and adjacent Arizona, where a large diversity of shrubs, trees, and cacti makes this region a green desert. The hyperhumid tropics, such as on the Pacific coast of Colombia, are dense forest, as is the *montaña* or cloud forest on the Andean flanks.

The savannas of the Orinoco basin extend over plains with a hundred inches of annual rainfall, as did those of Panama, in the eastern part now a luxuriant rain forest. There were savannas in Haiti from the semiarid west to the abundantly rainy east. Tropical America has alternating wet and dry seasons, but its grasslands, for the most part, were not in areas with a long and marked dry season.

The extratropical grasslands are humid, subhumid, and semiarid. In early American usage, they were called prairies, from the Great Lakes to the Rockies. Josiah Gregg's classic *Commerce of the Prairies* dealt with the Santa Fe trade between Missouri and New Mexico.

## TERRAIN

The grasslands in general are plains, whatever they are called: llano, savanna, pampa, champaign, prairie, steppe, or puszta. Some are former sea floors; some were made by deposits of ice, water, or wind during the Ice Age. For the most part, their soils are loams or clays, not sands. Their common quality is that they are plains and not super-humid. Where upland plain meets valley rim, the plant cover changes from herbage above to trees and shrubs below—that is, the woody growth reaches to the top of the valley sides, whether these are exposed to sun or are shaded. Relief, not climate, has given the pattern of vegetation of the plains. Where hilly tracts, such as terminal moraines, rise above the plains these also are, or were, partly wooded.

The Pennyroyal region in Kentucky is a gently rolling limestone plain, largely drained by subterranean solution channels. It is encircled by strata of shale and impure limestone that have been modeled by runoff into a belt of hills. The hill belt was well wooded. The Pennyroyal was a large island of grass, settled by stock-raising pioneer farmers. How it was changed in a few decades into a woodland has been told by David Dale Owen, early geologist of Kentucky. Owen, son of Robert Owen of the Utopian New Harmony community in Indiana, gave superior descriptions at mid-nineteenth century of ecologic changes in Kentucky, Indiana and the upper Mississippi Valley.[12] The settlers, unacquainted with the name "prairie," called the Pennyroyal the "Barrens" because it lacked trees, not because they thought it infertile.

The grass-covered plains, formed by the Ice Age from southern Wisconsin to the Ohio River, were known to the French as prairies, and the name passed to the American settlers. The plains beyond the Mississippi and Missouri were prairies, south to the Black Waxy Prairies of east and central Texas.

Grasslands in the far West occupied long intermontane basins: in California, the great Central Valley and lesser ones within the coast ranges such as Salinas, Santa Clara, Santa Rosa, and Napa valleys; in Oregon, the Willamette Valley. Oaks, solitary or in groves, grew here and there on the grassy floors. The grass cover extended somewhat up the flanking hills and commonly ended in a well-marked border against woodland or chaparral above. (This pattern also characterizes the Bitterroot Basin of western Montana, with a sinuous border of grassland against conifer woodland. In Costa Rica, the structural basin between the central mountain range and the one bordering the Pacific, called *Valle del General,* has tongues of savannas well up the mountain sides. Although now

---

12. Carl O. Sauer, "Geography of the Pennyroyal," *Ky. Geo. Survey,* Ser. 6, v. 25 (1927), p. 303.

largely wooded, they are still known as savannas, each by its proper name.)

A third and lesser kind of grassland is on smooth-topped ridges above wooded slopes. In the central coast ranges of California, ridge crests are rounded and capped with grass; one above Berkeley is named Baldy. The Ozarks, in particular at the west and north, have long, flat-topped ridges, remnants of the time before they were dissected. These were ribbons of prairies, narrow or broad.

The major exception to the association of grassland and plains is in Antioquia and adjacent parts of Columbia. Here the central and western cordilleras of the Andes are grassed over a mountain terrain of different kinds of bedrock and landforms, largely *tierra templada,* but extending well into *tierra fria.*

## VEGETATION

Interior open plains were known to the Spanish and French from the Pecos Valley of New Mexico to Lake Michigan. The behavior of buffalo herds was described, but not what they fed on. It was said that here and there grass grew as high as a man on horseback and that there were brightly colored flowers. Trees that grew along the valleys were quite clearly identified, as were the grapevines that grew on them, and the edible fruits; also named were fish and waterfowl. Plains were where the buffalo roamed.

The late alteration of grasslands began with the chance introduction of Old World plants, the manner unknown. The fertile limestone land of central Kentucky was known, almost from the beginning, as the Blue Grass. How this superior European pasture grass was introduced is not known, perhaps accidentally by French canoes from the St. Lawrence Valley. The prairie land to the west of the Blue Grass is the Pennyroyal, named, it appears, for a European mint. The California valleys were speedily populated with wild oats, burr clover, alfilaria, and mustard, brought from Spain to Mexico and thence with the missions to California, finding there a chance to multiply and dominate that they did not have in Mexico. Again the introduction was accidental.

The study of grasses began after the grasslands had been altered by civilization. By 1850 the prairies of the Midwest were mostly under cultivation or in pastures, by then largely of alien grasses or clover. Lately a few small, more or less undisturbed, prairie remnants have been made into reserves in Wisconsin, Iowa, and Mississippi. They are inadequate in size, but they are protected from grazing and seasonal burning, which the prairies were not in Indian time. Secondary roads, railroad rights of way, and town lots are refuges of prairie plants, such as big and little bluestem and switch grasses. At the margin of the prairies, less fertile and less suited to mechanized tillage, native grasses may persist. Stock-raising farmers are now finding that on such lands, native grasses are good feed for cattle at all seasons, especially during the dry fall weather, and that they can be cut for hay.

The Missouri Conservation Commission is encouraging the protection of the native tall grasses by its efforts to restore the range of the prairie chicken. An ecosystem includes animals and plants, as we are tardily beginning to understand. We even more slowly realize that it includes ourselves.

The Black Waxy Prairies of Texas were broken by the plow for cotton about the same time as the northern prairies became the corn belt. Their native vegetation was soon removed and is little remembered.

The ecology of the Great Plains was still little disturbed at mid-nineteenth century—a land of grass, buffalo, and Indians. Wagon trains, the transcontinental railroad, and slaughter of the buffalo began an alteration that became a catastrophe for the Plains Indians—their reduction to reservations. As the plains were emptied of their game and Indians, the generation of cattle ranges and drives followed, with overgrazing that became disastrous in the drought of the early nineties. The Homestead Act opened the plains to settlement by small farmers, wheat fields in the north, cotton in the high plains of Texas. Another drought in the 1930s brought the dust bowl years and additional loss of plant cover and topsoil, and thus the completion of a century of environmental ruin.

So long as the Great Plains were the range of buffalo, in greater numbers than the cattle that later grazed them, and also of herds of antelope and elk, the plant cover appears to have been in balance with its animal numbers, which were controlled by Indian hunting and the predation of wolves and coyotes. In addition to tall-growing bunch grasses, there was short grass that spread by stolon and seed to form broad patches of turf, highly nutritious dry as well as green. These were the preferred pasture of buffalo and antelope, perhaps a symbiotic relation of grass and grazer. Americans called this short grass "buffalo grass" *(Buchlöe)*. Farther south the Spanish name *grama*, introduced from Mexico, was applied to short spreading grasses that provided superior forage. They are species of *Bouteloua* and are considered to have been the principal forage over thousands of square miles in the southern Great Plains. In the high plains of the Southwest, several species of *Hilaria* of similar turflike habit and grazing quality are known by Spanish names: galleta, toboso, and curly mesquite grass (also called buffalo grass).

GRASSLANDS—THE RESULT OF BURNING

The prairie fire was part of the lore of the Midwest and is remembered as "Indian Summer," a dry time of late fall when the air was hazy with smoke. At that season Indians were accustomed to setting fire to the sere vegetation to assure good spring growth of forage for buffalo and other game. The practice had been observed by Frenchmen in the seventeenth century and was traditional with the prairie tribes. Indian farmers also set fires to clear for planting. In the dry months of spring, the Mexican countryside is filled with the haze of smoke from the burning of litter before planting the milpas. Indians set fires to aid in collecting plant and animal food. Indians set fires for smoke signals. Indians set fires; they did not put them out.

Arid lands lacked sufficient fuel to spread a fire, and in very wet lands, fires could not start. Elsewhere there was a sufficient time of dryness for litter to be inflammable, sufficient even if only a few weeks in the year, as in eastern Panama, which was largely open and populated country at the coming of the Spaniards and is now luxuriant forest.

Fires spread across plains until stopped by a barrier, provided in the prairie plains and the Great Plains by valleys sunk below the upland. These were wooded to their tops, the break from upland plain to valley slope being a marked vegetation boundary. The plains of our western intermontane basins are flanked by grassy foothills up which fire spread from the valley floor until stopped by a ridge. In the Coast Range, even-topped, rounded ridges were converted to grassland by fires spreading along them, having their start in the adjacent basin. With the major exception of northwestern Colombia, grasslands are geomorphic features.

Grassland replaces woodland when there is repeated burning at short intervals. This burning is not the conflagration of crown fires, but is the recurrent light burning of litter that suppresses young woody growth when it is most susceptible to flames. Reproduction of trees is thereby reduced or stopped, the surface of the ground is exposed to the sun and opened to colonizing by sun-loving grasses and herbs, freely seeding annuals or herbs reproduced from rootstocks, in either case surviving or benefited by burns. The mature trees are not replaced and the woodland in time becomes grassland. The terminal stage is shown by the open-growth, mature valley oaks in California, last of their lineage in grassland. The reversal of succession is found where burning has been stopped, as for example in our national parks, the meadows of the floor of Yosemite, for example, invaded by trees.

Fire of natural origin rarely accounts for grasslands. Vulcanism is limited to a few areas, and in these areas revegetation does not proceed by grass. Lightning has been given gratuitous credit for control of vegetation. In parts of our western mountains, lightning is the most common cause of forest fires, when thunderheads build up over dry mountains and lightning is discharged with little or no rain. These mountain fires bring about temporary changes in the cover; they do not form grassland.

To convert woodland into grassland, burning must be recurrent and at short intervals, for which man is the competent agent. There has been no evidence or reasonable explanation that climate determines the presence and the distribution of grasslands. Man, user of fire, from time immemorial has modified vegetation, made and maintained savannas, prairies, and other grasslands.

# III. The Road
## Back to
### Mexico

# 9. Origins
## of Southwest
## Culture

The notion of the independence and isolation of Southwest Culture would not have arisen, it seems to me, if, historically, Mexico had been the center from which anthropological studies had spread into North America. Scholars, coming into the Southwest from the North, have realized they were getting into something strongly different, and yet their curiosity has usually stopped at the International Border, and they have failed to see how much of this complex has, even in ancient times, moved into the Southwest from the South. Indeed, notions about the origins of Southwest Culture originated in the years when it was considered proper to infer endemism as dominant in cultural studies, to maximize development *in situ,* and minimize the significance of dispersal and diffusion. A familiar example is the postulated succession of stages from Basketmaker I to Pueblo V, all of this construed as the product of autochthonous "evolution."

It seems most appropriate to me, therefore, to reexamine the cultural scene of the Southwest, both historically and geographically, as a deep and wide zone of constantly interpenetrating peoples and institutions, most of whom and which can be seen to have origi-

---

"Origins of Southwest Culture" is an edited and abridged version of "Comments on Paul Kirschoff's Gatherers and Farmers in the Greater Southwest," *American Anthropologist* 56:553–556, 1964.

nated elsewhere. Such a reexamination will by definition involve the association of comparative archeology, ethnology, and linguistics, with due regard to geographic realities. It would be delimiting, moreover, to accept the terms "Arid America" and "Oasis America" as central to our study. I agree with the emphasis such terms suggest, but cultures are seldom the product of specific environments. A culture should be recognized in cultural terms, and not tied to strict environmental labels which, geographically and even genetically, are ultimately inaccurate and misleading.

From the physical geography of North America two elementary facts should be called to mind: the cul-de-sac of the two Californias and the funnel of Mexico with the Southwest as the lip of the cone. The Californias are imperfectly but very largely isolated from the rest of the continent by Sierra Nevada, desert, and the Gulf of California, and are culturally a technologically primitive backwater into which drifted various migrants and from which very little has issued to rejoin the main cultural streams. The Mexican funnel, however, received by way of the Southwest whatever was moving southward out of the North, and also from it issued most of the northward flow of impulses originating to the South. The Southwest is the northern gateway of the one great constricted corridor of the New World. Very few parts of the world have as emphatically and durably the quality of an obligatory passageway. Here one should expect to find a maximum of cultural ebb and flow, of displacement, interpenetration, blending, and, *per contra,* little opportunity for the development of cultural endemism. It has been for thousands of years a deep frontier between the primitive North and the advanced South, a major arena of acculturation, the strength of northern and southern impulses fluctuating, neither perhaps sweeping the other entirely aside at any time.

The Mexican funnel operated in considerable measure in three partitions, by movement along the Pacific coast lowlands, along the margins of the Gulf of Mexico, and through the middle. Mexican Gulf Coast connections with the Southwest are least known and perhaps, except by the large circuit of the Mississippi Valley, least important. Of what moved along the mainland west coast or through the middle we know all too little, because the critical arena of northwest Mexico remains the *tierra incognita* between our Southwest and central Mexico. It is for this great area, of which I have some knowledge from years long gone, that connecting and comparative studies are most needed, to which end some trial balloons are here released.

The whole agricultural complex has come out of the South. I know of nothing that has been added in the Southwest, considering the tepary bean and the domestic panic grass to have been developed well south of the border. The introductions were by different routes and probably at widely differing times. The squashes and the basic races of maize may have come by all three available routes. Further critical study of domesticated plant forms may be expected to shed more light on prehistory. The Bat and Tularosa cave materials have moved the appearance of agriculture in the Southwest far back in time. It should also be noted that both are very marginal sites for agriculture, not likely to have been occupied until long after more attractive Southwestern areas had been peopled by farmers and until adaptation to climatic extremes was achieved by slow selection. It is quite possible that the age of the introduction of agriculture into the Southwest is almost of the same order of time as the spread into Europe. That this was effected by colonists from the South rather than by adoption of agriculture by local collectors and hunters is unproved but reasonable, since the adaptive selection implies long and strong dedication to making a go of agriculture in difficult environments. Historically we know for the same area that collecting and gathering folk were living side by side with agricultural peoples without accepting agriculture. From California and the Gulf of California to Tamaulipas on the Gulf of Mexico the boundary between agricultural and non-agricultural living, quite sharp in many places, as often as not ran right across areas environmentally well suited to crop growing. Agriculture is a way of life that is more than a matter of food intake. Its acceptance usually involves large reorientation of culture, not merely the osmotic penetration of some plants and tillage skills.

Hohokam culture may well be a pretty direct importation out of the South. The engineering of Hohokam irrigation works (and also the elaborate hill *trincheras*) point to a structured society. Permanent irrigation structures, large compact pueblos, multistoried houses, and other qualities of "politic" living, as the Spaniards said, are recorded in early documents for a good deal of Sonora, both among Opata and Lower Pima pueblos. There are neglected bits of documentary evidence of advanced culture of other north Mexican spots widely scattered, from the mouth of the Conchos to Zape in Durango and Chínipas and Topia within the western Sierra Madre. Lumholtz' journey of discovery fifty years ago through the Sierra Madre, from Arizona to Jalisco, has not been followed up. Ethnology and language remain neglected. The zone of ignorance remains between the Southwestern archeology and the Sinaloan digs of Isabel Kelly and of Ekholm. Whether this intervening area is strewn with enclaves of the higher cultures or was continuously possessed we still do not know.

If our very competent American linguists are again beginning to turn to comparative philology, as we hope and pray, the geographic distribution of languages should throw light on Southwestern-Mesoamerican connections. The Hokan-Subtiaba grouping, if confirmed, would seem to represent the ruins of an ancient (southward) drift of peoples who once filled the Mexican funnel from the Gulf of California to lower Texas and down into the narrow spout in Nicaragua.

In historic time most of the funnel, except at the east, was occupied by diverse Uto-Aztecan-speaking peoples. The filiation of these languages may give the master key to the later prehistoric culture history. Mexican scholars continue to think that the Aztec migration myth is a blurred recollection of actual wanderings out of a remote northern homeland, and they may be right. I know no surmise as reasonable as this: that wave on wave of *Völkerwanderung* of these northern barbarians broke into the southern lands of sedentary agricultural folk, assimilating themselves to the more advanced culture of the lands they overran, but imposing their own language, rule, and some of their rude valor.

My thinking began to run in this line in the days when I was working in the Mexican northwest. The early Spanish missionaries were surprised to find that, having learned the speech of the Tepecano, they had a language wholly usable among not only Tepehuan but also the Pima and Papago; from the margins of Jalisco to the Salt River of Arizona, they said, ran one speech, a band of country a thousand miles long, winding through Sierra Madre and out onto the desert plains of Arizona. Only a narrow mountain break separates the Tepehuan from the Pima, another, the upper from the lower Pima. The lack of differentiation of language indicates no high age for their entry. Against the linguistic identity strong cultural differences stand out: some were little more than collectors and hunters; others, like the mountain folk of Maycoba and Yecora, lived much as do their neighbors, the Tarahumara; still others, such as the Nebome of the lower Yaqui were town dwellers, irrigators, "politic" folk. The entire complex appears as a late prehistoric drift in mass out of a prior home within the borders of the United States, some bands slipping along the inner margin of the Sierra Madre far to the south, some breaking through to the Yaqui, others spreading across southern Arizona. The latter absorbed the remnants of Hohokam, picked up some of the red-on-buff pottery techniques, and appropriated surviving irrigation works. The middle group, the Lower Pima, on reaching the Yaqui and its tributary valleys found a strongly surviving earlier high culture; the fusion came to be known as the Nebome, with Pima speech. Separation of Pima from Tepehuan may have been effected by a still later breakthrough of Cahita peoples, driving from Chihuahua plateau into the lowlands of southern Sonora and of Sinaloa and blotting out most of the prior lowland culture. For the Opata, several valley areas of especially strong survival of older culture lie in a matrix of mountain and steppe.

It is apparent that the hypothesis runs parallel in process to the inundation of Europe by Indo-European waves. In physical opportunity, cultural impulse, and resultant amalgamation, it is indeed similar. Study of northwest Mexico both from the direction of the southwest and that of Mesoamerica should establish the facts.

# 10. Aboriginal
## Population of
### Northwestern Mexico


THE EVIDENCE AND ITS USE

This paper is an attempt by an historical geographer to consider aboriginal density of population for one particular area. The older Spanish documents, concerned with Indian matters, have been examined as far as they are known. In the past half-dozen years, I have visited the several parts of the area repeatedly. The archives at Mexico, Parral, and Hermosillo have been searched for material on this area and the colonial documents copied have been gone over on the ground to which they relate. Previously, I have presented a redefinition of tribal limits and relations for the same area;[1] later, I hope to outline an Indian economic geography for northwestern Mexico.[2]

The population estimate herein arrived at is in apparent dis-

"Aboriginal Populations of Northwestern Mexico" is an abridged version of the original monograph which first appeared as *Ibero-Americana: 10* (University of California: Berkeley, 1935).

1. "Aboriginal Distribution of Languages and Tribes in Northwest Mexico," *Ibero-Americana*, no. 5 (Berkeley, 1933). The reader is referred to the study cites for the full bibliography of published and unpublished sources employed in the present paper, except as indicated in the text.

2. This study is one of a series made possible by support from the Board of Research of the University of California and by a John Simon Guggenheim Memorial Fellowship (1931).

agreement with the opinion of American anthropologists.[3] Modern students commonly have been inclined to discount early opinions of native numbers, but rarely have specified their reasons for doing so. I have found no general reasons for suspecting that the first observers were given to exaggeration. Least trustworthy were the chroniclers who had a case to defend, like Las Casas or Gómara, or who, like Torquemada and Beaumont, rewrote, with scant acknowledgment, the accounts of observers to fit their narrative. Emotional bias and romantic narrative, however, are not long concealed from the attentive reader and they have little to do with the record of the area examined. It was universally admitted in the period of colonization that the Indian population was declining at such a rate that its very survival was a question: Las Casas was attacked, not for his data on the destruction of the Indies, but for the aspersions he cast on his countrymen.

The documentary evidence here utilized consists for the most part of the accidentally preserved, routine items of colonial administration, such as missionary letters, annual reports to the superior of the missions, diaries of expeditions, reports on campaigns, and depositions taken for the information of the central government or in trials at court. The contributors in particular were Jesuit fathers, who converted and administered the greater part of the region. The Jesuits, here as elsewhere, were intelligent and careful observers of the land and its inhabitants. It would be possible, for example, to compile an excellent and detailed physical and cultural geography of the Spanish Northwest directly and entirely from the Jesuit sources. These non-apologetic documentary materials will impress any student with their truthfulness and acuteness of observation. In terms of disinterestedness and intimate knowledge of local situations the sources used rate high.

Total population was rarely taken and population figures usually must be arrived at by converting warriors, families, baptisms, or other items of the minister's record. The commonest, and best, con-

---

3. As summarized, for example, in Mooney, "Aboriginal Population of America North of Mexico," *Smithsonian Misc. Coll.,* vol. 80, no. 7.

vertible term is the family unit, at times expressed as family, at others as heads of families (*vezino,* in the local usage of the Jesuits, and in this connection applied to Indians), occasionally as houses. At present the average family size in this part of Mexico is a little less than seven. From comparison with other types of population data, it appears that a similar or slightly lower figure can be used for the aboriginal family. An average of six to the aboriginal family has been adopted in this study. Where Christianization was complete, baptisms apply only to the infants of Christian Indians, and annual baptisms may be converted into total population. A birthrate of forty to the thousand appears to give the proper rate of conversion, about the same rate which Dr. Aberle found among the Pueblo Indians and which she noted also for Scandinavian rural populations in the past.[4] This rate is near the maximum possible and will probably apply only to sedentary agricultural population not heavily affected by venereal disease.[5]

When the missionaries first entered a new area they were permitted to baptize at once all the small children "in the age of innocence," defined as four years of age and younger, provided the parents surrendered them for baptism. This gives another rough means of estimating population. Under present age distribution, approximately one-tenth of the population falls into these limits. For both types of baptismal record, the high ratio to total population, based on present large size of families, operates against an overestimate of aboriginal numbers, when applied to the latter. The children under doctrine are also occasionally mentioned (aged between five and twelve years) and are taken at about one-fifth of the population. The term *personas de administración* is obscure and has not been found usable; perhaps it applied to those of whom labor for the mission was expected. These rates of conversion are of course rough, but they support

---

4. "Frequency of Pregnancies and Birth Intervals among Pueblo Indians," *Am. Jour. Phys. Anthrop.,* 16:63–80.

5. The only reference I have seen is a remark by Father Pfefferkorn, missionary among the Pima in the mid-eighteenth century, that these Indians had little venereal infection.

one another and prove out as well as the meager figures permit.[6]

Spotted and unequal as the data are, they have cumulative weight by their common confirmation. In all the demographic record, as pieced together from varied sources, I have found no contradiction of importance. The items of population in the following pages are not selected on any other basis than that they were early records and that they could be put into numerical terms.

In great part the data apply to small and discontinuous areas, necessitating many interpolations, but having also the advantage that these small districts were well known to the reporter and that there is little or no uncertainty in respect to the limits of the area included. Interpolations, of course, have been undertaken only for other localities of similar culture and similar and known resource.

Of the hazards of filling in the blank spaces I am not unaware, yet they are considerably less than would be the error of regarding fragmentary figures as totals, an error that, I think, has been committed repeatedly in the estimate of past populations. I may claim a firsthand knowledge of almost all parts of the region considered, both in respect to its subsistence qualities and in respect to its place geography. Present rural numbers are, at least in this region, a useful guide in such interpolation. In very many areas the people are settled in the same villages that were inhabited at the coming of the whites, they have the same fixed area of land from which to draw their support, and the manner of subsistence either has not changed or the changes have been of a determinable degree and direction. Almost all the land farmed, and it is farming land which primarily determines density, is either alluvial or colluvial, and was equally available to the tools, crops, and tillage of the aboriginal and the present inhabitants. The crop system and dietary of the population today are

---

6. Large families among the original inhabitants are at least as probable among the present population. Modern hygiene and medical service scarcely touches the population of today. Raw, bacillus-laden cow's milk is now widely used in feeding infants and small children. Contagious diseases take a heavy toll of children, especially measles and diphtheria; also, in certain sections typhoid and smallpox. These diseases are all probably Old-World introductions.

not altered significantly from aboriginal conditions. These static economic qualities of the area justify comparison of present distributions with those of the past, provided no further invalidating elements enter into the situation.

## AREA AND TRIBES INVOLVED

Uto-Aztecan tribes occupied nearly all the area considered, the Seri being the only certain exception. From mid-Sinaloa southward lived the Tahue and Totorame, people of advanced culture, resembling in various aspects the peoples of southern Mexico. The influence of a higher culture, probably derived from the American Southwest, also can be recognized among some of the northern tribes, namely, the Opata, Chínipa, and in part the Pima, especially in the use of irrigation, here to be considered as a cultural acquisition rather than an environmental adaptation. The greater number of tribes were extensive farmers, with supplementary dependence on hunting, fishing, and gathering. Each agricultural tract was, and is, surrounded by a large body of wild, nontillable land. In such areas extensive stockraising has been introduced in modern times, but probably provides no more food than did the wild range. The Papago held a country with very meager possibilities of tillage, and were forced into a seminomadic life, planting their fields of maize and beans in the rainy season, and wandering about for the rest of the year. Some of the coast people, such as the Seri and the Guasave tribes, had no agriculture. Cultural level and environmental advantage are only in partial agreement in most parts of the region.

The area approaches cultural unity only in linguistic connections; in respect to physical qualities it is not at all a unit. The southern limit lies at the base of the volcanic plateau of Tepic, its northern one along the Gila River. Two natural regions are included: first, the lowlands along the Pacific, which merge into a land of wide basins and short, discontinuous ranges, and second, the deeply fretted margins of the great Mexican plateau, the land of great, branching canyons, called the *barrancas* of the Sierra Madre. The western lowlands experience great summer heat, the Gulf of California failing to temper the process of heating. There is a well-

-1

ABORIGINAL POPULATION AND DENSITY OF POPULATION
OF NORTHWESTERN MEXICO COMPARED WITH
POPULATION AND DENSITY OF POPULATION, 1920

| Tribe | Area (in sq. km.) | Aboriginal number | Aboriginal density (individuals per sq. km.) | Total population in same area, 1920 | Density, 1920 (individuals per sq. km.) |
|---|---|---|---|---|---|
| Totorame | 10,400 | 100,000 | 10.0 | 120,000 | 12.0 |
| Tahue | 13,400 | 70,000 | 5.2 | 70,000 | 5.2 |
| Cahita proper | 27,100 | 115,000 | 4.3 | 115,000 | 4.3 |
| Sinaloa and Ocoroni River | | 15,000 | | | |
| Cinaloa—Tehueco—Zuaque | | 40,000 | | | |
| Mayo | | 25,000 | | | |
| Yaqui | | 35,000 | | | |
| Guasave | 8,000 | 10,000 | 1.2 | 30,000 | 3.8 |
| Comanito and Mocorito | 7,100 | 30,000 | 4.2 | 40,000 | 5.6 |
| Acaxee | 15,000 | 30,000 | 2.0 | 40,000 | 2.7 |
| Xixime | 19,800 | 30,000 | 1.5 | 50,000 | 2.6 |
| Barranca tribes of Fuerte and Mayo | 14,000 | 30,000 | 2.2 | 55,000 | 4.0 |
| Chínipa | | 4,000 | | | |
| Guazapar and Témori | | 3,000 | | | |
| Zoe | | 3,000 | | | |
| Tubar | | 3,000 | | | |
| Huite | | 2,000 | | | |
| Varohío | | 7,000 | | | |
| Tepahue | | 3,000 | | | |
| Conicari | | 1,000 | | | |
| Baciroa, Macoyahui, etc. | | 3,000 | | | |
| Lower Pima | 38,100 | 25,000 | 0.6 | 40,000 | 1.0 |
| Opata | 42,500 | 60,000 | 1.5 | 70,000 | 1.7 |
| Seri | 20,400 | 5,000 | 0.2 | 20,000 | 1.0 |
| Jova | 7,800 | 5,000 | 0.6 | 8,000 | 1.0 |
| Pima Alto | 100,600 | 30,000 | 0.3 | 58,000 (Mexico only) | 1.0 |
| Totals | 324,200 | 540,000± | (Ave.) 2.6 | 716,000 | (Ave.) 3.95 |

marked summer rainy season, followed by mild and sunny winters. Rivers rising in the Sierra Madre cross the lowlands and have two flood periods, one in midsummer, another, more irregular, in winter and spring. In coast plain, range-flanked basins, and barrancas that drain westward from the high plateau the people live and always have lived concentrated on flood plain or on lower piedmont slopes, where water is available to the land and the growing season is long, or, in some places, continuous. The tilled lands are in general well suited to intensive and varied production. As one goes northward in Sonora the growing season is increasingly reduced by winter cold, reaching its minimum on the Arizona-Sonora border south of Tucson.

## SOUTHERN PEOPLES OF HIGH CULTURE

The early records of the southern coast, inhabited by the Tahue and Totarame, are scanty because of the nature of the Spanish conquest, effected in 1530–31 by Nuño de Guzmán with extreme and sustained barbarity and under cloak of well-considered secrecy. The immediate result was a catastrophic collapse of the native civilization, which provided Las Casas with one of his illustrations of the destruction of the Indies. I have presented elsewhere what is known about conditions at the time of the conquest,[7] and there expressed the judgment that the aboriginal density of population did not differ greatly from the present.

The reasons for this conclusion may be summarized as follows: (1) A reconnaissance was made of the more conspicuous prehistoric ruins, especially along the flood plains, which showed that the valleys were occupied by prehistoric settlements comparable in size and spacing to those of the present. (2) The surface horizons of these ruins indicated that they were occupied contemporaneously. (3) It was possible to identify a number of the ruins as inhabited at the time of the conquest. (4) In addition to the larger archeologic sites situated on or marginal to the flood plains, numerous small sites were found on higher, less desirable land. These were also occupied

---

7. "Aztatlán," *Ibero-Americana,* no. 1 (Berkeley, 1932).

by farmers, though in such localities farming is not carried on at present, the implication being that in aboriginal times it was necessary to farm land which is submarginal under present economic conditions, and that hence the pressure of population was once greater than it is now. (5) All the Spaniards who took part in the conquest and left a record found that the natives compared favorably in number and level of culture with those in the lands through which they had passed, namely, the densely settled regions of central Jalisco and Michoacán. They also noted the sharp lowering of cultural level to the north of Culiacán, where the ruder Cahita Indians were first encountered. (6) The contemporary documents are mainly by companions of Guzmán, partners in some degree of his crimes, and called to testify at the trial in which he was brought to book. These witnesses hardly can be considered as inclined to exaggerate the numbers of natives whom they encountered, since there was little armed resistance to excuse the Spanish excesses or place the conquerors in an heroic light. The tone of the testimony rather is apologetic.

One of the contemporary statements is selected for comparison with present conditions. The first anonymous witness in the Guzmán trial declared of the country between the head of the Culiacán River and the alkali lands which occupy the river delta that "the land was more densely peopled than had been seen in the Indies; nine leagues of it were lined with pueblos on both river banks, spaced at a distance of three-quarters or half a league, and each having from five to six hundred houses."[8] The impression of a greater population than in interior Mexico may have been owing to its riparian concentration. This area was similarly though less explicitly characterized by others of Guzmán's party. Numerous and large ruins below Culiacán show that settlements were closely spaced as described, some of them on slight, flood-protected "islands," others, as at present is also true, subject to brief inundation. This flood plain has a present population of about thirty-five thousand, probably not far from the estimate of the Guzmán witness. Is parity of population in 1530 and 1930 reasonable for this area?

---

8. "Icazbalceta," *Coll. Doc. Hist. Mex.*, 2:391.

The Culiacán Valley has been converted to commercial production more completely than any other valley in the subregion being considered. Canals have been dug for irrigation, sugar plantations and mills have been set up, and the town population has increased. The valley is self-sufficient in respect to food and it also has an important surplus of sugar and of winter vegetables. Irrigation was introduced for commercial plantations. It altered the form of agriculture rather than extended the agricultural area, substituted more valuable cash crops for subsistence crops, and relocated the population locally, but did not stimulate population growth generally. On the contrary, the areas of commercial plantation throughout this southern coast have lower densities of population than those localities which are on a basis of subsistence farming. The Culiacán Valley has about 0.9 hectares of harvested land per capita. Three other *municipios* to the south, with important commercial plantations, give the same density. The remaining six municipios, which are given over to subsistence farming, report only 0.3 hectares of harvested land to a person.[9] Personal observations indicate that a hectare of cultivated valley land feeds from four to five people under present conditions. The fields are under nearly continuous production and their fertility is maintained by floods.

The present population of more than two hundred thousand people, inhabiting the lowlands once belonging to the Tahue and Totorame tribes, does not owe its numbers to the improvement or extension of agriculture by the white man. After its nearly complete sixteenth-century ruin, the country has gradually filled up with people again, and is still capable of growth without modernization of its agriculture.

The aboriginal population may well have been as far along, or farther, toward reaching the subsistence limits of the area: (1) In the flood plains approximately the same lands are farmed which were farmed aboriginally. The fertility of the lands is unchanged. (2) Upland farming has receded as against prehistoric conditions. (3) The

---

9. These figures are derived from the 1926 census and deal with acres harvested, counting twice those fields which are planted twice a year.

people are fed by the same crops, principally maize, beans, and squashes. (4) Changes in method of tillage are not significant. Draft animals have replaced hand tillage in part, the feed they require involving a small reduction of the land area available for food. (5) Animal food in aboriginal times was obtained in sufficient amount by hunting in the scrub savanna and fishing in rivers and lagoons. Both types of resources have been pretty well wasted, especially in late years. The chickens and pigs of the modern villager provide an equivalent, but are scarcely to be considered as enlarging the subsistence basis. (6) Adequate facilities for the interchange of goods existed aboriginally in the *tiangues,* or organized markets. (7) Warfare is sometimes cited as an effective factor in limiting population growth among Indian tribes. There is no evidence of the sort locally. These lowland peoples were organized after a fashion into four states, Culiacán, Chametla, Aztatlán, and Sentispac, which held no serious, if any, enmity against one another, and which were stronger than their more savage neighbors. Their religious cult lacked the human sacrifices of the interior. There is no warrant of any sort for considering that they kept numbers down by killing one another off.

Ruins, documents, and the present manner of living from the land support the estimate that aboriginal and current population were of the same order of density.[10] To the Totorame, who held the provinces of Chametla, Aztatlán, and Sentispac, a larger total and greater density applies than to the Tahue in the province of Culiacán. Southward there is notable increase of rainfall and higher percentage of alluvial land. At the south the lighter upland soils were and are widely used for summer temporal planting; northward, drought restricts crop lands.

The destruction of native life by the conquest of Guzmán repeats the happenings in the Greater Antilles, among the Chibcha, and on

---

10. Torquemada's statement (*Monarquía Indiana,* 2:337) that at the beginning of the conquest the Spaniards declared the province of Culiacán to have more than six hundred thousand inhabitants, is a picturesque guess, without authority and without definition of the province of Culiacán. Antonio Tello's various figures also are not to be taken seriously. Both friars wrote about things that happened before their time and both embellished their chronicles with legendary and sensational accounts.

the coast of Peru. Wantonly the settlements were burned, the stores and crops wasted. The people were rounded up in droves and shipped south as slaves not only during the conquest but throughout the time when Guzmán's men held the country. Famine and pestilence followed after, a great epidemic being recorded for 1535. In 1602 the bishop of New Galicia came to visit this part of his see. He found that "the province of Tahue in other days was very famous and now its largest settlement has less than forty householders."[11] In all the Tahue villages of the Culiacán Valley he enumerated less than a thousand inhabitants. Jesuit records, however, involving the Culiacán River Indians, indicate a somewhat larger survival.[12] In the Jesuit Añua of 1596, thirty-five pueblos of Culiacán Indians were stated as visited, and in the following year there were eight hundred communicants in the same area. In 1610 the Indians had been concentrated into sixteen pueblos along the Culiacán River, and in them more than fourteen hundred were admitted to confession and four hundred to communion. Since at that time these rites were not administered to children and the record applies only to the Culiacán River, a minimum survival of twenty-five hundred on the Culiacán River, or five thousand Tahue all told, is indicated at the beginning of the seventeenth century.

EUROPEAN EPIDEMIC DISEASES

The Jesuits came to the west coast in 1590 and made their headquarters at the villa of Sinaloa on the frontier of Spanish occupation. They were assigned to convert and subdue the lands to the north, inhabited principally by Cahita tribes. Thereafter the Jesuit annals provide a good record of the succession of events on this northward-moving frontier. There is notable emphasis in the earlier annual reports, in particular during the first thirty years, on the ravages of epidemics, the most severe of which are noted below.

---

11. La Motà y Escobar, *Descripción geográfica de Galicia,* p. 101 (Mexico, 1930).

12. Unless otherwise noted, Jesuit reports are taken from *Memorias para la Historia de la Provincia de Sinaloa,* which forms volume 15, Sección de Historia, in the General Archive of Mexico (hereafter identified as M.A.G.).

In 1592–93 there was noted:

a most violent pestilence of smallpox and measles which entered the province of Sinaloa, spreading from settlement to settlement so that almost no one escaped. One beheld with compassion the houses filled with sick people, covered from head to foot with repulsive crusts. On some the skin peeled entirely from hands and feet; all were full of corrupt blood and matter, emitting a pestilential and insufferable odor. The people, burning with fever, fled to the fields and rivers in order to escape from the odor and heat in the houses. It appears that no more horrible thing has been seen, afflicting so many people at one time. The mortality was very great and the labor of burying exhausting.[13]

The Añua of 1601 reported a *cocoliztli* (unspecified epidemic fever) with a mortality of about half those who contracted it, children, however, being less affected. In the Añua of 1602 was stated:

This year there penetrated into this country the disease called garrotillo [diphtheria?] together with six or seven others, such as measles, smallpox, erysipelas and the spotted fever called tabardillo [typhus?], so that almost everyone has suffered one or more of them; for which reason a large number of people have died.

At the same time a furious epidemic of cocoliztli was reported in the Culiacán Valley. In 1611 the tabardillo again assumed epidemic proportions.

In 1617–18 another epidemic of cocoliztli spread through the country, mortality being especially high on the Yaqui frontier, where missionary work had then begun. The Añua of 1623 said:

The pestilence which has prevailed this year has been the greatest seen among the natives, a great number dying from the rigors of the sickness, which was followed by a famine such as has never been seen in this province.

---

13. Martin Perez in chap. 7 of *Puntos Sacados, Misiónes,* vol. 25, M.A.G. Antonio Ruiz' MS history has an account of the same epidemic. Also the Jesuit Añuas, where it is also stated that a famine followed the pestilence.

Father Juan Lorencio stated in 1625:

> For more than nine years God has visited his flock in the wilder-
> ness with hunger and pestilence, and particularly during the last
> two years the scourge has been general and most severe, so that
> the Fathers of these missions, when solicited for their annual
> statement, reported only the number of people died under their
> ministrations, which was in excess of 8600, not counting the
> many who died in the brush without succor. The number of sick
> was so great that in one pueblo three hundred were taken ill at
> one time, similar occurrences happening in other pueblos. Great
> mortality was also caused by a grievous famine which succeeded,
> a dozen entire pueblos becoming abandoned which previously
> were well peopled.

The epidemic and famine of 1625 was especially severe on the Yaqui
and other northern rivers (it was at least in part smallpox).

These reports are concerned only with the area from the Sinaloa
River north to the Yaqui, as brought under mission control in the
period 1590–1620. European epidemics probably preceded the
white man into this area, but their seriousness was certainly much
aggravated by the mission system. Prior to the missions these natives
(except so far as they had been reduced in *encomiendas*) lived in scattered rancherías, the houses being dispersed or in small clusters, of
airy construction, with open sun-shelters attached. With the best of
intentions the missionaries, by "reducing" the Indians to compact
pueblos and gathering them together regularly for worship, instruction, and joint labor, exposed them to contagion by European diseases. In founding a mission one of the first efforts was to build a
substantial church, about which clustered closely spaced houses for
the neophytes, the material of construction being generally adobe.
The Indians were thus brought into unwonted intimacy. The possibilities of infection could hardly have been increased more effectively
than by this congregation and by the daily assemblage for instruction and labor. The size of the church was usually just large enough
for all the worshipers to crowd into it. The protective isolation of
aboriginal living gave way quickly to almost ideal conditions for the
spread of disease, one European disease after another taking its toll of

a people who were lacking in immunity, hygienic measures, and medicines.

Famine normally followed on pestilence, presumably because the natives, caught in the epidemic, failed to plant their crops and consumed their supply of seed grain. Whenever a village became so diminished in population that there was room for its remnants in another village, the missionaries depopulated the site and transferred the remnants. The abandoned settlement then commonly passed into the hands of a Spanish grantee who used it for the raising of horses, mules, and cattle, the most readily negotiable product of the land on this frontier. Such encroachment by Spaniards on the native lands continued, thereby steadily narrowing the Indian bases of subsistence and eliminating the possibilities of recuperation. Of the degree to which partial sterilization of the natives by venereal diseases took place there is no information. Though the missions protected the Indians from the sudden and violent extermination that characterized the area to the south, they nevertheless brought involuntarily but surely the means of their continued diminution.

BAPTISMS, NORTHERN SINALOA
AND SOUTHERN SONORA, 1592–1631

| From 1592 | | In 1616 | 4,155 | In 1625–26 | 13,057 |
|---|---|---|---|---|---|
| to 1609 | 25,897 | 1617 | 4,665 | 1627 | 4,170 |
| | | 1618 | 4,497 | 1628 | 5,474 |
| In 1610 | 2,586 | 1619 | 7,421 | 1629 | 4,762 |
| 1611 | 1,745 | 1620 | 7,600 | 1630 | 8,697 |
| 1612 | 2,075 | 1621 | 11,340 | 1631 | 8,808 |
| 1613 | 1,613 | 1622 | 8,343 | | |
| 1614 | 5,420 | 1623 | 11,221 | Total, | |
| 1615 | 1,703 | 1624 | 6,000 | 1592–1631 | 151,621 |

GENERAL STATISTICS OF THE EARLIER JESUIT MISSIONS

A summary of early baptisms exists for northern Sinaloa and southern Sonora.[14] These figures relate mainly to the flood plains from the Mocorito River north to and including the Yaqui. The earlier bap-

---

14. *Misiónes,* vol. 25, M.A.G.

tisms were restricted to northern Sinaloa. In 1614 baptisms began among the Mayo Indians on the Mayo River, in 1617 among the Yaqui, and in 1619 to a small degree among the lower Pima. In the later figures some of the southern Opata are included. During this period missionary success was not notable in the hill lands of southern Sonora, and the nonagricultural coastal districts of Sinaloa were still only partly under control. The missionaries made repeated complaint of the fact that in many places the older Indians continued to reject Christianity. It is impossible to convert these figures into an estimate of the total number of Christian Indians for the period.

The Provincial was informed in 1593 that in the six valleys then known in Jesuit territory, the Mocorito, Sinaloa, Ocoroni, Fuerte, Mayo, and Yaqui, there were living more than a hundred thousand souls.

In 1622, Captain Martinez Hurdaide, reviewing his work as governor of this frontier, reported to the Viceroy[15] that he had brought the order of Spanish government to a hundred leagues of territory (from the Sinaloa River to the Yaqui) in which there lived more than one hundred eighty-five thousand Indians, of whom more than eighty thousand were of the Christian faith. His statement is supported by the Añua of 1623, which noted twenty-three parishes "and many of them have in excess of thirteen hundred households, the holy sacrament being administered to more than eighty-four thousand souls by twenty-three priests."

From the third decade of the seventeenth century is the following entry in the *Fragmental History*:[16]

El orden de los rios es desta manera:
el 1° que llaman de Mocorito con 3 poblaciones y vecinos 350
el 2° de Petatlan con 10 pueblos y vecinos 1550
el 3° de Cuaque o Cinaloa o Carapoa por otro nombre con 11 pueblos y vecinos 3,150
el 4° de Mayo con 10 pueblos y vecinos 3,650
el 5° de Yaqui con 8 pueblos y vecinos 5,250
el 6° y 7° rios de Nebome y Seriaripa con 8 pueblos y vecinos 2,400

---

15. *Historia,* vol. 316, M.A.G.    16. *Misiónes,* vol. 25, M.A.G.

el 8° rio de Aybino y Bacuca con 9 pueblos y vecinos 1,200
el 9° y ultimo (hasta donde ha llegado el estandarte de la predica-
cion del Evangelio) de los Sonoras y Huris con 800 vecinos.[17]

The text continues:

> The number of [adult?] inhabitants (*moradores*) of these rivers has
> been in excess of a hundred thousand; although at present it is less
> because of the sicknesses and pestilences which they have suffered
> on various occasions; but nevertheless it is very large and the
> families of those baptized number 18,350 without taking into
> account many others who are in rebellion or are as yet unsubdued.

The Añua of 1626[18] said that "those reduced are almost one
hundred fifty thousand souls, without innumerable others who are
seeking baptism." All these estimates refer to the same general country, beginning north of Culiacán at the Mocorito River, extending
thence north to the great bend of the Yaqui River, and involving but
little of the barranca country to the east.

CONCLUSION

The record, as interpreted, gives an aboriginal population between
Gila and Rio Grande de Santiago in excess of half a million, almost
three-fourths of the number now living in this part of Mexico. Bit by
bit, the theme has obtruded itself that aboriginal rural populations
and present ones are much the same. This, I believe, is not a sensational conclusion, but a quite natural one.

Population in such a country as Mexico cannot be expected to
conform to the growth that our western civilization has experienced.
The fields that feed the people today are the same that were farmed
aboriginally, the flood plains and colluvial slopes were as amenable

---

17. The Petatlan is the modern Rio Sinaloa, but the third river is now called
the Fuerte. The Nebome formed part of the Lower Pima; the Seriaripa is the
Sahuaripa; the Aybino is the Matape River. The Bacuca were the people of the
valley of Batuc, on the lower Rio Moctezuma. The last river named was the
Sonora, the Huri (Ure) being another branch of the Lower Pima, whereas the
Sonora were Opata. The figures for the last-named rivers have no significance,
since conversions were then only beginning on these streams.

18. *Misiónes,* vol. 25, M.A.G.

to primitive planting—stick and hoe—as they are to the simple plow and metal hoe of the present cultivator. On those lands there is no problem of fertilizing or crop rotation. No crops have been introduced that yield more food than did the native crops; indeed the crops are still primarily the immemorial crops of the Indian. Changes in tillage have taken place but they do not mean more intensive tillage.

If Indian families were small, whereas present Mexican families are large, a disparity would be introduced into the two scenes. Such evidence as we have, however, indicates that fecundity was about the same as at present. Nor is there evidence that health conditions have improved. It is still the law of the land that when one gets sick, either one gets better or one dies. We know of no diseases that have disappeared, but of numerous ones that have been introduced. There remains the possibility of intertribal wars as a possible depressant of aboriginal population, but with the exception of the enmity between Xixime and Acaxee, there is no record of serious hostilities. There is a static quality to the population scene; once, and now, again, it has been filled in similar manner by human habitations; between the two periods lies a disastrous decline and slow recuperation.

# 11. Colima of New Spain in the Sixteenth Century

## The Conquest of Colima

### ANTECEDENTS: ENTRIES TO THE SOUTH SEA

The Spanish occupation of Colima was an integral part of the design of New Spain, as shaped by Cortés. The men who were fresh from the plunder of the Aztec state were not slow to turn westward. Colima was important in the quest for mineral wealth, as a base for reconnoitering the unknown North, and for the long voyage to the East Indies. Events soon shifted attention away from this area, but for a brief period it was the farthest outpost of Spain in the great unknown, where Amazons were thought to hold the passage to Cathay or the Spice Islands.

The first Spanish approaches to the Pacific Coast from the highland of Mexico are poorly known, because the records are scanty and unclear. There were more important things to do in those breathless years than keep close account of every party that set forth to plunder and discover. History has preserved, however, the way in which

---

"Colima of New Spain in the Sixteenth Century" is an abridged version of the original monograph which first appeared as *Ibero-Americana: 29* (University of California: Berkeley, 1948).

EXPLORERS' ROUTES ON THE WEST COAST OF MEXICO, 1520–1524

Cortés turned to the task of getting a foothold on the west coast. (See map on facing page.)

In the spring of 1520, as part of the game of enmeshing the Aztec state, Cortés informed himself concerning the tribute that was brought to the court of Moctezuma, for the tribute rolls drawn up for subject districts served as guides to the economic geography of the country. It is most significant that in this way the Spaniards learned that gold was brought from afar, for the volcanoes about the Valley of Mexico yielded no metals. Cortés quickly sent soldiers, accompanied by Aztec guides, to view the so-called gold mines. The principal sources they sought lay southeastward, the chief direction in which both Aztec empire and trade had been expanding. Moctezuma indicated to Cortés several gold-bearing districts, lying southeast of Mexico City. One of these was near Sosola and Tamazulapa, in the upper Mixteca, to the northwest of the modern city of Oaxaca.[1] The expedition thither in 1520 is ascribed to Gonzalo de Umbría. The earliest accounts agree in this identification of the gold provinces of the south. The later historians, Bernal Diaz and Herrera, became confused over Sosola, which is still a place of some importance, and called it Zacatula. This confusion of the Oaxacan pueblo with the town at the mouth of the Balsas River has been repeated in histories to the present time. The two places are far apart, on entirely distinct routes, and there is no evidence that Zacatula or any other place on the Pacific Ocean was reached in these first reconnaissance expeditions, through which the Spaniards became familiar with the auriferous streams south of the central volcanic chain of Mexico.

When Aztec resistance was broken, Spanish curiosity was again directed south, extending the trails discovered the year before. The Aztec capital Tenochtitlán was laid waste in August of 1521 and Cortés lost little time in sending other scouting parties southward. The Third Letter of Cortés (May 15, 1522) gives the substance of what is known about such *entradas* as were directed to exploration, by then extended to the Pacific Coast.

---

1. *CC,* Second Letter, October 30, 1520, pp. 28, 51. These pueblos, under variant spellings, are identified also by Peter Martyr [Pietro Martire de Angleria], *De Orbe Novo* in *BAE,* II, 101; Gómara, *Historia de Mexico* in *BAE,* XXII, 354; and by Oviedo, *Historia general y natural de las Indias,* lib. 33, chap. vii.

At the date of writing, Cortés declared that he had succeeded in discovering (by proxy) the South Sea at three places.[2] He informed the king that one of these was the Tututepec (Tototepec) coast of western Oaxaca, which Pedro de Alvarado overran early in 1522. Somewhat earlier, soon after the fall of Tenochtitlán, but lasting probably into the winter of 1521–1522, two exploring parties followed up native reports of the southern ocean, one reaching the sea, according to Cortés, at a distance of one hundred thirty leagues, the other continuing for one hundred fifty leagues. The two parties proceeded in different directions.[3] Cortés identified one of these discoveries as having been made at Tehuantepec,[4] probably on the shorter of the two routes, for the shorter expedition was the one noted as passing through many large towns of high culture, precisely the condition of the intermediate Mixtec and Zapotec land. The history of Herrera named one Del Valle as discoverer of Tehuantepec.[5] Both the Del Valle and the Alvarado expeditions may be thought of as extensions of the Gonzalo de Umbria expedition of 1520, following fairly closely along what is now the Pan American Highway, the great, immemorial road south.

The third expedition by which Cortés had secured discovery of the South Sea was the one that traveled one hundred fifty leagues, too great a distance for any direct route to the Pacific. This party, we infer, made a long detour to get to Zacatula, near the mouth of the Balsas. Cortés said in his Third Letter that "in one of the three places where I discovered the sea, I have instructed that two medium-sized caravels and two brigantines shall be built," and he described the steps he was taking to send shipwrights to the proposed port and to have the necessary materials carried overland from Vera Cruz.[6] Though he did not mention the place by name, no other harbor need be considered, for we do know that such steps were begun at Zacatula late in 1522, and not at Tehuantepec or Tototepec. Gómara,

---

2. *CC,* p. 94.
3. Ibid., p. 90.
4. Ibid., p. 92.
5. Herrera, *Historia general de los hechos de los castellanos,* Dec. 4, lib. 4, chap. ii.
6. *CC,* Third Letter, p. 94.

moreover, identified the terminus of this exploration by name.[7] The Ixtlilxochitl *Relación* is also in agreement:

> Ixtlilxuchitl envió ciertos mensageros a Tehuantepe, Tzacatecan [misprint for Tzacatulan] y otras provincias . . . y con ellos fueron cuatro Castellanos por dos caminos que envió Cortés para que reconociesen la mar del sur . . . solo Tototepec se negó . . . Cortés teniendo muy entera relación de la mar del sur por los cuatro Españoles que fueron con los mensageros de Ixtlilxuchitl envió a Pedro de Alvarado [against Tututepec].[8]

Nothing is stated about the route followed to Zacatula. It is considerably closer to Mexico City than is Tehuantepec, yet Cortés apparently reckoned the route taken as twenty leagues longer. The more direct way would have been by Michoacán, but the evidence on Michoacán, presented below, shows that it had not been crossed at this time. The next best route was over the line of the present highway to Acapulco and then northwestward along the coast, this distance being slightly greater than that from Mexico to Tehuantepec. This circuitous route had the advantage of passing through regions under established Aztec authority extending to the vicinity of Acapulco and Zacatula, for the coast as far as Zacatula paid tribute to Moctezuma, whereas Michoacán was independent. It may be inferred that the tribute rolls again guided the Spaniards in the selection of their route—a route that avoids the descent of the Balsas Valley, with its difficult terrain and long stretches of sparsely inhabited country. The lower Balsas was also the frontier between the Mexican and Tarascan states and a zone of conflict, not of commerce. (In modern Mexico the boundary between Guerrero and Michoacán reproduces roughly the Aztec-Tarascan boundary.) Since the explorations of the white man followed Indian trails in general, and Cortés at this time relied on Aztec information and guides, it seems certain that they used the Aztec route to Zacatula, by way of Acapulco. Cortés may not have thought it worthwhile to tell the king that the

---

7. Gómara, op. cit., p. 395.

8. Ixtlilxochitl, *Decima tercia relación de la venida de los españoles* in Sahagún, *Historia general de las cosas de Nueva España*, IV, 285.

party reached the coast at a place called Acapulco, or by way of Yopelcingo, and that thence it proceeded along the coast in the direction of the unknown west to the farthest Aztec-controlled frontier place, where there was both harbor and good timber for shipbuilding.[9] There were so many things to tell that geographical explanations were usually omitted in these letters. At any rate, by the spring of 1522 Cortés had knowledge of the Pacific Coast from the Isthmus of Tehuantepec to the mouth of the Balsas River and was contemplating a shipyard and port at Zacatula, the farthest point west.[10]

## THE CROSSING OF MICHOACÁN

Meanwhile the Spaniards were also beginning to extend their reconnaissances west from the Aztec capital, across the volcanic plateau. Here also the sequence of steps is confused. In addition to the general chronicles we have the Indian account, collated around 1540 by a cleric under the title "Relación de las ceremonias y ritos—de Michoacán." This is the most explicit and perhaps the most objective record of the occupation of Michoacán by the Spaniards. This *relación* is paralleled by Herrera with respect to the preliminary steps:

(1) A Spaniard (Parrillas) reached the frontier Tarascan town of Tajimaroa from the Valley of Mexico on February 23, 1522, the exact

---

9. Oviedo merely paraphrases the letter of Cortés. Herrera adds some items that are confused. In his *Historia* (Dec. 3, lib. 3, chap. xvii), he states that when Cortés was seeking to discover the South Sea "he sent Francisco Chico, with three other Castilians and some Indians, in the direction of Zacatula with orders that they should reconnoiter the whole coast of the South Sea and discover if there were facilities for the building of ships. These went to Tehuantepec and to Zacatula, and to other towns and took possession of that sea and land." If only we had the documents that Herrera lumped together in this abstract! It is not necessary to assume that the four Castilians were one party and made a continuous coastwise exploration from Tehuantepec to Zacatula, nor that Herrera invented the statement. On minor matters he was often simply a careless compiler. Cortés made a definite statement that, aside from the Alvarado expedition to Tototepec, he had sent two parties, each headed by two Spaniards, to explore the Pacific shore by different routes. Tehuantepec and Zacatula, therefore, were the end points of two explorations. Apparently Rodrigo Alvarez Chico was in charge of the Zacatula party.

10. For the identification of Zacatula as one corner of the domain of Moctezuma, I am indebted to the work of Robert Barlow, *The Extent of the Empire of the Culhua Mexica,* Univ. Calif. Publ. Ibero-Americana: 28.

date having been remembered by the Indians because it coincided with an important native festival.

(2) Shortly thereafter, a small party under Montaño (who had made the ascent of Popocatepetl) came to the capital of Michoacán (Tzintzuntzan); parallel details of this *entrada* are given in Herrera's *Historia* and the Indian relación.[11] This was in the spring of 1522. Cortés apparently alluded to both visits in his Third Letter (May 15, 1522), relating information he got from Tarascans who escorted the Spaniards back to Mexico, rather than describing the routes or experiences of the Spaniards. The earliest hint of Colima is in a conversation Cortés held with the Tarascan visitors. He said: "Since I had recently had some notice of the South Sea, [i.e., from the Zacatula party] I inquired also of them if one could go by way of their country; and they answered 'yes,' but that to reach the sea it was necessary to go through the land of a great lord with whom they were at war, and that for this reason they could not at that time get to the sea." The statement can refer only to the Indian state of Colima, which was independent of Michoacán and the only coastal group of any military importance other than Aztecan Zacatula. The conjecture is that the Tarascans told Cortés of a way through their land to Zacatula. They must have known that white men had come from the southeast to the mouth of the Balsas. Events later in the year suggest that they may have said so, but that this was another item which Cortés did not incorporate in his report to the king. That there was no reference to the coast of modern Michoacán is not surprising. Access to it is barred by the extremely rugged mountains of Motín.

(3) The next item is as curious as it is obscure. The Indian relación says that the Tarascans who escorted the (second) Spanish party back to Mexico returned to Michoacán with still other Spaniards and that these other Spaniards collected a large body of Tarascans at the Indian capital, to set out for Colima. The Spaniards prudently remained behind at an Indian pueblo but "sent the chiefs and common people ahead to ask the lords of Colima that they come in peace to the place where the Spaniards had remained, but these sacrificed all [of

---

11. RM, pp. 84–87; Herrera, op. cit., Dec. 3, lib. 3, chaps. iii–vii.

the Tarascans] so that not one returned. Whereupon the Spaniards, despairing of their coming and of waiting for the messengers, returned to the city of Michoacán."[12] Such an expedition apparently did take place late in the spring of 1522: Herrera mentions the dispatch by Cortés of certain Spaniards from Mexico with the homeward-bound Tarascans, without indicating the purpose or result of this action.[13]

(4) Thus, during the first half of 1522, Cortés acquired enough information in Michoacán to warrant a major expedition and formal occupation. The three previous parties, incidentally, had followed the main road from the Valley of Mexico to Pátzcuaro, each one getting somewhat farther into the Tarascan country than the previous one. In the summer of 1522 Cortés sent one of his great captains, Cristóbal de Olid, to add Michoacán to New Spain. This was the second greatest native state of North America, but the way had been well prepared and no opposition was expected, or met. The Indian *relación* is most explicit on this entrada and dates the arrival of the Spaniards at Tajimaroa on July 17, another Tarascan feast day, in the rainy season. Their entry into the city of Michoacán was somewhat later and their stay there was reported as having lasted four months, which would be toward the end of 1522.[14]

With the activities of the Spaniards in the Tarascan capital we are not concerned here, beyond these facts, which are relevant to their further movements: Michoacán at first yielded handsome returns, by gift and later by extortion, both of silver and gold. As the objects of precious metal became more difficult to acquire, the Spaniards grew restless. Like the Valley of Mexico, the main Tarascan country is a land of young volcanoes and their detrital basins; it lacks metallic deposits. Much wealth had been accumulated in ornaments in the Tarascan temples and houses, but the source of the silver and gold lay somewhere beyond. Actually it lay mostly beyond and below the land inhabited by Tarascans, but in lands which they dominated

12. RM, p. 87.
13. Herrera, op. cit., Dec. 3, lib. 3, chap. vii.
14. RM, pp. 87–96.

politically. The home land of the Tarascans therefore interested the Spaniards less and less. What if it was good for farming and stock raising, healthful and invigorating? They, like Cortés, had not come to pass their lives as farmers and cattlemen. In his Fourth Letter (1524) Cortés said: "The land did not please them for purposes of settlement; they showed poor inclination to do so, and even set up certain disturbances for which some were punished, and therefore I ordered those to return who wished to do so, and the others I instructed to go with a captain to the South Sea, where I then occupied and where I now [Oct. 1524] hold, a town called Zacatula, and there I have on the stocks four ships, to discover on that sea all that I may."[15]

(5) The end of 1522, then, saw the authorization to abandon plans for a Spanish villa on Lake Pátzcuaro, with the recall of some of the men to Mexico and orders for others to go on to Zacatula. Meanwhile, materials for ships and Spanish artisans were on their way to Zacatula. The first lot of men and ships' fittings went from Vera Cruz to Zacatula over the Aztec route, if we may follow Ixtlilxochitl:

> Cortés viendo que los de la costa del mar del sur eran amigos acordó de enviar cuarenta españoles, carpinteros y marineros a Zacatulan para labrar dos bergantines, y descubrir toda aquella costa, y dos carabelas para buscar islas, que tenía noticia había algunos muy ricas; y para este pidió a Ixtlilxuchitl le diese algunos carpinteros y gente para que fuese con ellos, y que les llevasen el hierro, armas, velas, maromas y otras jarcias de unas que estaban en la Vera Cruz; todo lo cual hizo Ixtlilxuchitl, mandando a sus vasallos. . . [16]

The Tarascan Indian relación also gives information of the transport of heavy supplies through their country and with their help, in the late fall of 1522, and tells of sixteen hundred Indians, accompanied by two Spaniards, who carried ships' anchors down to Zacatula, leaving Michoacán (Pátzcuaro) in mid-November. They returned laden with cacao from the coast for Olid, and this return should be

15. *CC,* p. 97.
16. Ixtlilxochitl, op. cit., IV, 286.

placed at the beginning of 1523. This incident predates the division of Olid's party. Spanish shipbuilding was, therefore, being prepared at Zacatula before the end of 1522, and the villa was formally established in 1523.[17]

Soon thereafter the more adventurous of Olid's men set out for the coast, doubtless being more interested in the gold to be found there than in the business of helping Cortés build ships. Zacatula was the ostensible goal, but Cortés himself had had his eye for some time on the sources of the Tarascan silver and gold, and also on a rich coastal state beyond, called Colima. Olid's men undoubtedly had heard more of the precious metals beyond the rim of the plateau than had reached the ears of Cortés, back in Mexico. Why should they shut their eyes to the opportunity to see for themselves?

### THE OCCUPATION OF COLIMA, 1523

The original statement of the occupation of Colima is in the Fourth Letter of Cortés (October 15, 1524). It follows after the account of the division of Olid's settlers of Michoacán, one captain being sent with a body of troops to Zacatula.

> And this captain and company going toward the said [contemplated?] town of Zacatula, they had notice of a province called Colimán, which lies apart from the road they were to travel, toward the right hand, which is to the west, a matter of fifty leagues; and with the party that was with him, together with many allies from the province of Michoacán, he went thither without my permission and entered a matter of several days' marches, where they had some brushes with the natives; and although there were forty horsemen and more than a hundred foot soldiers, archers, and shield carriers, they were beaten and driven out, three Spaniards and many allies being killed. So they turned about to the said town of Zacatula. This becoming known to me, I ordered the captain brought to me under arrest and I punished his disobedience.

The unnamed captain has perplexed historians, as we shall see later.

---

17. Vazquez de Espinosa, *Compendium and Description of the West Indies,* p. 177.

Somewhat later Cortés sent another captain from the south to pacify the troublesome province of Yopelcingo (by miscopying spelled also Impilcingo), the early name of the area inland, northwest of Acapulco. The fact that the term "pacification" is applied to this area supports the inference that the original entry to Zacatula had been by way of Acapulco. Thereupon this captain was to continue onward to Zacatula, with orders that:

> with the men whom he was leading, and with whatever additional force he could take from Zacatula, he should proceed to the province of Colima, where, as I said in a previous passage, the natives had defeated a captain and soldiers proceeding from Michoacán toward the said town, and that he should attempt to secure this province by peace, and if not thus, that he should gain it by conquest. And so he went, and of the men whom he led and of those he levied there [in Zacatula], he assembled fifty horsemen and a hundred and fifty foot soldiers, and went on to the said province [of Colima], which lies from the town of Zacatula along the coast of the South Sea, a distance of sixty leagues. Along the way he pacified some villages that were hostile and got to the said province. At the place where the other captain had been defeated, he found many men-at-arms who were awaiting him, thinking they could do with him as they had done with the other, and so they opened the fight. It pleased our Lord that victory was ours, without the death of a single person, though many and also the horses were wounded. The enemy paid well for the damage they had done, and so great was the chastisement that without more fighting the whole land submitted, and not only that province, but also many others near by came to offer themselves as vassals of your august majesty. These were Alimán, Colimote, and Ciguatán. Thence he wrote me all that had happened. I sent him word that he should seek a good site, in which he should establish a town, and that he should name it Colimán, for the said province. I sent him nomination of *alcaldes* and *regidores* for it and ordered him to make an inspection of villages and population of those provinces, so that there should be brought to me all the account and secrets of the land that could be ascertained. He came and brought these things and a certain sample of pearls which he had found. In the name of your majesty I assigned the villages of these provinces to the settlers *(vecinos)* who remained

there, numbering twenty-five horsemen and a hundred and twenty foot soldiers. Among the relations which he gave of these provinces, he brought news of a very good harbor which had been found on that coast, at which I rejoiced greatly, for there are few such. Also he brought me an account of the lords of the province of Ciguatán, who affirm that there is an island entirely inhabited by women without a single man. At certain times men are said to come from the mainland, with whom they have relations. Those women who conceive, if they bear female children, raise them, and if males, they put them away. They say this island is ten days' journey from this province and that many have gone thither and seen it. They tell me also that it is very rich in pearls and gold. I shall attempt as soon as equipped to know the truth and to make full account thereof to your majesty.

Cortés' letter, written in October, 1524, refers to events of the previous year. In his *visita* of Colima in 1554 the *Oidor* Lorenzo de Lebrón de Quiñones copied a number of grants made to settlers of the newly acquired province of Colima, which were signed, that is, confirmed, by Cortés in Mexico during December of 1523. The "disobedient" captain, who undertook the first expedition against Colima, must have done so early in 1523. The successful occupation of the province and its subdivision among the members of the following expeditionary party probably occupied the summer and fall of that year, the ratification of grants being completed in Mexico before the end of the year. The events of the conquest and subdivision of Colima consumed, roughly, the whole year of 1523.

THE OPENING OF THE ROUTE
AROUND THE VOLCÁN DE COLIMA

The trails used from Michoacán and Zacatula to Colima are difficult, and the land through which they pass is of little account, except in spots. From 1524 on, better interior routes served to connect with Michoacán and Mexico. These passed around the flanks of the twin volcanoes of Colima. Thereafter, the older route by the Motín area fell into disuse, except as a local trail.

A part of this inner route was opened in 1522 and 1523, from the Tarascan settlements. It is possible that the gateway then, as since, was Jiquilpan (or Zahuayo), at the northwestern end of the Tarascan country (state of Michoacán). The sixteenth-century MS, "Relación of Jiquilpan," states that it was first entered by Olid in the year 1522. From Jiquilpan, an old main road leads southwestward to Mazamitla, a Tarascan outpost (now in the state of Jalisco) in the mountains south of Lake Chapala. This ancient road descends a widening valley to Tamazula and there branches into the basin of Zapotlán (Ciudad Guzmán) and to Tuxpan. This southeastern part of modern Jalisco was aboriginally part of the Indian state of Michoacán, though its ethnic composition was largely non-Tarascan. Later, it constituted part of the Spanish province of Colima. However, at the moment of the conquest, the land east, northeast, and north of the Colima volcanoes was known to the Spaniards as part of Michoacán.

The Spanish entry into the district of Tuxpan, Tamazula, and Zapotlán is part of the general overrunning of Michoacán by Olid and his men, who were apparently determined by the fact that here lay the main source of the Tarascan silver, a topic to be developed later. A brief statement in the "Relación de Tuspa" (MS, 1580) tells us about all that we know of the entry:

> Todos estos tres pueblos con sus suxetos eran del Cazonzi, rrey de la probincia de mechoacan, el qual se rrindio al capitan Xpoual de Oli, que fue el primer hombre que en ella entro, que le embio el capitan general don Hernando Cortés a la dicha conquista en el año de mill y quinientos y beinte y dos años y como el dicho rrey Cazonzi se rrindio con toda su tierra el dicho capitan general don Hernando Cortés los tomo para si y le sirbieron algun tiempo hasta que los pusieron en la rreal corona a quien sirben hasta oy.

It is true that this statement implies that the land that Olid entered means the whole of Michoacán. It also constitutes, however, a specific answer by representatives from the three towns to the formal question of who was the first Spaniard to discover the local area. It may be inferred, therefore, that the local officials designated Olid (possibly Olid in the sense of men of the party of Olid) as the first Spaniard to enter this corner of what was then part of Michoacán. Evidence is to be presented later confirming the original possession of these three communities by Cortés. We do not know that Cortés ever saw these pueblos, yet he held them from the first Spanish occupation, probably because of their importance as a source of silver for the Tarascans. Olid may therefore have gone to this area to take possession of it for Cortés' own use, or he may have sent a subordinate. By the end of 1522 Spanish possession seems to have been extended over the plateau west to the Colima volcanoes.

In 1524 Francisco Cortés came from Mexico to administer the province of Colima. We are told that he entered with his party via Tamazula and Zapotlán and thence continued through Tuxpan to Colima.[18] This seems to have been the first Spanish use of what was to be the *Camino Real* between Colima, Michoacán, and Mexico. This road was troublesome in the barrancas between Tuxpan and the plain of Colima, especially during the rainy season, but it soon became established as the Camino Real to Michoacán and Mexico. An alternative road around the west flank of the volcanoes, with other steep barrancas to cross, also became established by Francisco Cortés.[19] It passed from Zapotlán (Ciudad Guzmán) over the ridge that extends northwestward from the volcano by way of Zapotitlán and Mazatlan to the Colima lowland. This is still a pack road of some importance.

## THE ORIGINAL SPANISH SETTLEMENT

Cortés said that the original corporation of vecinos among whom he divided the pueblos consisted of twenty-five horsemen and one hundred twenty foot soldiers. Lebrón, a generation later, said that the Spanish settlers originally numbered more than one hundred twenty. [For full citation on Lebrón, see page 238.] In 1523 and for some time thereafter Colima and Zacatula were the only villas west of Mexico City. That such a number of Spaniards should have elected to

---

18. *NV,* pp. 285, 304. From the relaciónes of Amula and Tuxcacuesco: Two Spaniards from the troops of Francisco Cortés discovered Amula (next *cabecera* west of Zapotlán) and "returned thence to Zapotlán where they joined their captain, Francisco Cortés, who had come by way of Tamazula and from there they all went [on] entering from Tuspa as far as Colima." The Indians of Tuxcacuesco (cabecera adjoining Amula on the west) heard that two Spaniards of the party of Francisco Cortés were coming up to their town and went to Tamazula to carry the Spaniards in a hammock (or litter?).

19. Ibid.

form a villa in Colima indicates the high expectations then held of this particular frontier. The names of almost half of the original founders have been handed down, indicating a representative sample of Cortés' soldiers of fortune.[20] They belonged to all grades of the hierarchy of conquerors, from charter members to cadets.

There was a small group of the original Cortés party, the old guard of conquistadores: Juan Pinzón[21] and Ginés Pinzón,[22] both of Palos, and presumably of the famous family associated with Columbus; Cristóbal Cabezón,[23] from Almagro in New Castile; Juan de Almesto of Sevilla.[24] (His name figures in most of the local accounts, variously misspelled, for example as Inhiestra. The orthography is clear in Lebrón, and checks with *CyP.* ) Alonso Martin de Trejo, Rodrigo de Evia of Asturias,[25] Rodrigo Lepuzcano or Guipuzcano of Aragón,[26] Benito Gallego,[27] and Diego Garrido[28] "who came with Cortés and was sent back to Castile by order of the Captain General to take the account of the land. [Does this make him the bearer of Cortés' Second Letter?] He returned after the capture of the city [of Mexico] and helped to conquer the Province of Michoacán and that of Colimán." Martin Ruyz de Monjaras of Durango in Biscaya came over to Cortés from the party that Garay had sent to Pánuco in 1519.[29]

There was a larger group of the men of Narvaez who went over to Cortés in 1520. One of these was Juan Fernandez, a Sevillan, later *escribano* of the Villa de Colima, who was in the party that captured Cuauhtemoc and was the first to lay hands on the prince as he was fleeing in a canoe.[30] A distinguished citizen of Colima was Alonso de Arévalo, who had held a *repartimiento* in Cuba from Velázquez and

20. The principal document is "Vecinos y Pueblos en Colima en 1532," variously reprinted, here used in the edition of the AGN*B,* X, 5–23. The original was extant in Colima in the nineteenth century, but the copy made in 1846 that has come down to us is obviously dreadful with respect to the rendering of place names. The names in the text above are of persons mentioned by Lorenzo de Lebrón de Quiñones or for whom there is additional information in other contemporary documents.

21. *CyP,* Nos. 351, 478.
22. Ibid., No. 1085.
23. Ibid., No. 10.
24. Ibid., No. 1161.
25. Ibid., No. 85
26. Ibid., No. 481.
27. Ibid., No. 485.
28. Ibid., No. 356.
29. Ibid., Nos. 25, 294
30. Ibid., No. 72.

who had been with Grijalva in the discovery of New Spain. He became the founder of the most powerful family in the annals of early Colima.[31] Juan Bautista, a Genoese, had also been with Grijalva before returning with Narvaez.[32] Bartolomé Chavarin was another Genoese in Narvaez' party.[33] Martin Monje of Palos, later the owner of a principality in western Jalisco, was one of Narvaez' men who established Colima. Others were Francisco de Cifontes of Córdoba,[34] Gomez de Hoyos, Antonio de Castillo of Palos,[35] Rodrigo de Villasinda, Alonso Quintero (Arriaga?),[36] Anton de Santa Anna, Juan Bautista Rapalo,[37] Alonso del Rio, Pero Gomes,[38] Francisco Santos, Juan de Villacorta,[39] Gregorio Ramirez, and Pedro de Simancas.

Among the founders were also men of the party of the Navarrese Captain Dias de Aux, who came after Cortés had been driven out of Mexico by the Aztec uprising. Principal among these was Juan de Aguilar, later *alcalde* of Colima.[40] Others were Mateo de Ventemilla,[41] Bartolomé López,[42] and Alonso López,[43] who is identified by Icaza as having later become one of the notoriously wealthy men of New Spain.

Then there were the lesser founders, who came too late to New Spain to wear the accolade of the Conquest of Mexico, but still in time to "conquer" Michoacán and Colima—Hernán Ruíz de la Peña, Jorge Carrillo,[44] Martin Ximenez, Manuel de Caceres, Diego de Chavez, Alonzo Lorenzo,[45] and Juan Perez.[46]

Participants in the settlement of Cuba, companions of Grijalva, Garay, and Narvaez, men who fought at Tlaxcala, who marched into the city of Moctezuma when the white men were met as visiting gods and fought their way out as enemies over the causeway in the retreat of the Sorrowful Night, soldiers of Olid in the occupation of Michoacán, companions of Sandoval along the Southern Sea—such were the

31. Ibid., No. 193.
32. Ibid., No. 86.
33. Ibid., No. 480.
34. Ibid., No. 698.
35. Ibid., No. 483.
36. Ibid., No. 224.
37. Ibid., No. 482.
38. Ibid., No. 484.

39. Ibid., Nos. 342, 1171.
40. Ibid., No. 131.
41. Ibid., No. 174.
42. Ibid., No. 412.
43. Ibid., No. 144, and p. xlviii.
44. Ibid., No. 378.
45. Ibid., No. 1141.
46. Ibid., No. 96.

first citizens of Colima. They had been in the thick of every important event of the great conquest.

An inspection of the location of the earliest land titles provides a means of appraising the desirability of site in the eyes of the original colonists. It is important here to note that the most numerous and most powerful vecinos elected to take tracts of land that are of little esteem in the modern economy, and that soon lost their desirability. These were closely grouped along the coast plain and in the coastal mountains from the Motín Range of the coast of Michoacán to Puerto de Navidad in extreme southern Jalisco. The original site of the villa itself was, according to Lebrón, a league or a league and a half from the sea, perhaps in the vicinity of the modern Armeria.

In 1524 Francisco Cortés, cousin of Hernán,[47] became alcalde mayor. His pueblos were: Tecomán (probably adjoining the first villa to the south; the Valley of Tecomán was credited by Lebrón with an original population of four to five thousand men), Zalagua (on the Bay of Santiago, across from Manzanillo), and Tlacatipa and Chiametla (in the rough mountain country behind this bay).

The main pueblo of Cihuatlán belonged to Alonso López, later to appear as one of the notorious rich men of Mexico City. In the southeasternmost valley, Alima was originally granted to one Sancho de Orna.

The copies of *cédulas* depositing Indians in the charge of Spaniards during the years 1523 and 1524, as made by Lebrón, identify such places as extending from Amatlan, in the Motín Mountains, to the Valley of Cihuatlán. Situated mostly in the hills and mountains near the coast and behind the lower Colima River, they include Tecocitlan el viejo, Abacatitlan, and Queyatlan north of the river, Ospanauastla and Tecolapa south of the river.

Further important light is thrown on the earliest distributions by a list of places in the "Vecinos y Pueblos en Colima," which lists places that had at that time (1532) reverted to *corregimientos,* that is, they had been abandoned to the Crown through the death or disap-

---

47. Thus identified by Mexia in the *Residencia* of Cortés (MS copy, Bancroft Library) where this relationship was cited as indicating nepotism.

pearance of the grantees. By checking the uncertain spellings of this list with the pueblos of corregiments in the "Suma de Visitas" and Lebrón, the following are identified, namely from north to south: Tlacinique, Tlacauaua, Cuzcatlan, Contla, Tlala, Ecatlan, Coyutlan, Tamala, Petlazoneca.

All of the places named in the preceding paragraphs lay within twenty kilometers of the sea. Most of them are in or near the coastal mountains. The original hundred-odd Spanish grants lay along and close to the coast, principally between the Cihuatlán Valley and the Motín Range, the original villa lying about midway of this stretch. It is probable that a minor number of grants extended upcountry toward the modern city of Colima. With the exceptions of the Motín area and the provinces of Hernán Cortés, there is no evidence in Lebrón that the outlying "provinces" began to be occupied, or were ratified by grants, until after the establishment of the original settlement.

# The Aboriginal Provinces

## ABORIGINAL POPULATION

The aboriginal population may be estimated from the number of Spaniards who formed the original corporation of Colima. These were the recipients of grants of the Indian settlements from the Motín coast to the Valley of Cihuatlán, and inland toward the seaward base of the Volcán de Colima. It is perfectly apparent that these first grants did not include more than the present state of Colima, the *municipio* of Cihuatlán in Jalisco, and those of Aquila, Coahuayana, and villa Victoria in Michoacán. Together these political units had a population of approximately one hundred thousand in 1940. Actually the present-day political limits were not fully reached by the vecinos of the original villa of Colima.

The grantees fell into two classes, the hundred and twenty foot soldiers, and the superior twenty-five who furnished horses and arms and were entitled to appropriate recompense for their greater services. If the individual foot soldier received as *tributarios* an allotment of two hundred males of working age, this would represent a pueblo of approximately eight hundred Indians. A minimum of twice that allotment might be expected for the *caballeros*. On this basis the minimum Indian population in the triangle between the Motín, the Bay of Navidad, and the Volcán de Colima should have been one hundred and forty thousand, or forty percent greater than in 1940.

These grantees were not an underprivileged part of Cortés' army, but, as was shown above, a representative fraction of the conquistadores of New Spain. In 1523 they could pick where and what they chose out of the newly won empire. That they should have settled in Colima in the numbers indicated means that this coast looked promising for a comfortable living, and this meant there were plenty of Indians to do the work by which the Spaniards were to live. Therefore the estimate of Indian population given above may be low.

At the time of the Lebrón *visita* (1551–1554) there were still in existence one hundred and twelve Indian pueblos for the area of initial Spanish occupation, outlined above. These mid-sixteenth century pueblos represent an unknown but considerable contraction of the number at the time of the Conquest, as shown by Lebrón's examination of individual titles. There need be no doubt, therefore, that in this area there was made available at least one pueblo per Spaniard and, in numerous cases, several. Moreover, there were large Indian towns such as Alima, Tecomán, and Cihuatlán that had political and commercial functions. Environment and aboriginal culture both support the view that this *tierra caliente* was prosperous and populous.

Lebrón gave the following interpretation of early population conditions:

> The Province of Colima and the valleys and provinces annexed to it which are under the jurisdiction of that Villa formerly were densely settled with people when the Spaniards conquered it. According to the information that I was able to get, the number and quantity was so great that of one hundred units of persons there may now remain less than one, as appears from inspection of many of the valleys and provinces thereof, all of which I have

visited and seen in my own person, so that there is neither valley nor province thereof, which, according to the account that I made at the time I visited it, is not much reduced in number. To avoid prolixity I shall give some examples from which Your Highness may infer the rest.

For the Valley of Espuchimilco they assure me that in the pueblo of Espuchimilco alone, when first reduced to peace, there were four or five thousand men, and at present in the visita I found eighty, more or less.

The Province of Cihuatlán, which is at the Port of Navidad, had, at the time when they acknowledged the rule of Your Highness, which was some thirty-three years ago, so many pueblos and people that they were allotted to twenty-seven Spaniards, each of whom was given his pueblo and a sufficient number of persons for his comfortable support. At a minimum there should have been approximately fifteen thousand men. I found, at the present, one pueblo remaining in all that district, named Cihuatlán, and in it there were Indians from two or three other of the towns of old; from one, two; from another, four; and from the third, six; and in all there were no more than thirty-five, certainly a matter for thought and compassion.

In the Valley of Ticomán there were four or five thousand men and now there were listed one hundred and eight. This pueblo, because it is seven or eight leagues from Colima, appears to have been in some degree sustained, since it was always under your royal crown.

The Valley of Alima, I am told, was so great and well-peopled that the settled area and houses extended about a league or more. I found at present one small pueblo of about forty Indians, overworked and sickly. Around about, in the lands which formerly were theirs, plantations of cacao gardens have been placed by Spaniards.

The account of Lebrón should not be discounted too sharply without cause. He spent almost three years visiting villages throughout Colima, he saw the titles of the original allotments, he roused the opposition of the *encomenderos* by prying into their affairs, and he retained the complete support of the Viceroy Don Luis de Velasco. A soft or careless person would not have remained, as he did, in such an unpleasant job, nor would he have been selected by the good and great Velasco to continue such inspections elsewhere. Lebrón represented the interests of the Crown, which may be admitted to have been more concerned with determining the real situation in its colonies, than were the special interests of the encomenderos. The gradual disappearance of the native population in the coastal regions of this part of Mexico was a general phenomenon, which will receive later attention. For the most part, these lowlands, and some are rich and great, are only now in process of reoccupation. With respect to its resources, no part of the hot country is at present occupied as extensively as the highland.

We know that Cihuatlán was one of the centers of greatest interest at the time of the Conquest. If Lebrón determined that there were twenty-seven encomenderos in this one valley at the outset, there is no basis for saying that he falsified his statement. The Suma[1] recorded that the valley was greatly diminished in population "a causa de aver sido depositado en muchas personas." Whether that valley supported fifteen thousand men is a matter of opinion, and was so stated by Lebrón. He was in a better position to judge, one generation after the first Spanish settlement, than we are today. It is true that the Cihuatlán district has very rich land and good growing seasons and is at present an area of active immigration. For Alima I can give some measure of corroboration. This rich and broad river valley is very poorly developed and sparsely inhabited at the present time. I have walked over the ruins of a great aboriginal town, which appears to be the aboriginal Alima. Mounds and occupational debris stretch for about a league. There is at present only an occasional hut and small clearing in this locality, which formerly held a settlement of almost urban proportions.

Perhaps the clearest indication of former conditions is given by the area once known as the Valle de Milpa, including Autlán, in southwestern Jalisco. For this area we have the advantage of published results of intensive archeological study by Dr. Isabel Kelly, and a village-by-village visita made in connection with the entrada of Francisco Cortés in 1525, which she has also exploited with care in

---

1. Suma, No. 175.

her monograph.[2] Her intimate study of prewhite occupation com-
pares place by place the archeological site and the Conquest record. I
know of no other area in the New World for which there is available
an early sixteenth-century place-by-place visita, made immediately
after the Spanish penetration. Here for once we leave the field of
speculative and temperamental reconstructions, because we have a
record of the number of houses in each town and village. Dr. Kelly's
conclusion is that the present population of this area, today the best
settled and best developed in all of early Spanish Colima, "seems if
anything to be somewhat less" than at the time of the Conquest. I
should increase her aboriginal estimate by one-third, for the following reason. She says: ". . . it seems entirely legitimate to assume that
the total population could not have been less than three times that
figure"[3] (i.e., the visita figures of "hombres"). In modern Jalisco the
proportion of males between fifteen and fifty-five is almost exactly
one-fourth the total population. In an area aboriginally at a comfortable cultural level, such as the Valle de Milpa obviously was, there is
no reason for postulating disturbed sex ratios, or a diminished proportion of children and aged as compared with present conditions. If
a multiplier of four is used instead of three, and an apparent error of
one thousand in the transcription of males for Autlán is corrected,[4]
the 1525 population of the Valle de Milpa (with Autlán) should be
placed at around thirty-seven thousand or nearly one-half greater
than its contemporary population. Thus, perhaps not by coincidence, we have the same result as for original Colima.

For the remaining components attached to colonial Colima,
comparable data are not at hand. The Valle de Espuchimilco was
obviously more populous before the Conquest than it has been since,
and it is at present one of the most active areas of colonization in
Jalisco. It was visited only in part after the entrada of Francisco

---

2. Isabel Kelly, *The Archaeology of the Autlán-Tuxcauesco Area of Jalisco,* I: The
Autlán Zone, *Ibero-Americana, No. 26* (1945), pp. 4–19.

3. Ibid., p. 21.

4. Throughout the visita able-bodied males were estimated as two per house.
Yet in the enumeration of Autlán, 1,200 houses were converted to 1,400 males. I
infer the dropping of one thousand in the figure for males in the Roman notation,
perhaps in transcription from the Roman notation of the original.

Cortés and I am unable, in view of the greatly changed toponymy of the present, to identify which part was recorded. The pueblos of Martin Monje of colonial days, now stretching from Tenamaxtlán south beyond Union de Tula, were included only in small part in the visita of the Francisco Cortés entrada, and those visited had been in considerable part destroyed in the Conquest. It is apparent, however, that their population was smaller than at present. This may be explained in part by the fact that its inhabitants were rather primitive in comparison with their neighbors, and in part by the fact that this wide, cool, upland country is characterized by clay soils, which are well suited to plow cultivation, but were not well adapted to Indian cultivation. Here the site value has changed markedly under modern circumstances, but this is not true for the areas previously considered. The ancient provinces of Hernán Cortés, inland from the Colima volcanoes, I should judge to be more populous today than at the time of the Conquest, in part because of industrial developments, such as at Ciudad Guzmán.

The general picture as I see it is, therefore, that in the tierra caliente, population is not yet back to pre-Conquest levels, but that on the highland it has exceeded aboriginal densities. For the entire area of the visita of Lebrón, I judge that aboriginal totals were not far below contemporary ones.

## Notes on Aboriginal Culture

### COLIMA PROPER

The aboriginal western extent of Nahua speech, formerly claimed to be quite wide, has now been reduced (by Mendizabal and Jiménez Moreno)[5] to very modest proportions. Indeed, all that may be attributed to such western Nahua peoples is approximately the area of the present state of Colima. As is often true in Latin America, the modern political boundary coincides closely with an old ethnic limit. This Colima area, apparently an island of Nahua speech, is as

---

5. Miguel O. de Mendizabal and Wigberto Jiménez Moreno, *Distribucion prehispanica de las lenguas indigenas de Mexico* (Mexico City, Museo Nacional), map.

little understood as are similar islands in Central America. The language, which is somewhat divergent from Nahuatl or Aztecan, has not been studied, but is still spoken by a rapidly diminishing number of older people in several villages of the state, such as Xilosuchitlan, Ixtlahuacán, and Tamala. Lebrón declared that the original Indian town of Tuxpan lay where the Spanish village of Colima was relocated (at its present site). In that case, at least a part of the large Nahua-speaking group surviving to the present in Tuxpan would have immigrated to its present situation in Jalisco as the result of the Spanish Conquest. In other words, the Tuxpan Indians may be the chief survivors of the Colima Nahua.

It is probable that the land between the Volcán de Colima and the sea had not been brought completely under dominance by Nahua colonists, and that the latter were acculturated in their ways of living to the modes they found on entering the coastal areas. The later archeological horizons appear to indicate a great deal of cultural diversity and to have little to do with the Aztecan archeology of Central Mexico. There survived at the date of the Conquest a few apparently non-Nahua place names in Colima proper, such as Damasco, Iloli, Mazungatle, Avalaut, and Atlachaque. Lebrón, unfortunately, devoted most of his report to administrative problems and scarcely touched on ethnic matters. He did remark upon the extreme diversity of language he encountered in all parts of his visita, even asserting that in small pueblos three or four different modes of speech might be found, but he made no statement that could be localized.

The area of Colima proper does not seem to have been unified politically in Indian days. The central part was designated as the Provincia del Colimotl, named after a chieftain, and this seems to have been a political unit of some importance. That the Valle de Tecomán represented a separate unit is indicated in particular by the statement of Lebrón that it alone offered resistance to the Spaniards. The land to the west of the Colima River was referred to as the Provincia de Tepetitango, and the two border valleys of Alima and Cihuatlán (whence originated the story of the Amazons as brought by Sandoval to Cortés) were also identified as distinct provinces— political groupings of population.

Place names tell little about the mode of life. Xolotlan and Tamala refer to maize, and Chiapa refers to the cultivation of *chia* (*Hyptis* or *Salvia*), as Yxcatlan does to that of cotton. Somewhat interesting are the place names referring to garden trees: Abacatitlan (*ahuacate*), Xocotlan (probably *Spondias*), Zapotlanejo, and Quautecomatlan (perhaps only the wild Crescentia alata, though since this is very widespread in the area, it is not a likely source of a place name). Coyutlan probably refers to one of the great stands of coyol or coquito palms, still a conspicuous and somewhat mysterious feature along this coast. Xicotlan was a place of bees; Iztapa, of salt.

The Suma gives a consistent picture. Maize was paid as tribute generally, and where irrigation was practiced two crops a year were grown. Frijoles seem to have come mostly from the hill pueblos. Far and away the most important tribute was in cotton, or more generally in *mantas, camisas, toldillos* and *camas pintadas*. Cotton was probably the most important negotiable crop of the lowlands; Alima was noted for its cotton production, and special mention is made also of Tecomán. Both Cihuatlán and Tecomán seem to have excelled in the quality of their weaving, as might be expected from their more urban character. Cacao, by the time of the Suma, was grown mostly in *huertas* belonging to Spaniards, but it is certain that it was an aboriginal crop in the coastal margins as far north as Tepic. Turkeys were a common tribute. Honey was a major tribute, reported either by number of *calabazos* (the large form of Lagenaria gourd) or by *jarros* (pottery jars). Tepetitango and Quezalapa also paid *tepuzques* (copper and gold alloy), twelve of them worth one peso of *oro comun*. These two places are on the edge of a once important mining country, and the tribute may have represented Indian smelting or copper-gold ore. Salt and fish came from coastal villages.

What we know of old Colima is very meager, and we shall not know much more until the rich archeology is properly developed. Colonial exploitation swept aside most of the native ways. The stingless native bees are still kept in log hives in the houses of small lowland villages. Muscovy ducks and Mexican turkeys are common in Indian communities. There is an occasional patch of *yuca* (*Manihot*). The *ciruelas* (*Spondias*) are the usual summer fruit in settlements lacking irrigation. One selected type, known as the ciruela de Mispan, is sold widely in native markets. The pre-Conquest pueblo of Mispani has disappeared, but around its site there are gnarled stands of this large-fruited, greenish-skinned *Spondias,* which is apparently an old horticultural variety reproduced by cuttings. There is no assurance that the coconut was present in Colima before the Spaniard, although I think it probably was. The Ponce account stresses its importance, but apparently does not consider it introduced. The Ponce account was written only a few years after the Philippine trade was started. I judge the papaya to be post-Spanish in local distribution, but its humble relative, the *bonete* (*Jacaratia mexicana*), is a familiar fruit at the unirrigated village margins. It was well described in the Ponce account.

Fine ceramics, especially effigy jars, have been and are being dug up and peddled far and wide from this area and are thus lost to identification. A high culture was destroyed here, its remains still awaiting discovery and interpretation.

## THE MOTÍN REGION

In the mountains and coast of the Motín region of adjacent Michoacán, but originally a part of Colima, there is a preponderance of non-Nahua names such as Aquila, Maquili, Alimanci(nique)(?), Suchicin(ique)(?), Gualoxa, Tlatic(t)la(?), Motín, Motenpacoya, Maroata, Coyre, Pomaro, Giroma, Cachan.

We are better informed of this mountain land than of Colima proper because there are relaciónes of 1580[6] extant for all but the most westernmost part (Aquila and Maquili). These documents contain specific information on aboriginal conditions.

The reporters agree that there was a marked diminution of population from aboriginal levels by 1580. Alimanci was said to have exceeded three hundred, Cuzcaquahtla four hundred, Epatlan five hundred tributaries, or grown males. A number of local aboriginal languages were spoken, which were not named, but at least by the latter part of the sixteenth century Mexicano was in general use,

---

6. "Relaciónes de los Motínes," MS in RAHM, 12–18–3, no. 16.

though its form "was corrupt," a phrase that perhaps refers to the use of the Colima Nahua as a medium of intervillage communication. A few names are interpreted in the old records and may perhaps serve as linguistic clues.

| | |
|---|---|
| Borbitni, Yuitlan in Nahua | = place of feathers |
| Dibo, Ostupila in Nahua | = place of frogs |
| Yanum, Ostutla in Nahua | = place of skunks |
| Motin | = place of many ashes |
| Pomaro | = conversation of the gods |
| Vaasi | = idol in human form |
| Gatagui (also Catagui) | = sierra |
| Puhuhari | = sierra corcovada |
| Tagui | = sierra para hacer rozas |

The "Relaciónes de los Motínes"[7] sketch a land of steep mountains, deeply gashed by canyons, with spurs trimmed into formidable cliffs by the sea, and barrier beaches built across the valley mouths, enclosing salt lagoons behind. Land and sea breezes gave daily change to the coastal climate. Small alluvial floors formed valuable farm land, but of very restricted extent, and most of the area reminded one reporter of the wild Cantabrian Mountains of Asturias.

Of wild vegetation there were noted the deciduous and live oaks in the higher lands; palms, such as the noble *quascoyule (Orbignia?)* on the coastal slope and the fan-palm *zoyamichin (Acanthorrhiza?);* the copal-bearing *thecomahacat* and *suchicopal* species of *Bursera*, which only the people of Aquila and Maquili gathered for gum; brazilwood *(Haematoxylum)* in abundance; the wide-spreading *guanacastle (Enterolobium); and* the *quaolote (Parmentiera edulis).* These are familiar in the flora of the west Mexican coast and lower mountain flanks, mostly at the altitudes of the deciduous dry jungle forest, below the higher, oak-crowned levels. Cane *(otate)* grew in swampy places of fresh water and was important for construction. There is also note of a variety of seaweed that was collected for food from the ocean.

---

7. Ibid.

A more important plant group, of semidomesticated character, was mentioned. *Quelites,* or pot herbs, were cooked and roasted with *tamales* and *cacalotes.* The horticulture of these people may have consisted in the protection rather than in the planting of desirable fruits. "Wine" was important for ritual drinking and was made from ciruelas (*Spondias*) and maguey. *Magueyales,* stands of maguey, are mentioned but we cannot judge whether these were planted areas or merely protected patches assuring this major source of food, drink, and fiber. *Zapotes* were both white and black (*Casimiroa edulis,* and *Diospyros ebenaster*); the *Chicozapote (Achras zapote)* was common, as was the *mamey (Calocarpum mammosum),* the *guamochil (Pithecollobium dulce),* the *ylama zapote* and *anona* (probably both species of *Annona*). The list is the usual one of tropical coast fruits from Sinaloa to Central America.

The contemporary list of cultivated native crops is notable for its fullness. The Indians had small cacao gardens and they were generally supplied with ahuacates. Maize, beans, and squash were of course basic crops. Repeated reference is made to a white pulse called *chonetli,* "ground, dissolved, and cooked in water" and then used as a milky drink. The Spanish term *hava,* as distinguished from the *frisoles (frijoles),* separately named, indicates something larger than a white navy bean. Its use in times of hunger would indicate an inferior but drought-resistant legume. It may have been the white-seeded *Phaseolus coccineus,* or possibly *Canavalia ensiformis.* Chili pepper was grown and, as usual, the most desirable forms came from a temperate locality, in this case from Pomaro, yielding "a type unto itself which neither burns excessively nor is too short in pungency." Of starch foods there was, in addition, much yuca or manioc (*cuauhcamotes*), sweet potatoes, and the cultivated chia (*Salvia* or *Hyptis*). Tomatoes, peanuts, and pineapple are listed, and also cotton and tobacco or *piciete* (not *Nicotiana tabacum,* but probably *rustica*).

Faunal notes reveal a plague of blood-sucking bats, and of aggressive caymans, preying upon those who had to cross the streams, in particular the Río Motín. Rivers and sea provided a variety of fish, mussels, shrimps, prawns, and crayfish. In the mountains deer and wild pigs were hunted, and the brush yielded *faisanes grandes, negros* (curassow?), and lesser game fowl. Wild honey was gathered, but no bees were kept. Two domesticated animals were identified. "They raised birds native to this country which are larger than pavos"; this may be a reference to the keeping of turkeys. "They raised a breed of dogs to eat. These had very short hair and grew fat with little feeding, and they raised them in pens, and when they were fat they were killed and eaten in feasts. This breed of dogs has become extinct so that there is not one left." This refers to the little edible "hairless" dogs, aboriginally present as far north as southern Nayarit.

Salt, made from sea water, was an important product; the manner of getting it was described in some detail for Tlatica.

> They make salt in small quantities and with some difficulty, watering first the beach from jugs containing sea water. After two or three waterings they heap this watered sand into piles. The heaps made, they take jars *(ollas* or *tinajas),* and place one upon the other. The top jar has some small holes in its base, like the openings in flutes, on which are placed straw mats. Into the upper jar they then place such water-drenched sand until it is a little more than half filled, and then they turn [rotate?] it to expel the sea water and this water drips into the jar below and this filtered water comes out very wholesome and is drawn off into their jugs, which they take to their houses to boil, placing it on the fire until it is boiled down and converted into salt. This is the art and manner of making salt which they have in this pueblo and in those of Motín, Maruata, Pasnori, and Cachan because they have no natural salines, such as there are in other places.

The procedure seems somewhat complicated, but the beach sand probably absorbed certain salts, other than sodium chloride, and served as a partial means of purifying the table salt. Such base exchange would take place in particular if the sand carries, as it does locally, ferro-magnesian minerals.

Cotton was woven, but there is little said about clothes. In one locality loin cloths seem to have sufficed. In another, shirts, rude breeches, and thin cotton mantles were customary. Maguey fiber was used in making hammocks, ropes, and net bags dyed with colors.

Preparation of food included the light roasting and dry grinding of corn for pinole and the soaking and wet grinding into dough for tamales and tortillas. There is reference to the use of a flat woven pannier made of strips of cane and used for holding the corn dough.

Weapons were of greater interest to the Spanish reporter than clothes. In addition to bows, arrows, and quivers, throwing spears or darts were made of poles with fire-pointed ends. Their ingenious construction was chiefly directed to defense. The round shields, or *chimales,* so common in the north and throughout Jalisco, are well described:

> They were four or five hands wide, made of the cane called otate, split into thin pieces, and joining one strip with another, and so they proceeded to weave them with much skill, so that of these strips there resulted a woven fabric. Thereupon they wove another of the same dimension and fashion. Having finished weaving these two fabrics they joined them, placing one across the other, and sewing them with a back seam with great nicety, thus trimming the shield round. Having attached the handgrips the shield was finished and was a suitable arm for defending themselves from the stones and arrows of their adversaries. The shield was so strong that an arrow could scarcely penetrate it.

In another place reference is made to a practice of reinforcing them with a pithy gum—perhaps the same plant gum that is still used instead of nails and mortises to fasten chairs in this part of Mexico. A quilted cuirass was also common—called *ychcaxicoli,* "like a form of quilt made of a great quantity of cotton, tightly packed, to the thickness of a finger more or less. Thus woven, they made what they wished of the quilt, helmets, and jackets and thigh-coverings and other forms of armor as they wished, and if it was well made it could not be punctured by arrows." The reporter continues: "The people of this province were not excessively bellicose, nor yet given to such cowardice that they fled from their enemies; rather they knew how to resist and defend their houses and lands."

House building required first the setting of a series of posts, forked at the top. Into these forks the principal beam poles were tied with cords of bark. Rafter poles were then tied on to serve as the immediate frame for the roof. These in turn had small withes laid upon them and then finally a thick cover of grass tied on. The roof was the most important part of the house—probably much the same sort of long overhanging palm or grass thatch that still serves to keep out rain and sun and wind in this tropical coast. Both relations refer to *tijeras* on the roof—X-shaped timbers. Most likely these were "horses" set on the ridgepole to hold the thatch in place. All roof construction was tied on. Apparently mud-daubed wattle walls were employed in part.

Of further artifacts we are told that the people of this area made *equipales*—a name given in this section to drum-shaped chairs with diagonal braces of wood held by a plant bitumen. We are also told that they smoked pipes made of segments of cane and called *yaquales*.

The sum of these contemporary notes shows that because of its environment, the culture of the Motín region was somewhat lower than that of Jalisco and Tepic.

## COALCOMÁN (QUACOMAN)

Coalcomán was an Indian province inland from the Motín Range, for which a brief relación of 1580[8] exists, less adequate than the report on the Motín area. "The climate and quality of this pueblo is temperate, more cold than hot. It is a humid land, of many waters. The subject settlements are of different temperatures. One of them called Tehuantepec is a very cold land and all the rest are hot. Coalcomán is built in a great plain surrounded by very high hills covered with oak and pine groves." The central part of this area thus rose high above the tropical levels found in the deep valleys falling away to the south.

Again the report is of a once greater population that lived dispersed in the hills and valleys (*cerros y quebradas*). "The language is called neither more or less than the pueblo, *quaucomeca tlatalli,* which indicates (in Aztec) the language of the Quaucomecas. The people have a very obscure language, but generally all speak and understand the Mexican language." Most of its place names have come to us in a Nahua version, but Toquali, Patichani, and Olan seem to be aboriginal names.

---

8. "Relación de Quacoman," MS in RAHM, 12–18–3, no. 16.

The cultural data available are rather trivial, the reporter obviously thinking that Indians were of little account anyway. In this cooler land agriculture was mainly reduced to the maize, beans, and squash complex. Maguey, apparently cultivated, was an important element in the economy, for sweet syrup, wine, and vinegar, but also as fiber, including the making of blankets. The diversity suggests several species of agave. The notation: "White honey is produced in the montes where the natives have many beehives," is another record of native beekeeping, an activity common to the Maya country, Colima, and Sinaloa, the northernmost outpost of this culture trait.

A curious note on natural history is contained in the explanation of the name Coalcomán. It was thus called "because anciently, before the land was conquered, there were here some animals of the manner of red and black cows, which are said to have had very large horns (and of these animals at present there are none)." This cannot quite be dismissed as an idle tale, for Düsselhof, in archeological excavations in Colima, noted the occurrence of bones of large ruminants in underground burial chambers. We also heard such described, independently, by natives in several localities, who had excavated crypts for salable pottery. They were spoken of as bones of cows.

This area politically, though not ethnically, belonged to the Tarascan state. "In the days of their heathendom, say the natives, they recognized the Cazonzi, who was the natural lord of the Province of Michoacán, to whom they gave obedience and tribute." Tarascan power was in process of being extended to the coast. In the Motín report of the Tlatica Valley is this statement: "At times they were at war with the Tarascans, who occasionally entered, captured, killed, and ate [their people], and also they were warred upon by the Epateco [people of Epatlan], who are to the west seven leagues, which was an immigrant population from the province of the Tarascans that took possession in this land and coast of the sea, and were very great eaters of human flesh, as were the same Tarascans, and with the one and the other they [the people of Tlatica] had wars." It seems that the Coalcomán area was ruled by Tarascans, whereas the land beyond the Motín Range was only occasionally invaded, except for the Epatec coastal colony that had come from Michoacán. These "immigrants" to the coast may or may not have been Tarascan themselves, but they show that cultural influences had spread from Michoacán to the coast, across Coalcomán, at the time of the Conquest (possibly for the purposes of securing salt?).

## TAMAZULA, ZAPOTLÁN, AND TUSPA

The fringe of the Mexican plateau between the Volcán de Colima and the western mountain border of Michoacán, marked by the three important centers of Tamazula, Zapotlán (Ciudad Guzmán) and Tuspa (Tuxpan), is the connecting corridor both between Jalisco and Colima, and Michoacán and Colima. Aboriginally, and in early colonial days, its principal relations were with Colima proper, although its transitional and connecting relations to Michoacán and Jalisco are also marked.

The "Relación de Tuspa, Tamazula, y Zapotlán"[9] (1580) for these provinces stresses their populousness before the coming of the whites. Of Tamazula it was asserted: "In the time of their heathendom there was a much greater quantity of people, so much so that they claimed twenty thousand Indios and more." Tamazula itself was called a *ciudad* in the suit of Cortés in 1531 for the recovery of encomiendas taken by the First Audiencia.[10]

These Indians were regarded as more advanced than those in most of the peripheral areas of Colima. Those of Zapotlán were "of acute understanding and good dispositions." Their skills were appreciated and the Indians of all three towns were known as traders. Thus in the "Suma de Visitas de Pueblos" the Indians of Tuxpan are noted as "having many chief and rich merchants, a people polished and of high knowledge *(mucha razon)*," and similar statements are made for the other two.[11]

This area has generally been regarded as Nahua territory, yet it would seem to have been less so than the state of Colima. The Suma and also the "Relación de Tuspa, Tamazula, y Zapotlán" (1580), significantly, speak of Naguales, indicating the more ancestral form

---

9. MS in RAHM, 12–18–3, no. 16.
10. HC-RA, pp. 339–407.
11. Suma, Nos. 115, 551, 552.

of Nahua speech which Alonso Ponce called "naval or corrupt Mexican."[12] But Lebrón states that the original Tuxpan was situated where the city of Colima now stands! In the relocation of the villa from its coastal position to the foot of the mountains, these Indians were dispossessed of their land in order to satisfy the extensive needs of the villa. It seems that they transferred about 1525 to their present highland position east of the Volcán, thus greatly reinforcing, at the least, the Nahual element in that district. The relación of 1580 for this area observes that Tuxpan "has two different languages, which some of the inhabitants do not understand and all in general can speak the Mexican language. Their natural languages are called, one Tiam and the other Cochin." This suggests an earlier substratum of two, unclassifiable languages, with a pre- and post-Conquest overlay of the West Coast Nahual.

Of Tamazula the Suma records: "They are by language Pinol, [and/or?] Chichimecas, and there are Naguales and Tarascans among them." Thus, again, there is clear implication of an earlier stock overlain by Nahual and Tarascan. The 1580 relación for this area claims only one aboriginal language, here called Tamazulteca, plus Nahual and Michoacán (Tarascan). The problem of the Chichimecas may be the same as that for the state of Michoacán (e.g., the "Chichimec" background in the "Relación de las Ceremonios y Ritos de Michoacán").[13] Is Tamazulteca to be equated with Pinol (plural, Pinome), a name appearing mysteriously over a wide area in the western mountains? The Suma[14] places the Pinol first in Tamazula province and rates the general level of the population as advanced. There may be here a faint evidence of a pre-Nahua stock of high cultural level. The Ponce account[15] says the language of Tamazula was a "distinct speech called that of Xilotlancingo which runs for many leagues toward the South Sea." Xilotlan is a mountain district below Tuxpan toward Coalcomán. The Ponce account places Pinome south of Lake Chapala. This language therefore held the mountain border between Michoacán on one side and Jalisco and Colima on the other—a typical retreat location.

---

12. Op. cit., II, 112.      14. No. 552.
13. In CDIE, LIII.      15. Op. cit., p. 114.

For Zapotlán the 1580 relación lists four languages which the aborigines "used anciently and still use, these are called Mechoacan, Zayulteca, Zapoteca, and Nagual, [the last] is Mexican and in general all speak it. Formerly the pueblo was called Tlaynla that is to say a land of much maize, and, they say, that the first founder was the Lord of Michoacán." The Suma relates that the Indian traders of this place used different languages. The Ponce account[16] mentions Naval and Tzaulteca, which is Sayultec. Again, it may be inferred that there were two earlier linguistic and ethnic stocks, the one called Zapotec, from the name of the town, and the other Sayultec—a group that had a distribution of some importance around the nearby Sayula area of Jalisco. Nahual and Tarascan would then represent later comers, who were probably economically and politically superior.

All three of these "provinces" were political dependencies of the Tarascan state. According to the 1580 relación, "these three pueblos and their subject villages belonged to the Cazonzi, King of Michoacán, to whom they paid tribute." Of Zapotlán it was said "that they were governed by a chief who was designated by the King of Michoacán, to whom they gave obedience and whom they served and provided with food and built his house and sowed his crops." On the other hand they were enemies of the people of Colima, Cihuatlán, Autlán, Cuzalapa, Tenamastlan, and of Ameca, Etzatlan, and Ahualulco. This makes the aboriginal political geography clear. This upland country was the next to the last outpost of Tarascan power, and, according to the "Ceremonias y Ritos de Michoacán,"[17] one of the last to be brought into that political structure. Beyond, to the west and south, lay a series of small and probably mutually independent tribal aggregates, subject to raids from the Tarascan group. Each of the three districts had a head chief, who apparently was a Tarascan governor. But Tamazula "was the capital of all this province and subordinate to it were those of Tuxpan and Zapotlán and their dependent villages and also those of Amula which is outside of this province."[18]

---

16. Ibid., II, 115.
17. In CDIE, LIII.
18. "Relación de Tuspa, Tamazula, y Zapotlán," MS in RAHM.

The picture given of production taken from the 1580 relación is very favorable. Above all this was a notable land for maize growing. The ordinary food was maize, frijoles, venison, chile, and many kinds of cooked vegetables, with turkey added at feasts. Further enumerated as products are *chia (Salvia hispanica?), bledo* (amaranth), *verdulaga* (cultivated greens, *Portulaca?),* tomatoes, squash, and *piciete* (native tobacco, *Nicotiana rustica*). For Zapotlán and Tamazula *zoal* was identified as a crop. This is a name still used for cultivated grain amaranth. What distinction was in mind between zoal and bledo is not clear unless one name was applied to a grain amaranth and the other to a grain chenopodium. Turkeys were raised and honey was gathered from the mountains. Termed "wild," but perhaps better considered as naturalized, were guayava, ahuacate, sapotes, ciruelas, guamuchil *(Pithecollobium)*—there were many useful groves of these trees. An indigo plant dye was secured. The Ponce account[19] adds the fruit-tree called *bonete de abad (Jacaratia mexicana).*

Tribute paid to Michoacán included goods (mantas) of cotton, and blue skirts *(naguas),* feathers from parrots and other large birds, or, in another place, "great colored feathers." In view of their proximity to the cool mountain forests of the Volcán and the report to be given later from Cuzalapa, we may wonder whether *quetzal* feathers may be meant. Indian captives taken from adjacent areas were also given as tribute.

Especially noteworthy is tribute of silver "drawn very fine," paid to the Tarascan overlord. The natives adorned their idols with silver. Tamazula had ancient rich silver mines, and Zapotlán paid tribute in silver. The important question of native silver-working is considered later in discussing the further development of Spanish occupation.

A note on clothing found in the 1580 relación says that: "Anciently they wore a closed, narrow piece (manta) of white cotton which reached to their shins and over it a colored manta." Arms included bows and arrows, lances of moderate length of sharpened

19. Op. cit., II, 112.

wood, clubs of heavy wood, and shields; in warfare pennants of feathers were used.[20]

## AMULA

Although the pueblo of Amula was soon removed and dispersed from its early location, the name was commonly applied in the sixteenth century to the mountain and barranca country forming the present border of Jalisco, from Tuxpan to the Valley of Cihuatlán, and included the northern and northwest slopes of the Volcán de Colima. Since it was, on the whole, a country of strong relief and considerable elevation, it lacked for the most part tropical lowlands and extensive upland valleys suitable for cultivation. Alluvial fields in canyon floor and benchlike surface on ridges had to be supplemented by fields built precariously on sharp declivities. This is a land poor even for aboriginal conditions, more suitable as a refuge for a weak people than as a base for an aggressive and expanding culture.

The entire reach of the Amula region is unanimously recorded as being inhabited by Otomi. It is surprising to find Otomi so far west and one might be inclined to interpret this as a general term for simple mountain folk. It seems, however, that the evidence really indicates Otomi. In the Suma, Copala is peopled by folk who are

20. Certain religious notes are markedly reminiscent both of Mexico and Maya lands. Thus for Tuxpan (1580 relación): "They held the skies to be God and believed there were eight heavens. And some there were who were glad that they should be killed wearing the best clothes which they had and said that they wished to go to the sky to serve the sun. After they were killed, their clothes were taken, and they were beheaded, and cooked and eaten." For Zapotlán: "They had sorcerers to talk with the stone idol which they held to be god and there gave [us] to understand that the god answered them and they sacrificed to it some Indians which had been taken in battle and took out their hearts and with the blood anointed the stone which was held to be god. After this they beheaded the victims and stuffed the skins with straw and danced about and ate the human flesh." For Tamazula: "They held the sky which they called hihuite cozaquic (meaning green and yellow) to be god and understood there were nine heavens and there lived an aguapile or mistress whom they called Ehua cueye (señora) who had a petticoat of hides and whom they held to be their mother. For forty days there assembled the chiefs, whom they regarded as priests, after which they went to the neighboring hills and let blood from their tongues and ears which they sacrificed and thereupon heard a voice speaking to them."

"Otomis and poor," in Zapotitlan "the people are poor and are Oto-mis," Teutitlan is inhabited by "Otomis and they are very poor." The association here is with poverty, not with the barbaric manner of hill folk. In the Suma, tribal names are introduced sparingly, usually to set apart a group that differs markedly in economic status from its neighbors.

The relaciónes (1579)[21] leave no doubt that they mean Otomi speech. In the depositions for this area native ancients gave the prin-cipal statements, and still, at this relatively late date, spoke through interpreters. The Amula province was divided in the relaciónes into three parts—the Zapotitlan district to the east, Tuxcacuesco in the middle and Cuzalapa in the west, and information was gathered from the full reach of aboriginal Amula. The two ancients of Zapoti-tlan said: "The language which the people speak among themselves is Otomi, and this is spoken by all the natives of the subject villages of this pueblo; but generally they speak and use Mexican."[22] For the Tuxcacuesco and Cuzalapa districts there were also flat statements by the Indian spokesmen of each that the language was Otomi.[23]

The Ponce account does not name the language, but calls it simply a "lengua particular," which was also spoken in one pueblo of Colima, Zacualpan, the rest of Colima using Nahual or "corrupt Mexican."

The data on economy in the relaciónes indicate that the major support came from the highlands, though some of the barrancas were deep enough to provide some tropical crops. Thus an early chief of Zapotitlan had some groves of cacao, yet for their clothing the natives bartered goods for cotton from Colima. At Cuzalapa they could raise two crops of maize a year[24] and also paid tribute in jars of honey.[25] The relaciónes indicate the importance of maguey in the mountain eyries of the Zapotitlan area—"for wine, vinegar, honey,

---

21. "Relación de Ameca" and "Relación de Amula, Tuxcacuesco, y Cusa-lapa" in *NV.*

22. "Relación de Amula . . . ," *NV,* p. 287.

23. At Cuzalapa the name of a chief may be Otomi: *Ercape,* the flea that bites.

24. Suma, No. 169.

25. Ibid., No. 199.

rope, clothing, wood, needles, nails, thread, and balm for wounds." "Wine" was also made of ciruelas (*Spondias*) and, in Tuxcacuesco at least, dogs were raised for food.

Other memories of ancient days set down by their survivors in the relaciónes were: at Cuzalapa, where life seems to have been most primitive, the aborigines paid no tribute to their chief but only planted his crops. At Tuxcacuesco they remembered the war clubs that had been studded with stone points and the cotton armor of old, and that the ancient houses had been made of canes plastered with mud and covered with straw that was bound down by ropes *(mecates)*. The informants at Zapotitlan were most communicative and drew what appears to be a somewhat roseate picture of their past. (It is to be remembered, however, that Zapotitlan was in closest connection with the high cultures around the Volcán). Formerly, they said, they went very well clothed in cotton garments of many colors and designs and wore many necklaces of gold and silver. Their own lord was overthrown by the Cazonzi of Michoacán (which is confirmed by Tarascan records) who set over them three governors. Later, it was claimed this alien rule was overthrown and they again had a chief whose name signified "the man dressed in silver." Repeated reference to aboriginal silver in this area, immediately adjacent to Tamazula, suggests either the existence of a silver trade from the latter source, or, possibly, an extension of aboriginal silver-working into some nonvolcanic part of eastern Amula. A final note excerpted from Zapotitlan concerns the making of rafts from calabashes placed in a net of ropes, in which about a hundred calabashes were used.

## THE NORTHWESTERN BORDER

We are concerned here with three territories: (1) the temperate highland about Tenamaxtlán and Tecolutlan, falling away southward toward (2) the warm, fertile basin of Milpa and Autlán, and (3) to the west, from the latter across a mountain range, the tropical Valle de Espuchimilco.

For nearly every pueblo visited in the entrada of Francisco Cortés, the identification is that the people were Otomi. For Xiquitlan in Milpa there is an additional statement that there were ten or twelve houses of *naguatatos,* probably meaning Nahua-speaking group. In the Suma Milpa,[26] Xiquitlan,[27] and Zacapala[28] in the Valle de Milpa are identified as Otomi, and in the Espuchimilco area Apamila,[29] Xonacatlan,[30] and Coyutlan[31] are thus labeled. The 1579 "Relación de Tenamaxtlán"[32] has two native languages, mutually unintelligible. Only one non-Mexican word was noted, *pupuca,* the name of a deity (reproduced in stone idols), which puffed smoke from eyes and mouth. The Mendizabal-Jiménez Moreno map[33] places a Cuyuteca and Cacoma speech in this area, on the authority of sources unknown to me. Ponce's account identified a local language, Auteca, for Autlán and Zacapula.[34] The reporter for Tenamaxtlán in 1579 thought the native stock very tall and strong, an unusual comment on physique to be heard this far south. The Otomi question, which was raised for the Amula district, applies therefore also to the whole northwestern frontier.

As for cultural level, the 1525 entrada used the term "gente pobre" for each of the northern pueblos of Tenamaxtlán, Ayutla, and their surroundings, but not for any of the pueblos of the Milpa and Espuchimilco basins, with the exception of Tequezistlan where, it said, the up-country people were poor. The latter pueblo and Acautlan were settled in barrios. In the Milpa basin Autlán, Ayuquila, Xiquitlan, Tlacaltescal, Milpa, and Teutlichanga were noted as having *tiangues* (organized markets). By the time of the Suma only Autlán was rated as being of high culture, "gente de razon y rezia" and as having a good income. Milpa,[35] Xiquitlan,[36] Zacapala,[37] and, in

---

26. Ibid., No. 368.
27. Ibid., No. 816.
28. Ibid., No. 172.
29. Ibid., No. 41.
30. Ibid., No. 171.
31. Ibid.
32. "Relación de Tenamaxtlán," in *NV.*
33. In their *Distribucion prehispanica de las lenguas indigenas de Mexico.*
34. Op. Cit., II, 89, 96.
35. Suma, No. 368.
36. Ibid., No. 816.
37. Ibid., No. 172.

the Espuchimilco Valley, Apamila,[38] Xonacatlan,[39] and Coyutlan[40] were peopled by gente pobre; in Coyutlan the inhabitants were characterized as being "virtually irrational." It may be inferred that in the space of twenty years the natives had become much depressed in station, perhaps that a ruder substratum had largely replaced the people of higher culture. The system of *tiangues* did not accompany primitive living. Moreover, there is further evidence of this depression in the fact that in 1525 Milpa was a town of five hundred houses, with a large amount of maize under irrigation and groves of fruit trees whereas at the same time Autlán had twelve hundred houses (and two chiefs).

The apparent conclusion is that the Milpa-Autlán basin was originally an island of higher culture, with two centers of urban size. This view is well supported by Dr. Kelly's archeological studies, which also bring out relations to Cihuatlán and lower Colima. There are well-documented sources showing the presence of irrigated agriculture and fruit horticulture. At the time of the Suma, cochineal was produced and it may therefore have been an aboriginal culture. (In later colonial days the town was known as Autlán de la Grana, because of the importance of its cochineal industry.)

For the Tenamaxtlán area a simple level of culture is recorded. According to the relación of 1579 there were woods of large oaks and pines in the higher country, with mesquite in the valleys, as today. Oak served for making planting sticks, twelve to eighteen feet long, shaped like bakers' shovels. Pines provided torchwood for lighting. The shoots of fan palms were used for food, especially in time of shortage; their fibers gave cordage. The seeds of the *guasim* (probably *Leucaena glauca*) were eaten roasted with maize. The pods and seeds of mesquite were ground and stored as reserve supply of food. However, note was also made of two kinds of cultivated ahuacates, the black and the green-skinned ones of the size of quinces. Another stoneless fruit grown was probably an Annona. Guayava, guamuchil, and *Spondias* were also described, as well as *miltomates* and *jitomates*.

---

38. Ibid., No. 41.     39. Ibid., No. 815.     40. Ibid., No. 171.

SUMMARY OF ABORIGINAL CONDITIONS

The population of the entire area at the time of the Conquest I estimate very roughly to have been about three hundred and fifty thousand—two hundred thousand for the coast and tierra caliente in Colima proper, the Motín, Cihuatlán, Milpa-Autlán, and Espuchimilco, and a hundred and fifty thousand for the temperate and cool interior highlands: Tamazula, Zapotlán, Tuxpan, Amula west through Cuzalapa, the Martin Monje province, and Coalcomán. There were at least eight urban aggregations: in the lowlands, Alima, Tecomán, Cihuatlán, Autlán, and Milpa; in the highlands Tamazula, Zapotlán, and Tuxpan, each of them ranging from perhaps five to ten thousand inhabitants. Approximately a fifth of the total population therefore may have lived in centers larger and more complex than would have been formed by a wholly agricultural community.

The hot country was more highly developed and more densely settled than it is today. Irrigation was practiced more widely than was usual in this part of the world, giving two crops of maize per year, and making possible huerta culture, as for cacao, which does not grow in the local climate without much irrigation. The assemblage of cultivated plants lacked nothing aboriginally found in this part of the world. The maize-beans-squash complex was supplemented by sweet potato, sweet manioc or yuca, amaranth (possibly *Chenopodium*), peanut, chia, tomatoes, chile, a perennial cotton, piciete *(Nicotiana rustica)*, and the Lagenaria gourds. Pineapples were grown, and the cultivated fruit trees included cacao, ahuacate, ciruelas *(Spondias)*, chicozapote *(Achras zapote)*, zapote *(Calocarpum mammosum)*. More or less domesticated were annonas, huaje *(Leucaena)*, guayava, and bonete de abad *(Jacaratia)*. It is curious that no mention is found of the papaya among native fruits, but that in the accounts of the latter sixteenth century, *plátanos* (plantains) were not only a major foodstuff of the tierra caliente, but that they were placed in all the relaciónes under the heading of native fruits as distinguished from the introduced ones. If introduced by the Spaniards, they had not only spread exceedingly rapidly, but had become an intimate part of the native economy.

Highland agriculture locally could still use most of the afore-
mentioned crops, except cacao, pineapple, Calocarpum, and yuca.
Chicozapote and *Spondias* did not pass the lower margins of the
*tierra templada.* On the other hand the white zapote *(Casimiroa edulis)*
and black zapote *(Diospyros ebenaster)* flourish in the higher country,
and the former probably gave its name to the Zapotláns and the
Zapotitlans of the highlands. Chile and frijoles do better than in the
lowlands, and there is no doubt that these items were taken in quantity down to the lowland towns. Maguey was widely used for food,
drink, and fiber; there were probably several cultivated forms.

Dogs, bees, and, somewhat curiously, cochineal, which elsewhere is a cold land product, were important in the lowlands. Nowhere else is there an equal archeological record of the short-legged,
edible dog, commemorated also in the place name Ixcuintlan. Beekeeping in and around the houses was widespread, and honey has
been noted as an important source of tribute. These were the domestic, stingless bees, known from the Maya country to Sinaloa in the
lowlands. The muscovy duck and turkey were the familiar poultry.
In the highlands, the domestic animal economy was of much less
account, except possibly for turkeys. This may be due to a difference
in cultural attitude.

Mining and metallurgy are reserved for later discussion, because
above all else the native knowledge of mines and mining drew the
Spanish to this country. The larger highland towns, Tamazula, Zapotlán, and Tuxpan were commercial centers concerned with mining
operations in different degrees.

The simpler cultures were found for the most part in the poorer
lands, to the south in the Motín Range, and in the center—the
rough mountain country that stretches from the Volcán and Nevado
de Colima through the range of Cuzalapa toward the coast of Navidad. There were, however, more attractive highland areas, like those
around Tenamaxtlan, part of Amula, and Coalcomán (Quacoman)
that were left to the simpler folk. The general impression is that the
poor and difficult terrain harbored relic populations, known to history usually under the name of some local language of unknown
affiliation, or under the term Otomi. Such meager information as is

available on the Otomi indicates that they may really have belonged to that far-flung mountain folk of central Mexico, often regarded as ancient occupants, wherever they are found.

With the exception of the Autlán region, all of the high culture area had a strong overlay of Nahua speech and people. I do not think it can be regarded as more than that. In the Tamazula, Zapotlán, and Tuspa districts, it is fairly clear that Nahua speech had incompletely replaced older, local languages. Autlán archeology is closely related to that of parts of Colima; Colima spoke Nahua and Autlán did not. There is no indication that Nahua-speaking people were the producers of the high culture found locally. Instead, we may think that from wherever they immigrated they were acculturated into a preëxistent high, western, coastal culture. How old that culture was we have no present way of knowing, nor the date of colonization by the Nahua. The record of domestic plants and animals suggests that the basic culture was carried up along the coast from the south. At any rate, the last prehistoric event was the spread of Tarascan rule, and, in part, of Tarascan people, from Michoacán westward through Tamazula and Zapotlán into the province of Amula, and a lesser drive south along the western end of the Motín to the sea. The coming of the Spaniards probably stopped further expansion of Tarascan rule over this area.

# Gold and Silver
## as the Incentive for Colonization

Cristóbal de Olid and his men made a half-hearted gesture at organizing a Spanish community in Michoacán, which dissolved almost at once. Michoacán remained for some years longer an Indian land, unvexed by Spanish communities. Some of Olid's group drifted on to the Pacific, there to constitute first the nucleus of the town of Zacatula and then that of Colima. Thereafter, and until the coming of Nuño de Guzmán, Michoacán functioned, in Spanish terms, as a passageway to Zacatula and Colima. The Tarascan state did not oppose Spanish penetration or passage. From its treasures of rulers and temples the Spaniards acquired as presents and loot the greatest quantity of gold and silver that had fallen into their hands since the sack of Mexico. It was known to them, before they entered Michoacán, that from there came much if not most of the silver. Yet they pushed on through the Tarascan land, with little delay.

Cortés, who wrote most of the reports on the Conquest, was reticent about the resources of the newly-won land. He told his sovereign of the progress of his campaigns and of the moves he had in mind for the aggrandizement of the newly-won empire; he discreetly said very, very little about the wealth of the new lands and of their appropriation by the conquerors. Our knowledge of such matters must be pieced together from trifles.

Michoacán is principally a young volcanic country and hence predominantly of basaltic materials and residues of cinders and ashes. Toward the Pacific, especially in the barrancas, lower and older geological horizons are exposed, and in the mountain ranges along the coast these appear to form a far-reaching, outlying area to the south of the basin ranges that extend southward from Arizona. The Pacific versant exposes on the plateau margins and beneath the young volcanic materials there are older andesitic rocks which may carry ores of various metals. There, down slope, as toward the sea, still older rocks are uncovered, granitic masses, schists and other metamorphic rocks, which are traversed by veins of gold-bearing quartz. Here also a more tropical climate prevails, with deep weathering, more or less lateritic in character. There is therefore in the subsoil a residual concentration of gold particles.

As the Spaniards descended below the barren cover of the volcanic plateau they found gold concentrated in the channels of mountain and foothill arroyos, and also in the deep subsoils of terraces and hill flanks. These facts of stratigraphy and physiography had been practically known to the Indians and were quickly appreciated by the Spaniards.

The hundred and forty-five Spaniards who formed the initial colony of Colima did so primarily to get precious metals. There was no need of a villa here in order to have a port. Colima was not a harbor, and there was only casual interest in the nearby excellent harbors of Santiago and Navidad. Zacatula had been established for shipbuilding and as a base for maritime exploration. The necessary resource of Indian labor was at least equally at hand everywhere in the Tarascan country, in which no villa was set up, and the Tarascan country was eligible as a base for the exploration of the unknown north. Colima was not an especially good spot for northern explorations. Its position necessitated an arduous descent to the coast and from here all roads north followed arduous trails across much difficult terrain. Actually Colima was used as a base only for one such expedition, that of Francisco Cortés. At the time of the settlement of Colima the Spaniards were not interested in setting up tropical plantations. Had they been, they would not have chosen the farthest and most inaccessible end of their territory. It was not because of agricultural expectations, maritime advantage, nor, primarily, as a base of northern exploration that the Spaniards made of Colima the most remote and the principal town in the west of New Spain.

Yet Cortés lost no time in ordering a party to the occupation of Colima. Very probably he did not set forth all his reasons. From the Tarascans he had heard of a lord of Colima on the coast. A Spanish party bound for Zacatula disobeyed its instructions and invaded Colima. There must have been a strong attraction impelling them to do so, for these hard-bitten men were not given to arduous detours as a lark. Cortés was irritated at such unauthorized entry. He very quickly sent one of his captains with a strong force to make the official conquest and, although he makes the venture read as though its purpose was to punish the natives for opposing Spanish soldiers, even when these had been disobedient, the reason was probably more substantial. The loss to Spanish prestige was slight, if any; the official expedition was powerful, and it set out in order to occupy the land, not merely as a punitive force.

After the entrada had been made, the preliminary steps to permanent subdivision of the territory seem to have been taken at once. The large majority of the party set about establishing themselves promptly in Colima. Gonzalo de Sandoval returned soon thereafter to Mexico with the plan of allotment of Indian pueblos, which Cortés ratified by grants, some of which have been preserved in the visita of Lebrón. All of this may be interpreted as meaning that Cortés had advance information that this coastal area was an important, perhaps the major, source of the precious metals found in the land of Michoacán, and that the occupation was planned on the basis of prior knowledge. The story he wrote to the king about pearls on the coast and the land of Amazons beyond was a piece of embroidery that may have concealed his reticence about the essential facts. For although both Cortés and the hard veterans of the Mexican campaigns believed they were entitled to a major stake for their services, it was not out of curiosity about Amazons or for a little pearl fishing[1] that they decided to found a town on the coast of Colima.

Lebrón mentioned mining only because he considered it an important factor in the early decrease of population. Referring to the period of colonization, he said that the Spaniards seized large numbers of Indians, male and female, adult and children, for personal services in the gold mines in such fashion that they took great gangs (*quadrillas*), even of a thousand and two thousand Indians. These were in part "engaged in carrying supplies twenty and thirty leagues and farther to the Spaniards and to the slaves of the mines, so that a large number of people were regularly engaged in this labor and others in opening roads across sierras and montes for the said mines." A distinction was made between slaves, who worked the mines, and forced labor, which was used for supplying the mines and carrying the supplies. The slaves were probably Indians who had been charged with rebellion or resistance; the porters were taken at will from the encomienda Indians. That Negro slaves were not used is indicated by the statements below, which blame the decay of mining on the prohibition (after 1542) of the enslavement of Indians.

Early gold mining must have involved almost the whole of early Colima. The twenty-seven encomenderos of Cihuatlán Valley are understandable only on the inference that there were profits in sight by using local Indians to work placer deposits near that valley. The main attraction here lay in the metamorphic and igneous mountains

---

1. There was some pearl and mother-of-pearl collecting done in the early years, as the "Relaciónes de los Motínes" declares.

behind Cihuatlán, rather than in the alluvial fertility of the valley. The crowding of early grants in the Provincia de Tepetitango, in a rough mountain belt north of the lower Colima River, points to the attraction of placer mining in small arroyos and perhaps in the digging over of the residual cover of hillsides. The still extant Indian village of Juluapan, west of Colima, was first the property of Gomes de Hoyos "who was sustained by Indians and slaves in the mines."[2] Tepetitango itself was one of the very few pueblos still paying tribute in metal (tepuzque) in the 1540s.[3] Across the river in the Provincia del Colimotl the powerful Arévalo owned everything from Istlahuacán to the mountain headwaters of the Río de Alima. He was "supported by the Indians, who are near to mines and he has sent slaves with them to the mines."[4] To this day the natives in the old Arévalo lands still grind ancient potsherds to wash out the gold they contain. Placer mining still continues on a small scale in the arroyos along the borders of Colima and Michoacán. As late as 1536, Alima itself and Uepantitlan near the mouth of the same river, in the Valle de Alima, were supplying annual tribute to His Majesty in smelted gold.[5] The same tribute list declares that the tribute of food then collected from Tamazula, Zapotlán, Tuspa, Amula, and Tuxcaquesco was being "sold in the Province of Colima in the gold mines, to which the said pueblos are near."

For the Motín region the record is fuller, perhaps only because records in Colima proper are in all ways scant. Hernandez de Alvor[6] was a miner who included in his claim for satisfaction the loss of certain slaves in the Motín. Juan de Samano, in the Residencia taken after the return of Cortés from Honduras, deposed that during the administration of Estrada (*ca.* 1525) Indians were loaded with maize and other foodstuffs in the interior and thus driven more than forty leagues to the mines of Motín.[7] The royal grant of 1530 to Gerónimo

---

2. VC.
3. Suma, No. 680.
4. VC.
5. "Tribute List of March 1, 1536" MS in AGI, Audiencia de Mexico, Leg. 91 (58–6–5).
6. *CyP,* No. 817.
7. Joaquín García Icazbalceta, ed., *Colección de documentos para la historia de México,* 2 vols.; (Mexico City, 1858–1866), II, 176.

López referred to the Motín as the province "where the gold mines are." From Cortés' lawsuit in 1531 there are these statements: one witness had just returned from Motín "where the slaves of the Marqués were engaged in conveying gold," and said that Cortés maintained eight Christians in the mines of Motín who worked gold by means of slaves.[8] Diego Garrido was esteemed in 1532 for having good Indians at Epatlan "and they are good because they are adjacent to mines." Cabezon's property of Tuxtla (Uztutla) was in the Motín area; he too used slaves in the gold mines.[9] Aquila, Guabayutla, and other places in the Motín were paying tribute to His Majesty in 1536 either in gold dust or in smelted gold.[10]

The relaciónes of 1580 for the Motín and the Coalcomán areas recall the early days of gold mining. In the Coalcomán area there were mines

> especially in the pueblo of Yuitlan which is from the said pueblo [of Coalcomán] nine leagues. There are many mines, especially one from which was taken the whole wealth of gold, which is called the mines of Copala where anciently there was taken much gold. This at present is full of water and with very little labor it could be unwatered, so that much wealth in gold could be taken out. The natives say that since the slaves were freed, who were at that time in this province, because the Spaniards no longer had anyone to work for them, they ceased to work the said mines and thus they have been depopulated many years.

For the Motín coast the account reads:

> At the time when this land was discovered there were found gold mines in it in the mountain called Catagui [near Ostutla], in all its flanks and gulches and limits both on the east and west side. Here many conquerors and ancient settlers (pobladores) supplied themselves with fine gold and good. With the abundance of slaves and personal services which they had in those times gold was then worked. But, after the discovery of the mines of silver and still later, after the freeing of the slaves, the mines were given

---

8. HC-RA, pp. 364–366.
9. VC, p. 7.
10. "Tribute List of March 1, 1536."

up and not because there is no gold today, for it still can be found in the slopes of this sierra. There are no mines of silver here, nor have there been any such discovered, nor of any other metal.

These records may be read to indicate: first, that there was an original distribution of coastwise mining activity, at least from Cihuatlán to the mines of the Motín, which were producing within the first two years of Spanish occupation. The first villa was established in the midst of the oldest grants of Indian pueblos close to the coast. Second, that very shortly there took place an extension of activity inland, up the drainage of both the Colima and Alima rivers to include all the country not blanketed by the aggraded slopes of the Volcán de Colima. Lebrón thought the shift of the villa to its second site was made in order to have better access to the mines. Third, that gold was produced from stream sands and by digging in the hillsides. The latter method undoubtedly meant the collection of the residual gold in lateritic subsoil or from terraces. The reference to the Copala mines on the east side of the Motín, as having been filled with water and requiring unwatering, indicates that vein mining also was practiced. The tribute of tepuzque from the Tepetitango area indicates some smelting of copper-gold ores. Fourth, that the collapse of gold mining was ascribed to the freeing of the slaves and the loss of the services of the Indians. Lebrón spoke of the quadrillas of thousands of Indians who were used as providers and pack animals for the mines. Under such circumstances the restriction of mining to slaves was probably not carefully observed and the lot of slave and servant was about equally hard. The parallel is very close to the early mining history of the West Indies and the results were similar. Most of the coastal encomiendas were abandoned in a decade.

Another aspect of mining development concerns the search for silver. This area of New Spain may contain the most ancient record of Spanish silver mining in the new world, a record that has been overlooked completely by historians. In the following pages evidence is presented for silver production in the Tamazula region.

Published archeological knowledge of the country between the Volcán de Colima and the highland of Michoacán is as yet almost restricted to the notes of Lumholtz.[11] Of special interest is his description of a large cast silver figure. Brief reference has been made in the chapter on aboriginal conditions to the production of silver in this area and its payment as tribute to the king of Michoacán. Michoacán has been generally considered the source of silver for aboriginal New Spain. Speculations about the source of the silver wealth of Michoacán have always overlooked the fact that the area of ancient Michoacán was greater than that of the modern state and that the source did not lie at all within the territory populated by Tarascans. No silver mining within Tarascan Michoacán has ever been documented from the time of the Conquest. But the Tamazula, Zapotlán, and Tuxpan section was a part of the aboriginal state of Michoacán, and I may say here, from field observation and in anticipation of further inquiry, that the Tamazula vicinity has a site indicating aboriginal silver mining. We know that Tarascan officials held sway over this region. It may be that this area was taken over by the Tarascan state principally for its mineral wealth and that it was the most likely source of the Michoacán silver hoards. There is no evidence that points anywhere else. The possibility that the Tarascan state took over this mineral-bearing region would also help to explain the existence in these villages of a wealthy aboriginal merchant class.

A silver district of Michoacán appears in the Spanish records of the 1520s. Rodrigo de Albornoz, treasurer and co-governor of New Spain, wrote to the king under date of December 15, 1525, saying, "It is necessary to erect in the Province of Michoacán a plant in order that there may be smelted the ore from which the silver is produced and that, having been smelted there, it be brought here [to Mexico] for refining." He further states that the silver was then being produced by native Indians, by slaves, and by Christians.[12] In 1527 Luis de Cárdenas wrote the king that in the land of "Cazonzi, Lord of Michoacán, are the rich mines of silver from which Hernán Cortés took in the year '23 five hundred loads of silver. In addition Hernán Cortés made another law that under penalty of a hundred lashes no

---

11. K. S. Lumholtz, *Unknown Mexico,* 2 vols.; (New York, 1902).
12. *CDIE,* XIII.

Christian should go in there, and we know about this from the Indians who thus informed us." He related also the earlier plundering
of palaces and temples in Michoacán by Olid, charging Olid with
having robbed the temples of one hundred twenty-two loads of silver
and five of gold (note the proportions!), and added that later (Cortés
having left for Honduras) "the governor Albornoz placed his Indians
in these mines and in five days took out five hundred marks of fine
silver."[13]

In the suit brought by Cortés in 1531 to recover Huicicila and
Tamazula, witnesses testified that Cortés had held these places from
the time of conquest until the entry of Nuño de Guzmán, that in no
other part of New Spain at that time was silver mined, except in the
said Province of Michoacán,[14] and in the summary for the Audiencia
we have the statement, "Tamazula, donde hay las minas de plata."[15]
In a list of Cortés holdings and rents of 1535,[16] is the following entry:

Tamazula e Zapotlan e Tuspa:
    los pueblos de tamazula azapotlan e tuspa de que el dho mar-
    ques ha de hauer rresiduo dan de tributo rropa e mahiz para
    mantenimientos lo qual se venden en las minas e valen los
    tributos que dan en un año vendido en las dichas minas mill y
    quatro zientos pesos del dho oro de minas.
Amula Tuscacuesco: [This entry follows with an almost identical
statement.]

The "Tribute List of 1536" identifies the same pueblos as belonging to Cortés. At the time of the Suma they appear as *en cabeza de Su
Magestad*.

The testimony of the "Relación de Tamazula" 1580 is as follows:

Captain Cristóbal de Olid was the first man to enter. He was sent
by Captain General Fernando Cortés to its conquest in the year
1521 [should be 1522] and as the said King Cazonzi submitted
with all his territory the said Captain General Don Fernando
Cortés took them [the pueblos of Tuspa, Tamazula, and Zapo-

13. MS in AGI, Patronato, Leg. 16, no. 2, ramo 6.
14. HC-RA, p. 373.
15. Ibid., p. 399.
16. MS in AGI, Patronato, Leg. 17, ramo 21.

tlán] for his own and they served him for some time until they were placed under the royal crown (as corregimientos).

This, it is inferred, was the district from which Luis Cárdenas claimed that Cortés excluded all Spaniards so that he might exploit its silver mines undisturbed.

Cortés did block out for himself a principality in the west, including Tamazula, Zapotlán, and Tuspa, but also Amula and Tuxcaquesco, precisely the western dependencies of the Cazonzi. This was the only land west of Lake Pátzcuaro that Cortés bothered to take for himself. It was certainly not for any ordinary reason that he preëmpted this stretch, so far removed from the rest of his holdings, but apparently because it was the silver land of Michoacán.

Here is a final note from Fray Alonso Ponce[17] about Tamazula:

Here also is the famed mine of Morcillo, whose discoverer was a Spaniard by this name. From it, so it is said, there was taken so much silver that when Morcillo came to register it, the authorities took it for the king, and God decreed that because of this act they never more could find it. Nevertheless, when the Father Commissioner reached Tamazula the people affirmed that it was being worked, and that the discontinuance in times past was because it filled with water, and others said no, rather that it had become exhausted, and that now they were cleaning it out to see if it showed any metal.

Thus ends the record of the Tamazula silver mine.

The control of Cazonzi was extended westward primarily, I think, to acquire the silver of Tamazula. When Olid came to Michoacán he may have had instructions to find the source of the Tarascan silver and reserve it for Cortés. At any rate Cortés took over the Tarascan king's holdings in this area and established the practice of mining for silver. Later, a Spaniard named Morcillo achieved brief fame as its operator and thereafter the mine was forgotten, as the role of Cortés and of the aboriginal metallurgists has been forgotten until now.

---

17. Op. cit., II, 114.

# The Aftermath

By mid-century, when the Suma was compiled and Lebrón was engaged in his visita, the deterioration of the local situation was far advanced. Indeed, another chapter had been added to the destruction of the Indies. Many of the lowland pueblos had been abandoned or merged, and the rest were far along in their decline. The Alima lowlands and the Cihuatlán area had become almost empty of Indians at the time of the Suma, as had the foot slopes of the volcano around the villa of Colima. The hill sections, like the old Tepetitango district west of the Armería district and the poor hill section around Istlahuacán, were least diminished. For the tierra caliente as a whole I estimate that, by the middle of the century, more than eighty percent of the population had disappeared. Lebrón has been cited above with respect to some of the facts in the diminution of the native population. We may let him continue with his explanation.

After noting the ruin of the great Indian town of Alima, he went on:

> Round about it in the lands that formerly belonged thereto is a great abundance of privately owned cacao groves which Spaniards have set out there—which is a seed like piñons in Spain, much valued among the Indians. Might it please Almighty God that never had the Indians given themselves thereto, for I hold it certain that it has been in large part responsible for the diminution of the natives. For one reason, because the lands on which it must be planted are the best of all and the best irrigated among Indian lands and so necessarily [i.e., obviously] they have been appropriated for such use [i.e., cacao growing was expanded at the expense of the best food-producing area]. Second, the trees of the said fruit require such care and preference that continuously, or most of the time, they must have attention and labor, which cannot be had without great hardship to the natives. Thus they have died off like flies without their knowing of what nor why. In the account of these pueblos which I have given, Your Highness may be pleased to infer that such plantations exist in most of those provinces and seacoast, and the same situation, I was as-

sured, exists in the other coast districts, such as Zacatula and Compostela and others where Spaniards have taken up private cacao properties and gold mines. The Spaniards of our nation say that the people die off because it is seacoast and tropical country, which seems to me ridiculous, for it was such before the Spaniards came and the natives had such fierce wars among themselves that they killed one another in large numbers and sacrificed one another and yet the land was greatly peopled as I have stated before.

The causes that I hold certain to have been responsible for the diminution and collapse of the natives include the large sum and mass of slaves which the Spaniards took out from these provinces when they came there, for they took away a large number of Indian men, women, and children so that in many villages there remained only the ancient and useless. Also the personal services in the gold mines required large gangs (quadrillas), many of a thousand or two thousand Indians more or less. These were forced to labor with as little charity or consolation as though there were no Christianity or fear of God on the part of our nation. Again, [the diminution was] due to the great labors that these natives had to perform in carrying supplies of food for twenty, thirty leagues, and more for the Spaniards and slaves in the mines, in which task there was regularly occupied a great number of persons. Others were used in breaking roads to the mines through mountains and woods. This labor of carrying food supplies to the villa of Colima had been customary until I came and stopped it all while I was there. Since then, I am informed, my orders are no longer observed. It was quite usual for loaded Indians to go eight and ten days each way, crossing great mountains and strong rivers with a load of maize which, delivered in the villa for their patron, was not worth half a real, and a large part of which was used in raising hogs and horses, at the cost of life to the natives, who, when they had no more of a miserable food of powdered corn, which they are accustomed to carry, eat the roots of trees and water, and in this fashion it has happened that they have succumbed on these roads.

In many villages, having seen these hardships, those who did not die, so I am informed, followed a settled mode by which their women ceased to conceive and others abstained from their women according to the order of nature, and if there were some women that did conceive, these disposed of the offspring before it was born, saying that they would not see their children in the captivity and servitude in which they were. These and many other things and causes well known to me have brought about the diminution of these people which I certify to Your Highness. If commonly there had been as good treatment of the Indians both on the part of those who hold Indians in encomienda as well as on the part of the authorities who hold such in charge, as there is of the dogs born in the houses of the Spaniards, for which food is ordered and which the owner protects from harm, how much greater would be the number of natives! God, our Lord, is ill served by our sins.

The second part of the Lebrón report concerns the excesses and disorders in the management of the Indians by encomenderos, and awaits use by some future student of Indian administration. It is a sorry picture of overwork, neglect, uprooting, and dreary wastage of natives, especially in connection with cacao growing, gold mining, and the system of human burden-bearers. Nearly all the delightful foot slopes of the Volcán were used as stock pastures, stretching for leagues about the villa. On the way from Colima to Tonila, Ponce found "for almost the entire six leagues, many fallen edifices and ruined houses, manifest signs that all that stretch had been densely peopled."[1] The villa decayed also with the dearth of Indians, Lebrón finding "forty-eight married vecinos, of whom not ten reside there and of the original settlers most have died and the rest live away from the villa and province. Of the old vecinos only six remain, of which three live here at present. The other vecinos are recent arrivals and most of them mestizos and persons of little account."

The highland districts, and Autlán, suffered no serious collapse. The Suma indicates a population of approximately ten thousand for the mountain and barranca settlements of the Provincia de Amula. Autlán still had, in the Suma, in excess of four thousand inhabitants, Zapotlán five thousand, Tamazula and Tuzpa six thousand. Four of the original eight major Indian towns thus were still flourishing. Lebrón pointed out that these were the only places in the area of his

---

1. Op. cit., II, 110.

visita that had convents and ascribed their survival largely to the protection and ministrations given to the natives by the Franciscans. I think that some credit also belongs to Hernán Cortés, who held much of this area and thus kept it out of the reach of local encomenderos.

Indian survival was, however, also favored by environment. The highland communities fared relatively well, the lowland ones decayed here, as they commonly did in tropical America. Autlán is the one exception and Autlán lies in a sunny, dry, well-drained basin, separated from the coastal lowlands by a mountain range. Its healthfulness is today in marked contrast to the seaward areas. It may be that the white man brought malaria and gastroenteric infections to the lowlands or that he helped to spread them; the highlands remained relatively free from such diseases.

Finally, it may be noted that all the important modern towns of southern Jalisco, such as Zapotlán, Autlán, Tamazula, and Tuxpan, had been large aboriginal towns, strong in trading peoples (*mercaderes*). These, as well as the town of Avalos, formed a cluster of native trading centers without parallel west of the valley of Mexico. These urbanized Indians may have been more resistant to infection and the psychological depression incident to the Conquest. The industrial and commercial character of these places today goes back to pre-Conquest times.

*Note:*

In keeping with the original text of "Colima and New Spain in the Sixteenth Century," the following abbreviations have been used in the footnote material:

AGI     Archivo General de Indias, Seville.

AGNB    Archivo General de la Nacion, Mexico, *Boletín.*

CC      Hernán Cortés, *Cartas de relación sobre el descubrimiento y conquista de la Nueva España* in Biblioteca de Autores Españoles (Madrid, 1857–1880), XXII, 1–153.

CDIE    *Colección de documentos inéditos para la historia de España* (Madrid, 1842–1895).

CyP     *Conquistadores y Pobladores de Nueva España, diccionario autobiográfico sacado de los textos originales,* ed. Francisco de Icaza (Madrid, 1925), 2 vols.

HC-RA   "Juicio seguido por Hernán Cortés contras los Licenciados Matienzo y Delgadillo" in AGN*B*, IX, 330–407.

Lebrón  Lorenzo de Lebrón de Quiñones, "Relación sumaria de dozientos pueblos," MS in AGI, Patronato, Leg. 20, no. 5, ramo 14.

NV      *Noticias varias de Nueva Galicia, intendencia de Guadalajara* (Guadalajara, 1878).

RAHM    Real Academia de la Historia, Madrid.

RM      "Relación de las Ceremonias y Ritos de Michoacán" in *CDIE,* LIII (Madrid, 1869).

Suma    "Suma de Visitas de Pueblos" in Francisco del Paso y Troncoso, ed., *Papels de Nueva España . . .* (Madrid, 1905–1906), 6 vols. I.

VC      "Vecinos y Pueblos en Colima en 1532" in AGN*B*, X, 5–23.

# IV. The American
## Historical
### Geographer

# 12. On the Background
## of Geography
### in the United States

THE PERSISTENT NATURE OF GEOGRAPHY

Were I to begin this essay in the leisurely fashion of the earlier years of which I shall treat I might entitle it notes and reflections on the past state of geography in the United States, considered as public benefit and private gratification. The span I have in mind is most of the past century and the first decade of the present one.

On both sides of the Atlantic there is present interest in reviewing what geography has been concerned with in past times and what persons have influenced its directions. The *Geographische Zeitschrift* has been and now again is a forum for the history of ideas. John K. Wright took the Centenary of the American Geographic Society in review for his *Geography in the Making* (1952), a history of American geography as recorded in the activities and publications of that society. In 1954 the Association of American Geographers issued *American Geography, Inventory and Prospect,* with Preston James and Clarence Jones as editors. In the past year (1964) William Warntz has given an interpretation of its academic status in this country as *Geography Then and Now.* The content, organization, and context of geo-

"On the Background of Geography in the United States" first appeared in "Festschrift für Gottfried Pfeifer," *Heidelberger Geog. Arbeiten,* 15:59–71, 1967.

graphical ideas merit attention to remind us that there is continuity of interest, that the expression changes with the age, and that a world view has a point of view.

It is fitting to recall that geographical learning is as old as mankind. Hettner's definition of geography is applicable to all peoples of all times. The subject matter of geography begins with the distinction between proper names and common nouns, which is perhaps as old as the faculty of language. The proper name given to a particular place identifies its uniqueness and location and also calls attention to the need of such identification in a cultural context, as a place providing food, water, or shelter, perhaps as one to be avoided, as a landmark in getting from one place to another, as noted for a memorable event, or as having ritual significance. Place name is location in cultural connotation. Correct orientation by knowing direction and distance has been obligatory learning. Every language also has its vocabulary of common names for kinds of features of land, water, vegetation and plants, and of human occupance.

The Europeans who settled the northern part of the continent had less need to take over such Indian words than did the Spaniards to the south, northern Europe and northern America being similar in their physical geography and plant forms. *Bayou* and *muskeg* are two such words that supplied a lack in English and French. Spaniards brought Indian words such as *savanna, mangrove, cay* from the West Indies to Florida. The English and French freely accepted Indian proper names for lakes and streams and mountains, in contrast to the Spanish. As far west as Louisiana our physical toponymy is mainly Indian. From the Sabine to the Sacramento River it is Spanish, not because native names were lacking but because such was the Spanish manner.

A competent geography, both locational and topical, has been common to all people known to us. In the terms of Varenius, special and general geography are immemorial.

The nature of primitive geographies has had little study. Two of the early observers of the American West, H. R. Schoolcraft and J. W. Powell, turned their attention from the original objective of an appraisal of land and resources in the terms of their contemporary society to Indians and their ways and thus became pioneers of American ethnology. Beyond the functional quality of aboriginal geography and its recognition of classes of phenomena is found also an aboriginal *Weltbild* or cosmogony.

The exploration of the Americas by Europeans was carried out everywhere by native information and guidance. Not only were they shown where a stream could be crossed or a mountain pass lay but they were told about distant parts and the way to them. The routes of discovery were Indian routes of communication. I may give an example that determined the major direction of Spanish entry into the American Southwest. When Nuño de Guzmán landed at Pánuco on the Gulf of Mexico in 1525 he met an Indian merchant who had been engaged in trade with Pueblo Indians of the Southwest, a thousand miles distant. Nuño thus was told of another country that was like Mexico, Mexico meaning the valley of Mexico. This was the origin of the name New Mexico, supposedly a land of cities and wealth. Nuño did not follow up this information at the time, but when later he went five hundred miles west to the Pacific Coast of Sinaloa he started from there in search of that northern land, which was quite as far away and on an entirely different route. He set out on the most direct course with Indian guides. His failure to reach New Mexico had nothing to do with uncertainty of direction, which was as well known to the natives of the West as it was on the eastern coast. Indian trade, to an extent that has been little considered, gave wider geographical horizons, not only in the higher cultures. For example, tribes from remote parts of the Mississippi basin resorted to the Pipestone locality of Minnesota to get this prized material.

Modern geography has continued to give attention to the same questions as did primitive folk: the significance of position, the togetherness of things, the areal distribution of entities and aggregations, the utility of the environment. These are no minor matters that are easy to conventionalize. Environment and resource are cultural terms that express both technical capacity and social values. This may be overlooked in the material success of our western civilization by which we are inclined to universalize our culture. The "underdeveloped" parts of the world are those that have not yet been fitted into our pattern, which is one of "growth" or "progress" in measurable satisfactions, a mystique of numbers. As the social sciences have substituted symbols for individuals and communities we now have a contemporary school of "mathematical geographers" which would discard the age-old interest in making sense of the diversity of land and its life. A generalized humankind is to be subsumed by mathematical symbols and functions of spatial relation. I do not think that such sophistication is valid in concept, nor that it gives grace and truth to the geographical imagination. Geographers stray from their course when they turn from phenomenon and location to abstraction of numbers. I suggest therefore that this may be a proper time to consider the intellectual engagements of our elders.

## THE TIME OF FIELD SURVEYS

The nineteenth century was the great period of discovering what the territory of the United States was like. The men who did so rarely were called geographers but it was they who made the observations and organized these into an overview that gave superior substance to regional geography. Also they raised topical questions of importance. Largely they were sent to spy out the American Promised Land. They headed field surveys that were commonly called geological surveys, partly because a geographical survey had the more restricted meaning of topography and geodesy. The public interest that supported them wished to be informed of natural resources, mineral wealth, soil fertility, water, and vegetation. The sustaining objective was practical, how to occupy the land for gainful ends, but those engaged were not limited in what they might observe, think about, or record. The men who went out were young, of good liberal rather than technical education, raised on the eastern seaboard, and open-eyed to learn what they could of lands that were new to them. This was a chance for intellectual and physical adventure and they made the most of it. Earth science, natural history, Indian ways, archeology, and frontier life all came in for discerning attention. What they reported was not recast to bureaucratic restrictions.

The observations made in these sundry surveys have not had their deserved recognition as geography. There is no guide available for them except as to geological content. Geographers are likely to pass by titles that are given as geology. The places of publication in part were obscure government publications, documents of House or Senate of a particular Congress or of some federal office, or of a state survey of limited circulation and short life. The best available introduction is in Susan D. McKelveny, *Botanical Explorations of the Trans-Mississippi West* (1790–1850), published by the Arnold Arboretum of Harvard University in 1955. It is regrettable that no student of American geography has done a bibliography or anthology of these, the major documents of its most productive century.

As a provisional and slight sketch of this time, supported by examples that chance to be known to me, I should propose something like the following order. I should not give more than passing mention to Jedediah Morse, who wrote the indifferent compilations by which he has become titular father of American geography. Instead I should start with Thomas Jefferson, whose *Notes on Virginia* (1784) are a classic of geography, based on intimate, organized, and discerning observations. At that time also he had begun to plan the scientific exploration of the land beyond the Mississippi, then in French or Spanish hands. Jefferson spoke of these as "literary" groups that were to seek permission to pass through foreign territory. Whatever Jefferson may have had in mind of westward expansion of the boundaries of the United States, his scientific interest was real. In 1792 he proposed to the American Philosophical Society that a subscription be raised for an exploration up the Missouri River and west to the Pacific Coast. It got no farther than taking the French botanist André Michaux to Kentucky. In 1803 he sent Zebulon Pike to follow the Mississippi River to its source, only to be arrested by Spanish authorities. Meanwhile Jefferson had been coaching his young protégé and secretary, Meriwether Lewis, to prepare for the grand project which was planned, to follow the Missouri River to its source, cross the mountains, and find the best course to the shores of the Pacific. The party set out, in 1804. Jefferson's letter of preface to the journals of Lewis and Clark well describes his geographical interest.

The Mississippi and Missouri rivers were the main objectives of scientific exploration in the decades following, some by individual initiative, some to serve state or national ends. Henry Schoolcraft began on his own in 1817–18, his *View of the Lead Mines of Missouri* serving to guide my field study on the Ozark Highland. His next observations were of the upper Mississippi and adjacent parts, *Narrative Journal of Travels through the Northwestern Regions* (1821), and *Narrative of an Expedition through the Upper Mississippi* (1832), both rich in content and insight. Meanwhile he had become employed on Indian affairs which resulted in the publication of six folio volumes in 1856 on the *History, Condition, and Prospects of the Indian Tribes of the United States,* a major ethnogeographical as well as ethnological document.

Prinz Maximilian von Wied-Neuwied was in the United States from 1832–34, most of the time being spent on the upper Missouri River. The observations were published at Koblenz in two large volumes of text and two atlases of drawings in color by Karl Bodmer, these being landscapes, details of physical features, Indians of many tribes, and different activities. A reduced version of the translated text is available in Thwaites, *Early Western Travels.* The original is the handsomest and best informed representation of nature and life of the Missouri Valley when it was still Indian country.

A third talented observer of our interior was David Dale Owen, son of the Scot Robert Owen who had tried making a Utopian community at New Harmony, Indiana. I came to appreciate the sharpness of eye and mind of the younger Owen by using the field studies he made when he was State Geologist of Kentucky (1854–60). Years earlier, when federal land commissioner (1839) for what we know as the Driftless Area of Iowa and Wisconsin, he carried through a remarkable geographical survey, tucked away in House Document 239 of the 26th Congress. A later commission by the General Land Office (1847–52) resulted in his volume, *Geological Survey of Wisconsin, Iowa, Minnesota, and Part of Nebraska Territory* (1852), describing the condition of those parts in the time after Schoolcraft, when they were in vigorous process of being settled.

These were four men (for the artist Bodmer must be counted as a contributing geographer) of the quality of whose observations I happen to have some late field knowledge. It has been a good experience to see the past live again in their accounts, to note the changes, and to recognize the validity of their records.

Somewhat before the midcentury geological surveys were set up by various states. Reference has been made to Owen, whose first such appointment had been in Indiana in 1837. George Swallow, a graduate of Bowdoin College in Maine, became state geologist of Missouri in 1853 and so continued to 1861, when the Civil War put an end to the work. His reports were an important part of my early education, covering as they did the country in which I grew up and instructing me in reading its features and reconstructing its earlier condition. At about the same time Eugene Woldemar Hilgard became state geologist of Mississippi. Born in Zweibrücken in 1833, in 1836 he was brought to Belleville, Illinois, an early German settlement that I also knew in later years. In 1849, Hilgard was sent back to study at Heidelberg where he took his doctorate in 1853 *summa cum laude*. In Mississippi and across the river in Louisiana he became interested in the formation and fertility of soils, in vegetation as an indicator of soil, and in southern agriculture. He laid there the foundation of the soil science for which he was to be known later and for the great agricultural college he was to develop at Berkeley. The job of economic geography he did for the Census of 1880 will have notice below.

The Geological Survey of California is a superior illustration of the range of interest and the kind of personalities assembled. It began in 1860 and continued to 1874 under the direction of Josiah Whitney, always referred to as Professor Whitney. Whitney was educated at Yale and had gone on to study at Paris, Berlin, and Giessen. He acquired field experience in the copper country of Lake Superior and on a geological survey of Iowa. Whitney returned in 1875 to his professorship at Harvard, there to exploit his field experiences by writing on the Sierra Nevada and its auriferous foothills, on the physical geography of the United States, and on climatic changes of the Ice Age. His junior associate at Harvard was Nathaniel Shaler and in 1892 W. M. Davis was added as assistant in charge of undergraduate exercises. The staff Whitney brought together in California included William Brewer, of whom more later, the fabulous Clarence King, and Charles Frederick Hoffmann from Frankfurt, of whom Farquhar said that he "may well be called the progenitor of modern American topography." For a time also there was Ferdinand von Richtofen, the association continuing in lifelong friendship.

Brewer, who was second in command, kept a journal recently edited by Francis Farquhar under the title *Up and Down California in 1860–64* (University of California Press). It is of interest both for the survey and its men and for its vignettes of California of the time. Brewer (1828–1910) had been named to be botanist of the expedition. A New York farm boy, graduate of Yale, he had gone to Heidelberg in 1855 to study with Bunsen and a year later to Munich to work under Liebig. During vacations he tramped about Bavaria, Tyrol, and Switzerland, learning to know the Alps and their vegetation, cultural as well as natural. He prepared a major part of the systematic botany of the Whitney Survey and some of its geographical accounts. Brewer returned to Yale in 1864 as Professor of Agriculture, contributed reports to the Ninth and Tenth U.S. Censuses, which will have attention below, started the Yale School of Forestry and gave its first lectures on forest physiography. He deserves to be acknowledged as a pioneer in biogeography and agricultural geography as well as for his lively descriptions of early California, and for his early awareness of what have come to be called problems of conservation.

William Gabb of Philadelphia was one of the youngest members of the Whitney Survey. Brewer commented on his arrival that he was "grassy green but decidedly smart." Gabb was appointed at the age of twenty-two to do the paleontology of California. When I did field work in Mexican Lower California I first became aware of Gabb's competence as a geographer. After completing his assignment in the Whitney Survey he crossed the border in 1867 to ride to the end of that peninsula by crisscross traverses. He went on to the Dominican Republic to do a survey that is still the best account of its physical geography and placer deposits (*Transactions of the American Philosophical Society for 1873*). It is larded with good observations on island conditions of the time and a memorable long passage on the poor judgment of Columbus in locating Isabela, the first European town in the New World. His last field work was done in Costa Rica (*Proceedings of the American Philosophical Society for 1875*) as the result of which he died, age thirty-nine. In Costa Rica he acquired the fullest knowledge of Indian life that we have for that country and made numerous other original geographical observations, still in part the only ones of their kind. Gabb's contributions to Cretaceous paleontology are known. His high talents as pioneer geographer of nature and culture in Middle America deserve equal recognition.

The thesaurus of the several national surveys can be indicated here only by their succession: The U.S. Exploring Expedition (1838–42), directed by Charles Wilkes, primarily important for its work in Antarctica and Pacific Islands, was also concerned with our northwest coast. A Pacific railroad survey under the direction of the War Department engaged in field work from 1854–60, resulting in twelve large volumes and addenda called *Reports of Explorations and Surveys to Ascertain the Most Practicable and Economical Route for a Railroad from the Mississippi River to the Pacific.* The *U.S. Geological and Geographical Survey of the Territories* headed by F. V. Hayden began after the Civil War and is known to the public largely because of the photographs of the West taken by W. H. Jackson. Clarence King's *Geological Exploration of the Fortieth Parallel* began at about the same time. George M. Wheeler was put in charge of the *U.S. Geographical Survey West of the Hundredth Meridian* in 1871. These three independent surveys were absorbed into the U.S. Geological Survey, established in 1879. To the end of the century the geographical attention of the nation was directed to the West beyond the Mississippi River. A host of able observers were schooled in these surveys to record in diverse ways the nature and condition of the West. By text, map, and photograph they described the land they walked, rode, and camped upon. They were free to direct their own observations and to express their meaning as they saw it. Some were eloquent in description, some bold in interpretation. They were discoverers and knew themselves as such.

INTRAMURAL GEOGRAPHY

Others who had not been schooled in field camps contributed to the shaping of geographic thought and to the extension of such knowledge. These were library scholars in no invidious sense, men who thought of the inspection and ordering of data by charts, philosophers of physical or human geography. They had some benefit of what they had seen of land and sea but they were concerned with synthesis and interpretation.

Matthew Fontaine Maury (1806–73), naval officer lamed by an accident that ended his sea duty, was placed in charge of charts and instruments by the Navy and thus began in 1847 his wind and current charts of the seas that became foundations of oceanography and meteorology. These were followed in 1855 by his *Physical Geography of the Sea,* a classic of earth science (and as such reissued in 1963 in the John Harvard Library, with introduction by John B. Leighly). As Commander in the Confederate Navy during the Civil War and its agent in England, he was not permitted to return home. During the years of exile in London he engaged in writing school textbooks of geography. These were current in American schools to the end of the century, together with wall maps of his design. Maury developed trains of thought in text and map, attractively presented to young minds, concerning the distribution of physical and biotic phenomena about the earth, even including a section on man's influence on physical geography. Written for children, they are an original and competent outline of the nature of geography. Readmitted in 1868 to this country, his last years were given to teaching at Virginia Military Institute and to carrying out his *Physical Survey of Virginia,* in worthy continuation of Thomas Jefferson.

George Perkins Marsh (1801–82) no longer needs to be introduced to a student of human geography. He was wholly unknown to my student days, although *Man and Nature,* first published in 1864, went through a series of editions for forty years. The rediscovery of Marsh is mainly due to Lewis Mumford. After a hundred years it has appeared again as a classic in the John Harvard Library, with an introduction by David Lowenthal, who has placed geography further in his debt by his earlier biography, *George Perkins Marsh: Versatile Vermonter.*

Daniel Coit Gilman (1831–1908) certainly also deserves to be called versatile. In 1863 he was librarian, secretary, and professor of physical and political geography of the Sheffield Scientific School of Yale and distinguished himself in all three capacities. As a librarian of the old school he found time to read and he read geography with attention, in those Yale days that ended in 1872. John K. Wright has written an informed sketch on Gilman as a student of geography (*Geographical Review*, vol. 51, 1961). Gilman missed little of geographically significant work of the time. Petermann complimented him as a kindred spirit for the best articles on current geography overseas. Gilman's addresses of 1871 and 1872 to the American Geographical Society passed in summary review the current inquiries. The state surveys he commended as "the common form in these days for the manifestation of local interest in natural science." The Whitney survey he thought contributed the most important findings of the decade. He knew that Marsh was inquiring into man's role as a geographic agent and he knew also the as yet unpublished studies of Gabb in the Dominican Republic. In his last address to the Society he showed a series of manuscript maps that were being prepared for the Ninth Census, explaining the insights that could be gained by plotting census data on topical maps. This new form of inspection, he said, was being introduced by General Francis Walker from the example of the Prussian statistical office, in particular Meitzen's *Boden und landwirtschaftliche Verhältnisse des Preussischen Staats*. Gilman did not say so, but he had called this work to the attention of his friend Walker. Gilman never lost his interest in geography although his later years were given to the development of higher education and of scholarship. In 1872 he became president of the University of California, which began to merit that name under his administration. In 1875 he moved to Baltimore to found there the Johns Hopkins University, first in the United States to adopt the European model of a university as a place of scholarly studies instead of undergraduate teaching.

Francis Amasa Walker (1840–97) must be given an important place in American geography. By reason of a brilliant military record, his father's eminence as economist, and his own promise as scholar and administrator he was appointed in 1869 to the Bureau of Statistics, shortly to be its Superintendent. The Ninth (1870) and Tenth (1880) Censuses are monuments. In the latter he introduced most of the categories of enumeration that have served since. Distributional maps, such as Gilman had shown, were published in the

Ninth Census and were so favorably received that a Statistical Atlas was authorized and by dint of hard effort appeared in 1874. The atlas continued in later censuses to serve as principal documentation of economic and population geography. The old inclination to statistical geography that had flourished in the eighteenth century was given a powerful and novel assist. Numbers were expressed on maps as quantity or density by county units, providing an easy and attractive means of inspecting geographical distribution of anything that had been enumerated. Topical maps as representation of quantities became the most convenient base for economic geography, not wholly to its advantage because the census maps directed the main attention to numbers.

Textually the Census of 1880, consisting of twenty-two massive volumes, is the greatest single contribution to the historical geography of the United States. The participating scholars were the ablest of their kind and they were not restricted as to how they developed their themes nor in the use of maps and illustrations. They gave exposition of the conditions as they found them and also of what they knew of their past state. They are historical geography both because they are the fullest description of the United States of the time and because the authors placed their time into historical perspective. The first volume began with Walker and Gannett's *Progress of the Nation from 1790–1880* and the famous maps on the decennial changes in population density, followed by a series of maps on relief, temperature, and precipitation. These were examined as "influences of physical features upon the distribution of population," the term "influence" in this case indicating only the fit between population density and physical category, such as minimal temperature or summer rain. William Brewer had contributed a shorter memoir on woodlands and forests to the prior census and wrote a long one on cereal production and its history for the third volume of the Tenth. Hilgard filled the fifth and sixth volumes with his classic *Cotton Production in the United States,* fully justifying its subtitle "embracing agricultural and physico-geographical descriptions of the several Cotton States and of California." These were economic and regional geography at a new high level. Volume eight contains two pioneer field studies of Alaska and its Seal Islands, richly illustrated with colored plates and pen sketches, including fur-bearing animals, natives and their ways of living and hunting. Charles Sargent wrote the ninth volume on forests of North America and Raphael Pumpelly and his assistants the eleventh one on the mining industries and iron resources of the United States. These are some of the highlights of the most extraordinary inquiry that has been undertaken into the nature and conditions of life in the United States.

The genius of Francis Walker, who organized the great Census, is remembered by few. Its volumes of text gather dust in the documents sections of libraries. Walker's maps of decennial changes of population, however, continued to be reproduced in the Census Atlas and to serve textbooks of American history and geography.

## GEOGRAPHY IN COLLEGE AND UNIVERSITY

Arnold Guyot (1807–84) held the first chair in geography in the country, being thus appointed in 1854 to Princeton, a Presbyterian college. His background and persuasion was Swiss Calvinism. He studied at Berlin where he heard Ritter, Humboldt, and perhaps Hegel and did his doctorate on lakes. On his return to Switzerland he taught school and confirmed Agassiz' observations on Alpine glaciation. The latter urged him to come to America and helped him to get established here. Guyot was introduced to Boston by giving the Lowell Institute Lectures in 1849 (in French). These were published in book form as *Earth and Man,* well received and widely circulated. By subtitle this was a comparative physical geography of the world related to the history of mankind. The teleology was that of Ritter without the learning of Ritter. "All is order, all is harmony in the universe," Guyot wrote, because all is "the thought of God." The physical features of the earth revealed its divine plan and predestination was apparent in the homelands and living of different races. Guyot offered a full and simple gospel of environmental determinism. Secure in this belief, he did not need further to examine premise or evidence. As an observer he merely measured altitudes in the Appalachians and monitored weather stations. He wrote textbooks for elementary schools that set a new vogue of attributing the condition of mankind in different parts to their physical environment. His best contribution to elementary teaching was that he introduced Pestalozzi's principle that learning should begin with observing the home vicinity.

The second establishment of geography at institutions of higher learning came toward the end of the century. The prime mover was William Morris Davis, who had been advanced to a professorship of physical geography at Harvard in 1890. Davis undertook the mission to promote geographical education in this country. He was first and last a teacher, rigorous in a didactic discipline that proceeded through orderly steps of learning. Secondary education at the time was of special concern as preparation for college, for which purpose the National Education Association set up a committee in 1892 under President Eliot of Harvard. Its subcommittee of ten on geography made a report that was regarded by the general committee as going farthest in revision of its field, proposing this as "the physical environment of men," and based on a comprehensive conception of physiography, Huxley's term, here first thus given currency in this country. The Committee of Ten included T. C. Chamberlin, Israel Russel, and W. M. Davis, the hand of the latter most conspicuous in drafting the report.

At the same time Davis proposed to the young National Geographic Society the preparation of a series of essays which "should be accessible to the teachers of the land." These appeared under the title of *The Physiography of the United States,* were edited by J. W. Powell and consisted of ten monographs, three by Powell, and one each by N. S. Shaler, Israel Russel, Bailey Willis, C. W. Hayes, J. S. Diller, G. K. Gilbert, and Davis—an illustrious roster of geologists. In the conclusion to his monograph Davis reaffirmed his faith. "It is only after a clear perception of the forms of the land is gained by tracing out their development that the careful teacher or the serious student is prepared to undertake the discussion of the relation of geography to history." And again: "Today it is only by those who fail to see the direction of geographical progress, and who are ignorant of the progress already gained, that objection is made against the effort to bring every geographical fact under the explanation of natural processes."

This is pure Huxleyan doctrine plus Herbert Spencer. In support of these ends Davis also became the founding father in 1904 of the Association of American Geographers, assisted by a group of geologist godfathers.

In practice Davis limited himself to applying his view of a general order to land forms. These he organized as categories of his inclusive concept of the erosion cycle. Thereby to his mind, "rational explanation has replaced empirical generalization." His famous formulation of structure, process, and stage would provide a genetic classification of all land forms. This unifying concept of his was a construct of his mind. Description therefore was illustrative of his thesis instead of empirically informative. What he called explanatory description required identification of forms by terms of his system of explanation, and therefore the introduction of a new vocabulary. A Davisian description did not propose to give the reader data that were independent of his frame of reference. The block diagrams which he drew with art were theoretical models, not graphic descriptions. His thinking depended on stage and cycle, the metaphors of youth, maturity, and old age, and of rejuvenation by a new cycle. I think that Davis came to regard the difference between geology and physical geography as a different attitude toward time, the former being concerned with divisions and length of time, the latter with cycles for which length of time was indifferent. When he was on the Pacific Coast he would remonstrate if I talked of a surface as of Pliocene age instead of as being of a certain stage. A. Penck was Visiting Professor of Geography at Berkeley at the same time that Davis was such in Geology. Davis commented to me that the geographer was lecturing in the Department of Geology whereas the geologist was doing so in Geography, Penck being concerned with the history of Pleistocene glaciations and interglacials and their durations. This is water long over the dam. For years there was a division in American geography between the Davisian camp and others.

Geography was a basic subject in elementary schools and physical geography was being taught in secondary schools as a college entrance subject. Schools for the training of teachers, then called normal schools, required instructors in geography and therefore teachers of teachers of geography. The doors of universities began to open to geography because it was appreciated as part of a liberal education. The men appointed to university posts were expected to communicate significant geographical knowledge. That they would add to knowledge was hoped rather than demanded. Their first dedication was to win the interest and respect of students, which they might nourish by also being scholars. British thoughts on education entered into consideration, especially those of A. J. Herbertson of Oxford and to some extent H. R. Mill's inquiry for the Royal Geographical Society into geography at German universities.

Ralph S. Tarr combined at Cornell University the qualities of teacher and scholar. His textbooks at various levels were solid, well presented, and used in large numbers. His *Physical Geography of New York* was composed of a competent knowledge of literature and maps, a fair amount of observation, common sense interpretations, and addressed to the reader who might also be a teacher. As a student Tarr was interested in glaciation, to which his observations in Alaska are durable contributions.

Academic geography in the United States was shaped most strongly at the University of Chicago and through the personality of R. D. Salisbury. The university opened in October 1892 with a most remarkable lot of scholars who were attracted by the invitation to make a new university as they wished it to be. T. C. Chamberlin left the presidency of the University of Wisconsin to build the great Department of Geology and bring Salisbury with him as Professor of Geographic Geology. Their close association had begun when Salisbury was a student and was continued for life. They had studied glaciation together in the field and had taught together at Beloit and at the University of Wisconsin. At Chicago Chamberlin turned to hypotheses of the origin of ice ages, or orogeny, of continents, of the planet Earth, Salisbury being his interpreter and commentator, as is shown in the three volumes of their classic *Geology*.

From the beginning of the University of Chicago to his retirement Salisbury was a member and long the head of the Department of Geology. In 1903 he also became the head of the newly created Department of Geography. Always his courses in physiography continued to be listed under Geology but were required also of students in Geography. The gradual extension of interest in the direction of geography is apparent in the early years by fellows—H. C. Cowles in 1896, J. Paul Goode in 1897, W. W. Atwood in 1898, N. M. Fenneman in 1900. When the new department was organized in 1903 Goode became Assistant Professor, giving all the courses, those of Salisbury remaining listed under Geology. In 1905 H. H. Barrows, previously in Geology, became Assistant Professor of Geography. In 1906 Ellen Semple began lecturing for a part of the academic year, and introduced in 1907 her Principle of Anthropogeography. In 1908 W. D. Jones became assistant, and the following year W. S. Tower joined the staff. By such leisurely selection Salisbury built the first Department of Geography.

Salisbury will not be remembered as a scholar though he did able work on glaciation. He took great delight in teaching, not by lecture but by questioning. A class session was likely to be a Socratic dialogue in which I have never known his equal. A field excursion was the following-out of a trail of clues. Observations became evidence by no formal method but by asking whether they were material, competent, and relevant. He liked to bring up Chamberlin's recommendation of multiple hypotheses to be considered one by one until one was found, or a combination, that was satisfactory. He liked the word hypothesis, might commit himself as far as saying "as a rule" of experience, but indulged in no general theory, unless it happened to stem from Chamberlin. Salisbury, as I knew him, was especially pleased if a student came to the point of informed disagreement with him. He encouraged learning by independent field observation. At the end of my first year he sent me into the Illinois Valley to make a study for the state geological survey. When I asked how to go about it he answered that that was my business, that he would find out later whether I had seen and learned. He came down twice to visit me in the field, asking me to show him whatever I wished in the way of evidence. He listened to my expositions, asking occasional acute questions but giving me no assistance in interpretation. This was my job and it was up to me to come to my own conclusions.

Salisbury was a master teacher and superb editor, as I had the good fortune to learn. His clear and cool judgment was called upon heavily by the administration of the university, formally as dean of the graduate school of science, informally as its most trusted adviser. As academic statesman he had a lot to do with those golden years of a great young university.

The department at Chicago started as a teaching staff, giving courses intended primarily for teachers and others for the instruction of undergraduates. It remained with these preoccupations and thus its extracurricular activities turned to the writing of texts and the designing of school maps. Goode had skill, taste, and inventiveness as a maker of maps and stimulated students to use and make such. Information of staff for the most part was from secondary sources. Learning by going out to observe was left to physiography and plant ecology. Henry Cowles by his excursions to the dunes of Indiana and the marshes about Chicago introduced the incipient geographers to manner and meaning of ecological seeing in the outdoors classroom of which he was a genial and perceptive mentor. Wellington Jones had been with Bailey Willis in Patagonia and had a year with Alfred Hettner at Heidelberg. At his return he became the insistent advocate of geographical field study.

It was the tenor of the time to regard geography as the expression of physical geography in human activities. In the first announcement of courses in 1903 this was described as "structure, physiography, and climate as factors determining or affecting location . . . social and economic status of peoples." Barrows introduced the course in Influences of Geography on American History in terms of "geographic conditions that have influenced American history, as compared with non-geographic factors." His presidential address of 1922 to the American geographers, *Geography as Human Ecology,* popularized a term that had long been familiar on the campus. At the Chicago meeting of the Association of American Geographers in 1907 Goode gave a paper outlining "a course in the principles of geography with the purpose of emphasizing the interrelation of life and its physical environment. Essentially an elementary course in plant, animal, and human ecology." The concept of ecology was introduced by Cowles. Later it was taken up by sociologists at Chicago and modified as to meaning.

Ellen Semple stirred imagination and feeling with her fervor and eloquence as she set forth the continuity of environmental influence on history. Her view of historical geography was of the persistence of advantage or disadvantage of place, not one of change. She had been a student of history who found the key to its understanding by hearing Ratzel lecture. A native of Kentucky, she had studied the westward movement of settlement across the Appalachians and down the Ohio River, noting the continuing significance of routes and localities. This grew into her book on influences of geography on American history, used by Barrows as a text. The anthropogeography she introduced at Chicago was Ratzel at his weakest, the first volume of his *Anthropogeographie*. The second volume in which he considered cultural diffusion did not attract her attention.

The affirmation of the dominance of physical environment in human affairs did not lead to a promising body of knowledge. It was a mode of explanation that Barrows tried to keep within proper limits by making the distinction between "geographic" and "nongeographic factors." It was not realized that physical environment, site, and resource were terms of culture, not of nature, and that the study of habitat needed to rest on knowledge of culture. Reconsideration of the nature of human geography began when Ellsworth Huntington pushed environmental interpretation to the extreme, especially in his *Civilization and Climate* (1915).

# 13. The Formative Years
## of Ratzel
### in the United States

Geographers in the English-speaking world lately have been provided a proper perspective of the life and works of Friedrich Ratzel, the talented and many-sided human geographer who, having come to profess himself as such, said "the geographer is naturalist" *(Naturforscher)*. Fifty years after Ratzel's death Jan Broek read an appraisal of his work to the Association of American Geographers.[1] In 1961, Harriet Wanklyn (Mrs. J. A. Steers) published her well-tempered biographical memoir.[2] In 1969 Robert E. Dickinson gave him a major chapter in *The Makers of Modern Geography*.[3]

At the present time of methodologic stirring and agonizing the thought and observations of Ratzel have renewed relevance and counsel as to the nature of geography. He was greatly interested in the contemporary world but he never took on the narrow vision of an

---

"The Formative Years of Ratzel in the United States" first appeared in the *Annals,* Association of American Geographers, 61:245–254, June 1971.

1. This paper has not been published, but the abstract appeared as J. O. M. Broek, "Ratzel in Retrospect," *Annals,* Association of American Geographers, Vol. 44 (1954), p. 207.

2. H. Wanklyn, *Friedrich Ratzel: A Biographical Memoir and Bibliography* (Cambridge, England: Cambridge University Press, 1961).

3. R. E. Dickinson, *The Makers of Modern Geography* (New York: Praeger, 1969).

*ad hoc* geography. His contemporary and later critics were bothered by the reach of his attention beyond the order of systems, an evolutionist searching for natural law and, as well, a humanist concerned with non-periodic origin and diffusion of cultures, their practical and esthetic satisfactions, the latter not measurable. He came to the study of geography out of the natural sciences, newly invigorated and oriented by the doctrine of evolution. On occasion he indulged in eloquent acknowledgment of environment as limiting or stimulating human condition and has been thus remembered by geographers as an environmental determinist. He has suffered by the familiarity of this stance, which was indeed one likeness of the man and his time but showed him in only one, and lesser, attribute of his person.

THE YOUNG NATURALIST

In his early twenties Ratzel studied zoology and published on the comparative anatomy and systematics of worms, earth and marine. He read Darwin, Wallace, and Haeckel, and at the age of twenty-five wrote a book on evolution, *Sein und Werden der organischen Welt,* subtitled "A Popular History of Creation."[4] He began at Munich his long friendship with Moritz Wagner, who had developed out of field studies in Central America the thesis that evolution resulted when there was migration into new habitats and also that people and their ideas changed by their dispersal. Mrs. Steers has acknowledged the influence of the older naturalist on the young scholar. In later years Ratzel expanded the migration concept of Wagner to the diffusion and differentiation of cultures and of particular culture traits. This had major and lasting impact on the study of man by anthropologists, but less generally so by geographers, as Dickinson has well noted. Before he was thirty Ratzel had written a book and more than a dozen articles on biology and a book and several articles on prehistory of man, all before he came to the United States. He was very well read, made good biological observations, and was attentive to

---

4. F. Ratzel, *Sein und Werden der organischen Welt: Eine populäre Schöpfungsgeschichte* (Leipzig: Gebhardt und Reisland, 1869).

processes of origin and change in natural history, finding new meanings in a world relieved of theological constraint.

While studying marine life on the Mediterranean Ratzel wrote letters to the *Kölnische Zeitung* which were well received and earned him a position as traveling correspondent of that influential newspaper. The zoological letters were followed by others describing his travels in South Italy, a collection of both issued (1873–74) by the firm of Brockhaus as *Wandertage eines Naturforschers*.[5] The young naturalist wrote with uncommon grace and freshness of observation and opened for himself a career as a reporter. In 1870 he served in the Franco-Prussian War until disabled by wounds and then returned to travel in Transylvania and the Alps, resulting in a second volume of description. Meantime he continued his association with Moritz Wagner at Munich.

Ratzel had learned to identify and associate biotic elements, to note their interdependence, and to think about the processes of their differentiation. Man and his works were increasingly in the range of his attention. What was living together had assembled or been assembled there or had developed there. Being free of the old concept of creation he had begun to look into nature (and man) as of four dimensions and so to appreciate and understand geographical diversity as involving movement and time.

## THE AMERICAN YEARS

In 1873 Ratzel, age 29, was sent by the *Kölnische Zeitung* to report on life in the United States, to which he added an interesting reconnaissance of Mexico in 1875. This was the longest period he spent at travel observations, as it was also the last time that he went to lands unknown to him.

To the readers of the Rhenish newspaper the United States was of particular interest. For more than forty years a flood of emigrants had gone from lands along the Rhine to settle overseas. Large numbers had served in the Union forces during the Civil War, lately ended. The South was still in the time of reconstruction, beginning to insti-

---

5. F. Ratzel, *Wandertage eines Naturforschers* (Leipzig: Brockhaus, 1873–74).

tute a new social order. In the North industrial development was strongly under way. Railroads had become the dominant means of transport. Land settlement was extending west of the Missouri River. It was indeed an opportune time to report on the vigorously growing young nation.

Twenty years earlier Moritz Wagner and the Austrian botanist Karl von Scherzer had written of their travels in the United States. Ratzel also was informed of the travels and explorations of other Germans and of accounts in English and French, which he used. He had read well in preparation for his American journey. The Cologne newspaper, he acknowledged, conceived his travel as no small matter and gave him liberty of movement so that he could tarry wherever he wished and pass on where nothing attracted his attention.

A selection and revision of his letters to the *Kölnische Zeitung* was published in 1876 as *Städte- und Kulturbilder aus Nordamerika,* sketches of cities and culture in the United States.[6] They have not been reprinted nor translated. The newspaper sent him by way of San Francisco to Mexico, leading to a collection of letters republished as *Aus Mexico: Reiseskizzen aus den Jahren 1874 und 1875* (1879, reprinted in 1969 with introduction by Franz Termer, almost the last thing Termer wrote).[7]

In the introduction to the sketches of the United States Ratzel said that the nature of a people is most clearly expressed in its cities, that these hold what is best and highest in culture, that there the contact of minds makes history. Obviously Ratzel did not hold to Jefferson's views of a rural society. He praised the American spirit that had built fourteen cities of more than a hundred thousand people within that century, would continue in metropolitan growth, and, advancing ahead of other countries by new means of communication, would diminish the contrast between town and country. This

---

6. F. Ratzel, *Städte- und Kulturbilder aus Nordamerika* (Leipzig: Brockhaus, 1876).

7. F. Ratzel, *Aus Mexico: Reiseskizzen aus den Jahren 1874 und 1875* (Breslau: Kerns, 1878); neudruck des 1878 erschienenen Werkes mit einer Einführung von Franz Termer, Vol. 17 of Quellen und Forschungen zur Geschichte der Geographie und der Reisen (Stuttgart: Brockhaus, 1969).

"wonderland of culture" was providing new prospect as it fostered material progress by technical inventiveness.

The American cities were taking new forms. Boston, New York, and New Orleans had old quarters that reminded him of European cities, but about these were modern urban patterns of regular and ample plan such as had been applied first in Philadelphia and Charleston. The young cities of the west began as models of urban planning. The overall impression of American cities was of straight and wide streets, heavy traffic, small average size of homes (a sound preference for single family living), and the sharp division between residence and business streets. This happy condition was then changing in New York, where large tenement buildings were becoming numerous.

A rural aspect was preserved in the cities by planting rows of trees along the streets, lawns in front of the houses, and vines on the balconies, "even in the heart of New York and Boston and especially in Philadelphia. Even in San Francisco, despite the dry dune sand, undemanding eucalyptus have been planted. On the other hand flowers in the windows are uncommon. More than the green and shaded margins of the streets, the nearness to nature and the love of nature of the Americans is expressed in their beautiful parks and public gardens." Fairmount Park in Philadelphia and Central Park in New York astonished a European familiar with great parks, and the young cities of Cincinnati and St. Louis provided fine parks. American cemeteries departed from the melancholy of the European graveyard by making them places for recreation for the living, being parks in attractive locations. Public buildings in large part did not impress him, but the architecture of the great bridges did.

There are twenty-one sketches, arranged somewhat in the order of visit. The first and much the longest is on New York, beginning as usual with the nature of its site and the rationale of its location. The traffic of streets, such as the horse-drawn street cars, and the sanitary organization of the city, had attention, as did most of all the public school system, of which he approved. Next came a trip up the Hudson and a visit to Saratoga Springs in the fashionable season, when New York came to the country. He noted an encampment there of Indians from Canada, quite like a gypsy camp in Hungary. Boston, Cambridge, Philadelphia, and Washington were stressed as to intellectual life.

Richmond was the first city of the South visited, seen in postwar change to industries. Columbia was being rebuilt from the devastation of the war and was under Reconstruction government. Charleston and Savannah he appreciated as cities of evergreen trees and shrubs, live oaks hung with Spanish moss, magnolias and camellias, the cherry laurel he knew as mock orange, and hedges of a native holly *(Ilex cassine)*. In the Deep South houses had their narrow side toward the street, the long side, with a veranda of one or two stories (called *piazza*), facing on yard and garden in "retiring respectability."

Florida was becoming a winter resort for northern city people. One could travel by sleeping car from Boston to Jacksonville or by steamship from New York. More than forty thousand persons had come thus the previous winter. Thousands were moving into Florida to settle, enjoy the subtropical climate, grow oranges, and get away from city pressures. He took his first notes in Florida of rural life and of country stores, to him a new institution.

The journey from Jacksonville to New Orleans began with an overnight train ride of sixty-odd miles to Jessup, Georgia, a railroad junction of a score of houses in the pine woods. The arrival being on Sunday, when no trains ran, the day of rest was observed by the natives in going to church morning and afternoon, and by the passengers in boredom, the bar being closed. The journey to Macon continued Monday through the pine woods, passing an occasional sawmill and meager settlement on the railroad, poorly constructed and maintained. Macon in pouring rain left an impression of unsurfaced muddy streets, flanked by plank sidewalks, of many shacks and few substantial houses. The rain continuing when he arrived at Montgomery and the rail lines beyond being interrupted by floods, he settled down in a boarding house to become acquainted with southern life and countryside. The unusually high water of the Alabama River enabled steamboats to pass above Selma as far as Montgomery. Ratzel took passage on a sternwheeler to enjoy a three-

and-a-half day ride through flooded country to Mobile, which he found gay with flowers in homes and streets.

New Orleans still showed damages by the late war. The sugar and cotton plantations were partly abandoned, and its former river traffic had been largely diverted to railroads. Horse-drawn street cars diverged from the broad axis of Canal Street, splashing through the flooded streets. In spite of inadequate gutters, poor sanitation, water supply from cisterns and river, and the bordering swamps, the health conditions were not bad. The numerous markets had abundance of food, Texas beef and Gulf seafood, tropical fruits, bananas, pineapples, oranges, and coconuts from the West Indies. Locally grown Japanese persimmons were cheap. On the sidewalk outside of the markets Indian women, remnants of their tribe, offered baskets of large blackberries. Inside the markets an enticing variety of dishes invited the visitor to partake at rows of tables. The markets were his most attractive memory of New Orleans, along with its colored population; its gardens and city park were the most disappointing.

The trip up the Mississippi and Ohio rivers gave rise to a sketch which I think is one of the finest portrayals of American landscape. It would need to be reproduced in full to do justice to what he saw in the flood of water in changing light and direction, of the rarely broken solitude along the Mississippi River, its willow thickets, slender cottonwoods, and angularly branched sycamores, with the distant ragged skyline of cypresses. Except at Baton Rouge, Vicksburg, and Memphis they saw hardly a steamboat, and below Cairo met only five flatboats. The sugar plantations of Louisiana largely were in ruins; north of Louisiana the lowlands were mainly wilderness until they got to Cairo at the mouth of the Ohio where flour mills gave notice of a different agriculture. The Ohio River was a clear and decorous stream in a civilized land. Here cultivated fields lined valley floor and sides, orchards were in bloom, towns or villages usually were in sight. Sternwheel steamers pushed coal barges downriver and barges of iron ore from Missouri to the steel mills upriver. At intervals railroad bridges spanned the Ohio. River and land here resembled the European scene.

Great rivers and lakes determined location and growth of the cities in the interior. Cincinnati had the initial advantage by the early settlement of the fertile states of Kentucky and Ohio, being the largest western city to the time of the Civil War. It was the first to become a center of industry, manufacturing goods for the needs of the West and converting farm surplus in pork packing plants and whiskey distilleries. The lower part of the city, with factories and warehouses, occupied a "bay" above the reach of river floods. Residential districts extended into the heights of the surrounding hills, as in a great park, the houses largely of brick and of one family, the general aspect like that of a hilly Philadelphia. The city was well kept but subject to the smoke of its factory chimneys.

"St. Louis has become basically what it is on account of the Mississippi, in particular in its first decades, but is becoming less and less a Mississippi River town." Its former character as a southern city had been changed by northern immigration and a hundred thousand Germans, who found themselves most at home there. Industrially it ranked third after New York and Philadelphia. As products he listed flour, meat packing, iron, lead, leather, refined sugar, and cotton goods, but strangely omitted beer and tobacco. The waterfront he found unattractive, but the gently rising terrace behind, impressive in its great mass of houses and church steeples. Streets were less planted with trees than in eastern cities but the parks were admirable. Shaw's Garden and Tower Grove Park would arouse envy in Berlin, and there were beer gardens in great number.

Chicago, "one of the modern wonders," was the best example of a railroad city, the product of what could be called a natural law of commerce, the obligate convergence of land and water routes at the end of Lake Michigan. "Chicago is above all the creation of New England enterprise." Yankee drive made Chicago and dominated it, Germans contributing skilled labor. Less than three years after the fire that destroyed more than half of it he saw it rebuilt as the richest and handsomest city of the West. "Few events in American history present its people in such favorable light and demand such respect."

Denver had grown in fourteen years from a few poor shacks in a desolate spot of the High Plains to a city of twenty thousand, which he could more easily imagine as a future ruin than as a coming queen of the West. It could have had an attractive and suitable site at the foot of the Rockies, but there it was, in what he thought a dreary location, thriving because it had been terminus of the Kansas Pacific Railway and a junction of four more rail lines. Not advantage of location but routing of railroads had come to determine what settlements would become cities. Wide, unpaved streets with raised plank sidewalks were lined by young cottonwoods. A conspicuous trait of the physiognomy of Denver was the astonishing number of saloons, frequented by miners.

The rail journey from Cheyenne to San Francisco was described in sensitive attention to the configuration and tones of the landscape, the component vegetation of desert, bunch grass, and mountain forest. The rail route had been chosen for the convenience of terrain; the memorable scenery was at the approach to Salt Lake and in the descent of the Sierra Nevada to the valley of California. The train stopped for meals three times a day, giving welcome breaks and a feel of the country. The comfort and leisure of travel was at its best in this manner of conveyance and service. This was railroad construction and maintenance such as he had not known in the South, an example of American competence to plan, execute, and operate a large enterprise.

The bay of San Francisco was a wonder of nature's design when it could be seen, which was not often in the chill fogs of summer. Ratzel found the local climate of unexpected daily range and variability. The city, tucked in the lee side of the peninsula, was subject to much blowing sand carried by wind from the ocean beach and dunes. Its location had been determined by historical incidents that presented problems of inland communication which a different location on the bay would have avoided. Except for the blocks near California and Montgomery Streets, the buildings had a provisional appearance. Its hundred and fifty thousand inhabitants were about half American-born whites, almost half foreign-born whites, twelve thousand or more Chinese, mostly packed in the narrow quarters of Chinatown, and somewhat more than a thousand blacks. On the cultural side he noted the great Bancroft Library and the newly established Academy of Sciences; as to commerce, that the clothing store of Hastings (still existing) had covered rocks and fences from Oregon to Mexico with its advertising.

The final essay dealt with ruins. Towns sprang up with the construction of railroads, had expectation of growth and permanence, and were abandoned as the rails pushed farther. California had its short-lived gold placer towns, Colorado had shaft mines with stamp mills and smelters that stood abandoned. He described a long tramp into the Adirondack forest to an iron mine and smelter that had been active a generation ago and was being reclaimed by wilderness. The South had its ruins of the late war, such as the mansions of rice plantations on the coast of South Carolina. Along St. Johns River in Florida were remains of mansions and plantations said to date from English times and in the woods wild orange trees that had given rise to a belief that oranges were native to those parts. "America ages rapidly."

The Mexican trip (1874–75) began at Acapulco. The letters written to the *Kölnische Zeitung* were reworked as "unaffected aspects of nature and life," with acknowledgment to Humboldt and other Germans who had traveled there. From Acapulco he rode northwest through the coastal thorn savanna to Petatlán, then rode across the coast sierra and the Balsas depression to Huetamo, Tecámbaro, and Morelia, colonial capital of Michoacán. From here he traveled by stage *(diligencia)* to Mexico City and Puebla. He climbed the volcano of Orizaba on his way to Vera Cruz, took a ship to Minatitlán at the mouth of the Coatzacoalcos River, went up the river by dugout and completed the crossing of the Isthmus of Tehuantepec on horseback. From Tehuantepec he traveled the main road north to visit the ancient ruins of Mitla, the city of Oaxaca, around which Humboldt had made botanical exploration, Tehuacán, and came again to Vera Cruz. The concluding essay dealt with the characteristics of nature in the tropics, a worthy companion piece to Humboldt's classic.

Ratzel knew little of Indian culture or Spanish society, as Termer said, nor had he time to learn much. He reported in good outline what he saw and experienced without affectation or bias. His recognition of vegetation was very good, remarkable considering that he had never been in the tropics before. The naturalist registered well on things that grew, wild or cultivated, and on the small farmers and stock raisers.

BEGINNING THE ACADEMIC CAREER

Returned to Germany in 1875, Ratzel, on recommendation of his "fatherly friend," Moritz Wagner, offered himself as Docent in Geography at the *Technische Hochschule* of Munich, an institute of technology of university grade. The study he presented for habilitation was on Chinese emigration, as a contribution to cultural and commercial geography. The theme, it is inferred, came to him in California. It is an early use of the term cultural geography, proper and connected with Wagner's interest in migration. The publication has not been accessible to me; Mrs. Steers has cited its extensive use of the writings of British colonial officers of the nineteenth century. His first bold step as a professional geographer was concerned with a major topic of British empire and American development of the far West.

In those beginning academic years he completed the first volume of his handbook of the United States, *Physikalische Geographie und Naturcharakter* (1878), a formidable collection of 667 pages of organized data.[8] Ratzel knew little of forms and processes of physical geography. He knew something of the Ice Age, partly through contact with Agassiz, but there is little identification of glacial land forms in his descriptions of the United States as to location, process, or time. He spoke of drift, boulder clay, a bluff formation that resembled loess, of ridges of sand and gravel like the kames of Scotland, but gave little meaning to their distribution and relation. He dealt somewhat with what later were called physiographic regions and their geologic structure. The hydrographic section detailed the patterns of stream systems and lakes, added cold and hot springs and a bit on solution caves, a competent compilation of geologic field studies and use of existing maps. Climate was presented in terms of what was known by instrumental observations, spiced by weather experiences of travelers and explorers, showing that Ratzel was busy taking excerpts from a lot of reading. There is little that was original in the sections on physical geography.

---

8. F. Ratzel, *Die Vereinigten Staaten von Nordamerika* (München: Oldenbourg, 1878–93).

On vegetation he read Asa Gray, W. H. Brewer, Michaux, Engelmann, and other field botanists, but also contributed floristic determinations of his own, especially for California. Of the different theories of the origin of prairies he thought the best to be James D. Dana's—of precipitation as ineffective for tree growth. The mammalian fauna was characterized as mostly neo-arctic. The avifauna included neo-tropic forms, hummingbirds nesting as far north as Manitoba and parakeets as far as the Platte River, although these were becoming rare.

The volume ends with thirty essays descriptive of natural landscapes, largely based on his articles for the *Kölnische Zeitung*. They are representative landscapes from different parts, some rural, some wilderness; a composite of what he saw and what others had written. Having the eye of a naturalist, Ratzel registered well on vegetation that determined the aspect of the land as to tone and texture. The essay on autumn color in the northeastern states is a gem, describing how the different trees and shrubs change their leaf color and continue to do so to gradual fading and fall, in contrast to the paler colors and earlier fall of leaf of the deciduous woods of Europe. The pieces on the prairies, their woods margins, and park-like oak openings are illustrated by selections from earlier observers, among them James Fenimore Cooper, whom he rated a fine observer. (Cooper has been out of fashion because of his style, but his descriptions are remarkably acute.) Ratzel described the true prairies of the Midwest as floriferous meadows with a burst of rosy bloom in spring, followed by blue in summer, and changing to yellow and red in fall, stressing the diversity of *Compositae* and leguminous plants. About two-thirds of the coast plain of Virginia and Carolina were or had been woods of various yellow pines, the abandoned fields, exhausted by tobacco growing, in stages of repossession by secondary growth. In the deep South climbing and scandent vines occupied open spaces, among them honeysuckles, smilax (greenbrier), passion flowers, and a rose that covered young pines with white bloom (the Cherokee rose, not yet recognized as an immigrant from China). There are good essays on cypress swamps, the Rocky Mountain front near Boulder, the Great Basin and its oasis of the Humboldt River flanked by sagebrush, the valley of California with oak parks and expanses of wild oats and clovers, an ascent of Mount Dana, and a visit to Yosemite. This lot of essays is notable as to quality of perception and description.

His years of the late seventies at Munich were of great activity, largely focused on North America. The bibliography of his journal articles lists twelve in 1878, thirteen in 1879, and twenty in 1880, about half concerning America.

The second volume of *Die Vereinigten Staaten* was completed in 1879 and published in 1880 (762 pages) entitled *Kulturgeographie.* Its introductory section on "natural conditions of cultural development" describes an environmentalism tempered by awareness of alternative choices. The United States at the time had forty-five million inhabitants and might be expected to grow to two hundred million in the course of centuries. It was still engaged in careless waste of its resources, for which he introduced the term *Raubbau,* later repeatedly used. (This was a generation before Friedrich and Brunhes directed the attention of geographers to destructive exploitation, both having been strongly influenced by Ratzel.) The young nation, taking possession of a vast and great land, growing in strength by overcoming difficulties and doing great things, was looking confidently to a limitless future. Largely it was highly mobile and had not as yet settled down to make itself at home in the process of becoming "a new race."

The second section dealt with population, including Indians (sketchily treated here, without indication of his later insights of ethnology), immigration from Europe and dispersal inland, demographic increase, Negroes during and after slavery, and Chinese immigration. Agriculture was introduced by a discussion of soils and climate and the limits of cultivated plants. In wooded country American farmers chose land by kinds of trees that indicated fertile soil. They cleared and planted the land by intermediate steps that gave yield and saved labor, adding a footnote on the superior utility of the American axe. Other practices were used in settling the prairies, requiring use of draft animals and steel plow. In either case fencing was necessary. Years of arduous and varied labor were required and, labor being in shorter supply than land, exploitation of the natural fertility of the soil resulted, soon registered by declining yields. The losses of fertility by such *Raubbau* were great, a hundred million acres estimated as exhausted and abandoned, a good fourth of Virginia being in that condition. Hence in good part the continuing westward thrust of settlement. Crop rotation he noted as established only in the old settled farm lands of the East. Commercial fertilizers were used mainly in the South. On the Atlantic coast fish fertilizer plants, largely processing menhaden, had begun thirty years previously and were supplied by hundreds of ships. Import of guano was increasing, the largest single source being the islet of Navassa in the Caribbean, belonging to the United States (as it still does). Mineral fertilizers included phosphate rock, limestone, marl, greensand, gypsum, and salt.

The American farmer, independent owner of his land, was a social form and force unknown to Europe. Beyond the cotton and tobacco lands the rural economy was based mainly on maize, superior in yield and uses to the small grains. It was marketed mainly by feeding pigs, processed in packing plants, first developed at Cincinnati as a major industry.

Industrial initiative he thought had not given sufficient credit to the Dutch and Swedes in their introduction of sawmills and perhaps of grinding grain by windmills. In the nineteenth century labor-saving machines were designed in a diversity and efficiency without parallel elsewhere. The Americans were a nation of inventors of machines for farming, household use, and heavy and light industry. The Patent Office documented the pace of invention as, for example, more than two thousand patents for sewing machines had been given since 1854. Industrial enterprise was greatly benefited by the ease of credit. "American business lives on credit."

The section on transportation reviewed the navigation of rivers and lakes, the building of canals, and the revolution of shipping and travel by railroads. Ratzel traveled mainly by train, observing road-beds, rolling stock, and operation of service as comparing favorably with Europe. In treating of commerce he was impressed by the trait of "merchant sense," largely attributed to New Englanders, and apparent across the West in the flow and organization of trade to and from the country or general stores. Like the farmer, the storekeeper was a peculiarly American cultural phenomenon.

The fourth and final section dealt with political organization, church, the *geistige Leben,* and society. He regretted the drawing of geodetical boundaries for political divisions and had reservations about egalitarian voting, though not sharing the fears of Tocqueville. Protestant churches ranged from Episcopalian and Presbyterian luxury and ceremonial in the cities to extreme simplicity, revival meetings, camp meetings, and emotional preaching among Methodists and Baptists. New sects had appeal especially to the poor. New England Congregationalism had been of outstanding cultural influence in the West, as had Scottish Presbyterianism in the South. The Roman Catholic Church, largely urban and Irish, was strongly organized and well directed.

The materialistic preoccupation of the American people stressed practical relevance of knowledge, but its native talent *(Begabung)* was great, in part because there was favorable natural selection of those who had migrated overseas. Educational institutions were developing strongly, latterly including public instruction, from elementary schools to universities. (He thought that there was excessive attention to oratory.) The search for knowledge had been advanced by scientific explorations of the West (of which he made large use) and at the time was being developed by the Smithsonian and other government offices.

He was well read on American scholars and made an appraisal of American men of letters. Washington Irving had the manner of English gentry; James Fenimore Cooper was an authentic American, and Emerson, the most original mind, was a new type of man of letters. The latter, Cooper, Thoreau, and Bryant wrote splendid descriptions of nature. Whittier was quoted at length on the lack of Yankee pastoral poetry. Landscape painters were discovering the appeal of American scenes. Public architecture still was imitative of Old World designs. In music he thought the English lack of musical talent apparent.

Being a newspaperman, Ratzel considered the press as greatly different from that of Europe, much concerned with politics and, with rare exceptions, partisan, playing up the latest news, writing for mass appeal, and aiming at greatest circulation. Advertising had an importance and stridence unknown in Europe. Journalists were numerous in legislatures and politics, Lincoln having sent some in diplomatic service to Paris, Bonn, Constantinople, Rio, La Paz, and Cairo.

Perhaps this young people was evolving into a new "race." Transplanted to new habitat it ceased to be European and the offspring was different from its parents, perhaps more precocious and somewhat physically altered. Culturally, Anglo-American dominance was assured. The expectation of lasting German-American communities was an illusion; these were fading in the second generation and disappearing in the third. The structure of American society was shaped by the prestige of making and having money and by the readiness to leave home for a new place, giving the interior parts a "cultural physiognomy" of building for temporary service.

PERSPECTIVE AND PROSPECT

The samples I have taken out of a large context show the range and acuteness of a very able reporter. The impressions are sharply drawn and properly representative. He was a critical observer who came to learn about American ways, liking their freedom, confidence, and energy. The nation, founded on just and viable social institutions, had accomplished great things in material progress and might be expected to grow in grace and spirit. The lately ended Civil War had given great push to industry and innovation and urban growth. Natural wealth was being wasted in the careless exploitations he called *Raubbau,* but such excesses might be ascribed to youthful recklessness. Even this rich country had limited resources which it would in time learn to husband.

Ratzel returned to Germany before the opening of the Centennial Exposition at Philadelphia but took pains to be provided with information about it as an exhibit of American progress in technology, its new machines for collecting primary materials, processing them into products, and bringing them to the consumer. The centennial date was an appropriate milestone in the course of our national life. The period of occupying the land was changing to one of industrialization and urban growth. Ratzel was its first geographer. He carried out his inquiry in historical perspective, attentive to origins, dispersals, changes, and replacements, as a student of natural history should.

The biologist-journalist, develped into a geographer by his American experiences, made use of his earlier training. As a field naturalist he made identification of living things as to kind, association, and habitat. He had insights that later would be called ecology and also ethology, and applied these to man. The problem of location was always in his mind, as was Wagner's theme of migration, which gave direction to his thinking on cultural diffusion and innovation. As journalist he cultivated the art of description of landscape, natural and man-made, and thereby asserted the old prerogative of geography to aesthetic appreciation. *Kulturgeographie,* as he outlined it for the United States, extended beyond the material works of man to include its *Geist,* the spirit of its society, its traditions, aspirations, and its contributors to art and science.

The achievement of the first century had been great, the prospect bright. The young nation lived in expectation of unlimited growth in wealth and numbers. Moderation he thought would come with maturity. *Raubbau* of farm land, forest, and mines would be replaced by conservative management. The excessive mobility of the people in search of new opportunity of gain would change to permanence of habitation and the social amenities of communities. The "cultural nomad" was a phenomenon of the time, as was the addiction to advertising that cluttered newspapers and the out-of-doors. The late war had given powerful push to mechanical innovations, industrial plants, railroad building, and growth of buildings, but Ratzel was not thinking of such stimulus by future wars. Materialism was running at high tide in the seventies but might serve as means to a nobler civilization. What Ratzel thought of the prospects of the nation was reasonable optimism.

The richly rewarding time Ratzel spent in the United States and Mexico remained almost unknown to American geography. When the subject had academic attention in the nineties the founding fathers, such as W. M. Davis, R. D. Salisbury, and R. S. Tarr were physiographers and physiography was Ratzel's weak side. Later Miss Semple brought her interpretation of Ratzel to Chicago and to Clark University, but I am not aware that she knew the significance of his American period nor that she drew on the content of his American *Kulturgeographie,* which was in fact historical geography of grand design.

## THE CENTURY AFTER RATZEL

In the following half-century it did appear that the country was maturing properly. I grew up in that period, which in retrospect seems to have been a very good time in which to live. Rural America, except for the frontier of drought and where monoculture of cotton and tobacco was dominant, was living in fair balance with its land. Crop rotation was practiced, as was animal husbandry, supplemented by family garden and orchard. Country towns were viable communities of diverse services and attractive aspect. The devastation of forests was becoming a public concern. The National Conservation Commission in 1909 drew up a plan to control the exploitation of resources, in part already protected in forest reserves and national parks. Urban growth was seen to present increasing problems of crime and an exploited working class. People and materials were pouring by rail into cities in accelerating stages of industrialization. Urban civilization was developing strongly as Ratzel thought it would and should, but the country was still largely rural at the time of the First World War.

As we approach the end of the nation's second century we are in grave and unresolved crisis of destructive exploitation and urban malaise. Instead of moderation of material satisfactions, advance of technology has accustomed the people to want more things of brief appeal. The automobile industry became the giant of the nation by planned obsolescence. We have built an economy based on waste and boredom and both are overtaking us. Ratzel thought that advertising was too obtrusive; at present it dominates telecast as well as print. He thought the people would settle down and make homes; cultural nomadism has become the common way of life, by later name "New Frontiersmen." He thought the American landscape aged early; the age of "development" and "redevelopment," of tract housing and highway building, obsolescent at their completion, was still in the future. The pollution of air, of the land and its waters, and finally of the global ocean has been the incubus of technology as it has grown since his time and especially in the past three decades.

Ratzel's observations of a century ago are rich in themes of cultural geography of the United States that have had little attention by geographers.

# 14. The Fourth
## Dimension
### of Geography

At the beginning of this century geography was one of the basic
subjects in our elementary schools, as it had been for generations.
History was taught mainly to instruct the youth in the origin and
development of the United States. Geography dealt with the entire
world, its physical and cultural diversity expressed in regions, which
were most conveniently studied as countries. The political entity as
unit of study tended to be an eclectic choice of whatever seemed to be
its conspicuous aspect of nature and society.

The American Book Company, publishers of *McGuffey's Eclectic
Readers,* had Baron von Steinwehr, a cartographer and a general in
the Union Army, do a series of *Eclectic Geographies,* well illustrated
by maps and pictures, that set the pattern of school texts for decades.
The school geographies written by a Confederate officer, Matthew
Fontaine Maury, stressed physical geography and processes. Neither
author has had deserved attention in the shaping of American school
geography.

Geography as taught in the schools came under the criticism
that the pupils were drilled in place names and their location, in

---

"The Fourth Dimension of Geography" first appeared in the *Annals,* Association of American Geographers, 64(2):189–192, June 1974.

river systems, the height of mountains, boundaries and capitals of states. The meaning of toponymy was lost in rote memorizing, it was said. Learning place names and their association on maps was a dull matter, perhaps more so for teacher than student. The normal schools, our training centers for schoolteachers, felt the need of academic guidance for geography such as history had at universities.

Chairs of geography had been founded early at Princeton University (for the Swiss Arnold Guyot) and at the University of California (for the geodesist George Davidson, born in England). In 1892 a national committee was formed to inquire into the condition of geography in schools. T. C. Chamberlin, then President of the University of Wisconsin, was its Chairman, the report largely written by William Morris Davis of Harvard University. Chamberlin was the country's most distinguished geologist; Davis was in charge of physical geography in the Department of Geology at Harvard. The recommendation was of an inclusive physical earth science, from elementary through secondary schools, to prepare for entry to college and to be represented there.

In 1893 Chamberlin moved to the new University of Chicago, to form there a great school of geology, taking with him his junior associate, Rollin Salisbury, as Professor of Geographical Geology, to be given opportunity to introduce courses in geography of university level and to form a Department of Geography. Geography shared the university museum with geology. For almost three decades the cohabitation continued, Salisbury giving common instruction to all graduate students of geology and geography in physiography, and in dynamic and historical geology. Davis continued at Harvard as Professor of Physical Geography in the Department of Geology.

Geography in the United States was given its academic entry by geologists, who for years remained its sponsors and guides. Some of us started in geology and were attracted to the new direction of linking study of the face of the earth to its human occupants. We had a background of observing and identifying landforms as to kind and origin, in particular those of Pleistocene and Recent geologic time. We were accustomed to go out to see, name, and interpret features of the terrain; we would now learn how to gain understanding of the patterns of man's activities. After a year of graduate work, Professor Salisbury sent me in 1910 to do a study of the upper Illinois Valley. When asked for guidelines, he answered that I alone would determine manner and range of what I did in the field. That first untutored field season opened inquiries that have continued ever after. We started with some competence in the morphology of the land, which was important. Beyond that we were on our own.

The formative years of academic geography in the United States were greatly influenced by Davis and Salisbury, men of greatly differing temperaments. To Salisbury the earth sciences were an interdependent field. As I was learning to become a geographer I had the benefit of contact with paleontologists of large insight in paleogeography. Davis, on the other hand, was seeking to establish geography as a discipline that was freed of concern with chronology of time and change. The geologist dealt with the history of the earth and named its chapters and paragraphs. Davis formulated a theory of recurrent geographical cycles, of uplift, erosion, and wearing down to a peneplain, passing through stages of youth, maturity, and old age to rejuvenation in a new cycle. The cycle might be long or short, its length and position in time were irrelevant. Davis was our first and greatest maker of a system that replaced the complexity of events by a general order. Theory was illustrated by models, the block diagrams which he drew so well to show his concept of how the modelling of the land should pass from stage to stage. Davis continued to develop and expound the cyclic order that he thought he had discovered.

Meanwhile Ellsworth Huntington introduced climatic change as determining the course of mankind and became an advocate of climatic and other cycles, for which he tried to establish a chronology by tree rings. Another kind of environmental determinism was presented by Ellen Semple, who read history from the recent American past to classical antiquity as persistence of environmental advantage or denial. By both talented persons the human past was explained by favor or constraint of the physical environment, to which Huntington added racial selection. When Harlan Barrows at Chicago took over Miss Semple's lectures on American history and its geographical influences, he distinguished between what he called geographic and nongeographic factors, the latter added by man.

In these formative decades we, the young apprentices, were encouraged to study a selected region. We went out to learn what we could with a fair background of landforms and a liking of the landscape. We were expected to gain understanding by observing the relation of man to physical environment. We knew nothing of Ratzel's travels in the United States during which he became a geographer and returned home to write its *Kulturgeographie,* first of its kind. Cultural geography was an unknown concept, but to some extent we did what he did, stopped whenever we found something to engage our attention as significant by being there. By such reconnaissance we tried to describe the geographic pattern of human activity and interpret its meaningful assemblage, and began to ask how the things seen came to be together. A first exercise in learning that geography is spatial differentiation of nature and culture.

Regional geography was held to be the main concern. The chapter by Professor Davis in Mill's *International Geography* (1908 edition) presented the United States as a series of natural regions, distinguished by relief or climate, each having an economy proper to its physical nature. Each was delimited by boundaries, the whole country being thus subdivided. The natural region was taken as the basic unit for the study of human geography. Popular usage provided Davis with most of the regional names; he added more and supplied boundary lines. Professor Davis argued that our political boundaries largely were drawn by compass in advance of settlement, and were improper lines for the geographer. Instead, Davis found these in physical divisions, which he set up, largely by a combination of landforms and climatic regions. The regional pattern as outlined was inadequate and improper for the patterns of society and livelihood.

Geographers were and still are most numerous in the Midwest. It had been settled within a century by people of European stock, the earlier ones of colonial ancestry, those following largely immigrants from overseas. Their descendants lived on farms and in towns that had been occupied at the time of settlement and which retained qualities of their origin. These were evident and remembered, in part also were described in accounts of pioneer times. The then still living past, manifest in homesteads and habits and in place names, such as former groves and prairies, and names of their former homes, provided the historical base of the local geography. Regional studies involved depth of time, at least as far back as pioneer days. The physical background was reshaped by human agency in directions determined by differing cultural options. Human geography was beginning to be understood as cultural experience of a particular space, though not as yet so called by us.

At the beginning of the century changes in ways of living were going on with little uprooting of people or habits; we were becoming sedentary, attached to home place. The First World War brought large and increasing change. A technologic revolution was under way, staffed by engineers, chemists, and efficiency experts. The assembly line replaced the skilled workman. The gross national product became measure and goal of common commitment. Cities grew mightily and rural population began a decline that has continued to the present. The family farm, which grew diverse field crops by rotation, planted gardens and orchards, and raised livestock and poultry, was beginning to give way to specialized and mechanized agriculture. Small towns, the centers of rural communities, were becoming superfluous unless they developed industries.

During World War I numerous geographers were engaged in wartime services, such as the Shipping Board, which allocated cargoes by specific routes and ports. They dealt with tonnages of whatever kind from source to destination. They returned after the war to academic life, knowledgeable in the statistics of volume and the monetary value of the items of commerce. The universities were adding schools of commerce and business that had use for this sort of information, and geographers were available for such courses of instruction. They gathered statistical data, drew topical maps, and constructed graphs, all under continuing revision to be kept up to date. Things, people, places were quantitative aggregates to be related. Numbers in their spatial distribution were the common concern, which in the course of time became sophisticated to theories of spatial order, independent of real place or time. The new breed had little experience or need of the traditional interests of geography in the physical, biotic, and cultural diversity of the earth. It was not interested in the past beyond the short run of statistical series, but was concerned with projecting the future. The applied geographer attached to the world of business learned the use of statistics to chart the flow of trade. A few were beginning to construe an abstract world of hypothetical space and time.

In 1923 I moved from Michigan to California to gain experience of a different country, and also to get away from what geographers mainly were doing in the East, which interested me less and less as narrowing professionalism. I had begun to read seriously what German, French, and English geographers were learning about the world as long and increasingly modified by man's activities. *The Morphology of Landscape* [Sauer: 1925] was an early attempt to say what the common enterprise was in the European tradition.

John Leighly came with me to Berkeley to do his doctoral thesis on the historical towns in central Sweden. The third member of the staff was Richard Russell, native Californian, who introduced us to nature and life in California. Loren Post and Peveril Meigs were students at the university, joined a year later by Fred Kniffen and Warren Thornthwaite, and shortly by others—a young group finding its way into geography as an earth science in which the present became intelligible by knowledge of the past. The fourth dimension, time, was necessary to understanding and could not be replaced by stage, cycle, model, or environmental influence. This gradual learning involved reading works we had not known, the contributions to cultural geography by such men as George Marsh, Vaughan Cornish, Brunhes, Eduard Hahn, Ratzel, Gradmann, Schlüter, and *The Corridors of Time* by Peake and Fleure. The spread of mankind to the ends of the earth, *Gang der Kultur* in Hettner's phrase, reached back to remote cultural beginnings.

The University of California offered a congenial place to learn from related scholars. Geologists were engaged in geomorphic studies. Soil science had its origins here and the mapping of soils gave insight into the processes by which the land was formed. A group of naturalists was outlining the distribution and assemblage of the biota in historical depth, in fact historical biogeography. Historians studied the American and Spanish past of California and were well advanced in inquiring into the northern Spanish borderlands. Above all, anthropologists were our tutors in understanding cultural diversity and change. Robert Lowie in particular introduced us to the work of such geographers as Eduard Hahn and Ratzel as founders of an anthropogeography that I had not known. (At Chicago the lone anthropologist had been Frederick Starr, whose quarters were in our building; we knew him as a pleasant person but not as one from whom we should learn. There was no anthropologist at the University of Michigan.) Wider horizons were opened to us at Berkeley, perhaps wider than we would have found anywhere else.

California was an extraordinarily good example of natural regions of major interest to biologic evolution and survival, and as a pocket in which diverse Indian tribes had lodged. Because it was so well studied we looked beyond it for less known lands. These were nearby, across the Mexican border. Our first expedition was to Baja California, the earlier California described by missionaries and seafarers in Spanish days and since then largely disregarded, except by field biologists. We returned for a number of field seasons, ranging to the southern end of the long and sparsely inhabited peninsula. It was our field school of physical and human geography, out of which came a variety of studies. Former missions, in part ruins, were guides to reconstruction of past conditions and thus to include aboriginal life, here and there still existing. Also we began to go south along the Pacific mainland of Mexico, there learning about Indian crops and agriculture. By chance we came upon a forgotten prehistoric high culture that largely extended the archeologic limits of Mesoamerica. The presence of man and his works set the limits of human geography. We were learning cultural geography in depth in Mexico, and beyond, in Central and South America.

The dimension of time is and has been part of geographic understanding. Human geography considers man as a geographic agent, using and changing his environment in nonrecurrent time according to his skills and wants. We now know that he is not the master of an unlimited environment, but that his technologic intervention in the physical world and its life has become the crisis of his survival and that of his coinhabitants.

*V. The Agency*
  *of Man*
      *on the Earth*

# 15. Plants,
#     Animals
#     and Man

The paleography of man, which deals with the whole span of his existence, asks whence he came, the manner of his dispersal, and in what lands new ways of living were learned. It tries to understand the changing outlines and patterns of the *oikoumene* and also of the natural world, the spread and wasting of ice sheets, fall and rise of sea levels, climatic changes, alteration of vegetation and fauna. As a human geographer I have considered such topics from time to time. They are restated here in condensed and revised form. Also I have thought that enough is now known of the age of cultural innovations and of the course of the Ice Age to link Old and New World cultures in longer perspective.

## FAR REACHES OF HUMAN TIME

The human lineage[1] has now been traced back to beyond two million years. *Pithecanthropus erectus,* the "erect ape man," since determined to have lived half a million years ago, was not the intermediate he

---

"Plants, Animals and Man" first appeared in *Man and His Habitat,* R. H. Buchanan, Emry Jones and Desmond McCourt (Eds.), (Routledge and Kegan Paul: London, 1970), pp. 34–61.

1. See selection of my writings made by John Leighly under the title *Land and Life,* Part Three: "Human Uses of the Organic World," and Part Four: "The Farther Reaches of Human Time" (Berkeley, 1963, in paperback 1967). The

was thought to be at the time of his discovery, but a rudimentary human inhabitant of Java. *Australopithecus* of South Africa, named "the southern ape," is now recognized as hominid. When the Leakeys later found their famous and vastly old fossil at Olduvai it was placed in the human family tree as *Zinjanthropus*, "East Africa man," found by the potassium-argon clock as living one-and-three-quarter million years ago. The course of human evolution has been distinct from that of the anthropoids and began its particular direction before a time of which we have knowledge, perhaps, it has been suggested, to diverge before the apes began.

The human body differs in significant ways from the other primates, apart from cranial topography. The trunk and limbs are proportioned so that man stands, strides, and runs erect, using the legs alone for locomotion, the arms freed to serve whatever the hands find to do. The only real biped among his kindred, he has been a dweller and forager on the ground. To this terrestrial adaptation Sir Alister Hardy has added an appraisal of human anatomy, skeletal, muscular, and epidermal, as apt for swimming and diving, and has therefore suggested a partly aquatic habitat in his evolution. The hypothesis is attractive and has not had the attention it deserves. Some primates cannot swim, others do so reluctantly and frantically. Humans learn to swim readily and may do so as early as they learn to walk. When the Spaniards came to the tropical New World they were amazed by the daily swimming of the natives and their proficiency in water.

---

Bowman Memorial Lectures (American Geographical Society, 1952), and *Agricultural Origins and Dispersals,* reprinted as a paperback (Cambridge, Mass., MIT Press) with addition of three more articles. The references given in these two collections are not repeated here.

Knowledge of the relevant past is enlarging greatly. Karl W. Butzer, *Environment and Archaeology, An Introduction to Pleistocene Geography* (Chicago, 1964) is the latest synthesis. His emphasis is on the western part of the Old World, where the data are best and where he has contributed geomorphic field studies of notable originality on the association of land forms, soil development, and climate. Karl J. Narr, *Urgeschichte der Kultur* (Stuttgart, 1961) has stressed the ethos of cultures, the indications that material remains recovered by archeology give of ancient cultures, spiritual as well as material. Properly and prudently Narr has therefore also considered persistence in modern peoples of ceremonial traits concerning life and death, the spirit world, and "good" and "evil."

The Tasmanians, one of the most primitive cultures, astonished the European visitors by their skill at swimming and diving, by which means they got much of their food. The symmetry and grace of the human body, so different from the other primates, Professor Hardy suggests, may have developed in part by an ancestral habitat in water as well as on land.

The other primates are mainly vegetarian. Man, although lacking the powerful jaws and teeth of apes, is one of the most omnivorous of creatures. He eats, likes and is able to digest a great diversity of foods and is not driven thereto by famine as civilized observers have concluded at times from their own fastidiousness. The human stomach and intestines are extraordinarily competent and tolerant, somewhat limited in ability to consume raw starch in quantity. Of high intake of salt, and sensitive to a lack of iodine, mankind suggests an old affinity to the sea. Needing to drink often, the more so the drier and warmer the air, man could not range far from fresh water. This most naked of warm-blooded creatures, thin and sensitive of skin, lacking fang, claw and horny extremities, was restricted to a particular habitat outlined in his anatomy and physiology.

An African origin is generally accepted, present evidence favoring East Africa. The physical geography of equatorial eastern Africa is not greatly different from that of millions of years ago. The highlands of the African Shield bordered upon the Indian Ocean by an intermediate coastal lowland, growing broader or narrower as Pleistocene sea levels rose and fell. Vulcanism was active; in Olduvai Gorge, for example, the age of human sites has been determined by overlying volcanic beds. Climate is least subject to change in equatorial latitudes and in these parts it may have remained rather constant under the control of the seasonal reversal of monsoon circulation across the Indian Ocean. Thus the sedimentary beds exposed in Olduvai Gorge show evidence of minor climatic changes from somewhat more to somewhat less arid than at present. Olduvai has long been notable for its great number of vertebrate remains, indicating a scrub savanna within which there were gallery forests and marshes about watercourses and ponds. The early Pleistocene landscape resembled the present, a major difference perhaps being that grass savannas have largely replaced the mixed assemblage of drought-tolerant shrubs, trees, herbs, and grasses. The replacement continues at present by the practice of burning, carried on by man for a long time.

Olduvai has become the classic site that has reoriented thinking about human beings. It has brought us closer in time and location to the ancestral home but the habitat lacks the primal advantages that once favored man. The dry season is long and extreme. The herd animals and their predators and scavengers move far in search of food, as illustrated in the modern game reserve of the nearby Serengeti plain. The famous primordial camp site of Olduvai was at the edge of a small body of shallow water, with remains of the young offspring of large animals, of small waterside creatures, and of fish, all of which would be taken by hand or knocked down by club. A temporary camp at a watering place, its open situation was attractive as well to the herbivores and predators of the plains.

It is unlikely that such a marginal, exposed, and seasonally limited environment should have provided the sustenance and protection needed for the origin of the human lineage. The hominids whose presence has been found about Olduvai had stone implements of recognized type. They camped in the open and therefore knew how to safeguard themselves against the great cats for which they were attractive prey, easier to take than the fleet herd animals of the savannas. Olduvai man was in possession of developed skills that enabled him to venture into a land of hazard and seasonal provision. His presence became known by burial under a blanket of volcanic ash. He came from elsewhere.

The African savannas are currently in vogue as the first habitat of mankind, despite their severe seasonal limitations. Perhaps then, as now, they held great herds of large game. Primordial man, lacking the physique and the weapons to live by hunting skill, is imagined as trailing after the moving herds, picking off injured, infirm, and dead animals, competitor of jackal and hyena rather than of the feline predators. Thus he has been construed as living in small mobile bands dominated by the strongest and most aggressive male, with submissive females and their young in his keeping. The implied first basis of human society is masculine authority, band not family, and mobility not habitation.

The evidence of the human female is that human origins and society took a different course and came about in an environment other than that of the savannas. The period of gestation is about the same for humans and apes, but the human pelvis failed to enlarge so as to accommodate the foetus to physical maturity. The human infant is born in complete dependence on maternal care and long remains so. It does not cling to its mother, but must be carried; it is slowest in becoming ambulant; it must be fed longest. The juvenile stage is longest by far. Dependence becomes participation by continuing association of mother and offspring. Unlike other animal societies, there is no break at which mother and offspring lose such mutual recognition. When or whether the male parent became identified as such is less important. The enduring family is unique to mankind, and the recognition of kinship was first established maternally. Consanguinity, whether fact or fiction, is most elaborately structured among primitive peoples, suggesting that the recognition of relatedness was a basic concern, from the immediate to the extended family and to the community.

It was the role of the mother to see to providing the young with food and drink; to shelter them from harm by cold, heat, or wet; to keep them from straying and from accident. She taught them to recognize what was good or harmful and trained them until the boys were taken into the activities of the adult males. The men might roam and do whatever they wished, the women were constantly engaged in the care of their offspring, until the youngest became adult.

Mobility might suit the males but was a disadvantage to the women, who were responsible for the welfare of the family, as the keepers of the household. The primitive home, it may be stipulated, was as permanent as possible. The selection of a suitable site was of primary concern, to have food and drinking water close by and protection from weather and enemies. If supplies were available the year round and there was good shelter, the woman stayed put with their brood—sessile homemakers.

The biogeographer Moritz Wagner proposed a law of migration

as a supplement to Darwin's *Origin of Species*. Evolution, Wagner thought, would not produce diversity if the progeny stayed in the same habitat, divergent forms being suppressed by the dominant established kind. If variants moved into a new environment favorable to their deviation they might survive, increase, and become a successful new entity. The hominid primate departed far from his kindred. Premature birth, slowest and longest adolescence, lack of a pelt except for the head of hair, living on the ground, walking erect, a body well-designed to swim, omnivorous habit, in addition to a mind that has the capacity of thought, tell of a different destiny determined in a distant time. They supply clues also to a place suited to his origins and the development of human ways. Accepting the present evidence for an African origin in low latitudes, and holding the concept of bands roaming about the savannas as incompetent and irrelevant, a suitable ecologic niche is required and indicated.

## THE ATTRACTIVE SEACOAST

The African shores of the Indian Ocean have advantages for human beginnings that are lacking in the savannas of the interior. Waves have fashioned a varied coastline, trimming back headlands and building strands along the lowlands, the stand of the sea being notably higher at the time we are now considering. Good tidal range gave daily access to diverse foods available at the water's edge and at all seasons. The beachcombing life knew no lack and at times enjoyed additions to the daily fare of shellfish: sea turtles came to lay their eggs in the beach; sea mammals and fish were stranded occasionally; sea cows pastured in estuaries. Landward there was plant food to be had, in particular where surface stream, spring, or underground seep issued from the mainland behind. Here there was water to drink in dry as well as rainy season. The environmental setting is in strongest contrast to the savannas: there was no need to wander, no season of hunger, no tracking of mobile and elusive game. And there was almost no competition for food or danger from predators. Here was an ample and comfortable niche awaiting occupation and ready to provide the opportunity to increase in numbers and develop human society. This was the promised land for the primate variants who would survive by following a course that was reserved to them alone.

As a student of the forms of life in the sea, Professor Hardy was impressed by the design of the human body and its remarkable adaptation to swimming, thus extending the evolutionary perspective to include natation as well as erect carriage on land. This gets farther away from the old and familiar picture of primitive man as a shuffling, clumsy, ape-like creature.

A tidal, tropical seashore habitat satisfies all ecologic essentials including the provision of shelter. Cliffed coasts are likely to have recesses; driftwood piles up on low shores and marshy ground has stands of rushes and reeds. There was no need to wander. In choosing a place to live the first consideration was a dependable supply of fresh water. Next would come the appraisal of sufficient and varied food at all times, having the choice of a productive beach, tide pools, and perhaps tide-washed rocks and the presence of an adequate shelter. A well chosen place was permanently habitable, a home where the mother raised her brood. Local resources permitting, the family became a family cluster and perhaps a community in which living in association began the process of social organization. This seems to me a better-founded view of the origins of society than the contrary view of a wandering band held together by force.

As the seacoast was superior to the savanna in food, water, and shelter, it also offered more advantage of materials for the practice of manual skills. The tidal sea washes many kinds of objects ashore: shells, stones, wood, seaweed, the jetsam that rouses the curiosity of the beachcomber, young or old, an ever-changing assortment of things to pick up, play with, and keep as useful or ornamental. Salt-seasoned wood provided shafts for tools of many purposes, for digging, throwing, prising. Shells of many forms, sizes, and colors served as containers, tools and decorations. Headlands supplied stone shaped by waves into cobbles, rounded and selected for toughness by continued abrasion. Cobbles of a size to fit the hand were ready-made tools. The earliest known artifacts are such cobbles, also called pebble tools, partly dressed to have a cutting edge or a pointed tip by repeated directed blows of another rock. In materials and models the seacoast is a workshop, well stocked for the beginnings of technics. The protein and fat of marine animals was abundant and continually available. The coast was least preëmpted, being mainly beyond the range of other primates as well as of the great cats.

## THE USE OF FIRE

The earliest certain use of fire was by Peking Man during the Second Interglacial period, at a time when winters in north China were much like the present. It does not follow, as has been suggested, that this is approximately when man began to keep fire. Nor does the oldest record of cooking, which is by Neanderthal man, necessarily suggest a deferment of such use until that late time, as has also been implied. These finds were made in caves that gave good protection. Sites in the open air do not retain proof that fire was used over long periods. Now that the age of human existence has been so greatly extended, the question of eoliths needs to be restudied, for example those of the Red Crag on the East Anglian coast. The flints in question have been described as artifacts though this has been questioned or denied by some. Some of the flints are fire-crazed, which has been attributed to natural fires, on the assumption that lightning might have had such effect; supporting evidence, however, is not given. The objection that the flint objects are too old to have been shaped by human hands no longer holding, the resort to an unknown and improbable effect of lightning is gratuitous.

The capture of natural fire came about when human curiosity replaced the animal fear of fire. Of the two agencies, lightning and vulcanism, the latter may be the more likely. In East Africa very early hominids lived in a land of volcanic fire; the camp at Olduvai was buried by hot volcanic ash. The step from watching a land ablaze to taking a brand and using it may have been decisive of the course of mankind and history. Its ritual memory is continued in fire worship of various forms, in the keeping of sacred fire, in the priestly services of fire sacrifices, incense, and eternal flame.

Lacking fire, man was limited to living in lands without extreme cold. The alternative, that he covered himself with skins, implies that he was a fairly competent hunter and that he, or rather the women, knew how to dress skins so that they were soft and stayed thus, a craft beyond the capacities of rudimentary cultures. Possessing fire he could venture into harsher environments on his way to the ends of the earth and its domination. That he did so at an early stage is recorded in the distribution of his remains and stone tools, fairly legible across Eurasia as far back as the Second Interglacial (Swanscombe Man in England, Peking Man in north China), half a million years and more ago. It is suggested as a reasonable thesis that the presence of man beyond the tropics implies his utilization of fire.

The hypothesis of his seaside origins points the way as well to the routes of his dispersal. He could skirt the shores of desert interiors, discovering the same supply of food and other materials at all seasons and also finding water to drink. He could continue thus into temperate latitudes and beyond, depending on the harvest of seashore before he learned how to live inland, where seasonal contrast of supply was marked. (Also, in addition to his early presence by or near the sea, there are such interior sites as Heidelberg, Steinheim, and Choukoutien that raise questions about his ability to store food.)

Fire may be held as the greatest cultural achievement. It enabled the dispersal of mankind, which need not have been due to pressure of population, but to an inclination of a group to detach itself and find a new home, perhaps a pioneering bent that has been inherent in man and which has never been adequately explained in economic terms. Fire provides a place where the cognate group gathers after dark for companionship. Tropical nights are longer than is needed for sleep and nightfall brings the household together about the hearth for some time before it retires, as I well recall from Indian communities. The fireplace draws people into its circle of light and warmth to attend to small jobs, to talk or keep silent, to relax in company, to share a sensible propinquity that may be the oldest of social satisfactions.

It is incredible that early humans, whatever the disputed quality of their brains, should have sat about the fire generation after generation without experimenting with it, especially in relation to food. Roasting over coals or baking in hot ashes changes the taste and texture of animal foods. A place of high antiquity may be suggested for the clambake as a "sociable." Starchy roots and tubers were made easily digestible by heat, bitterness was removed from seeds and roots and some poisonous plants were found to be nutritious after baking. Dry heat was introduction to an empirical chemistry that enlarged the range of what was edible. Steam cooking antedated the fashioning of containers, perhaps by wrapping food in succulent leaves, encasing it in mud, or placing it in a covered pit of coals. The techniques can be inferred from the cooking skills of historic primitive peoples. Using fire, man learned to identify palatable plants and how to prepare them. The collecting of plants and the preparation of food for the household was the business of the women, who were the first botanists and organic chemists. They had to recognize the kinds that were safe to eat, the kinds that could be made palatable, and those that were to be left alone. The most primitive aborigines have this competence, a knowledge that was of survival value wherever a land became inhabited.

The contained fire of the hearth carries us back very far in human time. Its dispersal by setting fire to vegetation as a means of procuring food is perhaps also an ancient practice. Primitive people in modern times have done so where vegetation and climate permit, an effective means of collecting that does not require special hunting skills or arms. The spreading fire overtakes slow animals and suffocates others in their burrows. Repeated burning changes the character of the vegetation and may increase the harvest of animals and useful plants. In East Africa humans witnessed the killing of living things by volcanic fires and perhaps this set an example. However, we do not know that man altered vegetation extensively until the advent of the hunting societies that depended on big game.

THE LONG SPAN AND SLOW PACE OF EARLY MANKIND

The major divisions of prehistoric time were formulated a century ago by archeologists in western Europe as a succession of skills applied to stone and then to metals. The Old Stone Age included the time before stone was ground and polished. A very long period of rudimentary dressing of stone was recognized as Lower Paleolithic. This was followed by the Middle Paleolithic, represented by Mous-

terian culture and Neanderthal man, in its turn succeeded by Upper
Paleolithic, introduced by Aurignacian culture and Cro-Magnon
man, the first fully accepted representative of *Homo sapiens*. This
third "stage" is now considered to have begun between thirty and
forty thousand years ago and continued to within ten thousand years
before the present. The antiquity of human lineage now carries back
about two million years. All but the last one hundred fifty thousand
years are assigned to the Lower Paleolithic, and the greater part of
the remainder to the Middle Paleolithic.

The status of Lower Paleolithic man is read almost wholly from
his stone implements. These were made by percussion, shaping the
desired object by blows from another stone. Archeology has been
able to determine how they were made, largely how they were used,
and in part the cultural inventory to which they belonged. Temporal
and regional complexes and connections have been recognized.
There was some innovation of pattern, improvement in workmanship, and introduction of new tools. Percussion continued to be the
basic technique, though this did not produce specialized hunting
implements such as blades or spear points.

The extremely slow rate of innovation is considered by some to
reflect the capacity of the primitive brain. In this respect the origin
of speech has been of particular interest but it now appears to be
admissible anatomically as primordial. Certainly, implements of
Paleolithic age, which belong to the same type and are recognized
over a wide area, imply communication. In distinctive association
they are called cultures, and some of the earliest, such as the pre-
Chellean, are widely distributed. The testimony of the rudest lithic
cultures is that their makers had use of speech.

The time it took mankind to get to the end of his first chapter is
greater than we had thought, possibly because the human brain was
slow in developing. Stone implements continued to be made by
percussion, with some improvement of skill and diversity of form.
They have served the needs of the users adequately, and in the absence of other criteria it is unwise to use them as a measure of intelli-
gence. The bias of the lithic stages of culture is obvious. Lower
Paleolithic man extended his occupation to far parts of Eurasia and

Africa, hot, temperate, and cold, implying the use of fire and foresight in gathering stores against the seasons of want. The archeological record does not reveal his thoughts, or tell what he learned in fashioning wood and fibers to his service.

Nor may we postulate that population was sparse everywhere. Resources available to man's skills set the limits to his numbers. Waterside habitats were most richly and continuously rewarding on tidal coasts; Mediterranean shores, lake- and streamsides were also attractive. Such habitats could support goodly numbers and community living. During the glacial stages sea levels were low; their coastal plains are now submerged and lost to our knowledge. Also, the valley floors of such times have been buried by the aggradation that followed from rising interglacial seas. The worldwide swings of sea level during the Pleistocene have largely concealed the places most advantageous to human occupation.

## A WORLDWIDE MIDDLE PALEOLITHIC

With Neanderthal man and Mousterian culture a major change must be recognized. The type skeleton was found in a cave in the Ruhr region, the culture was established from caves in the Dordogne of southwest France. *Homo neanderthalensis* became the prototype of the caveman, brutish, ugly and backward, to disappear when *Homo sapiens* came on the scene. It was thought that perhaps he succumbed to the readvancing ice and superior sapient man. The older version has been under revision, and needs more. He has now been advanced to the status of *Homo sapiens neanderthalensis* and is given a span of about one hundred thousand years, beginning in the warm Third Interglacial (Eem) and continuing into the cold Fourth Glacial (Wurm/Wisconsin), less than forty thousand years ago. Also, the physical type and a generally Mousterian culture have become known far from the narrow part of western Europe to which they were thought to have been restricted. Mousterian culture ranged from Portugal into southwest Asia and far into Russia.

In Eurasia the continental icecap and mountain glaciers had their greatest extension in the Third Glacial (Riss). Boreal vegetation was established over unglaciated lowlands between northern icecap and interior mountains, persisted in part in the following interglacial, and again occupied the northern lowlands in the Fourth Glacial. Mousterian culture appeared during the Third Interglacial and continued long into the following glacial time. Across the northern lowlands of Eurasia the vegetation was more boreal, in part tundra, in part moor and heath, with low forest of willow, aspen, birch and northern conifers, browsed upon by reindeer, bison, forest horse, woolly mammoth and rhino. Marsh, lake and stream were populous with water fowl and beaver and there were salmon to be taken. Food and pelts were available for men who knew how to hunt and fish and how to get through the winters. These people did so, and they had northern Europe to themselves for a long time.

These are the earliest known people who are properly called hunters. They lived largely by the pursuit and killing of large game, an enterprise requiring cooperation. The animals were not in large herds nor do they appear to have been widely migrant. Hunting seems to have been a matter of bringing in game as needed to the place of living. Where available the people occupied rock shelters (abris), some of which were permanently occupied. Their implements show refinements and innovations, the most significant being the making of points for spears. The regional differences in kind and style suggest that there was provincial grouping. Ceremonial burials, from France to the Zagros Mountains, give the first indications of religion.

Neanderthal/Mousterian is now known to have been also present from Morocco east to the Zagros Mountains beyond Mesopotamia, over a long belt of summer dryness with plants and animals differing markedly from those north of the Alps and Pyrenees. The old view of a habitat at the edge of tundra forest is expanded to extend to the edge of desert lands. Instead of an origin in western Europe the bearers of this culture perhaps came west into Europe out of southwest Asia.

Recent archeological work has located Mousterian sites far to the northeast, in the Altai of the U.S.S.R. and in Chinese Mongolia.[2] In time they appear to correspond to Mousterian in western Europe. There is no report of human skeletons. The great culture of the

---

2. C. Chard, *Saeculum* 14 (1963), 170–2.

Middle Paleolithic thus appears to have been established across the north of Eurasia from the Atlantic into Mongolia. At the time in question the Scandinavian ice reached slightly across the Baltic Sea and eastward somewhat into Russia.[3] An ice-free lowland bordered widely on the Arctic Ocean to the east of Scandinavia, the great plains of Russia and Siberia being then covered by tundra and boreal forest. Here the woolly mammoth ranged, feeding in the open tundra on shrubs and herbs and retreating in winter into the woods for shelter and scant subsistence. The large historical commerce in its fossil ivory, taken for centuries from Siberia into China, attests its presence in numbers on Arctic plains in late Pleistocene time. Mousterian sites in European Russia indicate major dependence on mammoth-hunting. The people who could live on hunting, fishing, and plant food in northwestern Germany practiced a similar economy across Siberia. There is also some evidence of greater and more diverse plant growth at the time of the mammoths and of a milder climate in Arctic lowlands. This accords with a current theory of Pleistocene climates proposed by Maurice Ewing and William Donn, who suggest that the Arctic Ocean was open during glacial stages, ice-covered during interglacials. The Lamont Geological Laboratory dates the start of the Fourth Glaciation at somewhat more than one hundred thousand years, with a notable recession about fifty thousand years ago.

For long, most authorities accepted a post-glacial entry of man into the New World. The last major recession of the ice now is placed as within eleven thousand years. There was no difficulty in getting across Bering Strait. Mousterian culture had reached northeast Asia at a time when the woolly mammoth thrived on the Arctic plains, and the time is thought to fall within the span of European Mousterian. The unglaciated corridor south of the Arctic Ocean was never blocked. The reasons for denying earlier entry to the New World are various and obscure. The extension of Mousterian culture into farther Asia was not known until lately. The difficulty of migration by skirting the Sea of Okhotsk and Kamchatka was evident, the habita-

---

3. K. W. Butzer, op. cit. (1964), Fig. 63.

bility of the Arctic Plain and coast was not considered. Authority continued to reject the reports of early man in the New World, but this position is now untenable with the evidence provided by radiocarbon dating. It is now possible to determine age to about forty thousand years, or into the last part of Middle Paleolithic time and mid-Wisconsin glaciation (by the Lamon calendar). There is good evidence that men were living in North America that long ago, in particular in California and Texas.

The Santa Barbara channel coast of California has a long record of human occupance which the Santa Barbara Museum of Natural History has kept under close attention for many years, yielding a long and nearly continual record of human presence on mainland and channel islands. Santa Rosa Island, inhabited by endemic dwarf mammoths, has been examined most closely. Their bones are exposed by the erosion of marine terraces, some found in fire-baked, pit-like depressions. These have been proved to be baking pits in which parts of mammoths were roasted, the oldest beyond the range of radiocarbon dating. It has also been shown that the channel by which the island was reached was then almost as wide as at present and that water craft were needed to cross it.[4]

The Mojave Desert has long been of interest for a number of sites having implements of primitive workmanship and occupied at a time of notably moister climate. Excavation of one of these, at Yermo, is now nearly complete, and the consensus is that its age is no later than mid-Wisconsin.

In northern Texas, excavation for the Lewisville Dam north of Dallas exposed an ancient site with at least fourteen hearths and numerous bones of extinct and living animals. The charred wood samples were beyond the limit of the radiocarbon testing, then given as thirty-seven thousand years. The number of hearths and bones indicated a community that was more than a casual camp. Gravel pits in the highest terrace of the Trinity River to the southeast of

---

4. Phil C. Orr and Rainer Berger, "The Fire Areas on Santa Rosa Island," *Proceedings of the National Academy of Sciences* 56 (1966), 1408–16, 1678–82. The geochronology is summarized by Orr in *Proceedings of the Symposium on the Biology of the California Islands,* Santa Barbara Botanic Gardens, 1967.

Dallas have yielded three crudely-carved limestone boulders. Two represent human heads, the third may have been intended to do so. They were taken at different times from the bottom of the pit, bones of elephants, horse, camel, and ground sloth being found in the same horizon.[5] The height of the terrace and its fauna indicate pre-Wisconsin age, probably the Third Interglacial. The Trinity site resembles the situation at Frederick, Oklahoma, in the valley of the Red River, which adjoins that of the Trinity to the north. Here sand and gravel pits were worked commercially, also on the highest terrace. The extinct fauna was the subject of paleontologic study, but an earlier generation of anthropologists considered that the artifacts could not be contemporary in view of the then-current theory of man's post-Glacial arrival.

Both in Texas and in California the presence of man has now been established beyond the limits of radiocarbon dating, which in terms of archeology is within Middle Paleolithic time. In both states, geomorphical evidence also points to human presence well before the end of that period, high river terraces in the southwest indicating inter-glacial entry. No remains of human skeletons have been found, but in both the Old and New World mammoths were hunted and other big game of extinct forms. In late Pleistocene times the Mojave was not a desert and had surface streams flowing into lakes. The Santa Barbara coast was rich in shellfish and fish, and the land abounded in oaks bearing sweet acorns and in diverse nutritive shrubs and herbs. The valleys of north Texas about Dallas had woods of oak and nut trees, fish in the rivers, and small and large game. Pleistocene folk found good places to live in the New World at the time of Neanderthal/Mousterian in the Old World.

## HUNTERS OF THE END OF THE ICE AGE

The rapid melting of ice sheets between ten and eleven thousand years ago accompanied the shift to the modern pattern of climate

---

5. The heads are in the Texas Memorial Museum and are reproduced in Plate I, W. W. Newcomb, *The Indians of Texas* (Austin, 1964), which also gives an account of this site and of Lewisville.

with its extremes of hot and cold, wet and dry. It was at the waning of the Ice Age that the people of the *grande chasse* took over in Europe and in North America. In both continents they were immigrants, perhaps from unknown areas of the interior of Asia. They followed the moving herds of big game as organized hunting parties, and in Europe the later ones are known to have used skin tents. Their new technique of shaping stone by pressure-flaking produced blades and points of superior execution and design. The use of a new weapon, the dart thrower, was added to that of the spear. It gave precision at longer range to the practiced marksman and was useful for hunting both large and small game. These Paleolithic hunters engaged in mass hunts, driving a herd to a place convenient for mass killing, inferentially by fire drive.

They engaged mainly in hunting large game of kinds now extinct. Quarry and hunter ranged plains from southwestern France across Russia and Siberia into Texas and beyond, and apparently disappeared together. In northwest Germany and Texas they survived to about nine thousand years ago. Each culture was somewhat specialized in its pursuit of a dominant game. For example, the Gravettian people of eastern Europe and Siberia largely hunted mammoths, the Solutreans the forest horse, Magdalenian and Ahrensburg hunters followed herds of reindeer in France and on the north German lowlands. In the United States people belonging to the earliest known culture of the kind, makers of the fluted Clovis points, have been called elephant hunters because they hunted mammoths as well as other game. Their range was wide and centered on the high plains of New Mexico. They were succeeded by the Folsom hunters of giant, extinct bison, their name taken from the place in northeastern Mexico where a Folsom point was first found embedded in the skeleton of such a bison. The Folsom points are small and fluted, well designed for use by dart thrower. Their area of use centered on the Rocky Mountains side of the high plains, from Colorado southward. A third hunting culture, called Plainview from a locality in the Llano Estacado of Texas, came a little later. Here a kill of a hundred giant bison was found in an area of five hundred square feet. Plainview points have been found from Alaska to Mexico and east to Ontario.[6]

It is not likely that this hunting complex of vast extension across Eurasia and North America developed independently in different places. In every known case it employed the new, demanding technique of pressure-flaking to shape thin and sharply edged implements of specialized design. The laurel leaf blades in Texas are nearly identical in pattern with those of Solutrean France and quite as elegantly made. The introduction of the dart thrower, or throwing board, and the attachment to darts of points designed for greater penetration represents another technical advance that seems to have a single origin. The American participants came somewhat later than those in Europe; their end seems to have been at about the same time.

The reason for the disappearance of hunter and hunted has been sought in change of climate. Aridity became more widespread in the American southwest, between the Rio Grande and the Gulf of California, and this may have driven the mammoths from these parts. The same thing happened in inner Asia. The plains of North America east of the Rocky Mountains, however, continued to grow a great deal of palatable vegetation. The proposal that hunting was so severe as to kill out the game lacks merit. There was an ecologic upset later restored by a different fauna and vegetation. The disturbance became a continuing crisis; the repopulation of the plains set in slowly, for plants, animals, and man. The one agency that could operate thus is fire. The older fauna—mammoths, horses, reindeer and bison—inhabited woodland, brush and tundra, browsing rather than grazing. Hunters could prowl about such a herd and pick off individuals, but not cause them to stampede. Mass kills are characteristic of the Upper Paleolithic hunters, and can be accounted for by fire spreading over a wide front, before which the animals fled in panic. I know of no other competent explanation. The hunters had learned the art of setting fire during dry weather so that it spread downwind, driving animals before it to a place where they would bog down or fall

---

6. Ibid.

over a cliff or be trapped by a barrier. The use of fire drives has been known generally to hunters in historic time. Its continued employment suppresses the reproduction of trees and other woody growth, which are replaced by grasses, annual and perennial, and by annual herbs.[7] Plains woodlands thus became steppes and prairies, occupied by a different fauna. The competent agent was man, organized for mass hunting; I suggest the time when the practice was instituted as Upper Paleolithic.

The grasslands of the New World are plains, semi-arid, sub-humid, and humid, whatever the season of rain. They do not extend into arid lands but, as in the western Llanos of Venezuela and the eastern United States, they did develop in areas of abundant rainfall. The common quality is that they are plains. They end where the terrain changes to steep and irregular slopes. Wherever valleys have been cut into grassy plains between the Appalachians and Rocky Mountains, the valley sides remain wooded, usually to the top. The early white visitors and settlers knew that the prairies and their western extension across the high plains were caused and maintained by burning. Indians set fires; the hazy sky of late autumn is still known as Indian summer, recalling the time when that was the season of Indian burning.

The alteration may be outlined roughly thus: the American hunters, from Clovis to Plainview, had possession of the plains for perhaps three thousand years, in the course of which the vegetation of trees and shrubs, and the browsing game it supported, were converted to an altered biome dominated by grass and herbs. Herds of other grazing animals multiplied, such as the plains bison, known as buffalo in the American vernacular, the pronghorn antelope, and the

---

7. In Africa the savannas are still expanding by the practice of burning. They too are plains, they range from high to low rainfall, and their vegetation is considered to be the result of periodic burning. That this has gone on for a long time is suggested by their grasses, the most nutritious pasture of low latitudes. As our bison spread and increased the buffalo and grama grasses, so African grazing animals are thought to have been selective agents in the dispersal and perhaps in the evolution of nourishing grasses. More recently, the introduction of African grasses into the New World is causing a revolution in tropical cattle raising in Brazil and around the Caribbean.

American elk. Low growing, spreading grasses, such as buffalo grass and the grama grasses, palatable green or dry, and a lot of annual weeds were symbiotic with the later grazing herds and fire. Burrowing rodents, such as the prairie dog, became numerous. The older cultures were replaced by more "localized" archaic hunting and gathering cultures that had domestic dogs, used mortars and pestles, and to some extent polished stone. Bow and arrow were introduced later into the New World, in Texas, according to Newcomb, after the beginning of the Christian era.

## DIVERGENT WAYS OF CULTURE

The division of human time based upon different types of stone artifacts was conceived in western Europe. It was proper there, holds across northern Asia, and appears to relate to the early migrations into North America. But it is not valid for the world as a whole, nor is it a general evolutionary series of stages. Atlantic Europe lay at a remote end of the habitable world. Its history during that vastly disproportionate time called Paleolithic is one of immigrations from the southeast, south and east; it is not endemic in origin. There is a bias in the European Paleolithic scheme in its stress on the masculine provider as dominating society, culminating in the collective hunters of terminal Pleistocene time. Its record deals with interior lands and takes little account of the waterside, salt or fresh.

The Upper Paleolithic hunters did not carry on as bearers of change into Mesolithic and Neolithic times. Some may have sired later reindeer-hunting tribes of the far north, others became lost in the spreading farming populations. They were the last of their kind, not the link to the new era. In northwest Germany, for example, the Ahrensburg reindeer hunters were contemporaries of farmers and town builders in Anatolia. The Plainview hunters were killing giant bison on the Llano Estacado when different people were cultivating plants in Pueblo and Oaxaca.

The new way of life, centered on tilling the ground, has been moved back in time by recent archeological discoveries in upland localities of the Near East and Mexico and these earliest records date back from nine to ten thousand years. They do not establish either the place or the time of agricultural origins, using agriculture to include the cultivation of plants of any kind by any means.

When the last deglaciation began, somewhat more than ten thousand years ago, the sea level stood about one hundred feet lower than at present, except for high, northern latitudes. Continued melting of ice raised the level of the sea until it reached its present state about thirty-six hundred years ago, the approximate age of the present coastlines in major outline. Low coastal plains, such as those fringing the South China and Java seas, were submerged and salt marshes spread about their margins. Rivers were embayed except where they carried the greatest loads of alluvium, and upstream alluvial deposits buried the earlier valley floors. Over this span of seven thousand years the lowland habitations of man are lost, in part submerged under the sea, in part covered by alluvium. In the lower parts of the great alluvial valleys they were more recently buried, as has been demonstrated in the Mississippi River delta.

It is improper to infer from archeological sites that the origins of agriculture were in upland regions and are post-glacial. Nor are they to be tied into the lithic stages of cultural succession. A quite different cultural and physical context is required and is available. I refer to the invitation of living by the waterside, which I proposed as the primordial human habitat. Such opportunity continued through Pleistocene time, in time of high or low sea level, offering sustenance and security at all seasons. It gave invitation to take a fixed abode, a prerequisite to farming life. By turning from salt to fresh water man had to acquire a new manner of living. The chronometer of the tides was replaced by the rise and fall of streams, the seasons of growth and harvest, the time of flooding and drying of land. Water resources were still of major importance, those of the land adding new attractions. The changing course of streams, the margins that were marsh and swamp, the fertile flood plains, and the bordering uplands formed a different habitat which man might learn to know and utilize. He could explore and exploit it from a permanent base, learning steps in elaborating more varied skills and interests. Living in families is stipulated, with the women having charge of the household and being mainly responsible for procuring the plant food and learning to know the kinds and properties of plants. The bilateral nature of waterside living is the provision of animals from the water, of plants from the land.

There is no longer a place for a Mesolithic stage of cultural evolution from Paleolithic hunting to Neolithic farming. The great hunters of old were not ancestors of the tillers of the soil. While specialized hunters ranged the plains other kinds of people lived in other places and with different ways, collecting what their land and waters produced, including particular devices for taking animals on land and in water. The archeological record being scanty, primitive peoples that survived into historic times provide insights into ancient and widely distributed skills that give information of cultural directions other than the lithic categories of conventional archeology. To what extent were such artifices a cultural heritage communicated from a common ancient source? The question here concerns the context of simpler waterside cultures, remote from each other but of similar practices.

In America, the most primitive natives of whom the Spaniards had early knowledge were the Karankawas and their neighbors on the coast of Texas, the main account of which was related by Nuñez Cabeza de Vaca as a result of the wreck of the Narváez expedition in 1528.[8] These tribes moved according to the season from island and lagoon to mainland and streamside, collecting, fishing and hunting. In winter, tubers (duck potato, *Sagittaria*) dug from the mud bottom of fresh water were a staple, in autumn they gathered acorns. Oysters at one season, blackberries at another, were mainstays. Fishing was practiced in stream, estuary and lagoon, by spear and net, by weirs built of canes and by brush dams, from dugout canoes. Canoes were used for spearing fish at night by torchlight. Medicine men prepared plants to stupefy fish, which were preserved by smoking. Cooking was done in pits. Baskets were made by twining and mats were used to cover their conical huts. Some of these artifices recurred widely throughout the world among waterside peoples of advanced as well as of simple cultures, and adumbrate a large and old dispersal

---

8. Ibid. See Chapters 3 and 12 for a summary of the customs of the Texas coast tribes.

of a way of life other than the lithic orientation of archeological evidence.

The geographic distribution of water craft and the use of *barbasco* are of particular interest. The Spanish-Portuguese term "barbasco" applies to plants used to stupefy or kill fish in mass without impairing their quality as food. Plants of many kinds have been found to have such effect, commonly by paralyzing the gills. Root, bark, leaves, or fruit of a suitable plant are mashed and strewn on still or slowly moving water, and the fish are collected as they float to the surface, belly up. The operation is organized and often ceremonially directed. The active substances lose potency by dilution and loss of stability, and thus have a short-term effect. Under social control the practice provided and conserved a supply of food. Whatever the plant employed, the procedure was similar and distinct from the use of bait or any mode of attracting fish. The range of practice does not coincide with that of barbasco plants, which have a wide distribution. This manner of fishing was commonly used by the natives of Mexico, Central America and the Pacific coastlands of the United States but not in the Mississippi valley or in the Atlantic coast states, where proper plants and suitable clear and quiet waters are present. In South America, barbasco was prepared by many tribes in the Amazon basin, including those possessing a most primitive culture. In the Old World it was important in lands around the Pacific and Indian Oceans. This, then, was an ancient art, rooted in a substream of waterside habitats that were carried far about the world, with competent identification of drug plants. In more sophisticated societies, plants found to be narcotic to man were adopted into ceremonial use.

The hunters of big game were not discoverers of plant drugs, nor did they build water craft. Beyond the depth in which poles may be used, paddles or sweeps were needed to propel the craft, whether it be steered raft, dugout, reed bundle, bark, or plank boat. Boat and propulsion are associated artifacts of distinctive types.[9]

---

9. Clinton Edwards, "Aboriginal Water Craft on the Pacific Coast of South America," *Ibero-Americana* 47 (1965), includes notes on wider distributions of the several kinds.

Dugout canoes were the most widely used means of water transport, and in many parts the only one. The name *canoa* was adopted by Spaniards from the Island Arawaks, who fashioned elegantly made boats of tree trunks. They were seaworthy, fast and expertly maneuvered, the paddlers ranging up to several score in boats of state. Dugouts of elaborate design and large size were also used by Indians of the Pacific northwest. In simple form and small size they were the water craft of primitive peoples from California to the Amazon and La Plata basins. In the Old World they survived most strongly in Africa and around the Indian Ocean. The idea of paddling a hollowed tree trunk may have occurred independently to different peoples, but the patience and skill required to make a serviceable boat out of a tree, and to propel and steer it by properly designed paddles, require competent workmanship. Shaping a dugout was an exacting and tedious task of charring and scraping inside and outside to get balance, displacement, and steerage. A common and ancient origin is suggested.

Reed bundle floats were another approach to being water-borne. They were made of reeds, rushes, sedges or the like, tied into bundles, these in turn lashed into the shape of a slender boat, coming to a peak at one or both ends, somewhat like a gondola. The occupants are partly immersed in water but unlikely to sink or capsize. Propulsion is by paddles. Such floats, of very similar construction and pattern, have a greatly disjunct distribution, especially around the Pacific and Indian Oceans and their interiors. Considerable antiquity is inferred from their great geographic range, from New Zealand, Tasmania and Australia, Lake Chad, the Nile, Mesopotamia and Afghanistan, the Gulf of California, the coasts of Peru and Chile, Lake Titicaca, and Argentina:[10] from their use by very primitive peoples such as the Tasmanian, Seri and Uru; and their representation in the ancient art of Egypt, Mesopotamia and Peru. They are also said to antedate other boats on the Nile. Being a distinctive and complex artifact, independent invention seems as unlikely for the reed bundle float as for the dart thrower or bow and arrow. That they

---

10. Ibid.

are a substitute for the dugout in a country that lacked suitable trees appears to be an inadequate explanation—the Tasmanians, for example, with tall and straight eucalyptus at hand, made floats closely resembling those of Lake Titicaca. Dugout and bundle float are two different concepts adopted by different peoples.

## AGRICULTURAL ORIGINS

The earliest farming known to archeology dates back to between nine and ten thousand years both in the Old and New World, in Anatolia and South Mexico. It is found in interior locations, in climates of long, marked dry seasons, and it set seeds to harvest seed. This was the period when Upper Paleolithic hunters of big game still held the plains of Russia and Texas. The omission of the waterside people who fished, made boats and nets, dug tubers, processed plants for fibers and drugs, and had houses is a discontinuity of sequence. The rise of sea level with deglaciation submerged coastal lowlands and raised valley floors with alluvial deposits, and thereby covered most of the early record of this other manner of living.

In superior locations, food was available to waterside peoples the year round both from water and land. Living in permanent communities gave them the benefit of shared learning. Sedentary fishers, attentive to the use of plants, are indicated as the-first farmers. The waters yielded animal protein and fat, fleshy roots and shoots of plants, starch, sugar, and other supplements to diet. Digging roots is a transition from collecting to cultivating. A patch that has been dug for a particular kind of root is likely to leave parts that reproduce as individual plants; the more often the plot is dug the greater the reproduction. Root digging is incipient tillage. The next step was to take pieces of a desired plant to a convenient location and begin cultivation.

Vegetative propagation results from observing that a piece of a plant will grow and reproduce itself. Primitive garden culture was established by assembling desirable plants, which would grow from a tuber or part of root or stem. Attention is directed to the individual plant; an attractive variant is selected and multiplied. In the course of long selection some plants have lost the ability to bear seed and have become dependent on propagation by man. The plants adopted are perennials and may be used at all seasons as wanted, without need of storage. Such a planting economy is largely independent of a season of harvest.

The two great areas of this vegetative planting complex are southeast Asia with the islands beyond and the lands around the Caribbean Sea. In both, the interest in plant food has been directed mainly to starch and sugar. Mainland southeast Asia and Indonesia were the home of the ancestral yams *(Dioscorea)*, aroids including taro, *Musa,* sugar canes and other plants that supplied starch or sugar. Bamboos and pandans were planted for diverse uses. Vegetatively cultivated fish poisons include the famous *Derris* which yields rotenone.

In the New World tropics around the Caribbean, a great variety of roots was taken into cultivation and ameliorated for human use. Manioc *(yuca* in Spanish, *cassava* to the English) is a singular achievement, the greatest producer of starch, source of sure poison, with the capability to keep indefinitely when baked in cakes, and with extraordinary tolerance of dry weather and of wide variations of pH values in soils. The list of superior cultigen tubers is large and includes sweet potatoes, the taro-like *Xanthosoma*, at least one *Dioscorea,* arrowroot, *Arracacia,* and *Canna.* The pineapple was developed by vegetative selection. Diverse drug plants were grown for ceremonial use as narcotics and hallucinogens. Curare was prepared to poison darts. The great attention to toxic plants probably carries back to the ancient practices of drugging fish; some, such as *Lonchocarpus nicou,* having been vegetatively reproduced to the extent that their propagation depends on man.

Both great regions of vegetative planting cultures in Old World and New were much alike in food economy, plant techniques, and habitation. The people of these regions lived in permanent villages, easily provisioned from water and land, and with competent water transport. They built houses of wood, cane, and thatch; made nets, mats, baskets and wooden bowls, and experimented with plant poisons. Their economy was strongly focused on the use of plants.

In South America the practice of vegetative reproduction extended through and along the Andean lands, adding there such cultigen tubers as oca *(Oxalis)* and ulluco *(Ullucus)* and the great assemblage of potatoes, ranging from diploids through fertile and sterile polyploids. Northward the vegetative cultigen complex was replaced by the maize-beans-squash seed complex, beginning in the highlands of Central America. In Costa Rica vegetative propagation is still much used, and the markets are well supplied with its products. A perennial cucurbit, chayote *(Sechium),* which may be grown by cutting or seed, is a favored vegetable, both as fruit and root. The *pejibae* (peach palm), an ancient tropical cultigen, is selected by planting suckers as well as by seed. Vegetative propagation is practiced in Central America and from here south to the limits of agriculture in southern Chile. Costa Rica, at the meeting of the two agricultures, uses both kinds of propagation for the same plants.

The northern agricultural complex of maize, beans and squash reached from Central America to the Gulf of St. Lawrence. The southern root crops dropped out to the north, not because of climatic limits, but because the northern plant breeders were interested in seeds. The vegetation to the north did not lack edible roots. Mexico and the adjoining American southwest, for example, have wild potatoes, of current interest to potato breeding. These were dug and eaten but they were not cultivated or made the object of selection. Northward attention centered on the cultivation of annuals, plants of rapid growth in the season of summer rains, maturing with the onset of the dry or cold season. Planting and harvest time regulated the calendar of work and ceremonial. The plants grown provided a reasonably adequate diet. This manner of seed growing for seed harvest is known as the *milpa* system by its Mexican name, in contrast to the vegetative propagation by *conucos,* a term taken from the Arawaks of the West Indies.

The origin of the milpa is obscure. Recent excavations at Tehuacan and Oaxaca in Mexico have shown it to be far older than had been thought. In both places, plants grown by inhabitants of rock shelters included beans and squash, at a time when giant bison were still hunted in Texas. There was no maize, and when it appeared later its yields were for a long time so poor that this could hardly be its attraction. Collecting and hunting would seem still to have provided the chief means of subsistence, although the bow and arrow were not as yet known. That seed plants were grown meant permanent residence, at least from planting to harvest. These high interior basins with their short rainy season do not impress one as a place where a great departure in plant domestication would begin. Yet they are not far distant from coastal lowlands where fishing and conuco farming were practised. The wild kindred of the squashes and beans are native to southern Mexico and northern Central America, especially in the higher and drier lands. The position of the most ancient milpas, marginal to lowlands of conuco farming, suggests that as agriculture moved inland and upland away from productive streams and lakes, wild cucurbits, beans and other plants populated the clearings, were found useful, and became the object of attention and propagation. The cucurbits spread their vines over the cleared ground, the beans climbed up supporting stalks. Chayote, *Cucurbita ficifolia,* resembling a watermelon, and the scarlet runner bean *(Phaseolus coccineus)* are perennial vines with edible fleshy roots, perhaps linking them to conuco origins. Except for some cucurbits, the plants at hand gave little promise of becoming important crops. With patience, wild *Phaseolus* were bred into high quality and heavily yielding cultigens—the kidney and navy, lima and other beans of commerce. Four of the five cultivated species of squashes and pumpkins are attributed here, and after a long time of indifferent success, maize was made into the great staple grain.

The maize-beans-squash complex afforded a balanced diet that needed little supplementing by animal food. The plants also served as green vegetables, roasting ears of corn, green beans, green squash and squash blossoms. Milpa agriculture follows practices like those of conucos, probably derived from the latter. Selection is by individual plant, the desired pumpkin, ear of corn, or bean pod, choosing certain colors and large-sized seeds. The seeds are thrust into the ground in determined numbers and spacing. The planting is by heaping the earth into mounds. Until the agricultural revolution of the late 1930s, the American farmer followed the Indian manner of growing corn, placing the grains by mechanical planter and "hilling" the plants by cross-cultivation.

The earliest agriculture known in the Old World is in Anatolia and adjacent areas; the growing of small grains and pulses, keeping sheep and perhaps other domestic animals, the people living in villages or towns with cult shrines. Their condition was far removed from the beginnings of agriculture. There are wild relatives of wheat in those parts, some, such as einkorn and emmer, taken into cultivation. The breeding of bread wheats came later. Vavilov pointed out that in the domestication of small grains and pulses the elimination of shattering of the ripe seed heads and pods was important and that such change of cultivated forms increases westward from India. The hypothesis may be suggested that seed cultivation had its beginnings in the less-rainy monsoon land of India, in which attractive annual weeds, grasses and pulses had an advantage over perennial roots and stems and thus moved west through lands of scantier summer rain into the winter rain lands of the Levant. The amelioration of the seed crops was not by individual but rather by mass selection. The small grains, *Phaseolus* beans, peas, and lentils of the Old World were not increased in seed size nor diversified in color as was the case in the New World. Broadcast sowing is indicated before the plough was used.

The thesis of Eduard Hahn was that animals were domesticated for religious reasons, as symbols of a divinity or as themselves sacred, as necessary to the observance of cult, perhaps for sacrifice. Starting out to study the economic geography of dairying, he found that milking began as a ritual act, and only later came to be regarded as a source of food. His exploration of sexuality in religions as represented by particular animals opened new insights that still hold good. With few exceptions the domestication of animals, including herd animals, was done by agricultural peoples in ceremonial context. Ease of taming and propinquity to man were not involved in their adoption. Their profane uses derived from ritual origins. The man-avoiding jungle fowl of southeast Asia appeared in Homeric Greece as a means of divination and in the ritual of cock-fighting before it was bred to produce eggs. Horned cattle were kept as sacred animals before they found a place on the farm. That hunters penned game to assure themselves of meat and thus became stock raisers is a myth invented by materialist imagination. I know of no evidence that suggests an economic basis of the origin of animal domestication.

The history of mankind can now be seen in relation to the history of the Ice Age. The repeated spread and recession of glaciation successively changed the extent and aspect of the habitable world, and the chronology of these changes now can be determined in part. There still are greatly differing interpretations of the alterations of the climatic patterns, oversimplified as "cold" or "warm" stages. The most important fact of the rise and fall of sea level has had the least attention concerning its effect on the history of mankind. This concerns coastal lowlands and, as well, the valleys that are dependent on the level of the sea. The oldest known agricultural sites are in high interior locations. It does not follow, as has been thought, that agriculture began in such situations. At that time the sea stood about one hundred feet below its present state and the associated valley floors were correspondingly lower. At the last glacial maximum, sea level was three hundred feet or more below the present. The superior attractions of waterside living that I have inferred for the beginning of humankind apply also, I submit, to the origins of the agricultural way of life at a time well before any archeological record.

# 16. Human
## Ecology
### and Population

The human lineage as distinct from other primates we now know goes back millions of years, hominids living in interior East Africa two million years ago. This indefinitely long period of primitive learning and geographic dispersal, named the Lower Paleolithic by the technique and forms of its artifacts of stone, carried on to a hundred and fifty thousand years ago, by which time man was established over far parts of Africa and Eurasia.

The successful divergent of primate evolution shows by his anatomy and physiology evidence of his ancestral habitat, the ecologic niche of his origins. He lived on the ground, erect of carriage, walked flat-footed, his arms free and not used in locomotion. He lacked pelt, powerful jaws, strong incisors, great strength. He is omnivorous with a widely competent digestive system except for the ingestion of raw starch in quantity. The human infant is born in complete dependence on maternal care, remains so longest, and takes longest to grow to maturity. Sir Alister Hardy has called attention to the superior adaptation of the human body to swimming, absent in other primates.

"Human Ecology and Population" first appeared in *Population and Economics*, Paul DePrez (Ed.), (University of Manitoba Press: Winnipeg, Canada, 1968), pp. 207–214.

It would seem apparent that the usual attribution of human origins to African savannas is improper. These have strong contrast of rainy and dry seasons, wide movement of the herds of game with the availability of forage and water, a balance between fleet game and their predators and scavengers, all drifting across the land. The place thus assigned to man is that of scavenger and predator about the margins of herds, living on crippled, infirm, and young animals, in taking which he competed with carnivores and vultures. The humans are thought of as bands under the control of a strong and aggressive male. The construct is as socially unattractive as it is ecologically incompetent—a poorly equipped primate, handicapped by dependent and defenseless offspring, venturing into competition with the functionally specialized predators of the savannas, to which humans were convenient prey.

A different, proper, and convenient niche was available for human origins and increase, the forming of its society and the development of skills—the African shores of the Indian Ocean. Here there was no lack of food or water at any time, no necessity to be on the move, so disadvantageous to women and children. The tides gave a daily change of collecting range on beach and rock. Sea turtles laid their eggs on beaches. Fish and marine mammals were stranded occasionally. Estuaries offered a rich harvest as learning grew. Drinking water of stream, spring, or seep was at hand at all seasons. There were shells of many sizes and shapes, bones and carapaces, salt-seasoned driftwood, jetsam of many kinds to be picked up on the beaches. Waves detached rocks from headlands and ground them into rounded cobbles, tough and hard, ready to suit the hand. Abundant and diverse food was at hand and the materials and forms of stone, shell, wood, and fiber invited use and fashioning. The coasts were not preëmpted by other primates nor hunted over by the great cats. There was security here as well as opportunity. Adopting the Hardy thesis of the design of the human body for swimming, the origin of our kind took form in aquatic as well as terrestrial habitat.

By the alternate and better option human society was formed by the women. The primates in general are rather notorious for the inattention of the males to the young. The human female had the responsibility of caring for the young and doing so for so long that the succession of progeny remained linked to mother and each other. The human family is unique in its continuity and is based on the maternal bond. Not band but family is the basis of human society. The most primitive peoples have the most elaborate systems of kinship. The simple maternal family readily became an extended family group by succession of generations that remained in the same locality, the primordial community. That paternity was acknowledged and accepted is not basic to the origin of the family.

Seaside living gave opportunity for permanent habitation, an innate maternal desire. The man might roam, the woman sought a place where she could have shelter for her brood and adequate provision of food, water, and materials. The selection of a proper site resulted in permanent occupation, the household and home, the nascent sessile community.

Being amply supplied with food and other necessities, the primordial seaside community continued to increase in numbers. New sites of similar advantage were occupied and spread about the Indian Ocean to South Africa and to Java. Some are recorded in human remains as in Java, more by sites of worked stone preserved on high coasts. Primitive and early artifacts have been found and named as to type on sea margins of Morocco and Portugal. Rather widely distributed early Lower Paleolithic types are known as pre-Chellean, Abbevillean, and Clactonian from type localities on tidal seacoast or lower river course in France and England.

By the Second Interglacial, perhaps a half-million years ago, man had colonized far beyond tropic lands and well inland, as shown by the habitation of Peking Man. This has the oldest record of his use of fire, preserved there by the rock shelter under which the people lived. Lacking fire, ancestral man was limited by cold and also in his ability to make plant substances palatable and storable. The narrow range of the fireless human was changed into a wide world open to his successful entry when he began his promethean course by taking fire under his control. This I consider was the great achievement of most ancient man, the act by which he began to be the ecologic dominant, freed of climatic restriction. Again I should attribute this to the woman, keeper of the hearth where she learned the varied ways of cooking and at which her family was warmed. At the hearth she found that starchy roots became good food by heat, that bitterness was thus removed from root, stem, and seed, that poisonous plants were made edible, that meat and plants could be preserved. The presence of man beyond tropical climates implies, I think, his use of fire, for warming his living space, and for preparing and storing his food. Thus I should refer nearly all archeologic sites in Europe to the employment of fire, at a time beginning far earlier than that of Peking Man.

Middle Paleolithic time, again by definition and calendar made in France, covers the span from about a hundred and fifty thousand years ago to less than forty thousand (by current Pleistocene reckoning). The innovation was a new breed, Neanderthal Man, and a new culture, Mousterian, the two linked. Both were thought to have evolved in Europe and there was an idea that they were unable to survive the rigor of the last great ice advance. Instead it now appears that they did so and that their range was from western Europe into Mongolia, the Zagros Mountains, and other parts. It was an inland culture, making stone points to use on spears or javelins, perhaps the first to be somewhat specialized for hunting, but also inclined to cave dwelling or, rather, living under rock shelters. They are the earliest people known to have buried their dead and done so reverently. The range of this culture was from lowland tundra through mixed woodlands to the edge of the desert. Its ecology thus was likely to differ with the habitat with a bent to taking game. I know of no interest in aquatic resources and infer a widely spread population of small groups ranging over small areas and taking advantage of natural shelters.

During Middle Paleolithic time sea level fell by three hundred feet as glaciation increased and rivers discharging into the sea lowered their floors correspondingly. The places and manners of living of waterside peoples of coast and lowland valleys have since been buried under sea and alluvium and are lost to our knowledge. This record is almost a blank though it concerned the largest number of people and the largest concentrations.

The New World was entered by man during Middle Paleolithic time and it may have been entered repeatedly. Under the prevalent doctrine that the New World was not peopled until "after the end of the Ice Age" good evidence to the contrary continued to be rejected. Radiocarbon dating now is competent to determine age to about forty thousand years. There are sites too old to have radioactive carbon and others are pending. Pleistocene geomorphology thus is paying new and more serious attention to the California coast, the Mohave Desert, and high terraces of Texas rivers. Whether men began to settle the New World during or prior to the last glaciation has not been determined. At any rate, there now is ample time to fill the New World to its diverse environmental capacities and cultural divergences.

The Upper Paleolithic peoples again were first determined in western Europe, and the first held to be entitled to the name *Homo sapiens*. By current reckoning their time reached from thirty-five to nine thousand years ago, in rounded terms. These were hunters of big game, organized for *grande chasse,* as the Solutreans for hunting forest horse, Gravettians for mammoth, and Magdalenians for reindeer. They made fine blades and points of stone by the technique of pressure-flaking and had new precision arms in the dart thrower and bow and arrow. They engaged in mass drives, most effective by setting fires in plains, their preferred habitat. In North America a very similar way of life appeared and at about the same time—first the Llano/Clovis mammoth hunters, then the Folsom hunters of an extinct giant bison, and last the Plainview hunters of the same bisons. The blades and projectile points were as finely made by pressure-flaking as those of the Old World. The dart thrower was used but not the bow and arrow. These New World hunters of late Paleolithic time and type mainly occupied the high plains east of the Rocky Mountains but also lower plains to the east. In the European and North American plains the hunters and their major game animals disappeared at about the same time, the mammoths, horses and bison becoming extinct, the reindeer and perhaps their hunters withdrawing to more northern tundras.

An ecologic alteration of large extent is implied. The great game animals were woodland forms and, as such, unlikely to mass in large herds. The rapid recession of continental glaciation that set in about eleven thousand years ago was part of a major climatic change by which arid and semi-arid lands increased in extent with replacement of mesophytic by more xerophytic vegetation. Humid plains became semi-arid in parts and the forage of their woodland browsers was diminished. The interpretation that continuing hunting pressure with increased climatic disadvantage brought faunal extinction is hardly competent. The major grasslands are plains. This is the quality they have in common, not any quality of climate. Where there is a break in the plain, as by the erosion of a valley, the grassy vegetation changes, often abruptly, to brush or woodland, whatever the climate. Steppe, savanna, or prairie, the grassland is maintained by burning. If burning is stopped woody growth enters. The grasslands were formed by fire spreading across plains during dry weather and, doing so year after year, suppressing the reproduction of woody perennials. Man is the agent competent to do this and he has done so since the time of the Upper Paleolithic hunters. His pursuit of large game, such as elephants, giant bison, forest horse, added the use of fire drives by which the quarry was herded to a place convenient for the killing. Fleeing from the advancing fire they could be driven over a cliff or become bogged down in wet ground. Such mass kills are known from Texas to France. The woodland plains became grasslands, the earlier game and hunters were replaced by grassland fauna and other hunting people who continued to practice burning. In its heyday the Upper Paleolithic hunting economy supported, I should say, more than a minimal population over a large area. It faded away with the animals on which it had depended. The plains appear to have been slowly repeopled. In time the plains bison, pronghorn antelope, and other herbivores restocked North American plains with as great, perhaps greater, supply of game.

At a time when Magdalenian hunters flourished in Europe and the Plainview hunters in Texas, agriculture was being practiced in Anatolia and in southern Mexico. The oldest places in the Levant date back ten thousand years, perhaps more, those in Mexico a thousand years less. The big game hunters lingered in the north, but a very different way of life was under way to the south in both hemispheres. In the Levant some of the oldest sites known, such as Jericho and Chatal Huyuk, were towns of surprising size and construction. These people were unrelated to the hunters of the north and appear with developed cultures, as to cult as well as to production. They were growers of seeds that had been selected for cultivation, still for a good while of low yield, but sown, cultivated, and stored. Both in Old and New World these earliest known parts where tillage was carried on were in interiors of the land, the Levant having winter rains, Mexico the rainy season in summer, both in scant amount. Were such the areas and such the plants of agricultural origins?

The time was the onset of the last melting of the icecaps and probably that of the modern pattern of climates. Since the last maximum of glaciation, sea level had risen two hundred feet or more and would rise almost a hundred feet more to its modern level, reached about four thousand years ago or less. The valley floors opening to the sea were built up accordingly by alluvium. The lowlands once inhabited were submerged by water or buried by alluviation as the ice melted. As I have thought that these lowlands were from the beginning the particular domain of man, in which he learned and increased most, so I look to them as the hearth of agriculture.

Moving from salt waterside through estuaries to rivers and lakes gave new direction to the manner of living. The tidal zone of the seacoast has a counterpart in fresh water, in shallows, swamps, and flood plain—a greatly diverse, accessible, and useful massing of plants and animals. Here fish spawned, water fowl fed and nested, amphibious mammals pastured and bred, and edible roots and shoots could be taken. Canes, rushes, reeds, and lianas provided material for structures and textiles. Man could live in permanent communities and continue to increase.

The evidence for ancient invention is found in primitive peoples that have survived or did so into historic time. Those who lived by suitable waters made water craft of competent and characteristic design, both as to boat and paddle. The dugout canoe was in widest use in low and middle latitudes of both hemispheres. The boat-shaped reed bundle float, often miscalled balsa, was used in widely separated parts of the world, and in part in almost identical design by most primitive peoples, such as the Tasmanians and the Uru of Lake

Titicaca. Having boats, fishing in open water as well as water transport was available. A widespread practice was taking fish by barbasco, the discovery that certain plants spread over the water would paralyze or kill fish without impairing their edibility. This was done by macerating root or other part of a plant known to have this effect and by scattering from dugouts. The procedure required specific plant identification and manner of application and was common to peoples of primitive and high culture, especially in lower latitudes. The active substances being unstable and soon dissipated in running water, the use of barbasco did not deplete the fishing waters. In some cases it was under ceremonial control. Primitive fishing folk also used nets and spears, as in spearing fish at night by torchlight. They dug edible roots in shallow water and on land.

In situations of superior attraction provision from water was not limited. Animal protein and fat was in good supply, largely by fishing. Starch, sugar, and whatever else was needed for a balanced diet were secured from roots, shoots, and fruits, perennials of lowlands. The transition from collecting to cultivation was by vegetative reproduction and probably began accidentally. Digging is the beginning of tillage. Parts that are missed reproduce as separate plants; the more a plot is dug for tubers the greater its likely stocking. The midden or garbage heap gave a place for discarded roots and stems to grow. The step to planting was easy and was done by selecting individual plants. Knowing that the piece of the plant would be the same as the one from which it was taken, attention was directed to the desirable individual. Vegetative reproduction became the way to plant breeding by selecting preferred individuals. As such became domesticated forms some became dependent on man with loss of the ability to reproduce by seed.

In the Old World the great hearth of fishing and vegetative farming was in southeast Asia of abundant monsoon rains and many rivers, formerly discharging across lowlands now covered by the South China and Java seas and the Bay of Bengal. Densely populated today on a rice and fish diet, it had the means of feeding a large population before rice was introduced. The cultivated yams (*Dioscorea*) mostly belong here as do the aroids such as taro, all the plantains and bananas, sugar canes, barbascos, plants needed for ceremonies, many kinds of plants that have been grown by cuttings from time unknown.

In the New World a parallel fishing-farming culture occupied the Caribbean lands, south far into South America and west across Central America. Manioc, probably the most heavily yielding of all starch producers, is grown from stem cuttings, as is the sweet potato. The list of vegetatively grown providers of starch is large and includes an excellent aroid *Xanthosoma* (*yautia* and other local names), at least one native *Dioscorea* yam, and arrowroot. Fish poisons and narcotics were taken into cultivation. Agriculture was carried into the high Andes by the planting of tubers, especially of *Solanums* that were bred into the great diversity of potatoes. A tropical terrestrial bromeliad was made into the pineapple, rich in sugar and used to make alcoholic drink.

Both tropical regions of the two hemispheres were directed to the production of starch and sugar, continuing to rely on their waters for animal protein and fat. A great diversity of plants was taken into cultivation by vegetative reproduction and thus bred into cultigens of high yield. Ample, varied, and constant supply of food promoted the growth of human populations in sedentary communities and did so, it is proposed, before this was the case elsewhere.

The origins of seed cultivation are indicated as geographically marginal to the fishing-farming areas. In the New World the ancestors of the major seed crops, maize, beans, and squash, are thought to be native to central and southern Mexico and northern Central America, mainly in interiors of rainfall limited to summer. The recently extended archeologic record establishes the early cultivation of beans and squash with the absence of maize. When maize appeared it remained for a long time most unimpressive as to yield and quality. The squashes, grown for their seeds, seem to have been more rewarding than the primitive cultivated beans. These oldest Mexican records of seed growing give scant promise of the great and much later development of the maize-beans-squash complex. The inference is that this was an alternative direction northward and inland entered on where the physical conditions were ill-suited to the older cultivation. Seed farming, known as milpa agriculture in Mexico, had a long task in making the crop plants we know out of the wild ones. This was done by the same practices used in vegetative planting: (1) Individual selection, the particular squash, ear of maize, or bean desired being kept for seed. (2) Heaping the planting ground into mounds or, less commonly, into ridges. (3) Thrusting a determined number of seeds into the heaped earth at desired depth. This still was planting. Selection for size and color of seed, for size and form of ear, pepo, and pod, and for yield and growth resulted in time in the superior lot of plant forms that supported the large Indian populations of Mesoamerica.

A similar development is suggested for the Old World. Beyond the well-watered monsoon lands of southeast Asia and especially to the west, seed-bearing grasses and pulses came under cultivation. The process of domestication was not speeded by individual plant selection and planting in mounded earth as in the New World, the seed apparently being broadcast. The amelioration came by mass selection, plants of better yield and ripening at the same time providing more and more of the seed stock. Grasses became the small grains of cultivation—millets, wheat, and barley. Pulses remained small-seeded lentils, peas, and *Phaseolus* beans. In contrast to the New World these beans are small-seeded and not diversified as to color. Cucurbits had little attention and least so for their seeds. Flax and hemp were grown for oil and fiber. The attainments of the seed farmers of the Old World are less impressive than those of the New World except for rice, which developed into a great staple in the fishing and vegetative planting complex of the southeast. Animals were not domesticated for the purpose of producing food nor were they significant to human increase until historic time except in the regions of dairying.

Having fire, man went to the ends of the earth. Having fire, he disturbed the associated biota to his advantage. He helped to increase secondary vegetation of shrubs and herbs, heliophil and precocious, at the expense of forest denseness and shade and thereby increased mammals that browsed and grazed and seed-eating birds. I think that during most of his existence he had continuing success in making the world increasingly habitable to himself, by increase of fauna and flora useful to his needs. Very late in his history he domesticated plants and animals. By extending his occupation over the land surfaces and increasing his ecologic dominance, man was able to grow greatly in numbers, perhaps to an equilibrium with the sustenance available to the skills he possessed. The rise of sea level in late and post-glacial time, which continued to within four thousand years and submerged lowlands and flooded valleys, took place at the time when man learned how to grow crops and keep domestic animals, the connection if any being unresolved.

Ecologic equilibrium seems a more attractive thesis than Malthusian rate of population growth. War and pestilence have little relevance to simple societies. It is not proved that any human population breeds until it is arrested by famine. Fecundity is not fertility nor do we know much about either in "underdeveloped" or "primitive" conditions, such as the reduction of conception by ceremonial practices or abstentions.

# 17. The Agency
## of Man
## on the Earth

## THE THEME

As a short title for the present conference we have spoken at times
and with hope of a "Marsh Festival," after the statesman-scholar,
George Perkins Marsh, who a century ago considered the ways in
which the earth has been modified by human action (Marsh, 1864,
1874). The theme is the capacity of man to alter his natural environment, the manner of his so doing, and the virtue of his actions. It
is concerned with historically cumulative effects, with the physical
and biologic processes that man sets in motion, inhibits, or deflects,
and with the differences in cultural conduct that distinguish one
human group from another.

Every human population, at all times, has needed to evaluate the
economic potential of its inhabited area, to organize its life about its
natural environment in terms of the skills available to it and the
values which it accepted. In the cultural *mise en valeur* of the environment, a deformation of the pristine, or prehuman, landscape has
been initiated that has increased with length of occupation, growth

"The Agency of Man on the Earth" first appeared in *Man's Role in Changing the
Face of the Earth*, William L. Thomas, Jr. (Ed.), (University of Chicago Press:
Chicago, 1956), pp. 46–49

in population, and addition of skills. Wherever men live, they have operated to alter the aspect of the earth, both animate and inanimate, be it to their boon or bane.

The general theme may be described, therefore, in its first outline, as an attempt to set forth the geographic effects, that is, the appropriation of habitat by habit, resulting from the spread of differing cultures to all the *oikoumene* throughout all we know of human time. We need to understand better how man has disturbed and displaced more and more of the organic world, has become in more and more regions the ecologic dominant, and has affected the course of organic evolution. Also how he has worked superficial changes as to terrain, soil, and the waters on the land and how he has drawn upon its minerals. Latterly, at least, his urban activities and concentrations have effected local alterations of the atmosphere. We are trying to examine the processes of terrestrial change he has entrained or originated, and we are attempting to ask, from our several interests and experiences, relevant questions as to cultural behaviors and effects. Thus we come properly also to consider the qualities of his actions as they seem to affect his future well-being. In this proper study of mankind, living out the destiny ascribed in Genesis—"to have dominion over all the earth"—the concern is valid as to whether his organized energies (social behavior) have or should have a quality of concern with regard to his posterity.

ON THE NATURE OF MAN

The primordial condition of man setting our kind apart from other primates involved more than hands, brain, and walking upright. Man owes his success in part to his digestive apparatus, which is equaled by none of his near-kin or by few other similarly omnivorous animals as to the range of potential food which can sustain him on a mixed, vegetarian, or flesh diet. The long, helpless infancy and the dependence through the years of childhood have forged, it would seem, *ab origine* a maternal bond that expresses itself in persistence of family and in formal recognition of kinship, system of kinship being perhaps the first basis of social organization. When humans lost the mating cycle is unknown; its weakening and loss is probably a feature of domestication, and it may have occurred early in the history of man, eldest of the domesticated creatures.

Built into the biologic nature of man, therefore, appear to be qualities tending to maximize geographic expansiveness, vigorous reproduction, and a bent to social development. His extreme food range favored numerical increase; I question, for instance, any assumptions of sporadic or very sparse populations of Paleolithic man in any lands he had occupied. The dominant and continuous role of woman in caring for the family suggests further inferences. Maternal duties prescribed as sedentary a life as possible. Her collecting of food and other primary materials was on the short tether of her dependent offspring. Hers also was the care of what had been collected in excess of immediate need, the problem of storage, hers the direction toward homemaking and furnishing. To the "nature" of woman we may perhaps ascribe an original social grouping, a cluster of kindred households, in which some stayed home to watch over bairns and baggage while others ranged afield. Baby-sitting may be one of the most ancient of human institutions.

Implicit in this interpretation of the nature of man and primordial society, as based on his trend to sedentary life and clustering, are territoriality, the provision of stores against season of lack, and probably a tendency to monogamy. These traits are familiar enough among numerous animals, and there is no reason for denying them to primitive man. Shifts of population imposed by seasons do not mean wandering, homeless habits; nomadism is an advanced and specialized mode of life. Folk who stuffed or starved, who took no heed of the morrow, could not have possessed the earth or laid the foundations of human culture. To the ancestral folk we may rather ascribe practical-minded economy of effort. Their success in survival and in dispersal into greatly differing habitats tells of ability to derive and communicate sensible judgments from changing circumstances.

The culture of man is herewith considered as in the main a continuum from the beginning; such is its treatment by archeology. The record of artifacts is much greater, more continuous, and begins earlier than do his recovered skeletal remains. Thereby hangs the still-argued question of human evolution, about which divergent views are unreconciled. If culture was transmitted and advanced in time and space as the archeologic record indicates, there would appear to be a linked history of a mankind that includes all the specific and generic hominid classifications of physical anthropology. Man, *sensu latiore,* therefore may conceivably be one large species complex, from archaic to modern forms, always capable of interbreeding and intercommunication. Variation occurred by long geographic isolation, blending usually when different stocks met. The former is accepted; the latter seems assured to some and is rejected by others, the Mount Carmel series of skulls being thus notoriously in dispute.

Neanderthal man, poor fellow, has had a rough time of it. He invented the Mousterian culture, a major advance that appears to have been derived from two anterior culture lines. The Abbé Breuil has credited him with ceremonial cults that show a developed religious belief and spiritual ceremonial (Breuil and Lantier, 1951, chap. xviii). Boyd, in his serologic classification of mankind (1950), the only system available on a genetic basis, has surmised that Neanderthal is ancestral to a Paleo-European race. There is no basis for holding Neanderthal man as mentally inferior or as unable to cope with the late Pleistocene changes of European climate. Yet there remains aversion to admitting him to our ancestry. The sad confusion of physical anthropology is partly the result of its meager knowledge of hereditary factors, but also the result of *Homo's* readiness to crossbreed, a trait of his domestication and a break with the conservatism of the instinctive.

We are groping in the obscurity of a dim past; it may be better to consider cultural growth throughout human time as proceeding by invention, borrowing, and blending of learning, rather than by evolution of human brain, until we know more of biological evolution in man. The little that we have of skeletal remains is subject to unreconciled evaluations; the record of his work is less equivocal. The question is not, *could* Peking Man have left the artifacts attributed to him, as has been the subject of debate, but *did* he, that is, do the bones belong with the tools?

When primordial man began to spread over the earth, he knew little, but what he had learned was by tested and transmitted experience; he cannot have been fear-ridden but rather, at least in his successful kinds, was venturesome, ready to try out his abilities in new surroundings. More and more he imposed himself on his animal competitors and impressed his mark on the lands he inhabited. Wherever he settled, he came to stay, unless the climate changed too adversely or the spreading sea drove him back.

## CLIMATIC CHANGES AND THEIR EFFECTS ON MAN

The age of man is also the Ice Age. Man may have witnessed its beginning; we perhaps are still living in an interglacial phase. His growth of learning and his expansion over the earth have taken place during a geologic period of extreme instability of climates and also of extreme simultaneous climatic contrast. His span has been cast within a period of high environmental tensions. Spreading icecaps caused the ocean to shrink back from the shallow continental margins, their waning to spread the seas over coastal plains. With lowered sea levels, rivers trenched their valley floors below coastal lowlands; as sea level rose, streams flooded and aggraded their valleys. Glacial and Recent time have been governed by some sort of climatic pendulum, varying in amplitude of swing, but affecting land and sea in all latitudes, and life in most areas. The effects have been most felt in the northern hemisphere, with its large continental masses, wide plains, high mountain ranges, and broad plateaus. Millions of square miles of land were alternately buried under ice and exposed; here, also, the shallow seas upon the continental shelf spread and shrank most broadly.

This time of recurrent changes of atmosphere, land, and sea gave advantage to plastic, mobile, and prolific organisms, to plants and animals that could colonize newly available bodies of land, that had progeny some of which withstood the stresses of climatic change. The time was favorable for biologic evolution, for mutants suited to a changed environment, for hybrids formed by mingling, as on ecologic frontiers. To this period has been assigned the origin of many annual plant species dependent on heavy seed production for success (Ames, 1939). Adaptive variations in human stocks, aided by sufficiently isolating episodes of earth history, have also been inferred.[1]

---

1. As most recently by Coon, 1953.

The duration of the Ice Age and of its stages has not been determined. The old guess of a million years overall is still convenient. The four glacial and three interglacial stages may have general validity; there are doubts that they were strictly in phase in all continents. In North America the relations of the several continental icecaps to the phases of Rocky Mountain glaciation, and of the latter to the Pacific mountains, are only inferred, as is the tie-in of pluvial stages in our Southwest. That great lakes and permanent streams existed in many of the present dry lands of the world is certain, that these pluvial phases of intermediate latitudes correspond to glacial ones in high latitudes and altitudes is in considerable part certain, but only in a few cases has a pluvial state been securely tied to a contemporaneous glacial stage. The promising long-range correlation of Pleistocene events by eustatic marine terraces and their dependent alluvial terraces is as yet only well started. Except for northwestern Europe, the calendar of the later geologic past is still very uncertain. The student of farther human time, anxious for an absolute chronology, is at the moment relying widely on the ingenious astronomical calendar of Milankovitch and Zeuner as an acceptable span for the Ice Age as a whole and for its divisions. It is not acceptable, however, to meteorology and climatology.[2] Slowly and only bit by bit are we likely to see the pieces fall into their proper order; nothing is gained by assurance as to what is insecure.

The newer meteorology is interesting itself in the dynamics of climatic change (Shapley, 1953; Mannerfelt *et al.*, 1949). Changes in the general circulation pattern have been inferred as conveying, in times of glacial advance, more and more frequent masses of moist, relatively warm air into high latitudes and thereby also increasing the amount of cloud cover. The importance now attached to condensation nuclei has again directed attention to the possible significance of volcanic dust. Synoptic climatological data are being examined for partial models in contemporary conditions as conducive to glaciation and deglaciation (Leighly, 1949, pp. 133–34). To the student of the human past, reserve is again indicated in making large climatic reconstructions. Such cautions I should suggest, with reserve also as

2. Shapley. 1953; Willett, 1950; Simpson, G. C., 1934, 1940.

to my competence to offer them, with regard to the following:

It is misleading to generalize glacial stages as cold and interglacial ones as warm. The developing phases of glaciation probably
required relatively warm moist air, and decline may have been by the
dominance of cold dry air over the ice margins. The times of climatic
change may thus not coincide with the change from glacial advance
to deglaciation. We may hazard the inference that developing glaciation is associated with low contrast of regional climates; regression of
ice and beginning of an interglacial phase probably are connected
(although not in each case) with accentuated contrast or "continentality" of climates. One interglacial did not necessarily repeat the
features of another; nor must one glacial phase duplicate another. We
need only note the difference in centers of continental glaciation, of
direction of growth of ice lobes, of terminal moraine-building, of
structure of till and of fluvioglacial components to see the individu-
ality of climates of glacial stages. In North America, in contrast to
Europe, there is very little indication of a periglacial cold zone of
tundra and of permafrost in front of the continental icecaps. Ques-
tionable also is the loess thesis of dust as whipped up from bare
ground and deposited in beds by wind, these surfaces somehow becoming vegetated by a cold steppe plant cover.

The events of the last deglaciation and of the "postglacial" are
intelligible as yet only in part. *A priori* it is reasonable to consider
that the contemporary pattern of climates had become more or less
established before the last ice retreat began. Lesser later local climatic oscillations have been found but have been improperly extended
and exaggerated, however, in archeological literature. In the pollen
studies of bogs of northwestern Europe, the term "climatic opti-
mum" was introduced innocently to note a poleward and moun-
tainward extension of moderate proportions for certain plants not
occurring at the same time over the entire area. Possibly this expansion of range means that there were sunnier summer and fall seasons,
permitting the setting and maturing of seed for such plants somewhat beyond their prior and present range, that is, under more "continental" and less "maritime" weather conditions. This modest and
expectable variation of a local climate in the high latitudes and at the

changing sea borders of north Atlantic Europe has been construed by some students of prehistory into a sort of climatic golden age, existent at more or less the same time in distant parts of the world, without regard to dynamics or patterns of climates. We might well be spared such naïvely nominal climatic constructions as have been running riot through interpretations of pre-history and even of historic time.

The appearance or disappearance, increase or decrease, of particular plants and animals may not spell out obligatory climatic change, as has been so freely inferred. Plants differ greatly in rate of dispersal, in pioneering ability, in having routes available for their spread, and in other ways that may enter into an unstable ecologic association, as on the oft-shifted stage of Pleistocene and Recent physiography. The intervention of man and animals has also occurred to disturb the balance. The appearance and fading of pines in an area, characteristic in many bog pollen columns, may tell nothing of climatic change: pines are notorious early colonizers, establishing themselves freely in mineral soils and open situations and yielding to other trees as shading and organic cover of ground increase. Deer thrive on browse; they increase wherever palatable twigs become abundant, in brush lands and with young tree growth; ecologic factors of disturbance other than climate may determine the food available to them and the numbers found in archeologic remains.

The penetration of man to the New World is involved in the question of past and present climates. The origin and growth of the dominant doctrine of a first peopling of the western hemisphere in postglacial time is beyond our present objective, but it was not based on valid knowledge of climatic history. The postglacial and present climatic pattern is one of extremes rarely reached or exceeded in the past of the earth. Passage by land within this time across Siberia, Alaska, and Canada demanded specialized advanced skills in survival under great and long cold comparable to those known to Eskimo and Athabascan, an excessive postulate for many of the primitive peoples of the New World. Relatively mild climates did prevail in high latitudes at times during the Pleistocene. At such times in both directions between Old and New World, massive migrations took place of animals incapable of living on tundras, animals that are attractive game for man. If man was then living in eastern Asia, nothing hindered him from migrating along with such non-boreal mammals. The question is of fundamental interest, because it asks whether man in the New World, within a very few thousand years, independently achieved a culture growth comparable and curiously parallel to that of the Old, which required a much greater span. There is thus also the inference that our more primitive aborigines passed the high latitudes during more genial climes rather than that they subsequently lost numerous useful skills.

FIRE

Speech, tools, and fire are the tripod of culture and have been so, we think, from the beginning. About the hearth, the home and work-shop are centered. Space heating under shelter, as a rock overhang, made possible living in inclement climates; cooking made palatable many plant products; industrial innovators experimented with heat treatment of wood, bone, and minerals. About the fireplace, social life took form, and the exchange of ideas was fostered. The availability of fuel has been one of the main factors determining the location of clustered habitation.

Even to Paleolithic man, occupant of the earth for all but the last one or two percent of human time, must be conceded gradual defor-mation of vegetation by fire. His fuel needs were supplied by dead wood, drifted or fallen, and also by the stripping of bark and bast that caused trees to die and become available as fuel supply. The setting or escape of fire about camp sites cleared away small and young growth, stimulated annual plants, aided in collecting, and became elaborated in time into the fire drive, a formally organized procedure among the cultures of the upper Paleolithic *grande chasse* and of their New World counterpart.

Inferentially, modern primitive peoples illustrate the ancient practices in all parts of the world. Burning, as a practice facilitating collecting and hunting, by insensible stages became a device to im-prove the yield of desired animals and plants. Deliberate manage-ment of their range by burning to increase food supply is apparent among hunting and collecting peoples, in widely separated areas, but has had little study. Mature woody growth provides less food for man and ground animals than do fire-disturbed sites, with protein-rich young growth and stimulated seed production accessible at ground levels. Game yields are usually greatest where the vegetation is kept in an immediate state of ecologic succession. With agricultural and pastoral peoples, burning in preparation for planting and for the increase of pasture has been nearly universal until lately.

The gradually cumulative modifications of vegetation may become large as to selection of kind and as to aspect of the plant cover. Pyrophytes include woody monocotyledons, such as palms, which do not depend on a vulnerable cambium tissue, trees insulated by thick corky bark, trees and shrubs able to reproduce by sprouting, and plants with thick, hard-shelled seeds aided in germination by heat. Loss of organic matter on and in the soil may shift advantage to forms that germinate well in mineral soils, as the numerous conifers. Precocity is advantageous. The assemblages consequent upon fires are usually characterized by a reduced number of species, even by the dominance of few and single species. Minor elements in a natural flora, originally mainly confined to accidentally disturbed and exposed situations, such as windfalls and eroding slopes, have opened to them by recurrent burning the chance to spread and multiply. In most cases the shift is from mesophytic to less exacting, more xeric, forms, to those that do not require ample soil moisture and can tolerate at all times full exposure to sun. In the long run the scales are tipped against the great, slowly maturing plants—the trees (a park land of mature trees may be the last stand of what was a complete woodland). Our eastern woodlands, at the time of white settlement, seem largely to have been in process of change to park lands. Early accounts stress the open stands of trees, as indicated by the comment that one could drive a coach from seaboard to the Mississippi River over almost any favoring terrain. The "forest primeval" is exceptional. In the end the success in a land occupied by man of whatever cultural level goes to the annuals and short-lived perennials, able to seed heavily or to reproduce by rhizome and tuber. This grossly drawn sketch may introduce the matter of processes resulting in what is called ecologically a secondary fire association, or subclimax, if it has historical persistence.

The climatic origin of grasslands rests on a poorly founded hypothesis. In the first place, the individual great grasslands extend over long climatic gradients from wet to dry and grade on their driest margins into brush and scrub. Woody growth occurs in them where there are breaks in the general surface, as in the Cross Timbers of our Southwest. Woody plants establish themselves freely in grasslands if fire protection is given; the prairies and steppes are suited to the growth of the trees and shrubs native to adjacent lands, but may lack them. An individual grassland may extend across varied parent-materials. Their most common quality is that they are upland plains, having periods of dry weather long enough to dry out the surface of the ground, which accumulates a sufficient amount of burnable matter to feed and spread a fire. Their position and limits are determined by relief; nor do they extend into arid lands or those having a continuously wet ground surface. Fires may sweep indefinitely across a surface of low relief but are checked shortly at barriers of broken terrain, the checking being more abrupt if the barrier is sunk below the general surface. The inference is that origin and preservation of grasslands are due, in the main, to burning and that they are in fact great and in some cases, ancient, cultural features.

In other instances simplified woodlands, such as the pine woods of our Southeast, *palmares* in tropical savannas, are pyrophytic deformations; there are numerous vegetational alternatives other than the formation of grassland by recurrent burning. Wherever primitive man has had the opportunity to turn fire loose on a land, he seems to have done so from time immemorial; it is only civilized societies that have undertaken to stop fires.

In areas controlled by customary burning, a near-ecologic equilibrium may have been attained, a biotic recombination maintained by similarly repeated human intervention. This is not destructive exploitation. The surface of the ground remains protected by growing cover, the absorption of rain and snow is undiminished, and loss of moisture from ground to atmosphere possibly is reduced. Microclimatic differences between woodland and grassland are established as effect if not as cause, and some are implicit in the Shelter Belt Project.

Our modern civilization demands fire control for the protection of its property. American forestry was begun as a remedy for the devastation by careless lumbering at a time when dreadful holocausts almost automatically followed logging, as in the Great Lakes states. Foresters have made a first principle of fire suppression. Complete protection, however, accumulates tinder year by year; the longer the accumulation, the greater is the fire hazard and the more severe the fire when it results. Stockmen are vociferous about the loss of grazing areas to brush under such protection of the public lands. Here and there, carefully controlled light burning is beginning to find acceptance in range and forest management. It is being applied to long-leaf pine reproduction in southeastern states and to some extent for grazing in western range management. In effect, the question is now being raised whether well-regulated fires may not have an ecologic role beneficial to modern man, as they did in older days.

PEASANT AND PASTORAL WAYS

The next revolutionary intervention of man in the natural order came as he selected certain plants and animals to be taken under his care, to be reproduced, and to be bred into domesticated forms increasingly dependent on him for survival. Their adaptation to serve human wants runs counter, as a rule, to the processes of natural selection. New lines and processes of organic evolution were entrained, widening the gap between wild and domestic forms. The natural land became deformed, as to biota, surface, and soil, into unstable cultural landscapes.

Conventionally, agricultural origins are placed at the beginning of Neolithic time, but it is obvious that the earliest archeologic record of the Neolithic presents a picture of an accomplished domestication of plants and animals, of peasant and pastoral life resembling basic conditions that may still be met in some parts of the Near East.

Three premises as to the origin of agriculture seem to me to be necessary: (1) That this new mode of life was sedentary and that it arose out of an earlier sedentary society. Under most conditions, and especially among primitive agriculturists, the planted land must be watched over continuously against plant predators. (2) That planting and domestication did not start from hunger but from surplus and leisure. Famine-haunted folk lack the opportunity and incentive for the slow and continuing selection of domesticated forms. Village communities in comfortable circumstances are indicated for such progressive steps. (3) Primitive agriculture is located in woodlands. Even the pioneer American farmer hardly invaded the grasslands until the second quarter of the past century. His fields were clearings won by deadening, usually by girdling, the trees. The larger the trees, the easier the task; brush required grubbing and cutting; sod stopped his advance until he had plows capable of ripping through the matted grass roots. The forest litter he cleaned up by occasional burning; the dead trunks hardly interfered with his planting. The American pioneer learned and followed Indian practices. It is curious that scholars, because they carried into their thinking the tidy fields of the European plowman and the felling of trees by ax, have so often thought that forests repelled agriculture and that open lands invited it.

The oldest form of tillage is by digging, often but usually improperly called "hoe culture." This was the only mode known in the New World, in Negro Africa, and in the Pacific islands. It gave rise, at an advanced level, to the gardens and horticulture of monsoon Asia and perhaps of the Mediterranean. Its modern tools are spade, fork, and hoe, all derived from ancient forms. In tropical America this form of tillage is known as the *conuco,* in Mexico as the *milpa,* in the latter case a planting of seeds of maize, squash, beans, and perhaps other annuals. The conuco is stocked mainly by root and stem cuttings, a perennial garden plot. Recently, the revival of the Old Norse term "swithe," or "swidden," has been proposed (Izikowitz, 1951, p. 7n.; Conklin, 1954).

Such a plot begins by deadening tree growth, followed toward the end of a dry period by burning, the ashes serving as quick fertilizer. The cleared space then is well stocked with a diverse assemblage of useful plants, grown as tiers of vegetation if moisture and fertility are adequate. In the maize-beans-squash complex the squash vines spread over the ground, the cornstalks grow tall, and the beans climb up the cornstalks. Thus the ground is well protected by plant cover, with good interception of the falling rain. In each conuco a high diversity of plants may be cared for, ranging from low herbs to shrubs, such as cotton and manioc, to trees entangled with cultivated climbers. The seeming disorder is actually a very full use of light and moisture, an admirable ecologic substitution by man, perhaps equivalent to the natural cover also in the protection given to the surface of the ground. In the tropical conuco an irregular patch is dug into at convenient spots and at almost any time to set out or collect different plants, the planted surface at no time being wholly dug over. Digging roots and replanting may be going on at the same time. Our notions of a harvest season when the whole crop is taken off the field are inapplicable. In the conucos something may be gathered on almost any day through the year. The same plant may yield pot and salad greens, pollen-rich flowers, immature fruit and ripened fruit; garden and field are one, and numerous domestic uses may be served by each plant. Such multiple population of the tilled space makes possible the highest yields per unit of surface, to which may be added the comments that this system has developed plants of highest productivity, such as bananas, yams, and manioc, and that food production is by no means the only utility of many such plants.

The planting systems really do not deserve the invidious terms given them, such as "slash and burn" or "shifting agriculture." The abandonment of the planting after a time to the resprouting and reseeding wild woody growth is a form of rotation by which the soil is replenished by nutriments carried up from deep-rooted trees and shrubs, to be spread over the ground as litter. Such use of the land is freed from the limitations imposed on the plowed field by terrain. That it may give good yields on steep and broken slopes is not an argument against the method, which gives much better protection against soil erosion than does any plowing. It is also in these cultures that we find that systems of terracing of slopes have been established.

Some of the faults charged against the system derive from the late impact from our own culture, such as providing axes and machetes by which sprouts and brush may be kept whacked out instead of letting the land rest under regrowth, the replacement of subsistence crops by money crops, the worldwide spurt in population, and the demand for manufactured goods which is designated as rising standard of living. Nor do I claim that under this primitive planting man could go on forever growing his necessities without depleting the soil; but rather that, in its basic procedure and crop assemblages, this system has been most conservative of fertility at high levels of yield; that, being protective and intensive, we might consider it as being fully suited to the physical and cultural conditions of the areas where it exists. Our Western know-how is directed to land use over a short run of years and is not the wisdom of the primitive peasant rooted to his ancestral lands.

Our attitudes toward farming stem from the other ancient trunk whence spring the sowers, reapers, and mowers; the plowmen, dairymen, shepherds, and herdsmen. This is the complex already well represented in the earliest Neolithic sites of the Near East. The interest of this culture is directed especially toward seed production of annuals, cereal grasses in particular. The seedbed is carefully prepared beforehand to minimize weed growth and provide a light cover of well-worked soil in which the small seeds germinate. An evenly worked and smooth surface contrasts with the hit-or-miss piling of earth mounds, "hills" in the American farm vernacular, characteristic of conuco and milpa. Instead of a diversity of plants, the prepared ground receives the seed of one kind. (Western India is a significant exception.) The crop is not further cultivated and stands to maturity, when it is reaped at one time. After the harvest the field may lie fallow until the next season. The tillage implement is the plow, in second place, the harrow, both used to get the field ready for sowing. Seeding traditionally is by broadcasting, harvesting by cutting blades.

Herd animals, meat cattle, sheep, goats, horses, asses, camels, are either original or very early in this system. The keeping of grazing and browsing animals is basic. All of them are milked or have been so in the past. In my estimation milking is an original practice and quality of their domestication and continued to be in many cases their first economic utility; meat and hides, the product of surplus animals only.

The overall picture is in great contrast to that of the planting cultures: regular, elongated fields minimize turning the animals that pull the plow; fields are cultivated in the off season, in part to keep them free of volunteer growth; fields are fallowed but not abandoned, the harvest season is crowded into the end of the annual growth period; thereafter, stock is pastured on stubble and fallow; land unsuited or not needed for the plow is used as range on which the stock grazes and browses under watch of herdboys or herdsmen.

This complex spread from its Near Eastern cradle mainly in three directions, changing its character under changed environments and by increase of population.

Spreading into the steppes of Eurasia, the culture lost its tillage and became completely pastoral, with true nomadism. This is controversial, but the evidence seems to me to show that all domestication of the herd animals (except for reindeer) was effected by sedentary agriculturists living between India and the Mediterranean and also that the great, single, continuous area in which milking was practiced includes all the nomadic peoples, mainly as a fringe about the milking seed-farmers. It has also been pointed out that nomadic cultures depend on agricultural peoples for some of their needs and, thus lacking a self-contained economy, can hardly have originated independently.

The drift of the Celtic, Germanic, and Slavic peoples westward (out of southwestern and western Asia?) through the northern European plain appears to have brought them to their historic seats predominantly as cattle- and horse-raisers. Their movement was into lands of cooler and shorter summers and of higher humidity, in which wheat and barley did poorly. An acceptable thesis is that, in southwestern Asia, rye and probably oats were weed grasses growing in fields of barley and wheat. They were harvested together and not separated by winnowing. In the westward movement of seed farmers across Europe, the weed grains did better and the noble grain less well. The cooler and wetter the summers, the less wheat and barley did the sower reap and the more of rye and oat seeds, which gradually became domesticated by succeeding where the originally planted kinds failed.

Northwestern and central Europe appear to be the home of our principal hay and pasture grasses and clovers. As the stock-raising colonists deadened and burned over tracts of woodland, native grasses and clovers spontaneously took possession of the openings. These were held and enlarged by repetition of burning and cutting. Meadow and pasture, from the agricultural beginnings, were more important here than plowland. Even the latter, by pasturing the rye fields and the feeding of oat straw and grain, were part of animal husbandry. Here, as nowhere else, did the common farmer concern himself with producing feed for his stock. He was first a husband-man; he cut hay to store for winter feed and cured it at considerable trouble; he stabled his animals over the inclement season, or stalled them through the year; the dunghill provided dressing for field and meadow. House, barn, and stable were fused into one structure. The prosperity of farmstead and village was measured by its livestock rather than by arable land.

The resultant pattern of land use, which carries through from the earliest times, as recovered by archeology in Denmark and northern Germany, was highly conservative of soil fertility. The animal husbandry maintained so effective a ground cover that northern Europe has known very little soil erosion. Animal manure and compost provided adequate return of fertility to the soil. Man pretty well established a closed ecologic cycle. It was probably here that man first undertook to till the heavy soils. Clayey soils, rich in plant food but deficient in drainage, are widespread in the lowlands, partly due to climatic conditions, partly a legacy of the Ice Age. The modern plow with share, moldboard, and colter had either its origin or a major development here for turning real furrows to secure better aeration and drainage. Beneficial in northwestern and central Europe, it was later to become an instrument of serious loss elsewhere.

The spread of sowing and herding cultures westward along both sides of the Mediterranean required no major climatic readjustment. Wheat and barley continued to be the staple grains; sheep and goats were of greater economic importance than cattle and horses. Qualities of the environment that characterized the Near East were accentuated to the west: valleys lie imbedded in mountainous terrain, the uplands are underlain by and developed out of limestone, and, to the south of the Mediterranean, aridity becomes prevalent. The hazard of drought lay ever upon the Near Eastern homeland and on the colonial regions to the west and south. No break between farmer and herdsman is discernible at any time; as the village Arab of today is related to the Bedouin, the environmental specialization may have been present from the beginning—flocks on the mountains and dry lands, fields where moisture sufficed and soil was adequate.

That the lands about the Mediterranean have become worn and frayed by the usage to which they have been subjected has long been recognized, though not much is known as to when and how. The eastern and southern Mediterranean uplands especially are largely of limestone, attractive as to soil fertility but, by their nature, without deep original mantle of soil or showing the usual gradation of subsoil into bedrock and thus are very vulnerable to erosion. The less suited the land was or became to plow cultivation, the greater the shift to pastoral economy. Thus a downslope migration of tillage characterized, in time, the retreating limits of the fields, and more and more land became range for goats, sheep, and asses. Repeatedly prolonged droughts must have speeded the downslope shift, hillside fields suffering most, and with failing vegetation cover becoming more subject to washing when rains came.

Thus we come again to the question of climatic change as against attrition of surface and increased xerophytism of vegetation by human disturbance and, in particular, to what is called the "desertification" of North Africa and the expansion of the Sahara. A case for directional change in the pattern of atmospheric circulation has been inferred from archeology and faunal changes. I am doubtful that it is good case within the time of agricultural and pastoral occupation. Another view is that the progressive reduction of plant cover by man has affected soil and ground-surface climate unfavorably. Largely, and possibly wholly, the deterioration of the borders of the dry lands may have been caused by adverse, cumulative effects of man's activities. From archeologic work we need much more information as to whether human occupation has been failing in such areas over a long-time, or whether it has happened at defined intervals, and also whether, if such intervals are noted, they may have a cultural rather than an environmental (climatic) basis.

No protective herbaceous flora became established around the shores of the Mediterranean on pastures and meadows as was the case in the north. Flocks and herds grazed during the short season of soft, new grass but most of the year browsed on woody growth. The more palatable feed was eaten first and increasingly eliminated; goats and asses got along on range that had dropped below the support levels required by more exacting livestock. As is presently true in the western United States, each prolonged drought must have left the range depleted, its carrying capacity reduced, and recovery of cover less likely. Natural balance between plants and animals is rarely reestablished under such exploitation, since man will try to save his herd rather than their range. A large and long deterioration of the range may therefore fully account for the poor and xerophytic flora and fauna without postulating progressive climatic desiccation, for the kinds of life that survive under overuse of the land are the most undemanding inhabitants.

Comparative studies of North Africa and of the American Southwest and northern Mexico are needed to throw light on the supposed "desiccation" of the Old World. We know the dates of introduction of cattle and sheep to the American ranges and can determine rate and kind of change of vegetation and surface. The present desolate shifting-sand area that lies between the Hopi villages and Colorado River was such good pasture land late in the eighteenth century that Father Escalante, returning from his canyon exploration, rested his travel-worn animals there to regain flesh. The effects of Navaho sheep-herding in little more than a century and mainly in the last sixty years are well documented. Lower California and Sonora are climatic homologues of the western Sahara. Against the desolation of the latter, the lands about the Gulf of California are a riot of bloom in spring and green through summer. Their diversity, in kind and form, of plant and of animal life is high, and the numbers are large. When Leo Waibel came from his African studies to Sonora and Arizona, he remarked: "But your deserts are not plant deserts." Nor do we have hammadas or ergs, though geologic and meteorologic conditions may be similar. The principal difference may be that we have had no millennial, or even centuries-long, over-stocking of our arid, semi-arid, and sub-humid lands. The scant life and even the rock and sand surfaces of the Old World deserts may record long attrition by man in climatic tension zones.

IMPACT OF CIVILIZATION IN ANTIQUITY
AND THE MIDDLE AGES

Have the elder civilizations fallen because their lands deteriorated? Ellsworth Huntington read adverse climatic change into each such failure; at the other extreme, political loss of competence has been asserted as sufficient. Intimate knowledge of historical sources, archeologic sites, biogeography and ecology, and the processes of geomorphology must be fused in patient field studies, so that we may read the changes in habitability through human time for the lands in which civilization first took form.

The rise of civilizations has been accomplished and sustained by the development of powerful and elaborately organized states with a drive to territorial expansion, by commerce in bulk and to distant parts, by monetary economy, and by the growth of cities. Capital cities, port cities by sea and river, and garrison towns drew to themselves population and products from near and far. The ways of the country became subordinated to the demands of the cities, the *citizen* distinct from the *miserabilis plebs*. The containment of community by locally available resources gave way to the introduction of goods, especially foodstuffs, regulated by purchasing, distributing, or tax-ing power.

Thereby removal of resource from place of origin to place of demand tended to set up growing disturbance of whatever ecologic equilibrium had been maintained by the older rural communities sustained directly within their metes. The economic history of an-tiquity shows repeated shifts in the areas of supply of raw materials that are not explained by political events but raise unanswered ques-tions as to decline of fertility, destruction of plant cover, and incidence of soil erosion. What, for instance, happened to Arabia Felix, Numidia, Mauretania, to the interior Lusitania that has become the frayed Spanish Extremadura of today? When and at whose hands did the forests disappear that furnished ship and house timbers, wood for burning lime, the charcoal for smelting ores, and urban fuel needs? Are political disasters sufficient to account for the failure of the civilizations that depended on irrigation and drainage engineering? How much of the wide deterioration of Mediterranean and Near Eastern lands came during or after the time of strong political and commercial organization? For ancient and medieval history our knowledge as to what happened to the land remains too largely blank, except for the central and northern European periphery. The written documents, the testimony of the archeologic sites, have not often been interpreted by observation of the physical condition of the locality as it is and comparison with what it was.

The aspect of the Mediterranean landscapes was greatly changed by classical civilization through the introduction of plants out of the East. Victor Hehn first described Italy as wearing a dress of an alien vegetation, and, though he carried the theme of plant introduction out of the East too far, his study (1886) of the Mediterranean lands through antiquity is not only memorable but retains much validity. The westward dispersal of vine, olive, fig, the stone fruits, bread wheat, rice, and many ornamentals and some shade trees was due in part or in whole to the spread of Greco-Roman civilization, to which the Arabs added sugar cane, date palm, cotton, some of the citrus fruits, and other items.

## EUROPEAN OVERSEAS COLONIZATION

When European nations ventured forth across the Atlantic, it was to trade or raid, the distinction often determined by the opportunity. In Africa and Asia the European posts and factories pretty well continued in this tradition through the eighteenth century. In the New World the same initial activities soon turned into permanent settlement of Old World forms and stocks. Columbus, searching only for a trade route, started the first overseas empire. Spain stumbled into colonization, and the other nations acquired stakes they hoped might equal the Spanish territorial claim. The Casa de Contratación, or House of Trade, at Seville, the main Atlantic port, became the Spanish colonial office. The conquistadores came not to settle but to make their fortunes and return home, and much the same was true for the earlier adventurers from other nations. Soldiers and adventurers rather than peasants and artisans made up the first arrivals, and few brought their women. Only in New England did settlement begin with a representative assortment of people, and only here were the new communities transplanted from the homeland without great alteration.

The first colony, Santo Domingo, set in large measure the pattern of colonization. It began with trade, including ornaments of gold. The quest for gold brought forced labor and the dying-off of the natives, and this, in turn, slave-hunting and importation of black slaves. Decline of natives brought food shortages and wide abandonment of conucos. Cattle and hogs were pastured on the lately tilled surfaces; and Spaniards, lacking labor to do gold-placering, became stock ranchers. Some turned to cutting dyewoods. Of the numerous European plants introduced to supply accustomed wants, a few—sugar cane, cassia, and ginger—proved moderately profitable for export, and some of the hesitant beginnings became the first tropical plantations. One hope of fortune failing, another was tried; the stumbling into empire was under way by men who had scarcely any vision of founding a new homeland.

What then happened to the lands of the New World in the three colonial centuries? In the first place, the aboriginal populations in contact with Europeans nearly everywhere declined greatly or were extinguished. Especially in the tropical lowlands, with the most notable exception of Yucatán, the natives faded away, and in many cases the land was quickly repossessed by forest growth. The once heavily populous lands of eastern Panama and northwestern Colombia, much of the lowland country of Mexico, both on the Pacific and Gulf sides, became emptied in a very few years, was retaken by jungle and forest, and in considerable part remains such to the present. The highlands of Mexico, of Central America, and of the Andean lands declined in population greatly through the sixteenth and perhaps well through the seventeenth century, with slow, gradual recovery in the eighteenth. The total population, white and other, of the areas under European control was, I think, less at the end of the eighteenth century than at the time of discovery. Only in British and French West Indian islands were dense rural populations built up.

It is hardly an exaggeration to say that the early Europeans supported themselves on Indian fields. An attractive place to live for a European would ordinarily have been such for an Indian. In the Spanish colonies, unlike the English and French, the earlier grants were not of land titles but of Indian communities to serve colonist and crown. In crops and their tillage the colonists of all nations largely used the Indian ways, with the diversion of part of the field crop to animal feed. Only in the northeast, most of all in our middle colonies, were native and European crops fused into a conservative plow-and-animal husbandry, with field rotation, manuring, and marl dressing. The middle colonies of the eighteenth century appear to have compared favorably with the best farming practices of western Europe.

Sugar cane, first and foremost of the tropical plantations, as a closely planted giant grass, gave satisfactory protection to the surface of the land. The removal of cane from the land did reduce fertility unless the waste was properly returned to the canefields. The most conservative practices known are from the British islands, where cane waste was fed to cattle kept in pens, and manuring was customary and heavy. Bagasse was of little value as fuel in this period because of the light crushing rollers used for extracting cane juice; thus the colonial sugar mills were heavy wood users, especially for boiling sugar. The exhaustion of wood supply became a serious problem in the island of Haiti within the sixteenth century.

Other plantation crops—tobacco, indigo, cotton, and coffee—held more serious erosion hazards, partly because they were planted in rows and given clean cultivation, partly because they made use of steeper slopes and thinner soils. The worst offender was tobacco, grown on land that was kept bared to the rains and nourished by the wood ashes of burned clearings. Its cultivation met with greatest success in our upper South, resulted in rapidly shifting clearings because of soil depletion, and caused the first serious soil erosion in our country. Virginia, Maryland, and North Carolina show to the present the damages of tobacco culture of colonial and early post-colonial times. Southern Ohio and eastern Missouri repeated the story before the middle of the nineteenth century.

As had happened in Haiti, sharp decline of native populations elsewhere brought abandonment of cleared and tilled land and thereby opportunity to the stockman. The plants that pioneer in former fields that are left untilled for reasons other than decline of fertility include forms, especially annuals, of high palatability, grasses, amaranths, chenopods, and legumes. Such is the main explanation for the quick appearance of stock ranches, of *ganado mayor* and *menor,* in the former Indian agricultural lands all over Spanish America. Cattle, horses, and hogs thrived in tropical lowland as well as in highland areas. Sheep-raising flourished most in early years in the highlands of New Spain and Peru, where Indian population had shrunk. Spanish stock, trespassing upon Indian plantings, both in lowland and in highland, afflicted the natives and depressed their chances of recovery (Simpson, L., 1952). In the wide savannas stockmen took over the native habits of burning.

The Spaniards passed in a few years from the trading and looting of metals to successful prospecting, at which they became so adept that it is still said that the good mines of today are the *antiguas* of colonial working. When mines were abandoned, it was less often due to the working-out of the ore bodies than to inability to cope with water in shafts and to the exhaustion of the necessary fuel and timber. A good illustration has been worked out for Parral in Mexico (West, 1949). Zacatecas, today in the midst of a high sparse grassland, was in colonial times a woodland of oak and pine and, at lower levels, of mesquite. About Andean mines the scant wood was soon exhausted, necessitating recourse to cutting mats of *tola* heath and even the clumps of coarse *ichu* (stipa) grass. Quite commonly the old mining *reales* of North and South America are surrounded by a broad zone of reduced and impoverished vegetation. The effects were increased by the concentration of pack and work animals in the mines, with resultant overpasturing. Similar attrition took place about towns and cities, through timber-cutting, charcoal- and lime-burning, and overpasturing. The first viceroy of New Spain warned his successor in 1546 of the depletion of wood about the city of Mexico.

I have used mainly examples from Spanish America for the colonial times, partly because I am most familiar with this record. However, attrition was more sensible here because of mines and urban concentrations and because, for cultural and climatic reasons, the vegetation cover was less.

## LAST FRONTIERS OF SETTLEMENT

The surges of migration of the nineteenth century are family history for many of us. Never before did, and never again may, the white man expand his settlements as in that brief span that began in the later eighteenth century and ended with the first World War. The prelude was in the eighteenth century, not only as a result of the industrial revolution as begun in England, but also in a less heralded agricultural revolution over western and central Europe. The spread of potato-growing, the development of beets and turnips as field crops, rotation of fields with clover, innovations in tillage, improved livestock breeds—all joined to raise agricultural production to new levels in western Europe. The new agriculture was brought to our middle colonies by a massive immigration of capable European farmers and here further transformed by adding maize to the small grains-clover rotation. Thus was built on both sides of the north Atlantic a balanced animal husbandry of increased yield of human and animal foods. Urban and rural growth alike went into vigorous upswing around the turn of the eighteenth century. The youth of the countryside poured into the rising industrial cities but also emigrated, especially from central Europe into Pennsylvania, into Hungarian and Moldavian lands repossessed from the Turks and into south Russia gained from the Tartars. The last *Völkerwanderung* was under way and soon edging onto the grasslands.

The year 1800 brought a new cotton to the world market, previously an obscure annual variant known to us as Mexican upland cotton, still uncertainly understood as to how it got into our South.

Cleaned by the new gin, its profitable production rocketed. The rapidly advancing frontier of cotton-planting was moved westward from Georgia to Texas within the first half of the century. This movement was a more southerly and even greater parallel to the earlier westward drive of the tobacco frontier. Both swept away the woodlands and the Indians, including the farming tribes. The new cotton, like tobacco a clean cultivated row crop and a cash crop, bared the fields to surface wash, especially in winter. The southern upland soils gradually lost their organic horizons, color, and protection; gullies began to be noted even before the Civil War. Guano and Chilean nitrate and soon southern rock phosphate were applied increasingly to the wasting soils. Eugene Hilgard told the history of cotton in our South tersely and well in the United States Census of 1880. As I write, across from my window stands the building bearing his name and the inscription: TO RESCUE FOR HUMAN SOCIETY THE NATIVE VALUES OF RURAL LIFE. It was in wasting cotton fields that Hilgard learned soil science and thought about a rural society that had become hitched wholly to world commerce. Meantime the mill towns of England, the Continent, and New England grew lustily; with them, machine industries, transport facilities, and the overseas shipment of food.

The next great American frontier may be conveniently and reasonably dated by the opening of the Erie Canal in 1825, provisioning the cities with grain and meat on both sides of the north Atlantic, first by canal and river, soon followed by the railroad. The earlier frontiers had been pushed from the Atlantic seaboard to and beyond the Mississippi by the cultivation of tropical plants in extratropical lands; these were dominantly monocultural, preferred woodlands, and relied mainly on hand labor. For them the term "plantation culture" was not inapt. The last thrust, from the Mohawk Valley to the Mississippi, was west European as to agricultural system, rural values, settlers, and largely as to crops.

By the time of the Civil War, the first great phase of the northern westward movement had crossed the Missouri River into Kansas and Nebraska. New England spilled over by way of the Great Lakes, especially along the northern fringe of prairies against the north woods. New York and Baltimore were gateways for the masses of Continental emigrants hurrying to seek new homes beyond the Alleghenies. The migrant streams mingled as they overspread the Mississippi Valley, land of promise unequaled in the history of our kindred. These settlers were fit to the task: they were good husbandmen and artisans. They came to put down their roots, and the gracious country towns, farmsteads, and rural churches still bear witness to the homemaking way of life they brought and kept. At last they had land of their own, and it was good. They took care of their land, and it did well by them; surplus rather than substance of the soil provided the foodstuffs that moved to eastern markets. Steel plows that cut through the sod, east-west railroads, and cheap lumber from the white pine forests of the Great Lakes unlocked the fertility of the prairies; the first great plowing-up of the grasslands was under way.

Many prairie counties reached their maximum population in less than a generation, many of them before the beginning of the Civil War. The surplus, another youthful generation, moved on farther west or sought fortune in the growing cities. Thus, toward the end of the century the trans-Missouri grassy plains had been plowed up to and into the lands of drought hazard. Here the corn belt husbandry broke down, especially because of the great drought of the early nineties, and the wheat belt took form, a monocultural and unbalanced derivative. I well remember parties of landlookers going out from my native Missouri country, first to central Kansas and Nebraska, then to the Red River Valley, and finally even to the Panhandle of Texas and the prairies of Manitoba. The local newspapers "back home" still carry news from these daughter-colonies, and still those who long ago moved west are returned "home" at the last to lie in native soil.

The development of the Middle West did exact its price of natural resources. The white pine stands of the Great Lakes were destroyed to build the farms and towns of the corn belt; the logged-over lands suffered dreadful burning. As husbandry gave way westward to wheat-growing, the land was looked on less as homestead and more as speculation, to be cropped heavily and continuously for grain, without benefit of rotation and manuring, and to be sold at an advantageous price, perhaps to reinvest in new and undepleted land.

The history of the extratropical grasslands elsewhere in the world is much like our own and differs little in period and pace. Southern Russia, the Pampas, Australia, and South Africa repeat largely the history of the American West. The industrial revolution was made possible by the plowing-up of the great non-tropical grasslands of the world. So also was the intensification of agriculture in western Europe, benefitting from the importation of cheap overseas foodstuffs, grains, their by-products of milling (note the term "ship-stuff"), oil-seed meals. Food and feed were cheap in and about the centers of industry, partly because the fertility of the new lands of the world was exported to them without reckoning the maintenance of resource.

At the turn of the century serious concern developed about the adequacy of resources for industrial civilization. The conservation movement was born. It originated in the United States, where the depletion of lately virgin lands gave warning that we were drawing recklessly on a diminishing natural capital. It is to be remembered that this awareness came, not to men living in the midst of the industrial and commercial centers of the older countrysides, but to foresters who witnessed devastation about the Great Lakes, to geologists who had worked in the iron and copper ranges of the Great Lakes and prospected the West in pioneer days, to naturalists who lived through the winning of the West.

THE EVER DYNAMIC ECONOMY

As a native of the nineteenth century, I have been an amazed and bewildered witness of the change of tempo that started with the first World War, was given an additional whirl on the second, and still continues to accelerate. The worry of the earlier part of the century was that we might not use our natural resources thriftily; it has given was that we might not use our natural resources thriftily; it has given way to easy confidence in the capacities of technologic advance without limit. The natural scientists were and still may be often of the lineage of Daedalus, inventing ever more daring reorganizations of matter and, in consequence, whether they desire it or not, of social institutions. Social science eyes the attainments of physical science enviously and hopes for similar competence and authority in reordering the world. Progress is the common watchword of our age, its motor-innovating techniques, its objective the ever expanding "dynamic economy," with ever increasing input of energy. Capacity to produce and capacity to consume are the twin spirals of the new age which is to have no end, if war can be eliminated. The measure of progress is "standard of living," a term that the English language has contributed to the vernaculars of the world. An American industrialist says, roundly, that our principal problem now is to accelerate obsolescence, which remark was anticipated at the end of the past century by Eduard Hahn (1900) when he thought that industrialization depended on the production of junk.

Need we ask ourselves whether there still is the problem of limited resources, of an ecologic balance that we disturb or disregard at the peril of the future. Was Wordsworth of the early industrial age farsighted when he said that "getting and spending we lay waste our powers"? Are our newly found powers to transform the world, so successful in the short run of the last years, proper and wise beyond the tenure of those now living? To what end are we committing the world to increasing momentum of change?

The steeply increasing production of late years is due only in part to better recovery, more efficient use of energy, and substitution of abundant for scarce materials. Mainly we have been learning how to deplete more rapidly the resources known to be accessible to us. Must we not admit that very much of what we call production is extraction?

Even the so-called "renewable resources" are not being renewed. Despite better utilization and substitution, timber growth is falling farther behind use and loss, inferior stands and kinds are being exploited, and woodland deterioration is spreading. Much of the world is in a state of wood famine, without known means of remedy or substitution.

Commercial agriculture requires ample working capital and depends in high degree on mechanization and fertilization. A late estimate assigns a fourth of the net income of our farms to the purchase of durable farm equipment. The more farming becomes industry and business, the less remains of the older husbandry in which man lived in balance with his land. We speak with satisfaction of releasing rural population from farm to urban living and count the savings of man-hours in units of farm product and of acres. In some areas the farmer is becoming a town dweller, moving his equipment to the land for brief periods of planting, cultivating, and harvest. Farm garden, orchard, stable, barn, barnyards, and woodlots are disappearing in many parts, the farm families as dependent as their city cousins on grocer, butcher, baker, milkman, and fuel services. Where the farm is in fact capital in land and improvements, requiring bookkeeping on current assets and liabilities, the agriculturist becomes an operator of an outdoor factory of specialized products and is concerned with maximizing the profits of the current year and the next. Increasing need of working capital requires increased monetary returns; this is perhaps all we mean by "intensive" or "scientific" farming, which is in greater and greater degree extractive.

The current agricultural surpluses are not proof that food production has ceased to be a problem or will cease to be the major problem of the world. Our output has been secured at unconsidered costs and risks by the objective of immediate profit, which has replaced the older attitudes of living with the land. The change got under way especially as motors replaced draft animals. Land formerly used for oats and other feed crops became available to grow more corn, soybeans, cotton, and other crops largely sold and shipped. The traditional corn-oats-clover rotation, protective of the surface and maintaining nitrogen balance, began to break down. Soybeans, moderately planted in the twenties and then largely for hay, developed into a major seed crop, aided by heavy governmental benefit payments as soil-building, which they are not. Soil-depleting and soil-exposing crops were given strong impetus in the shift to mechanized farming; less of the better land is used for pasture and hay; less animal and green manure is returned to fields. The fixation of nitrogen by clover has come to be considered too slow; it "pays better" to put the land into corn, beans, and cotton and to apply nitrogen from bag or tank. Dressing the soil with commercial nitrogen makes it possible to plant more closely, thus doubling the number of corn and other plants to the acre at nearly the same tillage cost. Stimulation of plant growth by nitrogen brings increased need of additional phosphorous and potash. In the last ten years the corn belt has more or less caught up with the cotton belt in the purchase of commercial fertilizer. The more valuable the land, the greater the investment in farm machinery, the more profitable the application of more and more commercial fertilizers.

The so-called row crops, which are the principal cash crops, demand cultivation during much of their period of growth. They therefore give indifferent protection to the surface while growing and almost none after they are harvested. They are ill suited to being followed by a winter cover crop. The organic color is fading from much of our best-grade farm lands. Rains and melting snow float away more and more of the topsoil. There is little concern as long as we can plow more deeply and buy more fertilizer. Governmental restriction of acreage for individual crops has been an inducement to apply more fertilizer to the permitted acreage and to plant the rest in uncontrolled but usually also cash crops. Our commercial agriculture, except what remains in animal husbandry such as dairying, is kept expanding by increasing overdraft on the fertility of our soils. Its limits are set by the economically available sources of purchased nitrogen, phosphorus, potassium, and sulfur.

Since Columbus, the spread of European culture has been continuous and cumulative, borne by immediate self-interest, as in mercantilist economy, but sustained also by a sense of civilizing mission redefined from time to time. In the spirit of the present, this mission is to "develop the underdeveloped" parts of the world, material good and spiritual good now having become one. It is our current faith that the ways of the West are the ways that are best for the rest of the world. Our own ever growing needs for raw materials have driven the search for metals and petroleum to the ends of the earth in order to move them into the stream of world commerce. Some beneficial measure of industry and transport facility thereby accrues to distant places of origin. We also wish to be benefactors by increasing food supply where food is inadequate and by diverting people from rural to industrial life, because such is our way, to which we should like to bring others.

The road we are laying out for the world is paved with good intentions, but do we know where it leads? On the material side we are hastening the depletion of resources. Our programs of agricultural aid pay little attention to native ways and products. Instead of going out to learn what *their* experiences and preferences are, we go forth to introduce *our* ways and consider backward what is not according to our pattern. Spade and hoe and mixed plantings are an affront to our faith in progress. We promote mechanization. At the least, we hold, others should be taught to use steel plows that turn neat furrows, though we have no idea how long the soil will stay on well-plowed slopes planted to annuals. We want more fields of maize, rice, beans of kinds familiar to us, products amenable to statistical determination and available for commercial distribution. To increase production, we prescribe dressing with commercial fertilizers. In unnoticed contrast to our own experience these are to be applied in large measure to lands of low productivity and perhaps of low effectiveness of fertilizers. Industrialization is recommended to take care of the surplus populations. We present and recommend to the world a blueprint of what works well with us at the moment, heedless that we may be destroying wise and durable native systems of living with the land. The modern industrial mood (I hesitate to add intellectual mood) is insensitive to other ways and values.

For the present, living beyond one's means has become civic virtue, increase of "output" the goal of society. The prophets of a new world by material progress may be stopped by economic limits of physical matter. They may fail because people grow tired of getting and spending as measure and mode of living. They may be checked because men come to fear the requisite growing power of government over the individual and the community. The high moments of history have come not when man was most concerned with the comforts and displays of the flesh but when his spirit was moved to grow in grace. What we need more perhaps is an ethic and aesthetic under which man, practicing the qualities of prudence and moderation, may indeed pass on to posterity a good earth.

## References:

AMES, OAKES
   1939    *Economic Annuals and Human Cultures.* Cambridge, Mass.: Botanical Museum of Harvard University. 153 pp.

BOYD, W. C.
   1950    *Genetics and the Races of Man.* Boston: Little, Brown & Co. 453 pp.

BREUIL, HENRI, and LANTIER, RAYMON
   1951    *Les Hommes de la pierre ancienne.* Paris: Payot. 334 pp.

CONKLIN, HAROLD C.
   1954    "An Ethnoecological Approach to Shifting Agriculture," *Transactions of the New York Academy of Sciences,* Series II, XVII, No. 2, 133–42.

COON, CARLETON
   1953    "Climate and Race," pp. 13–34 in Shapley, Harlow (ed.), *Climatic Change.* Cambridge, Mass.: Harvard University Press. 318 pp.

HAHN, EDUARD
   1900    *Wirtschaft der Welt am Ausgang des neunzehuten Jahrhunderts.* Heidelberg: C. Winter, 320 pp.

HEHN, VICTOR
   1888    *Wanderings of Plants and Animals from Their First Home.* Ed. James S. Stallybrass. London: Swan Sonnenschein & Co. 523 pp.

IZIKOWITZ, KARL GUSTAV
   1951    "Lamet: Hill Peasants in French Indochina." (*Etnologiska Studier,* No. 17.) Göteborg: Etnografiska Museet. 375 pp.

LEIGHLY, JOHN B.
   1949    "On Continentality and Glaciation," pp. 133–46 in Mannerfelt, Carl Mison, et al. (eds.), *Glaciers and Climate (Symposium Dedicated to Hans Wison Ahlmann as a Tribute from the Swedish Society for Anthropology and Geography). (Geografiska Annaler,* Vol. XXXI, Häfte 1–4.) 383 pp.

MANNERFELT, CARL MASON, et al. (eds.)
   1949    *Glaciers and Climate (Symposium Dedicated to Hans Wison Ahlmann as a Tribute from the Swedish Society for Anthropology and Geography).(Geografiska Annaler,* Vol. XXXI, Häfte 1–4.) 383 pp.

MARSH, GEORGE P.
   1864    *Man and Nature.* New York: Charles Scribner & Co.; London: Sampson, Low & Son. 577 pp.

1874    *The Earth as Modified by Human Action.* New York: Scribner, Armstrong & Co. 656 pp. (2d ed., 1885. New York: C. Scribner's Sons. 629 pp.)

SHAPLEY, HARLOW (ed.)
1953    *Climatic Change.* Cambridge, Mass.: Harvard University Press. 318 pp.

SIMPSON, G. C.
1934    "World Climate during the Quaternary Period," *Quarterly Journal of the Royal Meteorological Society,* LX, No. 257 (October), 425–78.

1940    "Possible Causes of Change in Climate and Their Limitations," *Proceedings of the Linnean Society of London,* CLII, Part II (April), 190–219.

SIMPSON, LESLEY B.
1952    "Exploitation of Land in Central Mexico in the Sixteenth Century." (*Ibero-Americana,* No. 36.) Berkeley: University of California Press. 92 pp.

WEST, ROBERT C.
1949    "The Mining Community in Northern New Spain: The Parral Mining District." (*Ibero-Americana,* No. 30.) Berkeley. University of California Press. 169 pp.

WILLETT, H. C.
1950    "The General Circulation at the Last (Würm) Glacial Maximum," *Geografiska Annaler,* XXXII, Häfte 3–4, 179–87.

# VI. Published
## Writings

# Works in Print

*The treasure the scholar lays up on earth is largely the printed page.* —Letter to Earl J. Hamilton, March 18, 1943.

1911   *Educational Opportunities in Chicago* (Chicago: Council for Library and Museum Extension). "Second Year," 1912.

1915   "Exploration of the Kaiserin Augusta River in New Guinea," *Bulletin of the American Geographical Society*, Vol. 47, pp. 342–45. With Wellington D. Jones, "Outline for Field Work in Geography," *Bulletin of the American Geographical Society*, Vol. 47, pp. 520–26.

1916   "Geography of the Upper Illinois Valley and History of Development," *Illinois Geological Survey*, Bulletin No. 27.

1917   "The Condition of Geography in the High School and Its Opportunity," *Journal of the Michigan Schoolmasters' Club, 51st Annual Meeting, 1916*, pp. 125–29; *Journal of Geography*, Vol. 16, pp. 143–48.

"Proposal of an Agricultural Survey on a Geographic Basis," *Michigan Academy of Science, 19th Annual Report*, pp. 79–86.

1918   "Geography and the Gerrymander," *American Political Science Review*, Vol. 12, pp. 403–26.

"A Soil Classification for Michigan," *Michigan Academy of Science, 20th Annual Report*, pp. 83–91.

"Part I, Geography," in Carl O. Sauer, Gilbert H. Cady, and Henry C. Cowles, "Starved Rock State Park and Its Environs," *The Geographic Society of Chicago*, Bulletin No. 6 (Chicago: The University of Chicago Press), pp. 1–83.

1919    "Mapping the Utilization of the Land," *Geographical Review*, Vol. 8, pp. 47–54.

   "The Role of Niagara Falls in History," *The Historical Outlook*, Vol. 10, pp. 57–65.

1920    "The Economic Problem of the Ozark Highland," *Scientific Monthly*, Vol. 11, pp. 215–27.

   "The Geography of the Ozark Highland of Missouri," *The Geographic Society of Chicago*, Bulletin No. 7. Reprinted in 1974 by Greenwood Press and AMS Press.

1921    "The Problem of Land Classification," *Annals*, Association of American Geographers, Vol. 11, pp. 3–16.

1922    "Notes on the Geographic Significance of Soils—I," *Journal of Geography*, Vol. 21, pp. 187–90.

1924    "The Survey Method in Geography and Its Objectives," *Annals*, Association of American Geographers, Vol. 14, pp. 17–33.

   With J. B. Leighly, *Syllabus for an Introduction to Geography* (Ann Arbor: Edwards Brothers). Processed. Later editions to 1932.

1925    "The Morphology of Landscape," *Publications in Geography* (Berkeley: University of California), Vol. 2, No. 2, pp. 19–53. Reprinted in 1938.

1927    "Geography of the Pennyroyal," *Kentucky Geological Survey, Ser. 6*, Vol. 25.

   With Peveril Meigs, "Lower California Studies. I, Site and Culture at San Fernando de Velicatá," *Publications in Geography* (Berkeley: University of California), Vol. 2, No. 9, pp. 271–302.

   "Recent Developments in Cultural Geography," in E. C. Hayes, ed., *Recent Developments in the Social Sciences* (New York: Lippincott), pp. 154–212.

   Editor, "Vereinigte Staaten," in *Stieler's Hand-atlas*, 10th ed. (Gotha: Justus Perthes), sheets 95–100.

1929    "Land Forms in the Peninsular Range of California as Developed about Warner's Hot Springs and Mesa Grande," *Publications in Geography* (Berkeley: University of California), Vol. 3, No. 4, pp. 199–290.

   "Memorial of Ruliff S. Holway," *Annals*, Association of American Geographers, Vol. 19, pp. 64–65.

1930    "Basin and Range Forms in the Chiricahua Area," *Publications in Geography* (Berkeley: University of California), Vol. 3, No. 6, pp. 339–414.

   "Historical Geography and the Western Frontier," in James F. Willard and Colin B. Goodykoontz, eds., *The Trans-Mississippi*

*West; Papers Presented at a Conference Held at the University of Colorado June 18-June 21, 1929* (Boulder: University of Colorado), pp. 267–89.

With Donald Brand, "Pueblo Sites in Southeastern Arizona," *Publications in Geography* (Berkeley: University of California), Vol. 3, No. 7, pp. 415–59.

"Thirty-two Ancient Sites on Mexican West Coast," *El Palacio,* Vol. 29, pp. 335–36.

1931 "Geography, Cultural," *Encyclopedia of the Social Sciences,* Vol. 6, pp. 621–24.

With Donald Brand, "Prehistoric Settlements of Sonora, with Special Reference to Cerros de Trincheras," *Publications in Geography* (Berkeley: University of California), Vol. 5, No. 3, pp. 67–148.

Review of H. E. Bolton, *Anza's California Expeditions, Geographical Review,* Vol. 21, pp. 503–04.

1932 "Aztatlán: Prehistoric Mexican Frontier on the Pacific Coast," *Ibero-Americana* (Berkeley: University of California), No. 1.

Letter [on physical geography in regional works], *Geographical Review,* Vol. 22, pp. 527–28.

"Land Forms in the Peninsula Range," *Zeitschrift für Geomorphologie,* Vol. 7, pp. 246–48.

"The Road to Cíbola," *Ibero-Americana* (Berkeley: University of California), No. 3.

1934 "The Distribution of Aboriginal Tribes and Languages in Northwestern Mexico," *Ibero-Americana* (Berkeley: University of California), No. 5.

"Peschel, Oskar," *Encyclopedia of the Social Sciences,* Vol. 13, p. 92.

With C. K. Leith and others, "Preliminary Recommendations of the Land-Use Committee," *Report of the Science Advisory Board, 1933–1934,* pp. 137–61.

"Preliminary Report to the Land-Use Committee on Land Resource and Land Use in Relation to Public Policy," *Report of the Science Advisory Board, 1933–34,* pp. 165–260.

"Ratzel, Friedrich," *Encyclopedia of the Social Sciences,* Vol. 13, pp. 120–21.

"Ritter, Karl," *Encyclopedia of the Social Sciences,* Vol. 13, p. 395.

"Semple, Ellen Churchill," *Encyclopedia of the Social Sciences,* Vol. 13, pp. 661–62.

1935 "Aboriginal Population of Northwestern Mexico," *Ibero-Americana* (Berkeley: University of California), No. 10.

"The Problem of Life in the Tropics," review of G. C. Shattuck, et al, *The Peninsula of Yucatan, Geographical Review,* Vol. 25, pp. 346–47.

"Spanish Expeditions into the Arizona Apacheria," *Arizona Historical Review,* Vol. 6, pp. 3–13.

1936    "American Agricultural Origins: A Consideration of Nature and Culture," in *Essays in Anthropology Presented to A. L. Kroeber in Celebration of His Sixtieth Birthday, June 11, 1936* (Berkeley: University of California Press) pp. 278–97.

1937    Communication [in reply to one by Ronald L. Ives regarding Melchior Díaz], *The Hispanic American Historical Review,* Vol. 17, pp. 146–49.

"The Discovery of New Mexico Reconsidered," *New Mexico Historical Review,* Vol. 12, pp. 270–87.

Discussion [on influence of vegetation on land-water relationships], in *Headwaters Control and Use: Papers Presented at the Upstream Engineering Conference Held at Washington, D.C. September 22 and 23, 1936* (Washington: Government Printing Office), pp. 104–05.

"The Prospect for Redistribution of Population," in *Limits of Land Settlement: A Preliminary Report to the Tenth International Studies Conference, Paris, June 29–July 3, 1937,* pp. 7–24.

1938    "Destructive Exploitation in Modern Colonial Expansion," *Comptes Rendus du Congrès International de Géographie, Amsterdam, 1938,* Vol. 2, pp. 494–99.

"Theme of Plant and Animal Destruction in Economic History," *Journal of Farm Economics,* Vol. 20, pp. 765–75.

1939    *Man in Nature: America before the Days of the White Man. A First Book in Geography* (New York: Scribner's). Reprinted, Berkeley: Turtle Island Foundation, 1975.

1941    "The Credibility of the Fray Marcos Account," *New Mexico Historical Review,* Vol. 16, pp. 233–43.

"Foreword to Historical Geography," *Annals,* Association of American Geographers, Vol. 31, pp. 1–24.

"The Personality of Mexico," *Geographical Review,* Vol. 31, pp. 353–64.

1942    "The March of Agriculture Across the Western World," *Proceedings of the Eighth American Scientific Congress Held in Washington, May 10–18, 1940,* Vol. 5, pp. 63–65.

"The Settlement of the Humid East," in *Climate and Man, Yearbook of Agriculture, 1941* (Washington: Government Printing Office), pp. 157–66.

1943 "A Section of 'Notes and Queries'," *Acta Americana,* Vol. 1, p. 134.

1944 "A Geographic Sketch of Early Man in America," *Geographical Review,* Vol. 34, pp. 529–73.
Review of Paul Rivet, *Les origines de l'homme américain, Geographical Review,* Vol. 34, pp. 680–81.

1945 "The Relation of Man to Nature in the Southwest," *The Huntington Library Quarterly,* Vol. 8, pp. 116–25; discussion, pp. 125–30, 132–49.

1947 "Early Relations of Man to Plants," *Geographical Review,* Vol. 37, pp. 1–25.

1948 "Colima of New Spain in the 16th Century," *Ibero-Americana* (Berkeley: University of California), No. 29.
"Environment and Culture during the Last Deglaciation," *Proceedings of the American Philosophical Society,* Vol. 92, pp. 65–77.

1950 "Cultivated Plants of South and Central America," in *Handbook of South American Indians* (Smithsonian Institution, Bureau of American Ethnology, Bulletin 143), Vol. 6, pp. 487–543.
"Geography of South America," in *Handbook of South American Indians* (Smithsonian Institution, Bureau of American Ethnology, Bulletin 143), Vol. 6, pp. 319–44.
"Grassland Climax, Fire, and Man," *Journal of Range Management,* Vol. 3, pp. 16–21.

1952 *Agricultural Origins and Dispersals.* Bowman Memorial Lectures, Series 2. (New York: American Geographical Society). Reprinted with additions, Cambridge, Mass.: M.I.T. Press, 1969, in paperback as *Seeds, Spades, Hearths and Herbs,* 1972.
"Folkways of Social Science," in *The Social Sciences at Mid-century: Papers Delivered at the Dedication of Ford Hall, April 19–21, 1951* (Minneapolis: University of Minnesota Press), pp. 100–09.

1954 Communication [on Paul Kirchoff, "Gatherers and Farmers in the Greater Southwest"], *American Anthropologist,* Vol. 56, pp. 563–66.
"Herbert Eugene Bolton (1870–1953)," *Yearbook 1953,* The American Philosophical Society, pp. 319–23.

1956 "The Agency of Man on the Earth," in William L. Thomas, Jr., ed., *Man's Role in Changing the Face of the Earth* (Chicago: University of Chicago Press), pp. 46–69.
"The Education of a Geographer," *Annals,* Association of American Geographers, Vol. 46, pp. 287–99.
"Summary Remarks: Retrospect," in William L. Thomas, Jr., ed., *Man's Role in Changing the Face of the Earth* (Chicago: Univer-

sity of Chicago Press), pp. 1131–35.

"Time and Place in Ancient America," *Landscape,* Vol. 6, pp. 8–13.

1957 "The End of the Ice Age and Its Witnesses," *Geographical Review,* Vol. 47, pp. 29–43.

1958 "Man in the Ecology of Tropical America," *Proceedings of the Ninth Pacific Science Congress, 1957,* Vol. 20, pp. 104–10.

"A Note on Jericho and Composite Sickles," *Antiquity,* Vol. 32, pp. 187–89.

Review of Harold Gladwin, *History of the Ancient Southwest, Landscape,* Vol. 8, No. 2, p. 31.

1959 "Age and Area of American Cultivated Plants," *Actas del XXXIII Congreso Internacional de Americanistas, San José, Costa Rica, 1958,* Vol. 1, pp. 213–29.

Communication [on the scope of geography], *Landscape,* Vol. 8, No. 2, p. 31.

"Homer LeRoy Shantz," *Geographical Review,* Vol. 49, pp. 278–80.

"Middle America as Culture Historical Location," *Actas del XXXIII Congreso Internacional de Americanistas, San José, Costa Rica, 1958,* Vol. 1, pp. 115–22.

1960 Communication [on past and present American culture], *Landscape,* Vol. 10, No. 1, p. 6.

"Maize into Europe," *Akten des 34. Internationalen Amerikanisten-Kongresses, Wien, 1960,* pp. 777–88.

1961 "Sedentary and Mobile Bents in Early Man," in Sherwood L. Washburn, ed., *Social Life of Early Man* (Viking Fund Publications in Anthropology, No. 31), pp. 258–66.

1962 "Erhard Rostlund," *Geographical Review,* Vol. 52, pp. 133–35.

"Fire and Early Man," *Paideuma,* Vol. 7, pp. 399–407.

"Homestead and Community on the Middle Border," *Landscape,* Vol. 12, No. 1, pp. 3–7. (Somewhat abridged; for full text see "1963.")

"Seashore—Primitive Home of Man?," *Proceedings of the American Philosophical Society,* Vol. 106, pp. 41–47.

"Terra firma: Orbis novus," in *Hermann von Wissmann-Festschrift* (Tübingen: Geographisches Institut der Universität), pp. 258–70.

1963 "Homestead and Community on the Middle Border," in Howard W. Ottoson, ed., *Land Use Policy in the United States* (Lincoln: University of Nebraska Press), pp. 65–85.

John Leighly, ed., *Land and Life: A Selection from the Writings of*

*Carl Ortwin Sauer* (Berkeley and Los Angeles: University of California Press). Paperback edition, 1967.
"Status and Change in the Rural Midwest—A Retrospect." *Mitteilungen der Oesterreichischen Geographischen Gesellschaft,* Vol. 105, pp. 357–65.

1964    "Concerning Primeval Habitat and Habit," in *Festschrift für Ad. E. Jensen* (München: Klaus Renner Verlag), pp. 513–24.

1965    "Cultural Factors in Plant Domestication in the New World," *Euphytica,* Vol. 14, pp. 301–06.

1966    *The Early Spanish Main* (Berkeley and Los Angeles: University of California Press).
"On the Background of Geography in the United States," in *Heidelberger Geographische Arbeiten,* Heft 15 (Festgabe für Gottfried Pfeifer), pp. 59–71.

1968    "David I. Blumenstock, 1913–1963," *Yearbook of the Association of Pacific Coast Geographers,* Vol. 30 (Also in hard cover as Arnold Court, ed., *Eclectic Climatology* [Corvallis, Oregon: Oregon State University Press], pp. 9–11).
"Human Ecology and Population," in Paul Deprez, ed., *Population and Economics,* Proceedings of Section V (Historical Demography) of the Fourth Congress of the International Economic History Association (Winnipeg: University of Manitoba Press), pp. 207–14.
*Northern Mists* (Berkeley and Los Angeles: University of California Press). Paperback reprint, Berkeley: Turtle Island Foundation, 1973.

1970    "On the Quality of Geography," *California Geographer,* Vol. 10, pp. 5–10.
"Plants, Animals and Man," in R. E. Buchanan, Emrys Jones, and Desmond McCourt, eds., *Man and His Habitat* (London: Routledge and Kegan Paul), pp. 34–61.

1971    "The Formative Years of Ratzel in the United States," *Annals, Association of American Geographers,* Vol. 61, pp. 245–54.
*Sixteenth Century North America: The Land and the People as Seen by the Europeans* (Berkeley and Los Angeles: University of California Press).

1974    "The Fourth Dimension of Geography," *Annals, Association of American Geographers,* Vol. 64, pp. 189–95.

1975    "Man's Dominance by Use of Fire," *Geoscience and Man,* Vol. 10, pp. 1–13.

1976    "The Seminar as Exploration," *Historical Geography Newsletter,* Vol. 6, No. 1, pp. 31–34.

"European Backgrounds of American Agricultural Settlement," *Historical Geography Newsletter,* Vol. 6, No. 1, pp. 35–58.

1980   *Seventeenth Century North America: Spanish and French Accounts* (Berkeley: Turtle Island Foundation).

1981   *Selected Essays: 1963–1975.* Edited, with an introduction, by Bob Callahan (Berkeley: Turtle Island Foundation).

# Index

Aberle, Sophie B. de, 166
Acadians in Mississippi Valley, 20
Acapulco, Mexico, 185, 191
Acaxec Indians, 169, 180
Africa, 350; as man's original home,
  103–104, 109–112, 115–116,
  131, 135, 143, 291; tillage by
  digging in, 342. *See also*
  Mediterranenan; North Africa
Agricultural aid programs to
  developing countries, 361
Agricultural revolution of 18th
  century: in western Europe,
  40–44, 354; in New World,
  48–50
Agriculture: American, 8–15, 17–20,
  46–56, 51–53, 161, 342, 352;
  ancient, in Southwest, 161; in
  Culiacán Valley, Mexico, 172;
  earliest New World, in southern
  Mexico, 308, 324, 342; earliest
  Old World, in Anatolia, Turkey,
  308, 317, 324–325; European,
  26, 31, 38–39, 41, 127,
  345–347, 350; "intensive," 357,
  359–360; of northwest Mexican
  Indians, 168; seed, in Anatolia,

Mexico, and Central and South
  America, 315–317, 324–325,
  327, 344; vegetative
  reproduction in Caribbean, South
  America, and southwest Asia,
  313–315, 326–327, 342–344.
  *See also Conuco* agriculture;
  digging; Milpa system
Aguilar, Juan de, 196
Ahrensburg people of Upper
  Paleolithic, 127, 305, 308
Alabama, 11
Alaska, 253; in glacial stages, 119;
  and Seal Islands, 253
Albornoz, Rodrigo de, 231
Alders, 25
Alfalfa, 41
Alima (Indian town), 199, 200, 201,
  205, 222; as distinct political
  entity, 204; nearly empty by
  mid-16th century, 234; pays
  tribute to Spanish king in
  smelted gold, 228
Alvarado, Pedro de, 182, 184
American Geographic Society, 241,
  251
American Philosophical Society, 245

*Designed by Eileen Callahan.*
*Typography by Abracadabra.*
*Mechanicals by David Mattingly.*
*Printed by McNaughton & Gunn.*